Canadian Government and Politics in Transition

SIXTH EDITION

Robert J. Jackson
Doreen Jackson

PEARSON

Toronto

Editorial Director: Claudine O'Donnell
Acquisitions Editor: Darcey Pepper
Marketing Manager: Christine Cozens
Program Manager: Madhu Ranadive
Project Manager: Pippa Kennard
Manager of Content Development: Suzanne Schaan
Developmental Editor: Christine Langone
Production Services: Cenveo® Publisher Services
Permissions Project Manager: Erica Mojzes
Photo and Text Permissions Research: Integra
Interior Designer: Cenveo Publisher Services
Cover Designer: Carrie Keller, Cenveo Publisher Services
Cover Image: Matthew Cole/Shutterstock

Vice-President, Cross Media and Publishing Services: Gary Bennett

2   16

Library and Archives Canada Cataloguing in Publication

Jackson, Robert J., 1936-
[Canadian government in transition]
    Canadian government and politics in transition / Robert Jackson, Doreen Jackson. -- Sixth edition.

Revision of: Jackson, Robert J., 1936-. Canadian government in transition.
Includes bibliographical references and index.
ISBN 978-0-13-298461-4 (paperback)

    1. Canada—Politics and government—Textbooks. I. Jackson, Doreen, 1939-, author II. Title. III. Title: Canadian government in transition.

JL65.J318 2016   320.471   C2016-900242-X

ISBN 978-0-13-298461-4

Brief Table of Contents

Detailed Table of Contents

Preface

The sixth edition of *Canadian Government and Politics in Transition* provides a concise, current analysis of the country's most important political institutions, processes, and issues in the twenty-first century. The October 19, 2015, Liberal election victory was in large part due to a desire for change. While policy differences showed up to some degree in the party platforms, there was little objective evidence that voter choice was based on the detailed stances of parties and leaders. Justin Trudeau simply offered a clear, "sunny" alternative to Stephen Harper. Trudeau now has the opportunity to govern the country—a process quite different from campaigning in an election.

Textbook authors need to be scrupulously fair about the various parties and individuals in the political process and analyze political and state institutions with sophistication and without bias. They are not part of the process in the way journalists sometimes aspire to be. After all, democracy is a deliberative process and there are always conflicting viewpoints about people, process, and policy. When the political system is weak or broken, political scientists need to say so, and there is no doubt in our minds that many obstacles remain in the way of good governance in Canada.

In this book, we systematically describe and dissect the key elements of federal institutions, providing relevant history to help place them into context. We also address the major current issues and difficulties affecting Canadian governments today. Political and other leaders need fundamental grounding in the functioning of Canadian government, and this is best achieved at college and university, and certainly before citizens engage in the hurly-burly exercise of political action. Therefore, we provide novel analysis concerning:

- The October 19, 2015, general election and the victory of Justin Trudeau and his Liberal majority government
- The impact of three consecutive Conservative governments, especially the 2011 majority government of Stephen Harper, on Parliament, politics, and specific hot-button topics that make up the country's business
- The foreign and defence policies of the country as well as the security measures put in place after the terrorist attacks on Canadian territory and in the United States, and their impact on civil liberties
- Political issues of particular interest to young people, such as youth unemployment, funding for colleges and universities, and other relevant topics
- Controversial issues such as when the Constitution makes necessary and significant change virtually impossible and how Parliament, when it cannot find ways to legislate, often leaves important ethical decisions for the courts to decide
- The lack of serious media activities such as in-depth investigations of difficult policy issues while relying on titillating sagas about Senate scandals and prime ministerial arrogance

This book is intended for courses at the university and college level, for Canadian studies courses in the United States and abroad, for the general reader, and possibly for advanced politics and government courses in schools. As such, it is to a large extent about understanding the basic elements of our political institutions and processes.

Underpinned by studies of the economic and social environment, as well as the Constitution, federalism, and nationalism, the text distinguishes between types of institutions. State institutions include the executive, bureaucracy, legislature, the courts, and judicial administration, including police and prisons; political institutions include political parties, interest groups, and elections. We have added a new chapter on foreign policy. The book concludes with a chapter on ethics in Canadian government, a current and ongoing issue in politics and government.

Our method in writing this book has been to provide the maximum amount of information on Canadian institutions in a brief and orderly fashion, summarizing vast amounts of information, data, and ideas under multiple headings to facilitate easy access to the material. In so doing, we have also attempted to capture the excitement, vitality, and importance of Canada's political institutions and political leaders. The goals are to inform and to encourage critical thinking and active citizens.

As usual with our books, there is a degree of constructive criticism and balanced argumentation with an overall tone of optimism throughout. There are solid reasons to look optimistically to the future. Canada holds enviable relations among the world's states. Unity continues to be an underlying issue, but does not define Canada. Canadians have moved on to confront other challenges of the twenty-first century. Vital decisions about economics and public security will be made within the present federal institutions of Canada—organizations that are unlikely to undergo fundamental change for many years—despite honeymoon expectations of vast improvements in the way that Canada should be governed.

NEW TO THE SIXTH EDITION

We have added chapters and made numerous updates to the sixth edition of the text:

- Chapter 1, "The Game of Politics," focuses on the foundations of Canadian government and politics, but updates the current issues that Canadians argue and negotiate about.
- Chapter 2, "The Context and Ideas of Government," offers a new section on political ideas in politics as well as increased coverage of the issues concerning demography, class, Aboriginal peoples, and women as part of the external context of politics in Canada. Newly available census data are used to update social and demographic trends.
- Chapter 3, "The Constitutional Framework," continues to provide a concise overview of the current problems of constitutional developments in Canada and to include important new *Canadian Charter of Rights and Freedoms* cases.
- Chapter 4, "Contested Federalism," updates the often divisive issues and developments in federal politics, including shifting patterns of economic well-being.

- Chapter 5, "Québec Nationalism and Aboriginal Peoples," assesses past and current events and ideas in the area of nationalism and Aboriginal affairs.
- Chapter 6, "The Executive," and Chapter 7, "Parliament," have been totally reframed in light of the 2015 election of a Liberal majority government in Ottawa. The new institutions are analyzed.
- Chapter 8, "Public Administration," brings budgetary issues up to date, including recent Conservative budgets and Liberal proposals for change.
- Chapter 9, "The Administration of Justice and Human Rights," contains vital material on security policy, institutions, and civil liberties in light of the 9/11 aftermath and domestic terrorism in Canada.
- Chapter 10, "Parties and Interest Groups," and Chapter 11, "Elections and Political Behaviour," have been completely revised to reflect changes in political parties, political leadership, new electoral rules, and the 2015 election, with analysis of how well the electoral system works and how it might be changed.
- Chapter 12, "Canadian Foreign Policy," outlines Canada's foreign and defence challenges. It overviews all of Canada's historical military expeditions, as well as contemporary policies in Afghanistan, Iraq, Libya and Syria, and specific issues of political concern such as pipelines and Arctic sovereignty.
- Chapter 13, "Ethics in Canadian Government and Politics," succinctly studies issues related to ethics in government and politics and highlights the Senate abuse issues of the twenty-first century.

Throughout, this new edition of *Canadian Government and Politics in Transition* brings up to date the political events and research of recent years. These have been politically exciting times, with dramatic changes and policy evolution. The Conservatives have been reduced to Official Opposition status and the New Democratic Party has lost strength in Québec and Ontario. The 2015 general election reversed a decade of Conservative ascendancy in the country and ushered in a majority government under Justin Trudeau, son of former prime minister Pierre Elliott Trudeau.

PEDAGOGY

This textbook uses the following pedagogical aids to help students understand the material more easily and to reinforce concepts:

- Learning Objectives appear at the beginning of each chapter and list what students should accomplish after reading the material.
- Key Terms appear in boldface in the running text, with definitions located in the margins. The terms also appear, with corresponding page numbers, in the Glossary at the end of the book.
- Close-Up boxes provide topical issues and events for interest and discussion.
- Discussion Questions relevant to the topics discussed end each chapter; these questions will help students to test their knowledge of the material.
- Further Reading, found at the end of the book, provides a list of supplementary reading material.
- The Glossary, also at the end of the book, lists key terms with their respective definitions and first-reference page numbers.

SUPPLEMENT

The **Test Item File** for *Canadian Government and Politics in Transition* helps instructors to easily create and print quizzes, tests, and exams, as well as homework or practice handouts. It contains 40 questions per chapter, in Word format, in multiple-choice, fill-in-the-blank, short answer, and true/false formats, graded into three levels of difficulty (easy, moderate, and difficult), and is available for download from the password-protected section of Pearson Education Canada's online catalogue. Navigate to your book's catalogue page to access these supplements. See your local sales representative for details and access.

Acknowledgments

We would like to thank the following reviewers for their insightful and very helpful remarks: James Baker, Memorial College; Anne C. Charles, Conestoga College; Christian Leuprecht, Royal Military College of Canada; Eva St. Jean, Northern Lights College; Paul Whyte, North Island College; Nelson Wiseman, University of Toronto.

We are also indebted to Starla Strain for her sunny and loyal assistance as well as to excellent colleagues at both Carleton University and the University of Redlands for their interest and stimulation. Over many years, colleagues at both Oxford and Cambridge Universities have been another significant source of inspiration and friendship.

We are also grateful to our friends and colleagues at Pearson Education Canada who, once again, provided exactly the right mix of encouragement, expertise, and assistance. They include Matthew Christian, Claudine O'Donnell, Madhu Ranadive, Christine Langone, Pippa Kennard, Sarah Ellen Horsfall, Yasmita Hota, and Erica Mojzes. It has been a joy to work with professionals of such high calibre.

We dedicate this book to the many students—past, present, and future—whose perceptive questions about, and enthusiasm for, Canadian government and politics make teaching and research a worthwhile and satisfying vocation.

—Robert J. Jackson and Doreen Jackson

Carleton University, Ottawa

University of Redlands, California

February 2016

Yukon

Whitehorse

Northwest
Territories

Nunavut

Yellowknife

Iqaluit

British
Columbia

Newfoundland and
Labrador

Alberta

Manitoba

St. John's

Edmonton

Saskatchewan

Quebec

Victoria

Regina

Ontario

P.E.I.

Winnipeg

Quebec

New
Brunswick

Charlottetown

Fredericton

Halifax

OTTAWA

Nova Scotia

Toronto

Canada

Chapter 1
The Game of Politics
Concepts and Institutions

Learning Objectives

After reading this chapter, you should be able to

1   Define and distinguish between the concepts of state and nation, and politics and government.

2   Identify and explain key features that distinguish democratic and authoritarian states.

3   Distinguish between procedural and substantive arguments about democracy.

4   Identify the main features of Canadian democracy and discuss some of the problems the country faces.

Canadian democratic politics sometimes seems confused and pointless. There are winners and losers in elections: parties and individuals regularly come and go. However, despite all of the frenetic activity, there may not appear to be any concrete results or improvements for ordinary people. In fact, the following comment in Lewis Carroll's *Alice's Adventures in Wonderland* seems to depict how many people see politics.

> The players all played at once, without waiting for turns, quarrelling all the while ... they quarrel so dreadfully that one can't hear oneself speak—and they don't seem to have any rules in particular: at least, if there are, nobody attends to them ...

However, the democratic ideal in Canada is not frivolous. After all, it embodies the values and hopes of Canadians. Yet politics in Canada is in many ways analogous to a team sport. The stakes of politics are often seen as equivalent to the trophies and glory of sports and games. The winners in Canadian elections form the government while the losers are relegated to the sidelines.

The sports analogy holds in many respects. The players or politicians are in a collective game with winners and losers. The competitors are organized into teams known as parties or interest groups. All of them are required to play according to rules. Some rules are more precise and codified than others, but nevertheless they all determine to a large extent how the players organize and conduct themselves. As in sports, the rules vary from country to country. For example, Canada's monarchical democracy has little in common with Saudi Arabia's monarchical authoritarian regime. Canada has no experience with revolution or coups d'état.

As a rule, Canadian politics includes none of the body contact typical of hockey, football, or lacrosse. Possibly baseball, or a board game such as chess, would be more appropriate to compare with politics. However, sometimes even military or war analogies are needed. Former U.S. president Richard Nixon, for example, prepared an enemies list, and Canadian party strategists often develop "whisper lists" to spread false rumours during election campaigns, just as propaganda experts do during a war. Usually, however, the media depict politics between the government and opposition as something like a horse race, or as having the skill and finesse of chess. At the same time, despite what casual observers watching them may think, the players act in a context and with rules. Sports may be played on fields or courts; politics is played in the context of histories, economies, social structures (regions, ethnic groups, classes), and especially institutions.

The game analogy should not detract from the seriousness of politics. However, politics and games do share some characteristics. Both have rules or agreed-upon principles to provide limits to behaviour. In democracies, the broadest rules are called constitutions. Politicians may be able to change the rules. In both politics and games, players with their own interests and ideas contest or compete for power. The political players bring to their activities philosophies, strategies, and tactics about how to win at the political game. They prepare plans of attack. They contest for a purpose—they wish to obtain political power. In other words, as in games, there are stakes to be achieved.

Competitive games arose partly from the need to practise for war, but even then rules were devised to control behaviour. In ancient Greece, for example, a contest called pankration (which involved wrestling and boxing) outlawed biting, piercing the eyes, and other forms of bodily attack. The Romans even had rules for contests between gladiators, although in the final result human beings were killed to entertain spectators and emperors.[1] Today's Olympics are descendants of such early games. Amateur athletes are subject to a host of rules, including stiff penalties for drug use.

In politics, democracies tend to have more, and more highly developed, rules than authoritarian regimes, which generally have only minimal, crude regulations to control the behaviour of citizens who contest for political power. However, all states have rules and institutions that provide opportunities and constraints concerning political action.

GAMES AND INSTITUTIONS

institutions: Mechanisms of social order and cooperation; social structures that are organized to achieve goals for society.

Institutions direct and enforce the behaviour of politicians and public officials, and also implement the public policies that emerge from them. **Institutions** are social structures that are organized to achieve goals for society. They organize and restrict political players in the same manner that rules delimit the actions of players in sports and games.

The most comprehensive rules of a state or country generally are found in a constitution. When the Fathers of Confederation established the rules for Canadian government in 1867, they joined normative democratic principles with practical ideas about how government should function. In simple terms, they linked British parliamentary democracy with a federal division of authority—dividing powers between the federal government and the provinces. These basic rules still provide the framework for Canadian debates about what matters in politics. Since Confederation, the Constitution has determined which issues the state should resolve and which should be left for individuals or groups in the private sector to decide upon.

Comprehensive and formal rules, such as those found in constitutions, change only gradually over time. Much like the rules of some games, the elements of play may change slowly over time. Rules for some games, such as checkers and chess, change only rarely, while in other games, such as basketball, some regulations change every year. Rules in political games are designed to do both. Constitutions change slowly or rarely, while the rules about elections and parliamentary organizations may change often. Managers, coaches, and players should always play within the rules whether they like them or not. This does not mean that rules are never broken. They often are—just as they are in games. Penalties are meted out. To understand politics and governing, we must first know what the rules of institutions are, how they are intended to guide behavior, and whether they actually do so or not.

Institutions help to organize government and politics much like rules organize sports and games. Some people—say, short people—are defined out of professional basketball. If the height of basketball hoops were changed in relation to the height of the players, then, theoretically, players of any size could play in the pros. Unfortunately for the height-impaired, the rules are the same for short, medium, tall, and very tall players. The same thing is true in politics: formal and informal rules provide advantages to some players and groups and constrain others. They also limit which issues can develop, which individuals can play, and at what level. The rich, for example, have advantages in all political games.

Where do the rules come from in the first place? In contemporary professional sports, they are usually made by the owners of the teams, or in bargaining sessions between owners and players. In amateur sports, rules are determined by university or school sports officials. In government as well, the rules are set in many forums. As in chess, conventions may develop; rules may come from traditions and customs that are many centuries old. Rules also may be conceived and put in place by political players acting on their own assumptions and biases about the task of governing; they may even act according to their own selfish interests. However, participants in the political game are bound together by common interests just as other groups of people are united in developing and changing the rules for games and sports.

STATES AND NATIONS

This book is concerned with the game of politics that takes place within Canada. We are all familiar with the concept of Canada as a country or state, with clearly defined borders, a specific system of government and a legal system. However, when we use the terms *state*, *nation*, or *ethnic group*, the meanings can be obscure, interpreted differently by people. It is important to understand precisely what we mean by each of them.

Think about the various social groups to which you belong. Individuals belong to many organizations or institutions. At the most basic level, you may be part of a family. You may be a student of a college or university. You may belong to a church or a sports or recreation club. You may also belong to a certain town where you might pay municipal taxes. You also belong to a specific province or territory within Canada.

Within Canada, you are also probably a citizen—a formal member of the state—and therefore eligible to enjoy specified rights and privileges. States normally consider all persons born on their territory and their children to be citizens. Other individuals acquire citizenship through a specified process, such as residing in the country for a certain length of time and carrying out a formal duty such as swearing an oath of allegiance. In Canada, an immigrant may apply for citizenship after a total of three years' residence in the country—if the individual is at least 18 years of age, can communicate in English or French, and has basic knowledge about Canadian history, politics, and society (see Close-Up 1.1). Of course, many non-citizens also live in Canada: they are residents on an extended or short-term basis.

ethnicity: Primarily a subjective term used to describe groups of people who share customs, language, dialect, and/or cultural heritage, and sometimes distinct physical or racial characteristics.

Most people also consider themselves part of an ethnic group. **Ethnicity** is primarily a subjective characteristic of groups of people who share customs, language, dialect, and/or cultural heritage, and sometimes distinct physical or racial characteristics. When combined with religious, territorial, or political differences, ethnicity is a strong political force. Canada's earliest founders came from two ethnic groups, French and English, but they settled on lands that had originally been occupied by Aboriginal peoples.

nation: Politically conscious and mobilized group of people, often with a sense of territory, who may aspire to greater autonomy or even statehood.

Nations, like ethnic groups, are cultural entities. They are essentially subjective, involving a sense of "we-ness" or belonging. We define a **nation** as a politically conscious and mobilized group of people, often with a sense of territory, who may aspire to greater independence or even statehood. Nations are not the same as ethnic groups, nor do they necessarily correspond to the territory of a country. Some Québec leaders claim to represent a "nation," and so do many Aboriginal leaders.

Close-Up 1.1

What Should Citizens Know about Their Country?

The Angus Reid Group asked a sample of Canadians 200 questions about Canadian history, culture, government institutions, and laws similar to those that immigrants are required to answer before they are allowed to become citizens of Canada.* The results were embarrassing. They indicated that nearly half of Canadians would fail the citizenship exam. Here are some surprising results:

- 95 percent of respondents knew the title of the national anthem, but only 63 percent could recite the first two lines correctly.
- Only 8 percent could name the Queen as Canada's head of state; 57 percent believed that the prime minister fills that role.

Do you think that Canadians who cannot answer these kinds of questions are able to vote intelligently? Should they lose their citizenship? How can the level of understanding be improved? What basic questions should Canadians of voting age be able to answer about their country and their form of government?

Try the practice test for Canadian citizenship at www.cic.gc.ca/english/citizenship/cit-test.asp
Are the questions fair?

*The Dominion Institute National Citizenship exam survey of 1997.

English-speaking Canadians, on the other hand, usually proclaim their loyalty to the country as a whole, or perhaps to a territorial entity such as a city or province.

When we use the word **state**, we are referring to the political unit of an entire territory. A state is made up of a territory, a population, and a government. However, a state is also an abstraction that involves many institutions and rules. It is impossible to point at one institution or even a number of them and say, "That is the state." Actions may be carried out in the name of the state, as when laws are enforced, or when countries impose taxes or go to war, but even in a national emergency or a war, not all state institutions necessarily are united behind the government. Some institutions may even actively promote contradictory policies. This is often the case in Québec, for example, when Parti Québécois ministers may promote separation from Canada.

Max Weber, a famous German sociologist, defined the state as a set of institutions that "successfully upholds a claim to the monopoly of the legitimate use of physical force in the enforcement of its order ... within a given territorial area."[2] This means that the state is able to use coercive force to issue rules that are "binding" on all people within its territory. The state is also defined in terms of its relation to power, both external and internal. A state is normally considered to be **sovereign** when final authority rests in the national government so that it is able to make laws internally—for example, to tax its citizens—and also externally to conduct its own relations with the international community, free from outside interference by other states or governments.

Normally, people strongly identify with their state. They proclaim their love for it, sing about it, work to better it, and fight to preserve it. When citizens accept that a government has the right to make decisions for them, political scientists say that the system has **legitimacy**. When the government imposes higher taxes, Canadians pay them even though they may not want to because they elected the government to handle such matters, and therefore consider the policy to be legitimate. Legitimacy is closely linked to the concept of **authority**, which we may define as the government's ability to make binding decisions and issue obligatory commands. In the illustration above, the government not only has the legitimacy or right to impose higher taxes, but also has the authority to do so, because it has the legal system behind it to force individual citizens to pay taxes even though they may not want to.

state: The political unit of an entire territory; it comprises a territory, a population, and a government. It is also an abstraction that incorporates many institutions and rules.

sovereign: A sovereign state wields authority and power in that it is capable of maintaining order within its territory, is able to tax its citizens, and is also recognized by the international community as having the right to run its own affairs free from external interference.

legitimacy: When citizens accept that a government should, or has the right to, make decisions for them.

authority: The government's power to make binding decisions and issue obligatory commands.

POLITICS, POWER, AND INSTITUTIONS

Politics is as old as human history. Defined by the non-specialist as manipulation or the struggle for advantage, it is omnipresent in all societal relations. However, political scientists do not study all social relations; they are concerned primarily with organized dispute and its collective resolution through governmental institutions.

Two traditional definitions of politics contend in the literature. The more widespread of them, put forth by a Canadian, David Easton, is very abstract. He defined politics as "the authoritative allocation of values."[3] By values, Easton did not mean moral ideas, but rather the benefits and opportunities that people value or desire. The second, more restricted definition was conceived by an American, Harold Lasswell, who pointed out that politics always concerns "who gets what, when and how."[4] Our definition of politics combines the insights of both Easton and Lasswell:

politics: The activity that entails making binding decisions about who gets what, when, and how.

Politics is the activity that entails making binding decisions about who gets what, when and how. It is an activity through which contending interests and differences may be reconciled for the supposed advantage of society.

Since valued possessions such as wealth and status are invariably scarce and unevenly distributed, disagreements often arise as people attempt to satisfy their seemingly endless wants. These disputes give rise to organized political conflict that sometimes becomes violent. It is no wonder that some cynics adopt the definition of politics as "the systematic organization of hatred."

To reduce the endless conflict over power, mechanisms have evolved to make and enforce decisions for all members of society. We refer to these mechanisms as government. Politics and governing both concern organized dispute over power; whereas politics is concerned with influencing the governors, governing consists of public officials making decisions. Much of the dynamic character of politics comes from the pervasive conflict between the rulers and the ruled.

government: The organization of people for the resolution of dispute and conflict.

Government is thus the organization of people for the resolution of dispute and conflict. Even the simplest societies have some means of settling disputes. In modern societies, governments not only provide law and order but also make collective decisions for society and regulate many aspects of private and public affairs. Political scientists describe and analyze the institutions and also the behaviour that takes place in the political governance of states. Social processes that influence, or are influenced by, politics or governance are also part of the study of political science.

The concept of power is central to the study of politics. The word *power* comes from the Latin verb *potere*, which means "to be able." Thus, in the broadest meaning of the word, power is being able to achieve what one wants. Power has been part of the vocabulary of politics since the time of Niccolò Machiavelli, yet it remains the most perplexing issue within the discipline of political science. Where would our understanding of politics be without the notion that some individuals hold power over others?

power: The ability to influence (convince) and/or to coerce (force) others to accept certain objectives or to behave in a particular manner.

The essential problem stems from the difficulty of ascertaining whether power is absolute or relative. A person's ability to influence others to act in a certain way often relies more on bargaining than on the application of naked force. Thus, **power** should be understood to include the ability to influence (convince) and/or to coerce (force) others to accept certain objectives or to behave in a particular manner.

All stable states have governments that exercise authority—institutions that the people entrust to make binding decisions. Governments resolve disputes and conflicts that arise within society. They issue obligatory commands. They "steer" the country in certain policy directions, make rules that are legally binding on residents, and obtain resources to carry out their policy goals while attempting to preserve the viability of governmental institutions.[5] Without government, people would exist in a state of **anarchy**—a state of chaos.

anarchy: A lack of government within a society.

The formal institutions of government are the most visible elements of the governmental process. Institutions are social structures such as constitutions, parliaments, bureaucracies, and executives, structures that are organized to achieve goals for society. Formal institutions explain much about politics. They are important units of analysis—they shape the interests, resources, and conduct of political leaders, who in turn shape the institutions.[6] The way institutions are structured affects political action as well as who gets what, when and how. Power is shared among many political actors in Canada, such as politicians, civil servants, advocacy groups, and private individuals. Key players in the process are sometimes referred to as stakeholders.

LAW AND POLICY

Governments enforce their authority by making laws. **Law** consists of a special body of rules issued by government and backed up by the threat of state force. Not everything governments do is made into law. Governments also spend funds, set up structures and processes for consultation and decision making, and steer the country in particular policy directions. **Policies** are broadly based patterns of government action. Policies and law both concern values about public goals and beliefs about the best strategy for a country to take.

law: Consists of a special body of rules issued by government and backed up by the threat of state force.

policy: A broadly based framework within which decisions are taken and a pattern of government action or inaction.

Democratic countries set out their laws relatively clearly. They separate courts from politics so that judges can interpret the law in an impartial (non-politicized) manner. Recognized legal authorities such as the police enforce the law by arresting offenders and holding them accountable before the courts. A prison system removes individuals from society when they do not conform to the laws. The prison system is often not included in books about politics, but it should be. It serves several goals of the state, such as punishing wrongdoers, safeguarding society, and correcting the behaviour of inmates in preparation for their release.

Laws come in many forms, but all concern how individuals and groups relate to government. Most citizen contact with political authorities involves dealing with laws concerning issues such as taxes, pensions, business regulations, and administrative guidelines.

TYPES OF GOVERNMENT: DEMOCRACY AND AUTHORITARIANISM

States differ widely in how they are organized and what ideals they hold. Democratic systems normally differ from authoritarian regimes in the amount and quality of participation they allow citizens in making public policy. A **democratic political system** is a system of government that reconciles competing interests through competitive elections. An **authoritarian political system** is a system of government that imposes one dominant interest, that of a political elite, on all others.

democratic political system: A system of government that reconciles competing interests through competitive elections.

authoritarian political system: A system of government that imposes one dominant interest, that of a political elite, on all others.

Democracy is a very simple idea that is difficult, if not impossible, to replicate in the real world. The word comes from two Greek roots, *demos* meaning "the people" and *kratos* meaning "authority" or "rule." In ancient Greek culture, therefore, democracy meant that all people should rule. Today, such an ideal situation is impossible for large states and tends to occur only in smaller towns or face-to-face societies.

In the simplest model of democracy, elections provide popular sovereignty. The people elect a few of their fellow citizens to serve for a time as their rulers. After a period, the rulers must be judged by the citizens as to whether they have ruled properly. In the accounting process, known as an election, the people reward or punish the rulers by re-electing or rejecting them. Good government is assured because the elected ruler must satisfy the people in order to get re-elected. Politicians are therefore supposed to serve the national interests of a country rather than their own selfish desires.

This simple model is very important. If people believe in it and act accordingly, a country can operate successfully. We have seen that when citizens accept that a government should, or has the right to, make decisions for them, the political system has legitimacy and authority. Nevertheless, this model of democracy is quite simplistic and in some ways misleading.

Six ingredients are generally considered to be necessary for a state to be democratic:

1. *Free elections* in which people vote for their political representatives free from intimidation or harassment.

2. *Universal voting rights*, so that all adult citizens have the right to vote for their political leaders.

3. *More than one political party* from which to choose.

4. *Liberty and freedom of expression*, so that individuals and the media can speak freely to praise or criticize governments, politicians, and policies. Liberty and freedom of expression assure freedom of assembly and association as well as freedom of communications and the press.

5. Policy decisions are made by a majority of the people or elected body—this is known as the **majority principle**.

6. *Rule of law* is also a fundamental part of the democratic ideal. Equality is embedded in the democratic notion that all individuals should be treated alike under the law and in rules about "one person, one vote" in elections.

majority principle: System of government in which policy decisions are made by a majority of the people or elected body.

In Canada, we say that we are ruled by law and not by people. Laws are made by humans, but under the rule of law they are to be administered impartially. No individual (regardless of his or her political status) is to be above the law. As we shall see in Chapter 3, the **rule of law** is a guarantee that the state's actions will be governed by law, with fairness and without malice. It means that no citizen is to be deprived of due process or to be punished at the whim of an official. Courts are set up to ensure that the rule of law is upheld. We will discuss law and its specific relation with the Canadian Constitution in Chapters 3, 4, and 9, but it is important here to establish the links between democracy and forms of government. Democratic states and their governments use laws to regulate and control behaviour.

rule of law: A guarantee that the state's actions will be governed by law, with fairness, and without malice. No individual should be above the law, and no one ought to be exempt from it.

Democracy: Procedural and Substantive

There are two distinct ways to think about democracy in Canada. One is known as substantive, the other as procedural.

In the contemporary world, virtually all states—even many that are clearly authoritarian—boast that they are democratic. Democracy has become so linked with "goodness" that these states all want to be associated with it. When countries claim to be democratic, they tend to mean that they rule for the common good. They maintain that the people have a say, to some extent, in how they are governed. For them, democracy simply means good government, and that is seen as the essential purpose of government. This is known as a *substantive* view of democracy.

For others, however, democracy is *procedural*—it refers to the mechanics or procedures by which a country discusses and organizes political differences and deals with political strife. It also concerns the procedures whereby citizens are able to participate in politics. The simple model of democracy assumes popular participation in public policy-making. However, in the modern world citizens rarely participate directly in decision making. The model of democracy is an ideal that is rarely realized. Most systems today are **representative democracies**, democracies in which elected officials make decisions with the force of law because they have achieved legitimacy through some form of election. Democracy in Canada is not rule by the people themselves. It is representative democracy—rule by officials elected by the people.

representative democracy:
A democracy in which elected officials make decisions with the force of law because they have achieved legitimacy through some form of election.

Making representative democracy work requires complex structures and a mass public that is fairly knowledgeable about government and politics (consider Close-Up 1-1). Those in government also must reconcile their authority with public influence because they operate within a society that holds conflicting beliefs about the role of government.

Let us take one example. For conservatives, individual rights are conceived as guarantees against government interference in the lives of individuals and groups. A free market economy in which government direction is minimal characterizes the type of economic relations desired by conservatives. On the other hand, modern liberals and other progressives think of rights as entitlements that individuals receive from the state. They do not object to government management of the economy— they applaud it. From this simple conflict in beliefs, we can see that democracy must be about a set of procedures that enable governments to work despite differences in judgments about the desirable outcomes of government action.[7]

What is required for a democracy to be stable and successful? When communism collapsed in the Soviet Union in 1989, for example, democracy did not immediately flourish. Having long been deprived of the cultural roots of democracy and a society of groups, associations, and participatory institutions such as political parties and a free press, the new Russia developed in an uncertain direction. On the other hand, democracy in Canada has flourished since 1867, sometimes even under quite difficult circumstances.

Another question in the analysis of democracy concerns its substantive qualities. Democratic and legal ideas imported from the United Kingdom are fundamental in Canada. Does democracy tend to be the cause, or is it caused by, the values of liberty and equality held by Canadians? The principle of liberty appears to be required in democratic systems because it underlies notions about freedom of thought, assembly, and association as well as freedom of the press. The majority principle, the idea of competing parties, rule of law, and free elections also seem to be fundamentally interlocked with democratic ideas. Furthermore, equality is embedded in the democratic notion that all individuals should be treated alike under the law, and in rules about "one person, one vote" in elections. Are such values required to establish democracy, or are they a by-product of the establishment of democracy? Which comes first?

In this book, we consider democracy to be a *set of procedures and institutions*. While one would be remiss to overlook the values and philosophies that are associated with the democratic process, and while democracies are associated with specific values such as liberty and political equality, it does not mean that democracy can be equated with, or equal to, the "good life."

Canadian Democracy

Canada has very deep democratic roots. When the first settlers arrived in the early colonies of Canada, they brought with them a long history of experience with democratic ideas and institutions. Canadians established their own unique democratic institutions at Confederation in 1867. Their historical background had provided them with democratic traditions that created a firm soil in which Canadian democracy could flourish.

Canada, like other democracies, has both state and political institutions. **State institutions** are related closely to the Constitution and federalism. They include the executive, legislature, bureaucracy, courts, police, and prisons. **Political institutions**, on the other hand, structure democratic expression within states and relate more closely to citizen behaviour. Parties, interest groups, elections, and the media, for example, link the people to their state and provide ways of influencing state authorities. Both state and political institutions are important elements of Canadian democracy.

As a framework for their state institutions, Canadian leaders at Confederation in 1867 rejected the presidential model of government adopted by the United States and instead chose the **British model of parliamentary government**, with which they were familiar. This system had already been operating in the colonies in what is now Central and Eastern Canada for many years. The leaders set up a Parliament with two Houses—an elected lower House, the House of Commons, and an appointed upper House, the Senate—and eventually a governor general to represent the monarch. Each province was also given its own legislature, with a lieutenant-governor representing the Crown.

Canada's state institutions continue to operate within a framework of constitutional monarchy, not a republic as in the United States. In a **constitutional monarchy**, a monarch is head of state, and a constitution and laws of the state restrict the powers of the monarch and the entire executive branch of government. In Canada, the head of state is Queen Elizabeth II, who is also the Queen of the United Kingdom, Australia, New Zealand, and many other countries around the world, from the Bahamas to Papua New Guinea. Canada is a constitutional monarchy because the Constitution shapes the arrangements of political power. In a republic, on the other hand, there is no monarch. The government of the state is carried out by the people or their elected representatives. The head of state is often elected directly by the people, as in the United States.

In Canada, the Constitution outlines a federal system of government—one in which power and authority to govern is shared between the federal (central)

state institutions: Institutions that are related closely to the Constitution and federalism; they include the executive, legislature, bureaucracy, courts, police, and prisons.

political institutions: Institutions that structure democratic expression within states and relate more closely to citizen behaviour; they include parties, interest groups, elections, and the media.

British model of parliamentary government: A model of government with two Houses—an elected lower House, the House of Commons, and an unelected upper House, the Senate—and a monarch.

constitutional monarchy: A form of government in which the head of state is a monarch, but a constitution shapes the arrangements of political power.

government and the governments of the provinces. This means that Canada is a federation. A **federation** has a number of territorially based units, and the activities of government are shared between their regional governments and a central government so that each level of government has some activities on which it makes final decisions. The United States, too, has a federal system. Britain, on the other hand, used to have a completely **unitary system** in which the power and final authority to govern was centralized in one government, but regional governments now exist in Scotland, Wales, and Northern Ireland. Westminster retains the final authority, but many powers have been devolved to the regions.

The Canadian Constitution divides formal authority between a monarchical head of state and a governmental leader, the prime minister. Since the Queen resides in Britain, the monarch's titular and symbolic role is carried out in Canada by the governor general. This makes Canada different from other presidential systems like the United States, where the president is both the head of state and the political head.

The prime minister heads the *political executive*—known as the ministry and Cabinet—and is the effective head of government. The prime minister derives power from Canadian and British constitutional conventions that give authority to the person who leads the party with a majority or plurality of votes in the House of Commons. We examine the executive in detail in Chapter 6.

The Constitution also provides Canada with a representative assembly, the House of Commons, and an appointed upper House, the Senate. As we have noted, therefore, Canada has a representative democracy, in which the House of Commons represents the electorate. The members of the House are chosen by the people on the basis of one person, one vote. Such perfect equality is not always possible in practice, but it is an important goal.

The ministers who make up the federal Cabinet are responsible to the House for the actions of the government, and the House of Commons is answerable to the people. For that reason, we say that Canada has **responsible government**. If the ministers cannot keep the support of a majority of the members of the House of Commons, the government falls. A new general election is called and the people elect a new government.

Canadian democracy, then, is set up as a constitutional monarchy. The Constitution outlines a federal, parliamentary system with representative, responsible government. It satisfies all six criteria for a functioning democratic state that we noted in the list above. We discuss all of these ingredients of Canadian democracy in detail in the following chapters.

ISSUES CANADIANS ARGUE ABOUT

Since politics is about a struggle for advantage among competitors, it is not surprising that disputes are at the centre of Canadian politics. Politics is diffused throughout society and there are a great many competitions among individuals and groups. Because of this, it is possible to have a multitude of interpretations of what issues are significant in Canadian politics. The political agenda is created by interactions between society and the political system and by the decisions of those in power. The group or groups that dominate government determine what issues and policies to pursue based on their vision of what needs to be done and the

federation: A form of political organization in which the activities of government are divided between regional governments and a central government in such a way that each level of government has activities on which it makes final decisions.

unitary system: A form of government in which the power and authority to govern is centralized in one government.

responsible government: The prime minister and Cabinet are accountable to Parliament and may govern only so long as they retain the "confidence" of the majority of the House of Commons.

priority they give issues. It is important, therefore, that parties, legislatures, and bureaucracies include significant representation from all groups so that their voices can be heard and issues that concern them will not be overlooked or shunted aside.

At the national level, a few fundamental and complex issues tend to dominate federal politics. The list is always changing. Today, it would have to include immigration, medical services, the environment, youth unemployment, an aging population, global economics, national security, child poverty, and literacy, to name just a few. It is not possible to understand or evaluate Canada's political institutions without also understanding the key issues that our leaders are working to resolve, or even to understand the front pages of the country's newspapers.

While the issue of Québec nationalism and how to counteract its divisive force has subsided in the second decade of the twenty-first century, other groups—such as Aboriginal peoples, women, environmentalists, and other "identity" groups with their own issues—have taken its place. Our security is also challenged by new terrorism issues. The threats of communist aggression and nuclear war have diminished. In their place, new issues relating to terrorism, jihad, and other doomsday scenarios—such as the possible hijacking of an Air Canada jet or the destruction of Toronto's CN Tower—have gained prominence.

The state of the economy is an ongoing issue. Despite the tiny surplus the government showed in its revenue–expenditure ratio in 2015, Canadian governments have amassed a massive debt, which today stands at nearly $700 billion. This and a weak 75-cent dollar (relative to the U.S. dollar) are sources of considerable concern. There are different schools of thought about how, and whether, to reduce the national debt while also injecting a finite amount of funds into competing areas of need such as health care, pensions, infrastructure, and the environment. During the 2015 election the Liberal Party campaigned on a platform of running a small deficit of $10 billion annually for three years to stimulate the economy through infrastructure programs. This is a highly contentious and emotional issue, and one very important to the economic health of the country. How it is resolved may determine the future of the Canadian political system.

deficit: The amount by which government spending exceeds revenues in one year.

Just how healthy is the Canadian economy? To begin to understand the financial situation, one must be clear about two terms, *deficit* and *debt*. The **deficit** is the amount by which government spending exceeds revenues in a particular year—that is, how much more it spends than it takes in. For about three decades until 1998, Canada's federal government spent more than it took in, so that each year it had a deficit. When all of these deficits are combined, they represent the debt. The **debt** is the total amount of the accumulated deficits over the years since 1867. In 2015, Canada's debt is just over $693 billion (see Close-Up 1.2).

debt: The accumulation of deficits over the years.

In 2015, the federal government's books show that the deficit was reduced to zero and there was a small surplus, although the debt load and high-debt interest payments continued. A **surplus** refers to money that is left over after the bills for a particular year are paid. In recent years all four major political parties have argued over how to pay down the debt and also spend any surplus.

surplus: Money that is left over after a government's bills for a year are paid.

The issue of government finances is covered in detail in Chapter 8 on public administration, where we consider how the government's yearly budget is prepared and what options the minister of finance and the public service have at their disposal in this task.

Federal Government's Projected Situation for the 2016–2017 Fiscal Year in Billions of Dollars

Deficit: 0
Surplus: 1.7
Net public debt: 693.4
Debt as a percent of GDP: 29.3%

ISSUES AND INSTITUTIONS

Many difficult issues must be resolved in Canada through the democratic institutions that have been built since Confederation. Throughout the book we address these issues, showing how government institutions function and how choices are made in public policy. As we examine Canada's institutions and turn the kaleidoscope to focus on each of them, we show the different shapes, patterns, meanings, and interpretations possible about these vital structures of democracy.

In Chapter 2, we describe the context in which Canadian politics takes place. Chapter 3 examines the mega-rules about the political game in the Constitution, and in Chapter 4 the federal aspect of the Constitution and the financing of the federation are analyzed. These overarching structures and institutions of Canadian democracy are not without their advocates and their critics. Chapter 5 outlines and assesses the forces of nationalism, separatism, and regionalism in the country.

In the next four chapters we examine state institutions. Chapters 6, 7, 8, and 9 combine to make clear how executive, legislative, bureaucratic, and judicial institutions function and interact. Coercive structures also play a part in democracy, and organizations such as the police and prison systems are shown to mesh with these central government organizations. We analyze civil liberties as part of the discussion of the courts and international terrorism.

It is necessary to understand political as well as state institutions to have a complete view of how the Canadian democratic system operates. Chapters 10 and 11 therefore provide an overview of four political institutions—political parties, interest groups, the media, and elections in Canada. These four institutions link the mass public with state authorities. The 2015 election and its consequences are outlined and analyzed here. Chapter 12 shows how Canada functions in global politics and how issues concerning defence, trade, and the environment are interwoven at the domestic and international levels. Chapter 13 concludes the book with an examination of the controversial issue of ethics in Canadian government and politics. Politicians often struggle to cope with negative images, made worse by scandals like the recent ones that plagued both Liberal and Conservative governments. Are these perceptions deserved? What rules are in place to keep our leaders honest?

State and political institutions provide a set of coherent relationships among the elements of our democracy. Together they work to produce a viable system. All states have stresses and strains caused by divisions within their societies. Canada, too, must endure such crises, and elected representatives are responsible for finding answers to these and other issues for their constituents. To a large extent, it is in their hands whether the country will continue in its historic form or change, transform, or disrupt as it moves through the twenty-first century.

Discussion Questions

1. What do you consider to be the major issues and problems that the Canadian government must cope with in the coming years?

2. Is the analogy between politics and games a good one? Why or why not? Is politics as competitive as the games analogy implies?

3. Is Canada a state, a nation, or both? Justify your answer.

4. What are the basic components of democracy? Is democracy in Canada "rule by the people"? Why or why not?

5. Can Canada continue in its present form as it changes, transforms, and perhaps faces disruption in the mid twenty-first century?

Chapter 2

The Context and Ideas of Government

Cohesion, Division, and Identity

Learning Objectives

After reading this chapter, you should be able to

1   Describe the main geographical and demographic factors that help to shape politics in Canada.

2   Identify and discuss at least five factors that unite Canadians.

3   Describe the main political ideas and social, regional, and economic cleavages that divide Canadians into different groups.

4   Identify the main ethnic divisions in Canada and compare their relative political and social implications.

5   Describe the various ways that Canadians identify themselves and how this impacts on Canadian politics.

Games and politics have much in common. The context in which games are played creates a network of advantages and disadvantages for individual players and teams. Performance is affected by external factors such as the support of "home fans" or bad publicity, as well as by internal factors such as leadership and adherence to traditions and values of competition and fair play. Similarly, government and politics occur in the context of a wider society. They are nourished by ideas, people, and events and are shaped by various circumstances of geography, history, resources, region, and how people identify themselves socially and politically. Experiences of the past and expectations for the future affect both politics and government.

In this chapter, we examine the domestic environment of government and politics. This overview provides a picture of who Canadians are and what kinds of political issues concern them most. Canadians can be divided into overlapping groups based on such factors as gender, class, education, region, language, and ethnicity. The categories and groups that individuals belong to help to determine what they want and expect from the country's political institutions. As we shall see in Chapter 12, the global environment, particularly relations with the United States, also helps to shape and sometimes limit the ability of the Canadian government to satisfy these aspirations.

SHARED FUNDAMENTALS

Canadian politics cannot be understood without a basic knowledge of the geography that provides both obstacles and opportunities for the country's inhabitants and divides them into distinct provinces and regions. It is a myth that Canada is a young country. Among the world's states, Canada is not an adolescent but well into middle age. In 2015, at 148 years old, Canada has existed longer, for example, than Italy (unified in 1870) or Germany (1871). Fewer than one-third of the 194 countries now represented in the United Nations existed in 1945, when Canada was already 78 years old.

Geography

Canada is the largest country in the western hemisphere. At nearly 10 million square kilometres, it is the second largest country in the world after Russia. East to west, it stretches more than 5000 kilometres. The land is diverse, often inhospitable to settlement, and for the most part rich in resources. The enormous distances that separate the population sometimes contribute to regionalist mentalities and to an alienation from the federal government in Ottawa.

Physical geography also separates Canadians and limits where they can live (see Figure 2.1). The low, discontinuous chain of mountains and valleys of the northern Appalachian region traverses the eastern edge of the country north to south and,

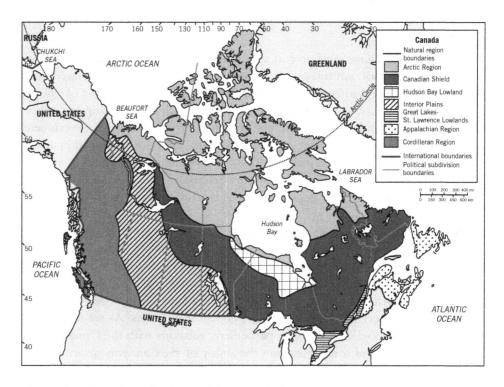

Figure 2.1 Canada's Physiographic Boundaries

along with the St. Lawrence River, separates the Atlantic provinces from Central Canada. Central Canada is dominated by the Canadian Shield, a region of formerly volcanic Precambrian-era mountains that takes up roughly one-half of Canada's surface area and extends from the Great Lakes, around the horseshoe of Hudson Bay, and north into the Arctic. The most fertile land in Central Canada lies along the shores of the St. Lawrence River and in southwestern Ontario, determining the location of large population centres. West of the Canadian Shield are the Interior Plains, which once formed the bottom of ancient lakes and seas. They are cut off from the coast by a belt of mountains more than 800 kilometres wide. This Western Cordillera includes coastal mountain ranges, high plateaus, and the Rockies.

Canada's climate is as diverse as its land mass. The Far North is characterized by long, harsh winters. The climate in the rest of the country is more hospitable but still the coldest on the continent, and extremely varied. Areas near large bodies of water enjoy more moderate climates than the inland areas and, because of prevailing westerly winds, the West Coast boasts lower temperatures than the East Coast.

The southern part of the Interior Plains and the lowlands along the southern Great Lakes and the St. Lawrence River are best suited to commercial agriculture. Elsewhere there is a wealth of non-renewable mineral deposits, from vast iron ore deposits in the eastern Shield to gold in the Yukon valleys. There are substantial deposits of zinc, nickel, gold, silver, iron ore, uranium, copper, cobalt, and lead. Major reserves of natural gas and petroleum, great hydroelectric power, and abundant supplies of clean water also exist throughout the country. Canada has 7 percent of the world's renewable freshwater resources but less than 1 percent of the world's population. In terms of renewable resources, lumber is a major asset. The Interior Plains provide one of the great grain-growing areas of the world. The once-plentiful fish stocks of the Atlantic and Pacific coasts are seriously depleted, but conservation methods are slowly restoring them.

Natural resources provide constant sources of conflict that governments must resolve. Who owns them? How and by whom should they be regulated and exploited? Who ought to benefit from them? These questions constitute a major focus of politics in Canada.

Economy

Canada has many economic strengths besides an abundance of natural resources, including a well-educated workforce, world-class banks, a stable political system, and peaceful borders. However, it exists in a competitive global environment and is highly vulnerable to events and circumstances in the outside world. The Canadian economy has always relied heavily on exports. Today these include mainly energy and forest products, agriculture products, minerals and metals, chemicals, fertilizers, and plastics. Although Canada's economy began to diversify to include consumer goods in the latter part of the nineteenth century, except for automobile products they do not constitute a substantial proportion of exports.

Being rich in extractive industries—energy and mining—can be a problem when a country is overly reliant on this sector for national well-being. A robust manufacturing sector is vital to balancing the economy when resource prices are low. Resource-rich Western Canada boomed when oil prices were high in recent decades. However, when oil prices declined sharply in 2014–2015, this placed the Canadian economy in a precarious position because the country had become overly dependent on the oil industry for growth. The value of the Canadian dollar soon fell below US$0.75.

While the resource and energy sectors strengthened, especially after 2000, the manufacturing industry in Ontario and Québec (including the initial processing and refining of primary products and the producing of finished goods) languished and declined, with innovative companies like BlackBerry and Bombardier becoming less competitive in world markets. The automotive sector also declined as companies and jobs moved to Mexico and other low-cost locales. Factories in Ontario closed, moved, or switched production to focus on the equipment and parts needed to build and supply Alberta's new oil rigs. By June 2014, the number of Canadian factory jobs was at its lowest level in 38 years of record keeping.

The downturn in value of the resource and energy sector in the West reduced the country's economic growth, and jeopardized the federal government's ability to reduce the deficit and debt. Alberta's economy threatened to slip into recession. Saskatchewan and Newfoundland and Labrador, other significant oil-producing provinces, also were negatively affected as oil prices plummeted. As the economy of the oil-producing provinces diminished and jobs evaporated, Canadians expected Ontario and Québec, which had benefited from the weakened oil prices, to pick up the slack, but they lacked the industrial capacity to respond fully. The falling value of the dollar caused by the collapse of the energy sector may eventually help to revive competitive industries and strengthen exports of manufactured goods, but the process will take time. Tensions about how to share financial burdens caused by economic stagnation among the provinces were exacerbated and politicized. (See Chapter 4 on Federalism.)

Canada has been striving unsuccessfully for years to overcome its legacy as a "hewer of wood and drawer of water." Many reasons have been given for its failure to expand its manufacturing sector, including a lack of innovation, too much protectionism, and a low appetite for growth and risk.

Demography

Although it is the second largest country in the world based on land mass, Canada is only thirty-fifth by population. In 2011, there were a meagre 3.7 people per square kilometre. Geography confines most of the population to a narrow band along the Canada–United States border, spread out like beads on a string. As a result, it has always been a challenge to develop transportation and communication links to unite Canadians and resist the seductive attraction of the large border populations in the United States. The Québec City–to–Windsor, Ontario corridor comprises only about 1 percent of the country's land mass but houses close to 62 percent of its population. Canadians are largely urban. More than 81 percent of them live in metropolitan areas (compared to about 16 percent at Confederation in 1867). The most populous urban areas include the Golden Horseshoe in Ontario, the Calgary–Edmonton corridor, Montréal and its adjacent region, and southern Vancouver Island and the lower mainland of British Columbia.

From just 3.5 million people at Confederation, Canada has grown to a population of more than 35 million—larger than Austria, any of the Scandinavian countries, Greece, Hungary, or Venezuela, to name only a few of the 194 countries of the United Nations.[1] However, in recent years, the country's population growth has slowed to less than 1 percent a year based on natural increase and immigration. Three basic variables affect demography: fertility, mortality, and immigration.

Fertility: As in most other developed countries, Canadian fertility rates began to decline in 1961, after the baby boom of the late 1940s and 1950s. In 2014, there were roughly 1.1 births per woman, but a rate of more than 2 births is needed to maintain the current population level.[2] Current social patterns and technical advances indicate that low fertility rates are likely to continue into the near future.

Mortality: Mortality rates are also changing. The average life expectancy at Confederation was approximately 45 years; in 2014, for those born in 2012, it was 82 years (84 for women and 80 for men). The lowest life expectancy correlates with unskilled and blue-collar workers, the unmarried, and Aboriginals.

Immigration: The main driver of population growth is immigration, which has always played a vital role in Canada's development. Canada has one of the largest proportions of foreign-born residents of any country in the world—double that of the United States. The first National Household Survey in 2011 revealed that more than one-fifth of Canadians were foreign born, the highest percentage in 70 years.

Canada's population, therefore, is widely dispersed and far from uniform. What unites Canadians? What ideas and aspirations do they share? The next section provides some answers to these questions. We then consider some of the most important lines of division that set Canadians apart from each other.

WHAT UNITES CANADIANS?

In 2017, for Canada's 150th birthday, the Trans Canada Trail will be complete, commemorating the many iconic Canadian journeys of voyageurs, explorers, pioneers, and heroes and allowing Canadians to walk and cycle in the footsteps of these nation builders. The land and water trails will link the country and provide the ultimate Canadian journey from coast to coast.

Canadians share this land mass, along with its economy, history, and political institutions. They also have many common interests, including maintaining basic personal freedoms in a peaceful, prosperous country. In the following chapters, we will examine Canada's major political institutions, including the Constitution, federalism, Parliament, courts, political parties, and police, and

The Trans Canada Trail.

Lake Louise Tourism/P. Zizka

consider the extent to which they and the issues around them are unifying or divisive. Next, however, we examine some of the most significant aspects of that shared political culture, including the values, attitudes, and ideas that help to unite Canadians.

Political Culture

What comes to mind first when you ask yourself what it is to be Canadian? Is it the land itself, the people, the values, national sports, the system of government, or something else that creates a bond between you and your fellow Canadians?

Citizens of all countries develop perceptions and expectations about their political system, and these provide the value and belief structures within which political decisions are made. Cultural values affect the rhetoric and biases of politics. They delineate the accepted parameters of individual and government political activity and enable organizations and institutions to function coherently.

political culture: The broad patterns of values, beliefs, and attitudes in a society toward political objects.

The broad patterns of values, beliefs, and attitudes in a society toward political objects are often referred to as **political culture**. Political culture draws individuals together; supports ideas, judgment, and action; constitutes the character and personality of a community; differentiates it from other communities; and encourages its members to seek common objectives. What citizens know and feel about their political system affects the number and kinds of demands they make on the system and also their responses to laws and political leadership.

The extent to which values and attitudes are shared greatly affects the sense of political community and therefore the degree of national cohesion and stability in a country. Deep cleavages within a state over issues such as language, identity, or economic well-being obstruct the sharing of values and contribute to political instability.

It is difficult to measure the strength of something as elusive as a sense of political community. However, as we shall see, Canadians exhibit similar values, attitudes, and behaviour toward the political system and government. The collective heritage of values, beliefs, and attitudes shared by Canadians is greater than the rhetoric of provincial autonomy and regional cleavages might lead a casual observer to believe.

Political Values and Beliefs

values: Shared beliefs that provide standards of judgment about what is right, important, and desirable in society. They are deeply held convictions.

To understand Canadian politics, we must identify the values and beliefs that support the political institutions of the country. **Values** provide standards of judgment about what is right, important, and desirable in society. Though generally taken for granted and not articulated, widely accepted values about what is good and worthwhile set the boundaries of acceptable behaviour and underlie citizens' attitudes toward specific political goals. They provide guidelines to define what is right or wrong, what is or is not acceptable.

Many values and beliefs pertain to *all* Canadians, while others are shared by only a few. Overarching values and beliefs that bring Canadians together include traditions of personal freedom and civil liberties, respect for the law, and the coexistence of heterogeneous communities. In April 1982, the *Canadian Charter of Rights and Freedoms* became the first comprehensive statement of fundamental values to be entrenched in the Constitution. The preamble sets out the premise that "Canada is founded upon principles that recognize the supremacy of God and the Rule of Law." The Charter then guarantees the fundamental rights of Canada's "free and democratic society." The implicit values of Canadians, as formalized in the Charter, are rooted in the Western political tradition and Judeo-Christian religious thought.

Many values of representative democracy are proclaimed in the Charter (see Close-Up 2.1). These include the right of individuals to four fundamental individual freedoms: freedom of conscience and religion; freedom of thought, belief, opinion, and expression, including freedom of the press; freedom of peaceful assembly; and freedom of association. Another value of representative democracy highlighted by the Charter is equality before and under the law, without discrimination. In the political sphere, equality presumes such related values as universal suffrage and elections contested by competing political parties that give voters alternatives from which to choose.

Another associated value recognized by the Charter is acceptance of the rule of law, with civil rights for all citizens. Still another *implicit* value of representative democracy— but one not recognized in the Charter—is majority rule. In Canada, governments are based on an ability to sustain a majority of votes in the House of Commons. Members of Parliament (federal MPs) are elected in a system that gives credence to the majority principle but in fact allows members to be elected by a *plurality*—that is, the winner is the individual who gains the most votes in an election. When there are more than two candidates, the winner often has considerably less than 50 percent of the votes.

Since it is deemed necessary to protect minority rights in Canada, some *collective* rights are also named in the Constitution. These include French and English minority language rights in the federal and Québec legislatures and courts and in New Brunswick. Canadians also value equality highly in questions concerning collective rights. Section 15 of the Charter states that there should be no discrimination based on race, national or ethnic origin, colour, religion, gender, age, or mental or physical disability.

There are many other values that affect how Canadians conduct their politics. For example, Canadians demonstrate considerable ethnic tolerance. They also agree to share economic well-being, distributing financial resources to less prosperous provinces and disadvantaged individuals. Canadian public policy ensures that all individuals have basic health care, pensions, and a host of other forms of social assistance. Canada has many characteristics of a caring society. Such social services are based on deeply held values that politicians ignore at their peril.

Close-Up 2.1

Values Proclaimed in the Charter of Rights and Freedoms

- Freedom of conscience and religion
- Freedom of thought, belief, opinion, and expression
- Freedom of peaceful assembly
- Freedom of association
- Equality before and under the law

- Acceptance of the rule of law
- Civil rights for all citizens
- No discrimination based on race, national or ethnic origin, colour, religion, gender, age, or mental or physical disability

Political Attitudes

Attitudes toward political objects are more differentiated and fleeting than basic values and beliefs, but they may also be more immediate determinants of political behaviour. Attitudes toward specific political issues of the day are ephemeral. These changing attitudes are often defined as "public opinion," and although they are important in determining short-term political behaviour, they are less helpful than fundamental values and beliefs in depicting the political culture of a country.

Canadians generally have enough basic information about political institutions to allow them to operate effectively at both provincial and federal levels of government. They also demonstrate a high degree of affect (emotional attachment) for both their country and their respective provinces. In a 2010 study of four regions (West, Ontario, Québec, Atlantic), respondents identified significantly more with Canada than with their province, except in Québec, where they identified more with their province.[3] On the other hand, studies also have shown that Canadians lack faith that politicians and the political system will respond positively to their interests.[4] Although attitudes generally fluctuate over a relatively short period and vary across the population, negative views about politicians have persisted in recent years.

Cynical attitudes about politicians do not prevent widespread support for the government in Canada or hamper political participation at either the federal or the provincial level of government, although they may affect how sparingly Canadians cast their ballots in most elections. As we shall see, voter participation has been declining since the 1970s (the 2015 federal election was an exception). On the whole, however, individuals comply with basic political laws, and major political groups rarely offer violent resistance to authoritative government decisions. Acts of Parliament are considered legitimate and almost always obeyed.

Shared Political Ideas, Customs, Traditions, Symbols, and Heroes

Shared ideas, customs, and traditions unite people, and so do symbols. Canada's early settlers brought with them political ideas that still form the basis of political thought in this country. Of these, the liberal ideas of British philosopher John Locke are widely accepted today. Ideas about the importance of the individual, free enterprise, and the right of the individual to pursue personal interests without government interference are firmly embedded in Canadian political culture. However, unlike in the United States, there are also strains of conservative thought that can be traced to settlers in New France as well as United Empire Loyalists who fled revolutionary America. Socialist ideas—holding that the state is responsible for its citizens and should provide for their collective well-being—can also be found throughout Canadian history.

The study of ideas in Canadian political thought is, in many ways, a search for a comprehensive "story" about what binds the country together. A central theme has been a search for Canadian identity. "Who are we?" is a common yet elusive question.[5]

Many Canadian **political customs**—the conventional and accepted practices that are part of the political system—come from Britain. They may not be written down as rules or laws, but they are followed nevertheless. As Canada matured, it also began to develop its own distinctively Canadian customs and traditions. In 1952, for example, Canadians abandoned the tradition of selecting a British citizen as governor general, allowing a Canadian to fill that office for the first time.

The *political values* of a country are symbolized by such objects as flags, anthems, leaders, national holidays, and historical heroes. These symbols help to enforce respect for, and emotional attachment to, political institutions. They can be a focal point for national unity by recalling the achievements, tragedies, and idealism of previous generations. As Canada transformed from a colony to a full-fledged state, the change was reflected in the country's *political symbols*. In the early stages, these symbols manifested a dual allegiance to Canada and Britain but gradually changed to reflect national pride and unity without reference to Britain.

The evolution of the Canadian flag is perhaps the best illustration. At Confederation in 1867, Canada was granted permission to fly the red ensign, the flag of the British Merchant Navy. Attempts to replace it with a uniquely Canadian flag began as early as 1925, but did not succeed until four decades later when a flag that features a stylized red maple leaf was selected. The maple leaf is a distinctively Canadian symbol with deep historical roots.

Other reminders of Canada's British heritage have come to the fore from time to time as new symbols have evolved. The first day of July, Canada's national holiday, was known as Dominion Day until November 1982. Although the word *Dominion* had been chosen explicitly by the Fathers of Confederation to mean sovereignty from sea to sea, many Canadians had come to feel that it smacked of colonial dependence, so Parliament changed the title of the holiday to Canada Day.

In many countries, a constitution provides a focus for pride and unity. This has not been the case for all Canadians. The *British North America Act*, the basis of Canada's written Constitution, was passed by the British Parliament in 1867. As a national symbol, it was a source of embarrassment to many Canadians in the twentieth century for two reasons. First, it could not be amended without British approval. Second, it contained no formal guarantee of rights and freedoms. As we shall see in Chapter 5, in the spring of 1982 a revised Constitution, now known as the *Canada Act, 1982*, was patriated, including the old *British North America Act* and a new *Canadian Charter of Rights and Freedoms*. However, this was done without the signature of the Québec government, and that is still a source of resentment for some.

Another predominant political symbol is the monarch. Canada is a constitutional monarchy, and the role of Her Majesty Queen Elizabeth II as sovereign of Canada and head of state is ceremonial. As queen, she personifies the country and is a symbol of allegiance, unity, and authority. The ability of this institution to serve as a unifying symbol for Canada's two founding cultural groups is limited, but for many the Crown and monarchy represent the best traditions in Canadian democracy.

Historical heroes, as well as sports and literary figures, also can be symbols of national pride and unity. Unfortunately, Canada's gradual evolution to statehood, as opposed to the dramatic (and bloody) revolution that happened south of the border, did not produce a large pool of charismatic heroes. As well, French and English

CP Photo by Boris Spremo

Modern hero Terry Fox was born in Winnipeg in 1958. His courage and determination in the face of cancer earned him widespread admiration and respect. In 2004, Manitoba renamed the August civic holiday Terry Fox Day in his honour.

Canadians each tend to cultivate their own separate symbols and historical memories. Hockey and Olympic sports heroes tend to be some of the country's most successful symbols of pride and unity, as are the national health care program and Canadian-style multiculturalism.

WHAT DIVIDES CANADIANS?

While there are many bonds that unite Canadians, other factors divide them. Differing ideologies provide the basis for fundamentally unique ways of looking at political issues and support different policy solutions. As well, several deep and relatively stable cleavages cut across Canadian society, creating different "layers" of Canadians with specific needs, interests, and prejudices. Some of these are based on age, class, gender, and region. Others are based on ethnicity, language, and religion. They divide Canadians into separate groups that coexist within the state. Group lines sometimes overlap. Each stratum or grouping of Canadians makes its own demands on governments. Some groups are cohesive; others are not. Some are politicized; others are not. Some have considerable power and influence; others have very little. These divisions are not necessarily unduly divisive politically, but they do demarcate special needs and interests and help to form the character and culture of the country.

Canadians do not have equal chances to succeed in life. They have different personal characteristics, abilities, and health, and are born into different social and economic circumstances. Factors such as gender, education, and socio-economic class to a large extent determine an individual's ideas and political orientations. They shape the experiences and opportunities of Canadians and influence how, and even whether, individuals wish to participate in the political process. Different political ideologies underpin Canadians' political ideas and orientations.

Some of the main factors that divide Canadians are political ideas, identity and ethnicity, age, economic class, region, gender, and religion. We consider each in turn.

Political Ideas

ideology: An explicit doctrinal structure that provides a particular diagnosis of the ills of society plus an accompanying "action program" for implementing prescribed solutions for them.

While many ideas unite Canadians, others divide them. **Ideology** is an explicit doctrinal structure that provides a particular diagnosis of the ills of society plus an accompanying "action program" for implementing prescribed solutions for these problems. Ideologies are associated to various degrees with particular political parties, structuring their rhetoric and conditioning their policy programs. Other than nationalism, which underpins the Bloc Québécois (and is discussed in Chapter 5), liberal, conservative, and socialist ideologies are the most significant of these forces in Canadian society.

These three ideologies have deep historical roots, and it is important to trace them briefly to understand their contribution to political thought in Canada. Liberalism and conservatism originated in Europe in the nineteenth century as philosophers and thinkers struggled to create logical and consistent patterns of thought about how to restructure the medieval social and political order that new technological developments were rendering obsolete. Socialism developed later but, again, in response to fundamental changes in economics. By the beginning of the twentieth century, the European political and ideological battlefield was a three-way contest, as the socialist ideology added socialist, labour, and communist ideas to those parties espousing liberalism and conservatism.

Liberalism Historically, liberalism was the ideology of a rising commercial class that resented the restrictions of the old feudal order on European society. The ideas it generated provided moral, political, and economic guidance. Morally, liberalism affirmed basic values, including freedom and dignity. Politically, it espoused basic political rights such as the right of representative government. Economically, it was dedicated to the right to private property, free trade, and free enterprise capitalism.

The historical root of *liberal* is the Latin *liber*, meaning *free* (man). The concept of freedom is at the heart of the liberal ideology. Early proponents of liberalism called for freedom (or absence of coercion) in all areas of life: social, political, and economic.

The English political philosopher John Locke (1637–1704) was the most influential of the early thinkers, who are generally referred to as classical liberals. Locke argued that all human beings have the right to life, liberty, and property and that they create government to protect and preserve these basic rights. If the government fails in this task, Locke said, the people have the right to overthrow it.[6] He wrote, "Freedom is . . . to have a standing rule to live by, common to everyone of that society and made by the legislative power erected in it."[7] Civil liberties, or freedoms such as freedom of expression, freedom of speech, and freedom to publish and disseminate one's ideas, have been enshrined in the constitutions of most liberal democracies.

Locke, and other liberals including John Stuart Mill (1806–1873), wanted to organize government to maintain law and order but not infringe on human rights. The way to accomplish that goal was to force governments to operate under the strict limits of a constitution. Locke believed that legislatures elected by the people (at that time still on a very limited franchise) should make decisions for society. He based his idea of representative government on the notion that political authority derives from the people. The

English political philosopher John Locke.

Scottish moral philosopher Adam Smith.

elected majority, he said, can make all decisions, but it must respect the natural rights of all citizens.

Liberalism also had important economic implications for the state. Scottish moral philosopher Adam Smith (1723–1790) expounded the principle of *laissez-faire*, which essentially means that there should be minimum intervention by government in economic affairs. Smith maintained that society is governed by natural laws, just as the physical universe is. One such law holds that prices in a free market are determined by supply and demand. Ideally, Smith reasoned, the government would leave the economy to adjust itself entirely through the free market.

Classical liberalism was later deemed harsh to the poor in society because it opposed redistribution of wealth. At the same time, however, it defended the principle of equality before the law for all individuals. Economic inequality was unavoidable, classical liberals said, but eventually the free market system would create wealth and raise living standards for everyone.

Modern liberalism has moved away from some of the tenets of classical liberalism. The new position is often called *reform* liberalism because it expanded or reformed the classical approach to the concept of freedom. Reform liberals moved away from the classical roots on three essential points:

1. The idea that government should be left to the propertied class was replaced by democratic principles of mass participation.

2. The concept of freedom was changed to recognize that the state might have to curb some liberties in order to provide a higher standard of living for the least well-off in society.

3. Reform liberals abandoned laissez-faire capitalism to accept the teaching of economist John Maynard Keynes (1883–1946), who argued in the 1930s that reliance on market forces could result in a permanent economic depression, so government action might be required to counter this possibility.

Reform liberals reconciled state action with their notion of individual freedom by arguing that economic intervention was necessary to enable individuals to fulfill their desires and make the market work effectively. They maintained that the government must play a regulatory role in protecting society. The governments of Canada, Britain, and the United States all followed this modern liberal reasoning after World War II.

Contemporary liberal values include respect for individual rights and freedoms, political equality, limited government, rule of law, minimum conditions of life guaranteed by the state, and modified economic freedom. In other words, modern liberalism favours minimal government intervention in the private lives of citizens but reasonable government intervention in economic affairs.

All parties in the Canadian House of Commons today espouse a kind of nineteenth-century liberalism in their stress on the market's role in the regulation of economic life. However, they all adapt aspects of Keynesianism and even aspects of the modern welfare state.

Conservatism Conservatism as an ideology originally justified the positions of the aristocracy and church in the old order of European society. These elements of society resisted the liberal ideology of progressive social change and defended the *status quo*. They sought to conserve such elements as power, property, status, and way of life. As it developed, this ideology took the term *conservative*, which comes from the Latin *conservare*, which means to save or preserve.

Irish scholar Edmund Burke (1729–1797) was the first major figure to define and clarify conservatism. Burke, along with other early conservatives, insisted that society must have a stable order and structure so that individuals will know their place in the community and live and work within those confines for the good of the whole. Change, they said, must be gradual. Burke believed that being a responsible

Irish scholar Edmund Burke.

member of society allowed an individual to achieve greater happiness than could be gained otherwise. Conservatives believed that it was not the individual but rather the social group that was more important. They accused classical liberals of being individualistic and selfish.

Whereas classical liberals were suspicious of state power and wanted to limit it, conservatives believed that state power was necessary in order to achieve social order. Burke therefore, for example, opposed extending the right to vote to the masses, and defended the hereditary aristocracy and established church. However, he viewed such power as including a responsibility to help the weak and less fortunate. In this way, conservatives were able to argue that their approach was better for the less fortunate of society than that of the liberals, who believed that everyone, including the poor, should be free to look after themselves. Burke and the early conservatives shared many views about the functioning of the market and economics with Adam Smith and the classical liberals.

Like liberalism, conservatism adapted and changed. After the World War II, when the old social order had been destroyed in Europe, conservatives gave qualified acceptance to the notion of the welfare state, but they still sought to preserve traditional moral values and a social structure that would provide leadership for society. European conservatism was never a strong part of American culture because the United States was founded and populated largely by liberals. There was no aristocracy or "old order" to defend. However, in the 1930s, those who opposed the welfare state philosophy of modern liberalism adopted the conservative label.

American conservatism thus stresses individualism, self-reliance, and a dislike for state interference, and it views the improvement of the human condition as the inevitable outcome of unrestricted interaction among self-interested individuals—in other words, American conservatives are similar to old-style liberals. European conservatism, on the other hand, ranks order and the common good of the community above individual freedom. The former Progressive Conservative Party of Canada espoused both the traditional and the American ideas about conservatism at various times in its history, while the Reform and Canadian Alliance parties essentially adopted the philosophy of U.S. conservatism. The Conservative Party of Canada today appears to be following a similar trajectory back to traditional and British conservatism.

Socialism Within the first few decades of the nineteenth century, the technological advances of the Industrial Revolution in Europe created a large urban working class that existed in wretched conditions. Socialists sought to ameliorate the lot of these workers by challenging the liberal idea that governments should not be directly involved in the management of the economy of the country. Socialism championed public ownership, a planned economy, and state intervention in market forces. Workers wanted help from a progressive state, but older philosophies held that the economy should be as free as possible of government control.

In the early years, socialism offered two versions of its doctrine: the *utopian* version found in Britain and France, and the *scientific* version of Karl Marx in Germany. The scientific socialists, led by Marx (1818–1883), dominated socialist thought by the end of the century. Within this group, however, a doctrinal split emerged. Those who wanted to work within the framework of parliamentary democracy became known as *democratic socialists*. Those who clung to the Marxist revolutionary prescription came under the label of *communist*. Both groups sought public control of the means of production and an end to the exploitation of labour under capitalism. However, communism went much further, to promise equalization of material conditions for everyone. In other words, they offered not just equalities of opportunity but equalities of outcomes.

Even before the breakdown of communism in the Soviet Union, there were significant changes to socialist thought. In Britain, nationalizing industries was no longer a key component of socialist doctrine. In 1995, Clause 4 of the British Labour party constitution (which called for nationalizing industries) was deleted, marking a major turning point in the development of socialism in political parties. Since then, the Labour party has espoused a completely diluted socialism—or not socialism at all, according to many commentators. In Canada, aspects of the socialist doctrine appear regularly in New Democratic Party (NDP) debates. On the whole, however, the party under Ed Broadbent (1975–1989) relaxed its relatively strict adherence to the socialist doctrine and has not returned to its strict ideological roots under subsequent leaders.

Ideology in Action in Canada Ideas derived from these main ideologies, and others such as nationalism and populism, have been taken up by political parties in Canada over the years with varying degrees of ardor and tenacity. There are two main schools of academic thought concerning ideology in Canadian political parties.

The first, somewhat cynical, school maintains that there have been no fundamental ideological differences between the Liberal and Conservative/Progressive Conservative (PC) parties over the years. As "brokerage parties," both place vote-getting ahead of ideology, and pragmatically and opportunistically follow public opinion polls in setting their agendas—rather like Tweedledum and Tweedledee. To a large extent, even the modern NDP adapts to brokerage-type policies and actions.

The second academic school says that the Liberal and Conservative parties both vie for the centre ground on issues but still maintain relatively consistent and distinguishable policy differences. For example, Liberals after 1900 were more sympathetic to Québec and French-Canadian interests, while Progressive Conservatives after 1957 were more sympathetic to Western interests. For many years, Liberals favoured lower tariffs, Conservatives higher tariffs. Liberals supported free trade, while the PCs objected to it. Liberals supported provincial rights, and Conservatives advocated strong central government. Clearly, such patterns did exist for specific periods of time, but not consistently. In fact, the two major parties reversed themselves on all of these positions throughout the twentieth century, especially on tariffs and free trade with the United States in 1988.

Both of these schools of thought are partially correct. Values based on a belief in a capitalist society, a market economy, and the right to private property are dominant in Canadian society, but not to the absolute exclusion of other perspectives. The main parties since Confederation—the Conservative, Liberal, and New Democratic parties—have reflected the broad ideological differences of conservatism, liberalism, and socialism but never strayed very far from the "liberal" opinions of the broader public.

Identity and Ethnicity

Beneath the veneer of Canada's national political culture there are many political subcultures. Cultural pluralism is encouraged by a number of factors, including the size of the country, many different ethnic groups, a sparse and dispersed population, and the federal system of government. An **identity group** consists of people who share a characteristic or characteristics that define them and set them apart from others. Age, class, region, gender, religion, and ethnicity are all subcultures that are components of social identity. Much of modern conflict is rooted in disputes over ideas and ideology based on these identity groups.[8] Nationalism, another component of social identity, is discussed in Chapter 5.

Ethnic groups are among the most significant subcultures are ethnic groups. **Ethnicity** is primarily a subjective characteristic shared by groups of people and reinforced by different customs, language, dialect, and cultural heritage, and sometimes distinct racial or physical characteristics. **Ethnic origin** refers to the ethnic or cultural group(s) to which an individual's ancestors belonged; it pertains to the ancestral roots or origins of the population and not to place of birth, citizenship, or nationality. Ethnicity provides a powerful sense of identity.

There are three major ethno-linguistic groupings in Canada: the two founding European nations, French and English, and Aboriginal peoples. The English-speaking majority today is culturally very diverse and becoming more so every year. The

identity group: People who share a characteristic or characteristics that define them and set them apart from others.

ethnicity: Primarily a subjective term used to describe groups of people who share customs, language, dialect, and/or cultural heritage, and sometimes distinct physical or racial characteristics.

ethnic origin: Refers to the ethnic or cultural group(s) to which an individual's ancestors belonged; it pertains to the ancestral roots or origins of the population and not to place of birth, citizenship, or nationality.

French live mostly in Québec but are found in smaller numbers dispersed throughout the country, particularly in New Brunswick, Ontario, and Manitoba. The third group includes various groupings of Aboriginal peoples. We consider each group in turn as well as a fourth group, visible minorities, that is growing rapidly.

Age

Age divides Canadians into groups with vastly different political interests and issues. Canada's population is rapidly getting older, and this has major social and economic implications. Consider that, in 1881, the median age was 20 years; by 2013, it was 40.2, an all-time high. The proportion of Canadians over 65 years of age has steadily increased since the mid-1960s, and accelerated at the beginning of the current decade.

Largely because of a low fertility rate, the proportion of Canadians over 65 years of age (15.7 percent in 2014) is projected to reach between 24 and 28 percent of the population by 2063. Meanwhile, the working population will decrease dramatically, thanks to the fact that baby boomers (born between 1946 and 1966) have begun to retire.[9] Canada's demographic dependency ratio (the number of persons aged 14 years and under, or 65 years and older, for every 100 persons aged 15 to 64 years) will increase from 45.9 in 2013 to at least 69.7 in 2063. By 2030, there could be just two workers for every senior Canadian.

Such an age imbalance increases financial pressures on working Canadians and raises questions about how best to support the elderly. The demands that are made on government reflect this shifting age stratification. Old Age Security (OAS) is one of the largest and most expensive federal programs. Beginning in 2023, the age of eligibility for OAS pension and Guaranteed Income Supplement (GIS) for poorer seniors will increase from 65 to 67 years. Will it go even further? Will the program exist at all when you retire?

With the country's current low birth rate of 1.1 births per female and an aging population, governments will have to decide if they should take in more immigrants to balance the effect of the low birth rate.

Class

class: Refers to a rank or order in society determined by such characteristics as education, occupation, and income.

Defining *class* is controversial and problematic. **Class** refers to socio-economic status and/or a rank or order in society determined by such characteristics as education, occupation, and income. These characteristics provide "objective" indicators, which are sometimes different from "subjective" or self-assigned rankings.

Class divisions based on wealth and income remain significant in Canada. Table 2.1 illustrates that there is a tiny elite, or *upper class*, of less than 2 percent of the population. These individuals hold the top positions in business, industry, the professional ranks, and the bureaucracy. The extensive wealth of these very few individuals and families in real estate, natural resources, communications, and various commercial enterprises, especially large corporations, sets them apart from other Canadians. People in this class earn a minimum of $150,000 a year. They tend to be university educated, male, and living in a married or common law relationship. In 2011, more than half of the top group lived in Toronto, Montréal, Calgary, or Vancouver. Most had studied business, health, or engineering and

Table 2.1 Distribution of Total Income of Individuals, 2011

Income Group	2011
Average income	$39 300
Median income	$29 000
Percentages	
Under $10 000	18.0%
$10 000 to 19 999	18.9%
$20 000 to 20 999	14.4%
$30 000 to 39 999	12.1%
$40 000 to 49 999	9.0%
$50 000 to $59 999	7.3%
$60 000 and over	19.4%
$150 000 and over	1.9%

Source: Income Statistics Division, Statistics Canada. The data are from CANSIM table 202-0402. http://www5. statcan.gc.ca

received substantial income from investments and self-employment. Since 1995, the after-tax income of the top income group has risen much more than it has for other groups (see Figure 2.2).

The vast majority of Canadians today are part of the huge *middle class*—sandwiched between the tiny economic elite and those who are economically

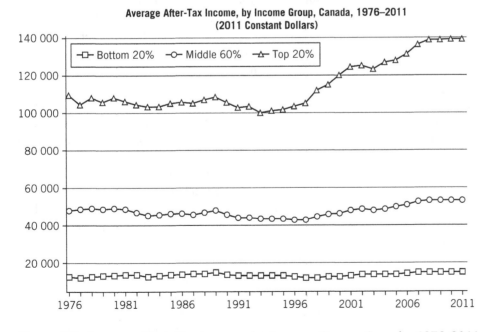

Figure 2.2 Average After-Tax Income, by Income Group, Canada, 1976–2011

Source: Employment and Social Development Canada (ESDC) calculations based on Statistics Canada, *Table 202-0703—Market, total and after-tax income, by economic family type and after-tax income quintiles, 2011 constant dollars, annual,* CANSIM (database).

deprived. The shape of the economic hierarchy, therefore, is not a pyramid; it is shaped more like a bulging onion. The median *individual* income was $29,000 in 2011, meaning that half of the population had an income above that level and half had an income below it.

The Canadian middle class is extremely heterogeneous in terms of income, occupation, and lifestyle. It can be subdivided into upper-middle and lower-middle class. The upper-middle tier is extremely varied—generally well educated and financially secure. It does not function as a single unit but has different economic interests and political demands. It includes groups such as lawyers, doctors, and business people.

The lower-middle class is generally considered to consist of those who do manual as opposed to white-collar work. As a whole, this group is less educated and generally earns less money than others in the middle class. Despite the fact that some of those in the lower-middle class are unionized, changes in the Canadian economy in the 1980s and 1990s dramatically increased unemployment in this group. The proportion of blue-collar jobs in the workforce increased only marginally, while unskilled and primary labour jobs in fishing, mining, and agriculture declined sharply. Early in the next decade, an oil boom increased jobs in the labour sector again, mainly in Alberta, but that too was short lived. An uncertain job market, combined with inflation and increased taxation, make individuals in this stratum particularly vulnerable to dropping into the lowest grouping of economically deprived Canadians.

Table 2.1 shows that 37 percent of individuals earn less than $20 000 per year, which makes them very vulnerable. There is no agreed-upon legal definition of poverty, and Canada therefore has no legal poverty measure. Sometimes it is measured by low income alone, sometimes by "basic needs" (which measure the minimum resources needed for well-being), and sometimes by "market-basket measures" (which estimate the income needed to meet basic needs). The different measures produce different statistics, but none provides a source of pride.

Generally, however, the poor in Canada are considered to be those who exist below the *poverty line*, a theoretical line set by Statistics Canada. This measure is called the **low income cut-off (LICO)**, and is based on a complicated and controversial formula.[10] In 2011, about 4 to 5 million Canadians, or about 9 percent of Canadians, were considered poor. Low income was determined to be an annual income of $30 945 for a family of four in a mid-sized town.[11]

Among those worst off are Aboriginal Canadians, one-parent families, children under 17 years of age, the single elderly, recent immigrants, and people with disabilities. Women are disproportionately represented among the poorest in Canadian society, particularly elderly women and single mothers. In 2011, there were 1.5 million single-parent families (more than 16 percent of all families). Women headed the majority of these families, and most were impoverished. Roughly one-third of all visible minority women and Native women were also in the low-income category. Poverty brings fewer educational opportunities, with all that entails (see Close-Up 2.2). It also brings shorter lives, higher mortality rates, poorer nutrition, more homelessness, more physical and mental illness, poorer and more hazardous working conditions, higher crime rates, and higher suicide and divorce rates. It is also the best predictor of juvenile delinquency.

low income cut-off (LICO):
An income inequality measure published by Statistics Canada that is often used to define a poverty line.

The Value of Education

Education is the primary means by which people achieve upward mobility and escape from the lower socio-economic classes and poverty. A university education does not guarantee financial success, but it certainly improves the odds. Higher education is associated with:

- Higher earnings
- Greater savings and assets
- Higher income in retirement

Together with occupation and income, higher education is also a principal determinant of social status. It increases political interest and awareness, expands opportunities, and develops the political skills necessary for effective political participation. Post-secondary education has almost become a necessity for holding high public office.

As well as directing students toward particular roles and class positions in society, educational institutions teach relevant facts, values, predispositions, and skills. They are the main community facility in which immigrant children learn one or both official languages and acquire basic citizenship training. Research indicates that education establishes a "receptivity to acquire further knowledge long after formal education has terminated."[12]

Canadians are staying in school longer. They are among the most highly educated in the world and perform well on international tests. Fifty-three percent of Canadians had at least some post-secondary education in 2012, and 28 percent had obtained a university degree. Canada ranks highest in post-secondary education attainment among the Organisation for Economic Co-operation and Development (OECD) countries but drops to seventh in the proportion of those with university education. Gender bias in educational institutions has greatly diminished so that women account for more than half of university graduates.[13]

The percentage employment by level of educational attainment for Canadians aged 25 to 44 years in 2014 was as follows:

Less than grade 9	49.2%
Some high school	61.0%
High school	75.8%
Some post-secondary	73.2%
Post-secondary	85.9%
BA	85.7%
Post-graduate	85.8%

Source: Statistics Canada, CANSIM table 282-0064 and Catalogue no. 89F0133XIE.

Unequal opportunity and poor distribution of wealth have significant implications for politics in Canada. The commodity boom that boosted the Canadian economy through much of the early 2000s did not distribute additional income to the country's poorest households. Instead, the income gap between the richest and the poorest Canadians widened.[14] The implications of this are particularly serious for children, as Close-Up 2.3 indicates.

There is no doubt that the economic elite exercises considerable influence in the development of the country. On the other hand, it is far from a ruling class. Political power in Canada is diffused downward at least to the middle class. The political decision-making process is extremely complex and virtually precludes control by one small group. Governments must maintain popular support, and this puts considerable power in the hands of the majority of Canadian voters.

Unfortunately, members of the lowest socio-economic stratum participate least in the political system, preoccupied as they are with questions of basic survival. A wide range of federal, provincial, and municipal welfare programs exists to help

Child Poverty

In 2014, UNICEF released "Report Card 12," a study examining child poverty and deprivation in the industrialized world. This was the first such study after the economic recession of 2008–2011, and it found that children in most wealthy countries had been severely hurt by the recession. In a few of the countries, government actions had helped to shelter children from the worst impacts, while in others conditions for children had worsened dramatically.

Canada ranked eleventh of 41 countries, in the middle category. The child poverty rate in Canada fell by 2 percent from 2008, lifting 180 000 children out of poverty. However, the child poverty rate was still 21 percent, and not all Canadian children fared equally. The most vulnerable among them slipped deeper into poverty. Levels of family stress increased, and when asked about whether they believed that children had sufficient opportunities to learn and grow, Canadians were pessimistic, ranking in the bottom third of the 41 countries.

Canada's child poverty rate is still unacceptably high and federal leadership is required. Social programs to buffer children from poverty need to be rethought, particularly in times of recession. As the UNICEF report concluded: "Countries should place the well-being of children at the top of their responses to the recession. Not only is this a moral obligation but it is in the self-interest of societies."[15]

Children are particularly vulnerable because they cannot speak for themselves and make demands on governments. What percentage of child poverty is acceptable in a relatively wealthy country? What Canadian government policies attempt to cut child poverty and poverty generally, and are they satisfactory?

them. However, these programs tend to be scaled back or cut when governments are having trouble balancing their budgets or when governments are ideologically inclined to do so. Young people are some of the worst hit by recessions, as reflected in youth unemployment (see Close-Up 2.4).

Of all government assistance policies, social security for seniors is one of the most controversial. As a population ages, it becomes more expensive to maintain. As older people retire, a bigger economic burden falls on the remaining workers. The government's plan for the elderly will have a great impact on today's young people. Government policy needs to determine how many retirees today's students will have to support when they are in the labour force and what proportion of their taxes will go toward supporting seniors—a difficult trade-off to make for even seasoned politicians and public servants.

Youth Unemployment

Youth unemployment for those 15 to 24 years of age is more than double that for Canadians as a whole. In December 2014, unemployment among youths was more than 14 percent, compared with 6.6 percent for workers aged 25 to 54 years. Recessions tend to worsen the unemployment rate for non-students relative to adults, but improve it for students.

What can and should governments do about this situation? What can youths do to protect themselves given these circumstances?

Region

Regionalism refers to territorial tensions brought about by groups that demand a change in the political, economic, and cultural relations between regions and central powers *within* the existing state.[16] It is such an important feature of culture and politics in Canada that it is a major focus of Chapter 4 on federalism as well as a major component of Chapters 10 and 11 on parties and elections.

Regional cultures, like political ideas, age, gender, class, and ethnicity, can divide Canadians. They develop where economic, ethnic, social, demographic, and other factors provide a unique identity within a particular geographical setting. Region is a very fluid concept that can be adapted to fit any particular circumstance. For example, some models consider three regions: the West, the East, and the North. Others delineate four: Western, Central, Atlantic, and Northern Canada. Still others consider more or fewer regions. Some studies use provincial models, and some are based on only two regions: Québec and "the rest." The point is that regions are often simply constructs that are useful for sociological or political purposes. Senate seats, for example, are regionally based, representing four regions (Maritimes, Québec, Ontario, and the West, with special status for Newfoundland and Labrador and the North). The most politically salient regions are those based on the political boundaries that divide the 10 provinces and 3 territories. These boundaries provide a framework for the loyalty and shared experiences of the people who live within them and their governments give voice to their demands and grievances.

Numerous factors promote and sustain regionalism. In Canada, people of different cultural and linguistic backgrounds settle in specific parts of the country and help to create cultural differences. Geography, physiography, and resource differences also form natural regions that foster among their inhabitants distinct viewpoints, loyalties, and attitudes toward political issues.[17]

Do Canadians identify more strongly with their country or their province? A recent study used the framework of four regions to answer this question. It found that in 2010, about half of Québec citizens identified more strongly with their province, while in Atlantic Canada and Western Canada fewer than 20 percent did so. Ontarians were the most nationalistic, with only 4 percent identifying more strongly with their province.[18]

When emotional connections to region or province are higher than they are to the country, it is dramatically easier for citizens to oppose the federal government. This happened in Québec with separatist challenges, and also sometimes in the West with alienation and disillusionment. The federal government had to address grievances and meet regional aspirations, balancing them with those of the rest of the country, in order to resolve tensions. Regions that are physically far from the government in Ottawa or that are not well represented in government are particularly vulnerable to regional discontent. Citizens feel ignored or cut off from power.

Canada has faced periodic demands from alienated regions. In the Atlantic region, there has always been fierce pride and independence, but these feelings have been mitigated by the area's need for federal financial assistance. As a whole, this region is consistently considerably below the national average in terms of per capita income and its provinces are major beneficiaries of equalization payments, discussed in Chapter 4.

regionalism: Refers to territorial tensions brought about by certain groups that demand a change in the political, economic, and cultural relations between regions and central powers *within* the existing state.

The fishing industry that traditionally sustained the Maritime provinces collapsed in the 1990s as stocks of groundfish fell dramatically, leaving an oversupply of fishers, trawlers, and processing plants. Resource industries have sustained New Brunswick, Newfoundland and Labrador, and Nova Scotia, but seasonal unemployment remains high. Newfoundland and Labrador has benefited greatly from offshore petroleum revenues, and Nova Scotia has done well with natural gas in the Sable Offshore Energy Project. The 2005 Atlantic Accord gave the two provinces the ability to keep the proceeds of offshore oil wells and not have that amount deducted from their equalization payments.

Discontent in Western Canada reflects a unique history and population composition. In Central Canada, a broad perception of national needs has been built around the two founding peoples because of historical relationships between French and English Canadians. This is not, however, the Western vision of Canada. Because the Western provinces were established later than those in Central and Eastern Canada by an ethnic population different from that in Ontario and Québec, the people there do not tend to state their political interests in terms of the early history of Central and Eastern Canada.

> *We have always had a sense of economic exploitation. This notion has marked all Political parties in the West. The cartoon that has captured these sentiments is one of A large cow standing on a map of Canada munching grass in Alberta and Saskatchewan.*
>
> Harry Strom, former premier of Alberta[19]

The thrust of Western discontent has hinged on a feeling of marginalization and alienation from the centres of economic and political power rather than on a desire for separation from it, as has been the case with Québec. Westerners were alienated when they did not have strong representation in government. As a region, they have strongly supported Conservative parties; when those parties were not in power, Westerners lost their voice. They expressed considerable dissent and alienation before Stephen Harper, from Calgary, became prime minister as head of the Conservative party in 2008, but since then their voice has commanded significant power and alienation has dissipated.

Regional cleavages, like ethnic frictions, divide Canadians, but they are not necessarily a threat to national unity. Analysis of Canada-wide data has shown that although regional loyalty is often high in Canada, it does not necessarily come at the expense of national loyalty.[20] In fact, outside Québec, feelings toward one's province and Canada are strongly correlated: positive feelings toward a province are often accompanied by positive feelings for the country. The more knowledgeable Canadians are about their country, the more sensitive they are to regionalism, and the more they tend to be cosmopolitan and feel warmly about others who differ from themselves.

The underlying problem of regional alienation continues to be easy to state but not easy to resolve. The combined population of Ontario and Québec considerably exceeds 50 percent of the entire country. Because of this, the outer regions of Canada often perceive that the federal parliamentary system represents only Central Canada and therefore, to an extent, is merely a regional government. Yet if democracy prevails—that is, if the rule stands that votes should count relatively equally—the most populous provinces and regions will, and should, always have a majority.

Gender

Gender, too, divides Canadians into groups with different political interests. Today, females make up slightly more than half of the population, and this affects not only social relations but also government actions, especially in the field of human rights. In recent years, other gender groupings have also won rights. In 2005, with the enactment of the *Civil Marriage Act*, Canada became the fourth country in the world to legalize same-sex marriage. In addition to new rights for gays, lesbians, and bisexuals, transsexuals are now allowed, under varying rules across the provinces and territories, to change their legal gender. These rights are protected by court decisions decided under Section 15 of the *Canadian Charter of Rights and Freedoms*, which states that individuals are equal before and under the law without discrimination based on sex and other attributes. Similarly, human rights legislation prohibits discrimination and harassment based on gender (see the court cases discussed in Chapter 9).

Males and females share many political values and goals, but significant differences also separate them. The two groups differ greatly on the extent to which they participate and are represented in the country's politics and also in the political issues that concern them. Throughout history, women around the world have often been treated as inferior to men. Discrimination was enforced by social customs and laws. At the beginning of the twentieth century, married women in Canada were still considered to belong to their husbands. Women were just beginning to enter universities, medical schools, and law schools for the first time. Some were fighting for the right to make contracts, own property, and work outside the home. Women were assigned, and generally accepted, primary responsibility for children and the family, while men worked outside the home. Initially, women were barred from such societal participation as owning property, holding public office, voting, and even higher education.

When women first began organizing to press for reforms on issues that concerned them, their impact on policy issues was limited. They were not even allowed to vote for their political representatives. Politics was the prerogative of relatively well-to-do males. Only slowly, over time, did women of different regions, religions, economic status, and backgrounds begin to come together to express what could be identified as women's issues and women's politics. There is still little unanimity among women on many political, social, and other issues.

In 1916, Manitoba, Saskatchewan, and Alberta were the first provinces to allow women to vote, followed by Ontario and British Columbia. Soon, all other provinces followed suit except Québec, where women were not enfranchised until 1940. Federally, women in the armed services voted in 1917, as did designated female relatives of soldiers who were abroad. A year later, all Canadian women were given the right to vote, though they did not have the chance to exercise it until 1921.

The 1921 election brought the first woman, Agnes Macphail, to the House of Commons (see Close-Up 2.5 and Close-Up 2.6)). It was difficult for women to participate in an occupation that required them to be far from home much of the time. They worked in parties but generally in affiliated auxiliaries rather than in the mainstream. Since the 1970s, their numbers have increased with almost every election, but as Table 2.2 shows, the Conservative and Liberal parties in particular have done a relatively poor job of recruiting female candidates. In the 41st Canadian Parliament elected in 2011, a record 76 women became MPs out of a total of 308—still only 24 percent

Some Firsts for Women in Canadian Politics

1921	First Canadian woman MP (Agnes Macphail)
1930	First Canadian woman senator (Carine Wilson)
1957	First Canadian woman federal Cabinet minister (Ellen Fairclough)
1982	First Canadian woman on the Supreme Court (Bertha Wilson)
1984	First Canadian governor general (Jeanne Sauvé)
1989	First Canadian woman federal party leader (Audrey McLaughlin)
1991	First Canadian woman premier (British Columbia, Rita Johnston)
1993	First woman prime minister (Kim Campbell)
2000	First Canadian woman chief justice (Beverley McLachlin)
2015	A record number of women were premiers (in six provinces and territories)
	First fully gender balanced federal Cabinet

of the House of Commons.[21] In both the 39th and the 41st Parliaments, the New Democratic Party caucuses were 40 percent female, the closest an official party has come to gender balance. In 2015 the victorious Liberal caucus was 27 percent female.

Once in Parliament, the next hurdle for women was to be appointed to Cabinet. This did not happen until 1957 (see Close-Up 2.5). Female representation in Cabinet increased slowly and fluctuated over the decades. In the 2011 Harper government there were only 12 women out of 39 Cabinet ministers, most of whom had minor portfolios. When the Liberals were elected in 2015, however, Prime Minister Trudeau appointed a fully gender-balanced Cabinet. In spite of this milestone, Canada still lags behind other countries in electing women to high office. In 2015, Canada placed 47th in a ranking of women in national parliaments.[22]

Table 2.2 Number of Female Candidates Nominated by and Elected for Federal Parties in Parliament, 2011 and 2015

	Women			
Party	Nominated 2011	Elected 2011	Nominated 2015	Elected 2015
Bloc Quebecois	24	1	22	2
Conservative	68	28	66	17
Liberal	90	7	105	50
NDP	124	40	145	18
Greens	99	1	135	1
Total		77 of 308		88 of 338

Source: Elections Canada, Women Candidates in General Elections—1921 to Date, http://www.parl.gc.ca/About/Parliament/FederalRidingsHistory/hfer.asp?Search=WomenElections&Language=E. 2015 data is provisional.

There is a larger number of women in Parliament now than there has been [in preceding Parliaments], but at this rate we would reach equality in 390 years.

Anne McGrath, Liberal party campaign co-chair[23]

For many years, women were not eligible to be appointed to the Senate. Carine Wilson was the first woman to win an appointment, but it took a long time for more women to join her. As of 2015, women made up about a third of Canada's senators. Leadership roles are still few and far between. Kim Campbell became prime minister before the 1994 federal election by winning the leadership of the governing Progressive Conservatives, but her party badly lost the subsequent election. In 1984, Jeanne Sauvé was appointed as the first woman governor general after having been the first female speaker of the House of Commons. Adrienne Clarkson became the second female governor general in 1999, followed by Michaëlle Jean in 2005.

Much of the impetus for women's gains in political life was generated by the Royal Commission on the Status of Women in 1970. Its report was a landmark for Canadian women in providing facts with which to argue their case and bring their concerns to the political arena. Special institutions followed: in 1972, the Office of Employment Opportunity and the National Action Committee on the Status of Women (NAC); in 1973, the Canadian Advisory Council on the Status of Women (CACSW)—government appointees who advise the minister responsible for women's concerns; and in 1982, the first federal–provincial conference on women's issues.

In Canada today, although much progress has been made, many groups still advance women's causes. NAC, for example, which began as an umbrella lobbying group representing roughly 3 million women, continues to be active, especially in rights-related questions. Initially funded by the federal government, it endured a series of financial cuts culminating in 2006, when the Harper government declared that NAC had completed much of its work. Since then, it has renewed itself and now is primarily financed through donations and membership fees.

Close-Up 2.6

The Famous Five

In December 1997, MPs voted to erect statues on Parliament Hill in Ottawa honouring the Famous Five, a group of women led by Emily Murphy. The group consisted of Alberta women who, in the late 1920s, challenged the legal definition of the word *persons*, which at the time included only men. Murphy's associates were Nellie McClung, Henrietta Muir Edwards, Louise McKinney, and Irene Parlby.

In 1929, the Supreme Court had ruled that women were not "persons," and therefore were ineligible to be appointed to the Senate. Murphy and her associates appealed this ruling to Britain's Privy Council, then the highest court for Canada. The women won, and the word *persons* was redefined to include both women and men. Women were finally allowed to participate in the political process by such means as running for office or accepting a Senate appointment.

The statues on Parliament Hill ensure that the five women are recognized for their contribution, alongside monarchs, dead prime ministers, and the Fathers of Confederation—the only other individuals to date to have been awarded statues on the Hill.

During the 1970s, the term *feminist* began to be commonly used to describe those who sought gender equality and an end to the subordination of women. Similar ideas were gaining ground in other countries, and the women's movement became an active and widespread expression of women's interests reaching across state borders.

Today, women are better educated, work more outside the home, enjoy a wider variety of job possibilities, and have greater social and political equality and legal rights than ever before. They have brought new issues to the government's policy agenda, including affirmative action, legal equality rights, equal access to opportunities, pay equity, sexual harassment, pornography, abortion rights, and child care. Women's contributions to political life are discussed in relevant sections throughout the text.

Canadian women do not speak with one voice. However, the women's movement in Canada has raised awareness about the position of women in various aspects of society, changed attitudes, and introduced many issues concerning gender identity broadly into the policy agendas of political parties. The movement has not tried to create a political party itself but has helped to improve legislation concerning women and promoted attitudinal changes about democratic participation.

Women's Key Issues Today

Poverty and Child Care: One-parent families (more than 80 percent of which are headed by women) are among the worst off in Canada. They desperately require government assistance, as do single women over age 65, who have the lowest incomes of any adult group. Policies that could help single-parent families headed by women include higher minimum wages, improved job training, literacy programs, employment equity, and available and affordable daycare.

Employment: In 1901, only 13 percent of Canadian women worked outside the home. In 2011, more than 62 percent of all females over age 15 did so (compared to 71.5 percent of all men over age 15).[24] Women now account for more than 47 percent of the Canadian labour force, yet many of those women earn less money than men. Job opportunities for women are improving, however. There are dramatically more women in professional occupations such as doctors, dentists, pharmacists, university professors, and lawyers than there were previously. In January 2012, women comprised 35 percent of all management positions and 23 percent of all senior management positions.

Policies that would help women in the employment sector include job security, benefits, and more convenient hours of work. Governments have not yet been able to place a value on the unpaid labour such as housework, caregiving, and volunteer work that preoccupies women much more than men. This work makes a major contribution to the economy but never shows up in official statistics or in tax or other credits for women.

Equality Rights: Women lobbied hard to have gender equality protected in the 1982 *Canadian Charter of Rights and Freedoms*. Without this clause, legislatures would have been able to override new rights for women by using the "notwithstanding clause." After the Charter, feminists continued to challenge laws that they considered discriminated against them. Women's groups are also vigilant in addressing how new constitutional and policy proposals will affect women's rights. For example, they were quick to support Native women in their quest to ensure that Aboriginal and treaty rights were guaranteed equally in the Constitution to male and female persons.

Abortion, Sexuality, and Assault Issues: There are many ongoing issues that concern women but on which there is no clear consensus. For three decades, feminists have sought to ensure that women are able to control what happens to their own bodies. Some accept abortions as a legal right. Others reject abortion rights. Pornography and prostitution issues are other concerns, but again, there is no agreement over whether governments should limit freedom of expression and the right to work as one chooses. Sexual assault, sexual harassment, and family violence are other ongoing issues, as are new debates over gender orientation.

Religion

A **religion** is an organized, institutionalized system of beliefs based on the superior authority of a supernatural being, or beings, a purpose of which is to instruct the faithful in morally responsible behaviour.

Religion provides a powerful sense of identity. It is an important force shaping political culture, and it is unlimited by state borders. A religion consists of a complex system of faith, beliefs, ethical principles, and laws. It also constitutes a belief system that involves issues of authority and justice that are factors in politics, and it is here that some societal clashes occur. Freedom of religion in Canada is protected by the Charter, but there is no state religion.

Christianity, mainly Roman Catholic and Protestant denominations, is the principal religion in Canada. However, large numbers of immigrants in recent decades have increased proponents of Hinduism, Buddhism, Sikhism, Judaism, and Islam so that together these smaller groupings today represent about 14 percent of Canadians (see Figure 2.3). Religion has rarely been a divisive force in Canada, but in recent years cultural clashes have arisen, mainly to do with issues of personal liberty (see Close-Up 2.7).

religion: An organized, institutionalized system of beliefs based on the superior authority of a supernatural being, or beings, a purpose of which is to instruct the faithful in morally responsible behaviour.

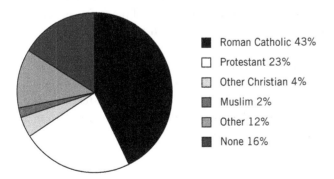

Roman Catholic 43%
Protestant 23%
Other Christian 4%
Muslim 2%
Other 12%
None 16%

Figure 2.3 Religious Diversity in Canada

Source: Data from Central Intelligence Agency, *The World Factbook*, 2013.

Do Canadians have the right to wear a niqab (a veil some Muslim women wear to cover their face) in public—even during a citizenship ceremony? Does it violate their personal liberty for the state to refuse such permission?

Prime Minister Harper: *"Covering one's face is not how we do things here."*

Liberal party leader Justin Trudeau: *"Prime ministers of liberal democracies ought not to be in the business of telling women what they can and cannot wear on their head during public ceremonies."*

In early 2015, in reply to a court challenge, a federal judge ruled that a ban on the niqab during a citizenship ceremony was unlawful because it did not allow citizenship candidates "the greatest possible freedom in the solemn affirmation of the oath." Led by Prime Minister Stephen Harper, the federal government appealed the ruling on the grounds that it was "offensive." NDP and Liberal leaders said that the appeal was not necessary. The government lost its appeal but said it would appeal the matter to the Supreme Court of Canada, and vowed to reintroduce the niqab ban within 100 days of re-election. The Conservative government's stand became a divisive pre-election issue.

Where do you stand in the debate? Is the niqab un-Canadian? Or is it an expression of religious or cultural expression that should be tolerated?

French-Speaking Canadians

As of 2011, 22 percent of Canadians claimed French as their mother tongue. Most of them were concentrated in Québec, with significant minorities in Ontario and New Brunswick. In Québec, 78.1 percent of the population claimed French as their mother tongue (94.4 percent claimed the ability to conduct a conversation in French). In Canada, only 21.3 percent claimed French as their mother tongue. This represents a very slow but steady decrease over the past three decades. Chapter 5 discusses modern nationalism in Québec, but here, we briefly note the history of the cultural division between French and English Canadians.

Relations between English-speaking and French-speaking Canadians have been characterized by long periods of relative tranquility punctuated by harsh conflicts. From 1663 onward, the political development of the colony of New France was dominated by French-style absolutism, modified somewhat by circumstances in the New World. Following the British conquest and the Treaty of Paris, which formally gave the French colony to Britain in 1763, the culture of New France was enveloped and preserved by the Roman Catholic Church, the French language, civil law, and the feudal landholding system.

From this inheritance emerged a distinctive political subculture, the most visible characteristics of which are the French language; a civil law code unique in Canada; and traditions, myths, and heroes based on early Québec history. The fear of assimilation that permeates politics in Québec, because of the minority status of francophones in Canada as a whole, also results from this early history.

Je me souviens.

Québec's official motto since 1883

One fundamental difference between the French and the English in Canada lies in the understanding of the term *nation*. Thus, while many anglophone Canadians view the Canadian state as one nation, with an enclave of French Canadians in Québec, francophones have a dualistic conception of a political system composed of Québec and "the rest of the country."[25]

This conception of Québec as a separate nation can be traced through the history of the province. In 1867, the Fathers of Confederation created a union that gave Canada every power a country needed to thrive. George-Étienne Cartier, who negotiated for Québec, supported this vision. He saw it as the responsibility of the provinces to preserve what he called "cultural nations"—cultures imported from England, Ireland, Scotland, and pre-revolutionary France. After Cartier's death, however, his Québec critics began to claim that Confederation was really a "compact" between French and English nations. This myth flourished and continues to thrive in parts of Québec. The **compact theory of Confederation** nourishes the notion of "two founding nations" and continues to provide French Canadians with a claim to equality rather than simple minority status within Canada. The word *compact* also provides a basis for claims that Québec has a right to withdraw from the original bargain.

It is generally accepted today that the Confederation arrangement was an implicit bargain between the French and English to create one strong political unit, a country that would protect the rights and assist the advancement of two culturally diverse peoples. Both English-language and French-language communities were to be protected. From the outset in Québec, both English and French were legal languages in the legislature and courts. However, in the other provinces, the practice until the 1940s was for English-speaking Canadians, wherever they were in the majority, to deprive French-speaking Canadian minorities of public-school facilities in their native language and to refuse them the use of their language in government institutions.

Several historical crises marked the breakdown of goodwill between the English and the French in Canada, causing frustration and eventually separatist movements. French Canadians find in these events the emotional justification to defend themselves as a distinct, culturally equal minority in Canada. The most recent such occurrence was the patriation of the Constitution in 1982 without Québec's agreement. It preceded two referendums in Québec on separation, both of which were close but failed. The provincial Parti Québécois (PQ) and the federal Bloc Québécois (BQ) rose as challenges to an integrated Canada. Both have been seriously weakened in the last decade, but they still seek the foundation of an independent, sovereign Québec.

English-Speaking Canadians

In direct contrast to the feudal traditions in New France, Canadian anglophone society was open to outside influences from the beginning. Among the early inhabitants of the northern British colonies were United Empire Loyalists fleeing the American Revolution. Their numbers soon surpassed the fewer than 15 000 British colonists already in Canada. The Loyalists brought with them many attitudes still prevalent in English-Canadian society: some aspects of the liberal American tradition but also anti-American sentiments and a corresponding loyalty to the British Crown.

Over the years, the composition of the "English-speaking" element of Canadian society has changed dramatically from its origins of primarily British immigrants. English-speaking Canadians now encompass individuals from over 200 different

compact theory of Confederation: The notion of "two founding nations," which provides French Canadians with a collective claim to equality rather than simple minority status within Canada.

Table 2.3 Origins of Immigrants to Canada by Region, 2006 to 2011	
Source	**Percent**
Asia and the Middle East	56.9
Europe	13.7
Caribbean and Central America	12.3
Africa	12.5
United States	3.9

Source: Data from Statistics Canada, Immigration and Ethnocultural Diversity in Canada. http://12.statcan.gc.ca/nhs-enm/2011/as-sa/99-010-x/99-010-x2011001-eng.cfm

ethnic groups, including more than 6 million persons categorized as visible minorities. Respondents to the National Household Survey (NHS) in 2011 claimed ancestry that included, in order of population, Canadian, English, French, Scottish, Irish, and German. Other ethnic origins that surpassed 1 million people included Italian, Chinese, First Nations, Ukranian, East Indian, Dutch, and Polish.

Canada accepts more immigrants per capita than any other member of the G7. Data from the NHS 2011 show that there were nearly 7 million foreign-born Canadians in 2011, or 20.6 percent of the total population. The leading country of birth for new immigrants was the Philippines, followed by China and India (see Table 2.3). Ontario is by far the largest centre for nearly all ethnic groups (almost one-quarter of Ontario's population is composed of immigrants), followed by British Columbia, Alberta, and Manitoba. At the other extreme, in Newfoundland and Labrador fewer than 2 percent are immigrants.

Because of ethnic diversity, Canadians have "layered" cultures. When immigrants choose Canada, they learn to speak English or French and the cultural layering begins. The United States is often viewed metaphorically as a "melting pot," because it was thought to have been built through shared experiences and commitment to similar political values. Canada, on the other hand, can be seen more as a tapestry, because separate parts of the whole remain so distinct. The Canadian ideal has been to encourage different cultures to exist side by side in harmony and tolerance. As the flow of immigrants to Canada continues, the challenge will be to maintain a balance between unity and respect for diversity as part of Canadian political culture.

During a high immigration period in the later 1940s and the 1950s, cultural pluralism gained popularity in Canada. The country pioneered the use of the term *multicultural* and adopted policies to deal with it. **Multiculturalism** in this context means that ethnic customs and cultures should be valued, preserved, and shared within the context of Canadian citizenship and economic and political integration. In the early 1970s, the federal government formally adopted a policy of multiculturalism. It defined Canada as being multicultural within a bilingual English–French framework. The *Canadian Multiculturalism Act* was passed in 1988 to assist ethnic groups that wanted to maintain their identity and share their culture with all Canadians. It sought to welcome and help all cultural groups to contribute to Canada.

multiculturalism: A policy that assumes that ethnic customs and cultures should be valued, preserved, and shared within the context of citizenship and economic and political integration.

By 1978, the new multicultural policies were reflected in a more liberal *Immigration Act*, which declared that immigration policy would be based on principles of non-discrimination, family reunion, humanitarian concern for refugees, and promotion of national goals.[26] An average of roughly 250 000 immigrants were admitted to Canada each year from 2001 to 2013. This approximate level of intake continues, and about two-thirds of Canada's population growth comes from international migration.

In recent years, as the sources of immigrants changed, multiculturalism has come under considerable criticism. French-speaking Canadians tend to fear that it will undermine their place as one of the two founding nations. Other groups argue that multicultural policies perpetuate the stratification of Canadian society, do not encourage enough integration, and decrease social and economic mobility. Still other critics contend that by supporting ethnic differences, the government divides Canadians, encouraging immigrants to separate themselves from mainstream culture.[27] The debate became heated in 2015 when the Liberals pledged to bring 25,000 refugees from Syria in a short period of time.

A study by Statistics Canada in 2013 showed that young immigrants (age 25 to 34 years) had higher rates of unemployment and earned less than their Canadian-born counterparts.[28] Some feared that as immigrants fell behind economically, social cohesion would disintegrate. To help counter this, in 2014 the government revised immigration rules to favour those with certain trade skills. The new rules included a revamped points system that places greater emphasis on an immigrant's youth and fluency in the two official languages, how closely credentials match those in Canada, whether employment is already arranged in Canada, and whether the immigrant's specific skills are in demand. It also considers adaptability, as indicated by time spent previously in Canada.

In the past, studies have shown that immigrants to Canada have assimilated relatively quickly into mainstream society and identify strongly with Canada, much better than they do in other countries. In Europe, for example, multiculturalism is ill defined and controversial.[29] In Canada, the new immigration rules are designed to ensure that this pattern of integration continues even as the sources of immigrants change.

The Canadian commitment to cultural diversity is strong. Surveys conducted by Environics dating back to the 1980s show that Canadian attitudes about immigration and multiculturalism have held steady or grown more positive over the past three to five years.[30] Multiculturalism unites Canadians by helping to combat two threats: American cultural domination and separation by any province or region. Multiculturalism is not to be feared if it is interpreted as encouraging members of ethnic groups to be proud of their own group's contributions to Canadian society. In this interpretation, multiculturalism is a voluntary, marginal differentiation among peoples who are equal participants in one country. It implies moderation—a middle ground—between melting pot assimilation and limitless ethnic division. The formal adoption of bilingual and multicultural policies by the government enshrines ethnic tolerance among other important values of Canadian political culture. It means that an individual can have more than one cultural identity and still be Canadian. Canada is not one piece of unbroken cloth, the same colour and texture throughout. The tapestry metaphor for the country holds true: a rainbow of interwoven colours, held together by a common thread. Canadians are strengthened, not impoverished, by their plural identities.

Visible Minorities

The *Employment Equity Act* defines **visible minorities** as "persons other than aboriginal peoples, who are non-Caucasian in race or non-white in colour." As of 2011, more than 6 million Canadians identified themselves as a member of a visible minority group—over 19 percent of the total population (see Figure 2.4). Their percentage is growing quickly; 78 percent of the immigrants who arrived between 2006 and 2011 were visible minorities, with the result that one out of every five Canadians now identifies as a member of a visible minority.

South Asians constitute a quarter of the visible minority group; the second largest group is Chinese at 21 percent, and Blacks are third at 15 percent. More than half of Canada's visible minorities live in Ontario and British Columbia. Seven out of 10 live in Toronto, Montréal, or Vancouver.

Despite Canada's integrative and pluralist model, ethnic cleavages persist. Ethnic visible minorities tend to integrate less easily into Canadian society than do white European immigrants. In part, this is because they struggle against racist attitudes in the population. **Racial discrimination** is the imposition of handicaps, barriers, and different treatment on individuals because of their race. Fed by prejudice and negative stereotypes, it creates a vicious cycle in which mainstream society is fearful and suspicious and the minority group is withdrawn and defensive. Often minority groups become concentrated in specific neighbourhoods or geographical areas, and this tends to reinforce their social and ethnic differences.

Institutional discrimination creates an additional hurdle for visible minorities, manifesting itself in high levels of unemployment and exclusion from certain sectors of the economy. Incidents of racial bigotry in Canadian history include the shameful internment of Japanese Canadians during World War II and the often-shabby treatment of Native peoples. Racist ideologies are condemned but persist.[31]

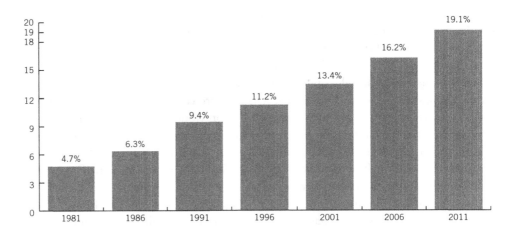

Figure 2.4 Percentage of Visible Minorities, Canada, 1981 to 2011

Source: Adapted from the following Statistics Canada publications: *Canada's Ethnocultural Portrait: The Changing Mosaic, 2001 Census*, Catalogue 96F0030, January 21, 2003; *The Daily*, April 2, 2008: www.statcan.ca/Daily/English/080402/d080402a.htm; and Statistics Canada, Table 2, www12.statcan.gc.ca.

Since the 1980s, systemic discrimination has been studied and addressed by public policy solutions. The problem has not been eliminated, however. It is clear that attitudinal changes need to be addressed continually to foster awareness, understanding, and tolerance—particularly since Canadians must anticipate an even greater mix in the population in the years to come.

Aboriginal Peoples

Another ethno-linguistic division lies between Canada's Aboriginal peoples and other Canadians. Native peoples make up 4.3 percent of the total population of the country. In 2011, 1.4 million Canadians claimed Aboriginal ancestry, including First Nations (status and non-status Indians), Inuit, and Métis (see Figure 2.5). First Nations make up about 65 percent of Aboriginal inhabitants. Between 2006 and 2011, the population with declared Aboriginal ancestry grew dramatically, by 20 percent compared to 5 percent growth for Canada in the same period. The Aboriginal population is therefore younger. Approximately 46 percent are under age 25, compared to 29 percent for the total Canadian population.

About half (45 percent) of registered Indians live on reserves, while the majority of non-status Indians (75 percent) and Métis (71 percent) live in urban areas. The Assembly of First Nations (AFN) represents those living on 615 reserves. In 2013, a federal court ruled that Métis and First Nations people living outside reserves should be considered Indians under the Constitution.

Aboriginal peoples live in all provinces and territories, but the largest populations are in Ontario, British Columbia, Alberta, Manitoba, and Saskatchewan. Their numbers are small in Yukon, the Northwest Territories, and Nunavut, but they form a very large percentage of the total population there.

The three Aboriginal groups are distinctive descendants of Canada's first inhabitants. They share a long history with other Canadians and their governments. For many decades, this relationship was fraught with injustices related to land and a lack of

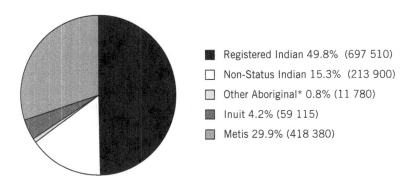

Registered Indian 49.8% (697 510)
Non-Status Indian 15.3% (213 900)
Other Aboriginal* 0.8% (11 780)
Inuit 4.2% (59 115)
Metis 29.9% (418 380)

Figure 2.5 The Aboriginal Population (identity based), 2011

*Other Aboriginal refers to respondents who reported more than one identity group, and those who reported being a Band member with no Aboriginal identity and no Registered Indian Status.

Source: Aboriginal Affairs and Northern Development Canada, aadnc-aandc.gc.ca. Based on Statistics Canada, 2011 National Household Survey, AANDC tabulations. CUDN 5242964.

respect for Aboriginal values and traditions. Today, issues emanating from that relationship remain the basis of many grievances that include historical maltreatment, lack of respect for and understanding of Aboriginal cultural heritage, and territorial and economic deprivation.

Aboriginal people share a unique history based on a hunting-and-gathering economy. Their values tend to be collectivist, based on an organic concept of community in which individuals are a specialized part of a whole society. Decision making is generally consensual, not majoritarian. Traditional leadership tends to be diffuse, with different leaders in different areas of specialization.

The Royal Proclamation of 1763, which outlined the territory acquired by Britain from France, clearly defined Indian rights, but the British rulers generally ignored it. The British depended on Indian tribes in the War of 1812 against the United States, but did not include them in the peace settlement. After Confederation, the federal Parliament was assigned legislative jurisdiction over Indians and the lands reserved for them.[32] Canadian governments, like the colonial governments, took away Native land by treaty or trickery. Shortly after Confederation, Parliament passed legislation designed to assimilate Aboriginals, and forced their children to leave home and live in residential schools where many were abused physically, mentally, and sexually.

The term *Indian* was legally defined in the first *Indian Act* in 1876. This Act aimed to suppress Indian traditions and extend government control over status Indians on and, to a lesser degree, off reserves. Although it was amended many times, the current Act, passed in 1951, still reflects those early biases and intentions.

The Inuit in Canada, scattered throughout the Arctic in eight distinct communities, were never subject to the *Indian Act* and were largely ignored by government until 1939, when they officially became a federal responsibility. Since then, they have been classified as "Indians" for the purposes of the Constitution. Because of their northern location, the Inuit have been largely bypassed by economic and political modernization—notwithstanding the creation of Nunavut, which gave them a territory of their own to govern.

The *Indian Act* was intended to integrate Aboriginal peoples within Canadian society by providing a range of social programs. All Indians receive the same benefits as other Canadians, such as family allowances and pensions, and status Indians also have the right to a wide variety of benefits in the field of taxation, education, health care, and housing. However, without constant employment such assistance has left them dependent on governments.

Most First Nations people on reserves live in abysmal social conditions, with high rates of tuberculosis and water and sewage problems on many reserves. Aboriginal children are far more likely to be living with a single parent, and half of the foster children in Canada under the age of 14 years are Aboriginal. According to AFN national chief Shawn Atleo, they are more likely to go to jail than to graduate from high school (more than 50 percent fail to graduate).

Alcoholism and depression plague many Native Canadians as they strive to cope with the loss of their traditional lifestyle. A reserve in northwestern Ontario became notorious in 2011 as the "suicide capital of the world." The Pikangikum reserve had a suicide rate about 20 times that of Canada as a whole, and by far the highest rate in the world. In 2014, the Royal Canadian Mounted Police (RCMP) reported that more than 1000 Aboriginal women and girls were homicide victims between 1980 and 2012, and that 164 more were missing.[33]

Supreme Court decisions and recent governments have been trying to adapt the principles of the Royal Proclamation of 1763 about the fair treatment of Aboriginal peoples and respect for their rights and to provide practical solutions. Although improvements are being made slowly, the gap between Canada's Aboriginals and their fellow Canadians remains wide and constant.

In 1996, a Royal Commission on Aboriginal Peoples said, in essence, that the relationship between Aboriginals and non-Aboriginals in Canada should "be restructured fundamentally." When Paul Martin became prime minister in 2003, he established the first Cabinet committee on Aboriginal affairs, chaired by himself, and set up a new Aboriginal affairs secretariat within the Privy Council. Ten years later, the Conservative government had different priorities. Its 2007 budget cancelled the Kelowna Accord, an agreement reached by the preceding Liberal government, the provincial and territorial governments, and Native groups to increase funding for various Aboriginal programs. Instead, the 2007 budget decreased the funding. The Conservative government did, however, recognized that the *Indian Act* should be replaced by a modern legislative framework that would provide for the devolution of legal and democratic responsibility to First Nations to manage "their own affairs within the overall constitutional framework of the Canadian state."[34]

In 2008, as a result of a class action suit two years previously, the Harper government apologized to Aboriginal peoples on behalf of the government and all Canadians and paid nearly $4 billion in compensation to 80 000 victims of notorious, now closed, residential schools.[35] It also set up a Truth and Reconciliation Commission to examine the school situation. This gave the people most affected by the abuses of the residential schools an opportunity to have their stories heard and recorded. In 2015, the report delivered a wide range of recommendations, some largely cosmetic or symbolic, along with others that needed considerable funding, such as improved health care on reserves. However, Justice Murray Sinclair, who headed the Commission, feared that the recommendations might once again be "consigned to dark spaces on dark shelves in dark corners of dark libraries."[36]

Education is seen as the answer for improving the lives of First Nations people. In 2014, Bill C-33, negotiated by Prime Minister Stephen Harper and AFN National Chief Shawn Atleo, established a framework to enable First Nations control over elementary and secondary schools on their reserves, and proposed $1.9 billion in federal money to bridge the gap between the funding from provincial governments for First Nations schools and other schools. The federal government proposed to retain final say about much of how education would be managed. First Nations groups were divided and angry over the deal. Previous historic treaties had been negotiated with the Crown, but the governor general had not been a party to this agreement. Many Aboriginals considered this to be a betrayal of the nation-to-nation principle they believe in. They also wanted to adjust the curriculum to include their own language and culture. Chief Atleo was forced to quit as a result of Bill C-33. The education bill stalled, and the future of First Nations education remains uncertain.

There are many areas where conflicts and controversies have arisen and continue to arise between Aboriginal peoples and other Canadians. In Chapter 5, we examine the long-standing controversy over Aboriginal rights, land claims, and resource development on Aboriginal lands. Many other conflicts have to do with special regulations for Native peoples, such as the right to hunt and fish where and when other Canadians cannot, or the issue of tax exemption for status Indians. Since 1995, status Indians have been required to pay income tax on employment income earned outside of reserves.

Historically, when assimilation was the official government policy, Indian babies were frequently removed from their homes and adopted by non-Aboriginals. Other issues have been the right to have gambling casinos on reserves and cigarette and other types of smuggling through Indian reserves on the Canada–United States border. Occasionally, development has gone ahead on disputed land, causing violent confrontations. An example occurred in Oka, Québec in 1990, when a dispute over land led to an armed confrontation between Mohawks and Québec's provincial police.

Yet another issue that brings First Nations people into conflict with other Canadians is Aboriginal justice. Disproportionate numbers of Aboriginals are incarcerated in Canadian jails. To rectify this, in 1995 the federal government amended the *Criminal Code* to make it more lenient in sentencing Aboriginals who transgress Canadian laws and allow them to be punished in more appropriate ways. At the same time, more Aboriginal police officers are being recruited.

Discussion Questions

1. What circumstances serve to unite Canadians? To divide them?
2. Can the French and English concepts of *nation* be reconciled?
3. Is multiculturalism a disruptive or an integrative force in Canadian society?
4. Does gender stratification affect you personally? Explain how and why.
5. Who are Canada's Aboriginal peoples and what are some of the cultural and economic issues that separate them from other Canadians?
6. How do you rate Canada as a place to live? Justify your answer.

Chapter 3
The Constitutional Framework
Rules for Government and the Political Game

Learning Objectives

After reading this chapter, you should be able to

1 Define *constitution* and *constitutionalism*.

2 Trace the development of Canada's Constitution from Confederation in 1867 to the *Constitution Act, 1982* and on to today.

3 Distinguish between types of law.

4 Outline the five formulas for amending the Constitution.

5 Outline six kinds of basic rights and freedoms protected by the *Canadian Charter of Rights and Freedoms*.

A constitution establishes the formal rules and principles for government and the game of politics. It provides specifically designed state organizations and a set of principles about governing. It also outlines the relations between society and the state and establishes the importance of particular institutions. These principles distribute power among citizens, guide deliberations between the rulers and the ruled, and grant leaders the legitimacy required to act authoritatively.

In this chapter, we define and explain the key ideas used to organize the game of politics. Constitutions, rights, and the rule of law are outlined, as well as the key institutional arrangements set out in the Canadian Constitution. Since the rules of the game of politics evolve over time, this chapter analyzes the development of the Constitution from 1867 until today, including its successes and failures. New paradigms, or very significant changes, in society and politics framed how constitutional questions were debated. They led to seismic reforms, sometimes even masquerading as unassailable new and conformist ideas.

CONSTITUTIONAL PRINCIPLES

A **constitution** is a body of fundamental rules, written and unwritten, under which governments operate. Modern constitutions outline at least the key institutions of government organization and list rules that restrain political leaders from engaging in arbitrary action. Any law that contravenes constitutional law may be declared invalid, with judges and courts acting as referees.

constitution: A body of fundamental rules, written and unwritten, under which governments operate.

Constitutions may be written or unwritten. A **written constitution** is the fundamental state law set down in one or more documents. An **unwritten constitution** consists of customs, conventions, or statutes and is not written down in one comprehensive document. Canada has a written constitution—the *Constitution Act, 1982*. The 1982 constitutional amendment codified all past constitutional laws, including the original *British North America Act, 1867* (*BNA Act*), into one document. It also provided a *Canadian Charter of Rights and Freedoms* and set up amendment formulas for future revisions of the constitution.

Constitutional Laws and Conventions

There is also an "unwritten" aspect to Canada's Constitution. Because of Canada's British heritage, many important parts of the constitution are not written down. These include principles such as how the governor general names the prime minister and many other rules about the relations between the executive and Parliament.

In Canada, as a result, we make a distinction between **constitutional law** and conventions. As constitutions develop over time, the norms of a society become incorporated into the rules for governing, but they are not all written into constitutional documents. In fact, it would not be possible to write down all of the rules for conducting state affairs in a constitution. A constitutional **convention** is a custom or practice that, while not necessarily a legal necessity or even enforceable by a court, is nevertheless based on accepted norms and reasons and should be taken into consideration.

Since conventions are not laws, courts cannot make final, legal determinations in conflicts that involve them. Conventions can be enforced only in the sense that a government would lose the support of the people if they were not obeyed. If the legislature is dissatisfied with a particular convention, it can simply replace it by statute law. Of course, it, too, must follow the constitutional rules. In 1982, for example, the Supreme Court of Canada determined that obtaining provincial agreement for the federal government's request to Britain to pass a constitutional amendment was a convention and not a law. Further negotiations between the premiers and the federal government then took place in an effort to solve the dilemma that the Supreme Court had enunciated.

Individual and Collective Rights

Constitutions may also convey **rights**—that is, entitlements owed to individuals or groups as duties by governments. Many constitutions contain statements about such values as natural rights, religious beliefs, and political rights such as freedom of speech and assembly. Canada's Constitution contains *both* individual and collective rights.

Individual rights are defined as individual claims against the state such as life and liberty. All individuals should be treated equally before the law, and individual rights are based on the principle that the government should draw no distinction among citizens based on their cultural, social, religious, or linguistic backgrounds. The *Canadian Charter of Rights and Freedoms* includes the fundamental principle of individual rights.

Collective rights are entitlements or duties owed to certain groups by the state. They call for distinctions to be made among groups to ensure equality of condition or bargaining power. For example, the *BNA Act* provided educational rights for some specific denominational groups and language rights for other groups. In short, some groups were given rights and entitlements while others were denied them. The *Canadian Charter of Rights and Freedoms* also lists collective rights for specific sectors of society.

The Rule of Law

A constitution implies the **rule of law**—a guarantee that state actions will be governed by law, with fairness and without malice. No individual should be above the law and no one ought to be exempt from it. As noted in Chapter 1, adherence to the rule of law and to a constitution are primary distinguishing features of democracies. The courts are the guardians of the rule of law and as such should be beyond improper influence. The principle of the independence of the judiciary is firmly established, with a British history of several hundred years.

In addition to certain general goals, the rule of law provides a guarantee of impartiality and fairness. The authority of the state is to be exercised rationally and without malice, with all citizens protected from the abuse of power. The rule of law means that no citizen, no matter what his or her transgression, should be denied the due process of law. No individual or institution should be exempt from it, and all should be equal before it. Adherence to this principle also means that no government or administrative official has any power beyond that awarded by law. The rule of law is a fundamental principle without which any constitution, written or unwritten, would be meaningless.

Common Law and Statutory Law

Canada incorporated much of its legal tradition from Britain and France. **Customary law**, or what came to be known as British **common law**, was brought to Canada along with other traditions. Common law, also known as unenacted or case law, consists of a body of established rules based on the principle of *stare decisis*. **Stare decisis** is the principle of following precedents (previous court decisions) set down in earlier court cases, a principle that binds lower courts to follow decisions made by higher-level courts. Nine provinces (excluding Québec) and the territories use common law as the basis of court judgments.

Another form of law came to Canada via the *Code civil des Français* or *Code Napoléon* of France. A **code** is a body of legislative laws brought together in a single body to provide a relatively complete set of legal rules. To codify laws is to arrange them into a written systematic body, as opposed to unwritten traditions. The *Code civil du Québec* is used only in Québec and performs the same function that common law does in the rest of Canada. Unlike common law, the *Code civil* is a written law. It is stated more in terms of principles and rationality than common law is.

When common law is insufficient or conflicts with contemporary norms, it may be amended by statute law. **Legislative (statute) law** consists of the authoritative rules set by the Parliament of Canada or the legislative assemblies of the provinces or territories.

As new problems are brought before the courts, judges refer to the constitution, statute law, and previous legal decisions that are deemed relevant in order to apply them when making their own judgments. If there are no appropriate constitutional rules, statute laws, or precedents, or if there are no laws that precisely fit the case, judges are forced to rely on common sense and reason. They may even appeal to doctrines based on natural law—the recourse to God or nature in establishing legal principles—or their judgments may be based on contemporary norms, customs, and values. Existing principles are thereby broadened, and the body of case law is expanded. Judicial review or interpretation is thus an important source of Canadian law.

The relationship between statutory and common law was historically defined by the **doctrine of parliamentary supremacy**, a basic premise of British parliamentary democracy. In Canada, it means that all legislatures have the authority, in theory, to repeal or modify any principle set out in common law. However, this power is not absolute. The Supreme Court can declare a law **ultra vires**. This means that the law in question is beyond a legislature's jurisdiction on the basis of the Constitution, especially Canada's federal division of powers. The entrenchment of individual and group rights in the *Canadian Charter of Rights and Freedoms* also limits parliamentary authority by placing certain rights beyond the reach of any legislature.

doctrine of parliamentary supremacy: A basic premise of British parliamentary democracy. In Canada, it means that, subject to the Constitution, all 11 legislatures have the authority, in theory, to repeal or modify any principle set out in common law.

ultra vires: A legislative act that is beyond a legislature's jurisdiction on the basis of Canada's federal division of powers.

Key Institutional Arrangements

Apart from stating fundamental principles, written constitutions also describe the organization of government. Some are remarkably detailed, outlining the entire government structure and the relative powers and limitations of the various institutions in the political process. At a minimum, most written constitutions outline the powers and duties of the executive (Chapter 6), the legislature (Chapter 7), the judiciary (Chapter 9), and sometimes other institutions such as the bureaucracy or the military.

The evolution of federalism—the division of power between federal and provincial units—is discussed in detail in Chapter 4. Here, however, it is important to note that federalism requires a "federal bargain," an agreement in which the parties agree to give up a degree of autonomy in exchange for becoming part of a more powerful political entity. Therefore, it is usual for federalism to be based on some kind of written document or constitution that enshrines guarantees and concessions to the various levels of governments. The provisions and limitations defined in that document help to shape the nature of federalism. This is the case in Canada.

It is important to remember, however, that a constitution is only a legal code about how government *ought* to operate. In practice, a constitution may be set down and then ignored. The institutions it defines may be used, suspended, or even demolished. Some constitutions list philosophical platitudes that have little, if any, bearing on how the political system actually works. One must understand how constitutions and institutions operate in the real world, not just on paper.

DEVELOPMENT OF THE CANADIAN CONSTITUTION

Constitutions are not static; they evolve and change over time. They are a product of their historical development as well as contemporary values, beliefs, and attitudes about how the country *should* function.

Important aspects of Canada's unwritten constitution evolved in Britain for many centuries before Confederation. The British colonists who immigrated to Canada brought with them concepts of basic constitutional principles, such as the rule of law and the right of opposition. The *BNA Act* was Canada's first constitution. It ensured that Canada was to have a form of government "similar in principle to that of the United Kingdom." This meant that certain institutional arrangements concerning the formal executive were to be reproduced in Canada, and that the British parliamentary system was to be used. Important elements of the Canadian Constitution were therefore already implicitly in place before the Fathers of Confederation met at Charlottetown in 1864.

The *BNA Act* was the product of lengthy, complex negotiations over the terms of union. All representatives tried to obtain concessions and guarantees that would protect matters of vital local concern to them. For example, French Canadians sought protection for their culture and language as the price for joining the union, while Nova Scotians argued for economic concessions and subsidies.

The authors of the *BNA Act* had to take into account a monarchical form of government, two dissimilar linguistic groups, and complex financial situations. They decided to graft a federal system of government onto the British heritage of representative and responsible cabinet government. In doing so, they created a division of jurisdiction between two levels of government, federal and provincial (see Chapter 4).

British North America Act, 1867

The *BNA Act* was not intended to establish a truly independent state; the formal authority of Canada continued to rest with the British monarch, and the Act itself could be amended only by the British Parliament. Rather, the Act was designed to enable the colonial provinces to join in a political union. Provinces that already were established kept their colonial constitutions, and those that joined after Confederation received their constitutions from the Ottawa government. As we have seen, the English-speaking provinces inherited the common law tradition from the United Kingdom, while Québec kept its system of civil law based on French traditions such as the *Code Napoléon*. Criminal law, on the other hand, was made a federal responsibility and therefore is similar throughout the land. Some general principles, such as liberty and the rule of law, were protected by common law and hence were not included in the *BNA Act*.

The Canadian Constitution is not highly detailed in all areas. Even vital procedural matters concerning the governing of the country go unmentioned; for example, the Cabinet is not mentioned explicitly. Canadian government relies heavily on British conventions such as "responsible government," which requires the government to resign when it is defeated in Parliament over a major issue. Of course, many specific issues that preoccupy governments today were not covered in the 1867 document.

What the Constitution does is to sketch, in rather uninspiring prose, the machinery of government and the basic terms of federalism. It is reasonably detailed with respect to the machinery of formal executive power and on matters concerning the division of authority between the federal and provincial governments.[1] The authors of the document intended to create a strong central government. They gave the federal government responsibility for the important topics of trade and commerce, defence, and foreign affairs, and left for the provinces jurisdiction over education, welfare, and other matters considered to be of lesser and local interest. As we shall see in the next chapter, the responsibilities of the provinces became relatively more expensive and complex over time and, when legal disputes developed between the two levels of government, the British law lords often sided with the provinces. At times, the *BNA Act* has been a very restrictive document that has created an impasse in federal–provincial relations.

The relative power of federal and provincial governments is dependent on the financial strength of the two jurisdictions. In a federal state, revenue sources must be divided reasonably between the two levels of government, or federalism will wither. Therefore, a key decision is how to distribute funds to the provinces while maintaining federal control of the national economy.

The *BNA Act* gave the federal government the ability to raise money by any system of taxation while, from the beginning, provincial authorities were restricted to collecting revenue through direct taxes or the sale of natural resources. (*Direct taxes*, such as income tax, must be paid directly to a government by the individual or firm assessed, while *indirect taxes*, such as sales tax on commodities, are collected and the money passed along to the government by other persons or institutions.) Thus, it appeared from strict interpretation of the *BNA Act* that the provinces could not levy a sales tax that would be passed along to consumers. However, through the ingenious device of making vendors tax collectors for the provincial governments, the rules of the *BNA Act* were evaded, and the provinces were able to employ both types of taxation. This was important because many growing areas of financial responsibility were awarded later to the provinces. Today, both levels of government use direct and indirect taxation.

Other Constitutional Documents

Although the *BNA Act* was the centrepiece of Canada's early written constitution, there were other relevant documents. Besides the various amendments to the *BNA Act* and the *Statute of Westminster 1931*, the Canadian Constitution before 1982 could be said to have included the Royal Proclamation of 1763; the *Colonial Laws Validity Act 1865*; the various acts admitting new provinces to the federal union; letters patent concerning the office of the governor general;[2] and a whole range of acts, common law precedents, and orders-in-council. Together, these made up the essentials of the Constitution from 1867 to 1982.

Interpreting the Constitution

Judicial Committee of the Privy Council (JCPC): The superior court of the United Kingdom, which until 1949, when the Supreme Court of Canada was established, was the court of final appeal in Canada.

Every political system requires a court or an arbitration process to interpret clauses of its constitution and resolve disputes over jurisdictional authority. Until 1949, when the Supreme Court of Canada was established, the court of final appeal in Canada was the **Judicial Committee of the Privy Council (JCPC)**, the superior court of the United Kingdom. For the most part, it defined federal authority narrowly and provincial authority widely. The emergency powers of the federal government, expressed in the "Peace, Order, and good Government" clause, granted extensive residual power to the federal government but were interpreted by the JCPC in a way that obstructed the centralizing intentions of the drafters of the *BNA Act*.[3] The rulings of the JCPC on Canadian federalism were very controversial. Many Canadians complained that the British law lords were too far removed from the political realities of Canada to render appropriate decisions.

The JCPC lost its position as Canada's court of last appeal in 1949 when the Supreme Court of Canada became the arbiter of constitutional review. The Supreme Court, with nine federally appointed judges, is Canada's highest court for civil, criminal, and constitutional cases. (See Chapter 9 for more on the court system.) In more recent times, the provinces have been reluctant to take jurisdictional matters to the Supreme Court because of its alleged pro-centralist bias. For a time, disputes between the federal and provincial governments tended to be resolved outside the judicial process, through the mechanism of federal–provincial conferences or diplomacy.

This is not to argue that the Supreme Court is irrelevant on federal issues. On the contrary, there have been many very important decisions by the Court on matters such as offshore oil and mineral rights and resource taxation, not to mention rulings on the federal government's plan to unilaterally patriate the Constitution. The Supreme Court has also been the arbiter of controversial cases involving civil rights and liberties in interpreting the *Canadian Charter of Rights and Freedoms* (see Chapter 9). Extremely important questions about whether Québec has the right to unilateral independence and whether the Senate could be reformed independently were recently referred to the Supreme Court for judgment (see Chapter 5).

Constitutional Amendment

It is important to be able to amend the Constitution, but also not to be able to change it too easily. Constitutional changes can take place through formal amendment or judicial interpretation. For political scientists, a **"rigid" constitution** is one that is difficult to amend, whereas a **"flexible" constitution** can be amended easily and adapted to changing circumstances. Although there are arguments both for and against the use of either type of amending formula, it is clear that all constitutions must provide *some* means to adapt themselves to new circumstances. Canada's amendment formula was, and remains, quite rigid.

The *BNA Act* did *not* contain a procedure for constitutional amendment within Canada. Instead, Canada had to appeal to Britain if it wanted to make any constitutional changes and have a bill passed in the British Parliament. Over time, the British role was diminished. In 1931, the *Statute of Westminster* established that the British Parliament could not legislate for Canada except at the request of the Canadian government, thus clarifying Canada's independence. At the time, the British government tried to persuade Canada to adopt a specific amending formula and thereby cut its last tie with the United Kingdom. Unfortunately, Canadian politicians could not agree on a formula, so the British Parliament remained responsible for constitutional amendment in Canada long after the country gained its independence.

"rigid" constitution: A constitution that is difficult to amend.

"flexible" constitution: A constitution that can be amended easily and adapted to changing circumstances.

On several occasions after 1931, the Constitution was amended in the United Kingdom after a request from Canada. Among these amendments was the 1940 amendment giving the federal Parliament jurisdiction over unemployment insurance, the 1951 amendment giving Parliament shared power over old-age pensions, and the 1960 amendment changing the retirement age of judges. For all of these, provincial agreement was achieved before asking the UK to amend the Constitution. On the other hand, no provincial agreement had to be reached (nor was it) when representation in the Senate was amended in 1915, nor when representation in the House of Commons was altered in 1946, 1952, and 1974.

In other words, a constitutional convention developed with regard to amendment of the *BNA Act*. The British Parliament always accepted the amendments that originated in a Joint Address from both Houses of the Canadian Parliament. On amendments that affected the federal balance of power, the provinces were always consulted and agreed to the proposals. On the other hand, no substantial amendment was ever made at the request of any province or group of provinces, since the British Parliament accepted only communications that arrived by way of the federal Parliament.

Not all constitutional change required the passage of British legislation, however. From the beginning, the provinces were allowed to amend their own constitutions in all spheres except those concerning the powers of the lieutenant-governor. The *British North America (No. 2) Act, 1949* empowered the federal Parliament to amend the Constitution except with regard to provincial power, rights, and privileges; the rights of minorities with respect to schools and language protection; the extension of the life of Parliament beyond five years; and the necessity to call at least one session of Parliament per year. These important exceptions prevented Ottawa from amending anything that touched on the nature and division of federal and provincial responsibilities.

From 1931 until 1981, strenuous efforts were made to cut the remaining ties to Britain. The difficult question in Canada was never *whether* we should have our own Constitution but *what* it should be. **Patriation**, or bringing the constitutional documents home, involved two seemingly insoluble conundrums for Canadians: how much provincial participation should be required and what type of amendment process should ensue.

patriation: Bringing a constitutional document to its home country.

Though minor efforts to find an acceptable constitutional agreement started as early as the 1930s, it was not until the 1960s that serious discussions on this matter took place between the federal government and all of the provinces. Two proposals almost succeeded: the Fulton–Favreau formula of 1964 and the Victoria Charter of 1971. In each of these cases, the essential stumbling block to finding an amendment formula was Québec's desire to be treated differently from the other provinces. Many Québeckers still argue that federalism is not a process involving 10 equal provinces working under one federal system but rather a union of "two founding peoples," and that both should have a veto over constitutional amendments. This view is premised on the idea that the Canadian Constitution is a "compact" between two cultural groups, the English and French provinces. By extension, a large number of Québécois argue that only the Québec state can protect francophone interests.

BRINGING THE CONSTITUTION HOME

The long and at times bitter debate over "bringing the Constitution home" ended in 1982 with the passage of the *Canada Act* by the British Parliament. Patriation of the Canadian Constitution was primarily symbolic, in that it did not involve significant changes in provincial or federal jurisdictions. However, it did include an entrenched *Canadian Charter of Rights and Freedoms* and an amending formula that had serious implications for both federal and provincial authorities.

The events leading up to patriation are crucial to understanding Canada's present Constitution and its problems. The catalyst for the final round of constitutional negotiations leading to patriation was the Québec referendum on sovereignty-association. In May 1980, Premier René Lévesque's *indépendantiste* Parti Québécois government sought authority to negotiate sovereign political status for Québec, with continued economic association with Canada. Québec voters ultimately rejected Lévesque's plan in a referendum by a margin of 60 to 40 percent. However, during the referendum campaign federalists pledged that Canada would begin a process of constitutional "renewal" to address the concerns of Québec citizens.

The concept of "renewed" federalism, while vague, allowed Liberal Prime Minister Pierre Elliott Trudeau to resume his efforts for patriation, a goal he had pursued since his first election as prime minister in 1968. He proposed to unilaterally patriate the Constitution with an entrenched *Canadian Charter of Rights and Freedoms* and explicit equalization and amendment formulas. Of the 10 provincial governments, only New Brunswick and Ontario supported the initial federal government proposal.

Six provinces took the issue of patriation to the Supreme Court. Its judgment offered both sides a measure of support. By a vote of seven to two, the judges ruled that the federal government could "legally" and "unilaterally" submit the constitutional resolution to the British Parliament for passage. However, by a vote of six to three, the Court also ruled that there was a constitutional convention requiring provincial consent and that Ottawa's proposed process "offended the federal principle."

The patriation package was thus tossed back into the political arena. In November 1981, a federal–provincial conference produced an agreement between the federal government and nine of the provinces (again Québec was the exception). The tenth premier, Lévesque, was enraged that the signators had made a deal without Québec and commented bitterly that this agreement would have incalculable consequences for Canada.

The major compromise that produced the agreement between the federal government and nine provinces was the inclusion of a **notwithstanding clause** in the Constitution, a clause that would allow Parliament or a provincial legislature to override many Charter provisions by a simple declaration to that effect when passing legislation. This provision also included a "sunset" clause requiring a renewal of the exemption every five years. Supporters of the notwithstanding clause argued that it provided an important political check, as it maintained the pre-eminence of legislative power in the event of "awkward" court rulings. Critics, on the other hand, argued that it circumvented the very purpose of an entrenched Charter, which is to give the courts the authority to protect fundamental individual freedoms in the event that legislatures and governments fail to do so. The dispute continues, and the clause has been used only three times.

notwithstanding clause: A clause in the Constitution that allows Parliament or a provincial legislature to override most Charter provisions by a simple declaration to that effect when passing legislation.

Another compromise leading to the agreement at the 1981 conference concerned the amending formula. An **amendment formula** is the procedure required to change a constitution. A proposal on federalism preferred by the provincial first ministers was accepted. It called for amendments affecting federal jurisdictions to be made by a joint resolution of both the Senate and the House of Commons, as well as by a resolution of the legislative assemblies of at least two-thirds of the provinces, representing at least 50 percent of the population of Canada. In addition, it granted dissenting provinces the right to opt out of all amendments that affected their status and powers.

There were several other compromises concerning the *Canadian Charter of Rights and Freedoms*. The case of Aboriginal peoples is an example. Recognition of their treaty rights was originally excluded from the Charter because several provinces were concerned that Aboriginal land claims might impede provincial control over natural resources. However, after intense lobbying by Aboriginal groups, recognition of these rights was restored.

Another important lobbying effort ensured the absolute rights of women. Section 28 of the Charter—which simply stated, "notwithstanding anything in this Charter, the rights and freedoms referred to in it are guaranteed equally to male and female persons"—was eliminated in one of the early agreements at the 1981 conference. In response, the Ad Hoc Committee of Canadian Women on the Constitution was formed. In just three weeks, it successfully lobbied all 10 provincial premiers to reverse their stand on the issue, and the clause was restored.

The British Parliament was presented with the Canada Bill in mid-February of 1982. The bill was supported by the federal government and nine provinces, but not by Québec. It eventually passed the British Parliament at every stage by large majorities. On March 29, the Queen gave royal assent to the *Canada Act*, 115 years to the day after the *BNA Act* had received royal assent. In Ottawa, on April 17, 1982, the Queen proclaimed the *Constitution Act, 1982*, completing the patriation process. At long last, Canada had a comprehensive and amendable constitution. However, this success did not come without more problems. The events outlined in Close-Up 3.1 are perhaps symbolic of the difficulties.

Québec and Constitutional Patriation

Québec's political leaders and government continued to reject the 1982 constitutional reform. They claimed to be the sole spokespersons for Québec on this matter, ignoring

---

Close-Up 3.1

The Perils of Keeping the Constitution

Two copies of the Constitution were signed in 1982 by Queen Elizabeth II. One was immediately spotted by rain during the outdoor signing ceremony. The second was damaged in 1983 when a man protesting against U.S. cruise missile tests poured thick red paint on it. Repairs were quickly made, but a pinkish-orange spot still covered 20 percent of the document. Later, because of an air-conditioning failure at the archives, or perhaps because of the restoration work, the document began to curl up in its frame.

Is there a moral to this story?

the facts that Prime Minister Trudeau was a French Canadian, one-third of his Cabinet was from Québec, and 74 of 75 members of Parliament (MPs) from Québec at the time were Liberals, almost all of whom supported patriation. Still, Québec's opposition to patriation prompted some critics to question whether the Supreme Court's call for "a substantial measure of provincial consent" had been achieved.

Premier Lévesque made several arguments against patriation of the Constitution. He argued that Québec's cultural security was threatened by the restriction of the province's exclusive rights in linguistic matters. He said the Charter's guarantee of access to English-speaking schools contradicted Québec's Bill 101, which restricted admission to English schools in that province to children who had at least one parent educated in Québec's English system. Lévesque also criticized the new Constitution's failure to recognize "in any tangible way" the character and needs of Québec as a distinct national society. Finally, he disliked the amending formula's removal of what Québec considered its traditional veto over constitutional changes. While the new constitutional proposal did provide financial compensation in the important areas of education and culture, the amending formula did not guarantee financial compensation for provinces that choose to opt out of other programs initiated by constitutional amendments.

The Québec government acted to exempt the province from the provisions it disliked in the newly patriated Constitution. It attempted to ensure that Québeckers' fundamental freedoms and legal and equality rights would be subject only to the provincial charter of human rights, not to the *Canadian Charter of Rights and Freedoms*. In 1982, it introduced and passed Bill 62 in the National Assembly. According to the provisions of that bill, a new clause would be appended to each Québec law, stating that it would operate "notwithstanding" the provisions of the Charter.

However, the notwithstanding clause does not apply to language-of-education articles in the Constitution. To bypass this obstacle, Québec relied on Section 1 of the Constitution, which states that the federal Charter guarantees the liberties it sets out "subject only to such reasonable limits prescribed by law as can be demonstrably justified in a free and democratic society." The Québec government hoped to prove in court that Bill 101's provisions could be justified on these grounds. However, in 1984, the Supreme Court rejected its argument that the threat to the survival of the French language in North America justified Bill 101's restrictions on English school enrolment. The Court ruled that the section of Bill 101 limiting eligibility to English-language schools in Québec was "incompatible" with the constitutional guarantees set out in the *Canadian Charter of Rights and Freedoms*.

In late 1988, the Supreme Court again had to rule on the constitutionality of certain clauses of Bill 101. This time it ruled that the law prohibiting business signs in languages other than French was against the Charter's provisions on freedom of expression and speech. The Québec government invoked the notwithstanding clause to escape from this section of the Charter. It then introduced Bill 178, which required French to be used on outdoor signs but allowed English on indoor signs provided that French was "prominently" displayed. Once more, Québec's language law sparked intense criticism.[4] However, these arguments over language were quickly overshadowed by discussions concerning the Constitution as a whole. (Language issues are discussed in Chapter 5.)

THE NEW CANADIAN CONSTITUTION

On April 17, 1982, the *Constitution Act, 1982* subsumed and replaced the *BNA Act* as Canada's Constitution. While none of the changes affected the main structure of central government or federalism, some of them greatly changed how Canadians govern themselves. The most important of the changes were the new amendment formulas.

Amendment Formulas

There are now five legal formulas for amending the *Constitution Act, 1982*.

- The *first formula* concerns amendments that require unanimous consent. It deals with amendments to the office of the Queen, the governor general, and the lieutenant-governors; the right of a province to have at least as many seats in the House of Commons as it has in the Senate; the use of the English and French languages; the composition of the Supreme Court of Canada; and amendments to the amending formulas.

  Amendments in these areas must be passed by the Senate and the House of Commons (or by the Commons alone if the Senate has not approved the proposal within 180 days after the Commons has done so), and by the legislature of each and every province.

- The *second formula* includes amendments that deal with taking away any rights, powers, or privileges of provincial governments or legislatures; the proportionate representation of the provinces in the House of Commons; the powers of the Senate and the method of selecting senators and their residence qualifications; the constitutional position of the Supreme Court of Canada (not including its composition, which is covered under the first formula above); the extension of existing provinces into the territories; and the *Canadian Charter of Rights and Freedoms*.

  Amendments in these areas must be passed by the Senate and the House of Commons (or by the Commons alone if the Senate delays more than 180 days), and by the legislatures of two-thirds of the provinces with at least half the total population of all provinces (excluding the territories). In reality, this means that any four less-populous provinces, or Ontario and Québec together, could veto any amendments in this category, and that either Ontario or Québec would have to be one of the seven provinces needed to pass any amendment.

- The *third formula* deals with matters that apply to one or more but not all provinces. Amendments in these cases must be passed by the Senate and the House of Commons (or the Commons alone if the Senate delays more than 180 days), and by the legislature or legislatures of the particular province or provinces concerned. These include changes in provincial boundaries or changes relating to the use of the English or French language in any province or provinces.

- The *fourth formula* concerns changes in the executive government of Canada or changes in the Senate and House of Commons that are not covered by the first two formulas. Such amendments can be made by an ordinary act of the Parliament of Canada.

- The *fifth formula* concerns amendments that can be made by individual provincial legislatures alone. In the original *BNA Act* (Section 92), provinces could amend their own constitutions, with the exception of the office of the lieutenant-governor. Section 92(1) was repealed and this amendment clause moved to Section 45, which places the provinces in a position equivalent to that of the federal government.

The first three amending formulas *entrench* specific parts of the written Constitution. **Entrenchment** means to embody provisions in a constitution so that they are protected and can be changed only by a formal amendment procedure. Neither Parliament alone nor any provincial legislature has the power to alter them. All changes must be made according to the particular constitutional formula that applies. There are also maximum and minimum time periods in which constitutional amendments must be passed.

entrenchment: Means to embody provisions in a constitution so that they are protected and can be changed only by a formal amendment procedure.

The constitutional amendment system now in place is quite rigid, so that the chances of further major changes to the Constitution by amendment are minimal. The right to amend the Constitution is finally in Canadian hands, but those hands are fairly firmly tied by rules that make major amendments almost impossible. Despite constant efforts and even a national referendum, there have been no amendments made under either the unanimity rule or the two-thirds and 50-percent rule. In 1996, Parliament passed legislation allowing Québec, Ontario, British Columbia, and any two Atlantic or Prairie provinces to veto any further constitutional change, and although this was not constitutionalized, it added even more symbolic rigidity to the amendment process.

Only 11 minor amendments to the Constitution were completed between 1982 and 2015. The first, in 1984, fleshed out Section 35 by calling for consultations with the Aboriginal peoples of Canada. The second, in 1985, modified the federal electoral formula. The third, in 1987, dealt with the entrenchment of the denominational school rights of the Pentecostal Assemblies in Newfoundland. In 1993, the fourth amendment established the equality of English-speaking and French-speaking communities in New Brunswick. In 1994, the fifth change amended the Constitution so that Canada could be relieved of the obligation to provide steamboat service to Prince Edward Island upon completion of the bridge joining the island to the mainland. Then, in 1997, the sixth and seventh amendments were passed, both concerning education in Newfoundland. (The second of these amendments did away completely with the system of denominational schools in that province.) The eighth amendment, also in 1997, replaced religious school boards in Québec with linguistic-based boards. The ninth change occurred in 1999 when the federal Parliament gave representation in the House of Commons and Senate to Nunavut. The tenth, in 2001, changed the name of Newfoundland to Newfoundland and Labrador. Finally, the eleventh modified the federal elections apportionment and put in place the *Fair Representation Act* of 2011.

The *Constitution Act, 1982* also included the following important changes.

Natural Resources The provinces obtained wider powers over their natural resources. Each province now controls the distribution within Canada of the primary production from its mines, oil wells, gas wells, forests, and electric power plants, provided it does not discriminate against other parts of the country in prices or supplies. The federal government can legislate on these matters, however, and in case of conflict, the federal law prevails. The provinces can levy indirect taxes on their mines, oil wells, gas wells, forests, and electric power plants and primary production from these sources. Such taxes must be the same whether the products are used within the province or exported to other parts of the country.

Aboriginal Peoples Three provisions related to Aboriginal peoples were included:

1. The Charter "shall not be construed so as to abrogate or derogate from any Aboriginal, treaty or other rights or freedoms that pertain to the Aboriginal peoples of Canada."

2. The existing Aboriginal and treaty rights of the Aboriginal peoples of Canada are recognized and affirmed (this includes status Indian, Inuit, and Métis peoples).

3. The prime minister of Canada was to convene, within one year of patriation, a constitutional conference of first ministers of the provinces, at which constitutional matters affecting Aboriginal peoples would be on the agenda.

Equalization The *Constitution Act, 1982* now states that the federal government and Parliament and the provincial governments and legislatures "are committed to promoting equal opportunities for the well-being of Canadians, furthering economic developments to reduce disparities in opportunities, and providing essential public services of reasonable quality to all Canadians." The federal government and Parliament are also "committed to the principle of making equalization payments to ensure that provincial governments have sufficient revenues to provide reasonably comparable levels of public services and reasonably comparable levels of taxation."

Canadian Charter of Rights and Freedoms

The 1982 Constitution included the *Canadian Charter of Rights and Freedoms*. Historically, as we have seen, civil liberties in Britain and the colonies were protected by common law and parliamentary supremacy. It was widely believed that neither the British government nor its master, Parliament, would infringe on individual freedoms because both were held in check by traditions, customs, and political culture. Following this tradition, Canada also relied on the rights provided by British common law and, after 1960, on legislation known as the **Canadian Bill of Rights**, which listed some fundamental freedoms but never entrenched them in the Constitution.

Did Canada Need a Charter?

Why did Canada need an entrenched Charter when it had existed as a free society for more than a century without such a document? The answer is that, despite the rule of law and British traditions, Canada has not always adequately protected citizens' rights. In 1937, Québec passed the Padlock Law. By that legislation, the Québec government banned the propagation of "Communism and Bolshevism" by padlocking any premises allegedly used for such purposes. The law gave Premier Maurice Duplessis the ability to move arbitrarily against groups opposed to his regime. In

Canadian Bill of Rights: Legislation passed in 1960 that listed fundamental freedoms but was never entrenched in the Constitution.

1938, the Alberta legislature enacted the Press Bill, which allowed the government to force newspapers to reveal the sources of unfavourable comment. In 1953, Québec restrained the freedom of religion of Jehovah's Witnesses by restricting their right to hand out pamphlets without permission.

Although the courts subsequently overturned these three restrictive pieces of legislation, the judges' decisions did not lessen, but rather strengthened, the argument for entrenching basic rights in the Constitution. The court rulings were not based on the fact that the legislation represented a violation of fundamental rights, but rather on the notion that provincial governments did not have the right to restrict civil liberties because of the constitutional division of powers. In all of these cases, the courts declared that the actions were ultra vires—that is, not within the provincial jurisdiction.

Another notable violation of basic rights in Canada's history was the internment of Japanese Canadians during World War II. Under the *War Measures Act*, thousands of people of Japanese descent were uprooted from their communities and placed in camps for the duration of the war for "security" reasons. Decades later, in 1970, Prime Minister Trudeau again invoked the *War Measures Act*, this time in response to terrorist activities in Québec by the Front de libération du Québec (FLQ). This action, which suspended civil liberties and allowed the arbitrary detention of hundreds of suspects, became a major symbol of government violation of basic human rights in Canada.

To prevent such violations of civil liberties from occurring again, the *Constitution Act, 1982* provides the *Canadian Charter of Rights and Freedoms* with both substantive and procedural rights. **Substantive rights** are fundamental rights as defined in a constitution. **Procedural rights** are rights of citizens to access certain processes such as a fair trial. They are devices to protect individuals from arbitrary action by governments. In 1988, the *War Measures Act* was replaced by a new law, the *Emergencies Act*, which again authorized special and temporary means to ensure the safety and security of Canadians. That law, however, allows for parliamentary review.

substantive rights: Fundamental rights as defined in a constitution.

procedural rights: Rights of citizens to access certain processes such as a fair trial. They are intended to protect individuals from arbitrary action by governments.

What Is in the Charter?

The Charter begins with a short introduction or preamble followed by 34 sections. The first section defines the limits of Canadians' rights and freedoms, stipulating that they are "subject only to such reasonable limits prescribed by law as can be demonstrably justified in a free and democratic society." This elastic clause allows the courts to determine the validity of laws within very wide parameters.

■ The Charter protects *fundamental freedoms*, including those of conscience and religion; of thought, belief, opinion, and expression; and of peaceful assembly and association. The basic democratic rights named in the document include the right of every citizen to vote; a five-year limit on the terms of federal and provincial legislatures, except in times of real or apprehended war, invasion, or insurrection; and the requirement for legislatures to meet at least once every 12 months.

■ The Charter also protects *mobility rights*, the right of Canadian citizens to enter, remain in, and leave Canada, and to move to and work in any province. However, these rights are limited by recognition of provincial residency requirements as a qualification for receiving social services. Affirmative action programs to ameliorate the conditions of an individual who has been socially or economically disadvantaged are also allowed.

- *Legal rights* such as the traditional right to life, liberty, and security are listed, along with new legal rights provisions. For example, unreasonable search or seizure and arbitrary detention or imprisonment are prohibited. A detained individual is guaranteed the right to be informed promptly of the reasons for detention, to have counsel without delay, and to be instructed of that right, as well as to have the validity of the detention determined and to be released if detention is not justified. Individuals who are charged with an offence have the right to be informed without delay of the specific offence, and to be tried within a reasonable time. They have a right against self-incrimination, and are to be considered innocent until proven guilty by an impartial and public hearing. Evidence obtained in a manner that infringes on an individual's rights and freedoms is to be excluded, but only if its admission would "bring the administration of justice into disrepute."

- The Charter further provides *equality rights* guaranteeing that every individual is equal before and under the law without discrimination, particularly without discrimination based on race, national or ethnic origin, colour, religion, sex, age, or mental or physical disability. However, affirmative action programs aimed at improving the conditions of groups discriminated against are allowed.

- The importance of *linguistic rights* is acknowledged. English and French are recognized as Canada's official languages and are awarded equal status in institutions of the federal Parliament and government. Both languages are also recognized in the province of New Brunswick. Thus, in Canada's Parliament and New Brunswick's legislature, both languages may be used in debates and other proceedings. Federal statutes and records, as well as proceedings of the courts, are published in both languages. Individuals have the right to communicate with any head or central office of Parliament or the government of Canada in either official language, and the same right is extended to other offices where there is significant demand.

- The Charter also provides *education rights*. All citizens of Canada who received their primary education in Canada in either French or English can exercise the right to have their children educated in the same language in the province in which they reside. However, this right is applicable only "where numbers warrant"—that is, where the number of children warrants the provision of public funds. Except in Québec, *minority* language education rights are also guaranteed to the children of Canadian citizens whose first language learned and still understood is that of the English or French linguistic minority of the province in which they reside—*even* if the parents received their primary education outside of Canada.

- The Charter includes a variety of *other specific rights*. The rights of Aboriginal peoples are not to be diminished by the Charter's provisions; for example, the provision that guarantees language education rights in French and English may not be interpreted to deprive the Indian people of James Bay of their right to educate their children in Cree. More broadly, the Charter may not be used to deprive anyone of existing rights and freedoms, and its interpretation must recognize Canada's multicultural heritage. Significantly, in recognition of Canada's federal nature, the Charter states that neither level of government gains power as a result of its provisions.

Despite this impressive list of rights, not all of them are inviolable. Remember that the Constitution was patriated only through political compromises. These included an agreement by the leaders to allow restrictions on citizens' rights in two general ways:

1. In Section 1, the Charter states that the rights and freedoms are guaranteed "subject" to "such reasonable limits presented by law as can be demonstrably justified in a free and democratic society." This means that the courts are allowed to decide that federal or provincial legislation that restricts freedoms is valid or invalid according to *their* definition of "reasonable limits." The Supreme Court, for example, has allowed the Ontario legislature to impose film censorship as long as the criteria it uses are prescribed by law.[5]

2. Section 33 allows each provincial legislature and the federal Parliament the power to enact laws to override certain Charter provisions. As we have seen, they may pass legislation counter to the Charter on fundamental freedoms and legal and equality rights by attaching a notwithstanding clause. Such bills become inoperative after five years and must be passed again if they are to remain valid. Section 33, however, cannot be used to override democratic and mobility rights.

Since the Charter became law, many of its provisions have been challenged in the courts. This has had both positive and negative effects. On the one hand, citizens have been able to ask courts to declare laws unconstitutional when they saw even a potential infringement of their rights. On the other hand, judges have interpreted and clarified many legal provisions and applied them to laws that had previously been passed by Parliament. Critics of the Charter argue, among other things, that it confers too much power on lawyers and judges, enabling judges who are not elected to strike down measures enacted by the democratic Parliament. We examine human rights highlights from these controversial Charter cases in Chapter 9.

THE MEECH LAKE ACCORD AND LANGEVIN AMENDMENT

Although the Constitution was patriated in 1982, unfinished constitutional business remained. In particular, Québec's objections had still not been met. The new federal Progressive Conservative government, elected in 1984, conducted months of bargaining with the provinces to design amendments that would secure Québec's political assent to the *Constitution Act, 1982*.

In the initial bargaining sessions, Québec premier Robert Bourassa demanded five constitutional amendments, known collectively as the Langevin Amendment:

- Recognition of Québec as a "distinct" society
- A formal voice for Québec in Supreme Court appointments
- A Québec policy on immigration
- Limits to federal spending powers in areas of provincial jurisdiction
- A veto on constitutional amendments affecting the province

While it was generally agreed that Québec should have these demands met as part of "renewed federalism," the nine other premiers *also* made requests for changes concerning the Senate, federal spending power, and the constitutional amending formula. In the end, the federal government and all 10 provincial premiers agreed to all five Québec demands in what became known as the **Meech Lake Accord**. A political agreement on Senate reform also was reached, but it was *not* to be part of the constitutional amendment at that time.

Many serious flaws in the accord soon became evident. In Parliament, the Liberals submitted eight amendments and the NDP two, but not one of them was accepted. In spite of this, Parliament passed the Meech Lake Accord with little dissent. However, since the Meech Lake amendments called for major constitutional revisions, it required the approval not just of Parliament but of *all 10* provincial legislatures as well. This requirement proved impossible to achieve.

The essential criticism of the secretly negotiated accord was that, in the pressure to win over Québec, important federal powers that would have weakened Parliament were given away. Critics contended that the Meech Lake Accord was handing over so much power to the provinces that Canada would be transformed from a federation into a weak confederacy. Québec nationalists and some regionalists countered that the accord was a positive affirmation that cooperative federalism could work.

In the final analysis, the Meech Lake Accord was defeated because it required unanimity from the provinces, and two provinces (Manitoba and Newfoundland) did not pass the necessary resolution before the ratification deadline of June 23, 1990. Symbolically, it was Elijah Harper, standing in the Manitoba legislature with a white feather in his hand, who blocked the accord. Aboriginal demands, he said, should also be met before the Constitution was amended.

When the proposals did not obtain provincial unanimity, the whole package was dead. Life went on, but the Québec independence issue, dormant since the 1980 referendum, was revived.

Post-Meech Efforts at Constitutional Change

Following the death of the Meech Lake Accord, numerous government-sponsored conferences, symposia, federal–provincial meetings, and even a Royal Commission were held on the Constitution. On September 24, 1991, Prime Minister Brian Mulroney introduced a new constitutional package in a publication called *Shaping Canada's Future Together*. This time, comments and proposed changes were encouraged.[6]

The proposals in the document were examined at length by a Joint House and Senate Committee on a Renewed Canada (known as the Beaudoin–Dobbie Committee) in order to produce yet another set of proposals. The committee presented a revised set of proposals on February 28, 1992, but Québec remained aloof and disdainful. Neither the government's position nor the Beaudoin–Dobbie proposals were formally presented to Québec and the other provinces, but members of Québec's political elite turned them down in principle. As for the Official Opposition in Ottawa, Liberal leader Jean Chrétien was sufficiently disillusioned to suggest that a moratorium on constitutional reform be considered.

Despite these reports and public consultations, the federal government still had no acceptable proposals. Public cynicism and criticism were growing and the Progressive

Conservative Party was falling apart. On June 23, 1990, Lucien Bouchard left the Cabinet to form the Bloc Québécois, a separatist party that would operate in Ottawa's Parliament. Québec's Liberal government, meanwhile, continued to be bound by Bill 150, which called for a provincial referendum on sovereignty by October 26, 1992.

Québec's most divisive input into the constitutional debate was a report that proposed a drastic decentralization of the country, maintaining that Québec should "exercise exclusive discretionary and total authority in most fields of activity." It wanted 22 domains to be in the exclusive power of Québec, including communications, energy, industry and commerce, regional development, and income security. Ottawa would be assigned only currency, customs and tariffs, debt management, and transfer payments.

In Ottawa, the federal government, nine provinces, two territorial governments, and Aboriginal leaders came to a new, tentative agreement, called the Pearson Agreement, on July 7, 1992. This deal included a Triple-E Senate (equal, effective, and elected) for the West, self-government for Aboriginal peoples, and a veto and "distinct society" recognition for Québec. Once again, in their totality, the proposals would have greatly weakened federal authority. Québec representatives neither attended the meetings nor agreed to the proposals.

THE CHARLOTTETOWN ACCORD AND THE 1992 CONSTITUTIONAL REFERENDUM

The Pearson Agreement drew Québec premier Robert Bourassa back to the bargaining table. Québec representatives met with Prime Minister Mulroney, the other nine premiers, and the leaders of the territories and the Aboriginal communities. They emerged with a complex and highly controversial constitutional deal, known as the **Charlottetown Accord** in August 1992. It consisted of an agreement in principle (not a legal text) about what changes should be made to the Constitution and what further political accords would be negotiated. The leaders agreed to put the tentative principles to the Canadian people in a countrywide referendum two months later on October 26, 1992.

Charlottetown Accord: An August 1992 agreement in principle on what changes needed to be made to the Constitution; rejected in a countrywide referendum.

The deal called for major innovation in the way Canada is governed. It included a Canada clause, a new division of powers, new Aboriginal self-government clauses, a social and economic union, and institutional changes in the House of Commons and Senate.[7] The most important proposal was that a definition of **distinct society** be added to the Constitution in a new clause stating that "Québec constitutes within Canada a distinct society, which includes a French-speaking majority, a unique culture and a civil law tradition." The proposals also affirmed the role of the legislature and government of Québec "to preserve and promote the distinct society of Québec."

distinct society: A term that the Charlottetown Accord wanted to be added to the Constitution to describe Québec: "Québec constitutes within Canada a distinct society, which includes a French-speaking majority, a unique culture and a civil law tradition."

Once again, critics argued, the proposals were too decentralizing and too multi-layered to allow effective and efficient government. They found hundreds of concrete amendments hidden in the global suggestions. Not only were the proposals vague, but the overall result of the relations among them was completely unknowable. Again, the proposals created the possibility of a checkerboard Canada in which Canadians living in different provinces would not share the same benefits and opportunities.[8]

An example from the Constitution makes this clear. The residual clause, "Peace, Order, and good Government," which has been used when necessary to give powers to the federal government, was to be weakened by giving power over "non-national matters" to the provincial authorities. This suggested that topics such as the environment could be considered as strictly a provincial matter, so that federal regulations might no longer apply equally across the country. As well, as part of the compromise, the federal government proposed to withdraw from several specific jurisdictions. Some withdrawals were reasonable; others were controversial.

Another major area of concern was that the reform proposals would have created a complicated Rubik's cube of federal institutions.[9] The proposed Senate was too powerful compared to the House of Commons. It would have had the right, for example, to ratify major order-in-council positions, a right denied to the House of Commons. Also, under the new proposals, a new layer of appointed government, the Council of the Federation, would have been added to the political system. Such a council undoubtedly would have been in constant conflict with the elected Parliament of Canada.

Instead of streamlining government and making it more efficient and less expensive, the Charlottetown Accord threatened to generate even more problems. However, all three federal party leaders approved the package. The opponents of the accord appeared weak and disunited. They included Jacques Parizeau, leader of the Parti Québécois, and Lucien Bouchard, leader of the Bloc Québécois; Preston Manning, leader of the Reform Party; and a few provincial Liberals such as Sharon Carstairs in Manitoba. However, the real leader of the "No" side proved to be former prime minister Pierre Elliott Trudeau, who attacked the constitutional deal with fervour and logic. Trace the constitutional highlights in Close-Up 3.2.

The third national referendum in Canadian history was a divisive event. In the final analysis, six provinces (Québec, Nova Scotia, Manitoba, Saskatchewan, Alberta,

Close-Up 3.2

Canada's Constitutional Highlights

A: Actual Constitutional Developments

1867: *British North America Act* (now the *Constitution Act, 1867*) enacted

1931: *Statute of Westminster* enacted; Britain could no longer legislate for Canada except at the request of the Canadian government

1949: An amendment to the *BNA Act* widened the scope of the Canadian Parliament's authority to undertake further amendments

1949: Supreme Court of Canada became final court of appeal

1961: *Canadian Bill of Rights* enacted

1964: Fulton–Favreau formula rejected by Québec

1971: Victoria Charter rejected by Québec

1980: Québec referendum on sovereignty-association defeated

1981: Supreme Court ruled Trudeau's constitutional resolution was valid but violated political convention

1981: First ministers made three significant changes to resolution; package was rejected by Québec

1981: Constitutional resolution was passed by Canadian Parliament

1982: *Canada Act* passed by British House of Commons and patriated; the *Canadian Charter of Rights and Freedoms* and an amendment formula became part of the Canadian Constitution; Québec did not sign

1984–2015: Eleven minor changes to Constitution

B: Constitutional Developments and Proposals (also see Chapter 7)

1987: The Meech Lake Accord failed

1991: The Spicer Royal Commission on Bilingualism and Biculturalism reported

1992: The Beaudoin–Dobbie Joint House and Senate committee report published and was followed by constitutional conferences

1992: The Charlottetown Accord was approved by federal and provincial leaders, then massively rejected in a countrywide referendum

1995: Québec referendum on independence held; sovereignty very narrowly defeated

1996: Parliament passed legislation: (1) on the distinct society clause; (2) allowed Québec, Ontario, British Columbia, and any two Atlantic or Prairie provinces to veto any further constitutional change; (3) Liberal federal government committed not to use its spending power to create new shared-cost programs without consent of majority of provinces

1997: Calgary Declaration—attempt by nine premiers to restart constitutional negotiations with Québec

1998: Supreme Court answered three questions about Québec separatism

1999: Federal Parliament passed *Clarity Act* and Québec responded with its own legislation

2003: Election of federalist Jean Charest as premier of Québec; separatist constitutional challenges from Québec stopped, temporarily at least

2006: House of Commons passed resolution saying that Québécois form a "nation within a united Canada"

and British Columbia) voted decisively against the accord and only Newfoundland, Prince Edward Island, and New Brunswick voted strongly for it. Ontario very narrowly supported the deal, while Yukon voted against it and Northwest Territories voted for it. At the national level, 72 percent of the Canadian electorate cast their votes and defeated the proposal by 54.4 percent to 44.6 percent. The Charlottetown proposal was dead. It had been designed mostly to accommodate provincial interests, and its defeat prevented Canada from becoming even more decentralized.

Have Canadians patriated the Constitution only to be mired in constitutional deadlock? The amendment procedures may prove too rigid to resolve divisive issues. The constitutional dilemma of how to solve regional aspirations and Québec's precise demands while retaining a viable federal government continues to be the most vital political challenge facing Canadians, but there is little desire to reopen negotiations (see Close-Up 3.3).

The new Liberal government in 1993 relegated constitutional reform to the back burner. Prime Minister Jean Chrétien took the stand that many issues between the federal government and the provinces could be solved outside the Constitution. This has been the case, for example, with changes in the relationship between the federal government and Aboriginal peoples. Some Aboriginal groups have achieved much of what they had wanted to be included in the Charlottetown Accord without a constitutional

Constitutional Fatigue

The constitutional fatigue that was shared by many Canadians gave rise to the following popular joke:

Two prisoners on death row were asked what their last wish would be. The first said he would like a steak and a beer. The second said, "I'd just like to debate the constitution one more time," to which the first prisoner groaned, "Then just kill me right now."

amendment. Others have not. However, larger problems in federal–provincial relations—in particular, the future of Québec in Canada—continue to plague Canadian politics (see Chapter 5). In 1999, the *Clarity Act* was passed, essentially concluding that a Supreme Court ruling in 1998 was correct; the federal government would never accept an unambiguous and unilateral declaration of independence from any province, including Québec. In 2006, the House of Commons passed a symbolic resolution that the Québécois are a "nation within a united Canada."

Despite federal–provincial bickering, the Constitution of Canada clearly is strong and not about to topple. When asked to decide on the Charlottetown Accord, Canadians were skeptical. Those who attempt to convince Canadians that the country and the Constitution do not work will have to be more persuasive, and be clear that they are not merely pushing their own agendas for things such as secession, devolution, asymmetry, or even themselves.

The next chapter focuses on the federal system and how it works. Decide for yourself whether—and if so, how—it needs to be reformed in a major way.

Discussion Questions

1. Why do countries need a constitution?

2. What were the basic obstacles to the 1982 patriation of the Constitution, and what compromises were reached to try to solve them? Why did Québec not agree with those compromises?

3. What were the main additions to the Constitution when it was patriated in 1982? Was it wise to patriate it without Québec's approval?

4. Describe and evaluate the current formula for amending the Constitution.

5. What attempts has the federal government made since 1982 to convince Québec to sign the patriated Constitution? Explain why, in your considered opinion, these attempts have failed so far.

6. How has the *Canadian Charter of Rights and Freedoms* affected equality and other rights in Canada? Are fundamental rights better protected now? Has the Charter protected civil liberties in an era of global terrorism? (Consult Chapter 9.)

Chapter 4

Contested Federalism

The Division of Powers and Financial Resources

Learning Objectives

After reading this chapter, you should be able to

1   Distinguish between unitary, confederal, and federal systems of government.

2   Outline the basic distribution of powers between the federal and provincial governments in Canada.

3   Trace the shifting pattern of power in Canadian federalism from 1867 to the present.

4   Explain four key problems at the root of federal–provincial financial arrangements.

5   Describe how the federal government currently distributes money to the provinces.

Federalism is a complex, political game. The basic idea of federalism has been traced back in history to the fusion of ancient Israelite tribes. In North America, its first occurrence is thought to have been among the Five Nations of the Iroquois. The contemporary concept of federalism, however, is best dated to the eighteenth century when the United States' Constitution established the first modern federal system of government. Federalism there was based on two main ideas: The distribution of government power on a geographical basis and the philosophy that unity and diversity can coexist. The U.S. federal system has been a model for other states, including Canada, Australia, and Switzerland.

Federalism sets up a multi-dimensional game of politics with powerful political actors at various levels of government. In this chapter, we examine the ideas that underpin the federal union and the legal foundations of federalism in Canada: The division of powers between Ottawa and the provincial capitals as well as the funding of the union. There is no doubt that controlling taxpayers' money is one of the most, if not *the* most, important and contentious ingredients in federal politics.

THE CONCEPT OF FEDERALISM

We learned in Chapter 1 that a *sovereign state* wields authority and power so that it is capable of maintaining order within its territory. It is able to tax its citizens and run its affairs free from external interference. A sovereign state is recognized as legitimate by its citizens and by other countries.

All sovereign states distribute the power to carry out governmental functions across their territories in some manner. There may be one strong, central government supplemented by local authorities, or the central government may be weak because authority is divided and shared with regional governments. In some countries, the constitution gives all final decision-making authority to one level of government. In others, the constitution provides for more than one level of final authority over the same people in the same territory.

Most of the world's states have centralized, one-level political arrangements called **unitary systems** in which the constitution provides for a single level of sovereign power in the country. The central government may delegate powers to regional or local administrative units, but it alone remains, in constitutional terms, the supreme law-making institution. If other levels of government—such as in cities and regions—exist, they are under the constitutional jurisdiction of the unitary government. Examples of unitary governments today include France and Japan.

In **federal systems**, legal powers are divided between a central government and regional governments in such a way that each level of government has some activities on which it makes final decisions.[1] This means that there is more than one level of government over the same geographical territory. In federal systems, the constitution specifically divides jurisdictional powers between the central government and the regional government(s). Neither level of government owes its authority to the other. Both federal and provincial legislatures may make laws that have a direct impact on citizens. This is the case in Canada.

There are over 15 times more unitary than federal states in the world. However, although there are only 25 federal states, they contain approximately half of the world's population. In a federal system, each level of government has more or less complete authority over some specific spheres of activity, while there may be a degree of overlapping jurisdiction on a few others. These rules determine how centralized or decentralized a country actually is (see Figure 4.1).

The Canadian Constitution outlines a federal system of government with jurisdictions divided or shared between the federal Parliament and the provincial

unitary system: A form of government in which the power and authority to govern is centralized in one government.

federal system: A system in which legal powers are divided between a central government and regional governments in such a way that each level of government has some kind of activities on which it makes final decisions.

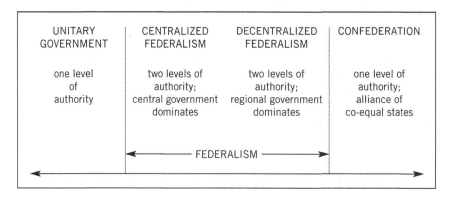

Figure 4.1 Continuum of the Degree of Centralization of Authority

Source: Adapted from concepts proposed by William H. Riker in *Federalism: Origin, Operation, Significance* (Boston: Little, Brown, 1964).

assemblies. Within that broad framework, however, the Constitution leaves much undefined, or loosely defined. Many administrative rules are left for the politicians of the day to make, based on historical and economic considerations and political judgments.

Since federal and provincial governments govern the same people and the same territory, there is constant rivalry between them. Political conflicts often arise over authority and jurisdiction. Most of these disputes concern who should make and who should pay for decisions. However, there are also serious quarrels over whether all of the provinces are, or even should be, equal in every respect, or whether some do receive, or should receive, special treatment from the federal government.

Federalism, therefore, is constantly changing. Developments in federalism affect the lives of every Canadian. The many social services and programs available to Canadians today are the result of agreements between federal and provincial governments. Some programs are supported by only one level of government, but the majority require financial cooperation between two levels. Just as too many cooks can spoil the broth, the federal system complicates many vital issues such as economic planning and control of inflation. On the other hand, it also brings government closer to the people, allowing provinces and regions to retain a degree of control over particular aspects of their development and the day-to-day lives of their residents.

ORIGINS OF CANADIAN FEDERALISM

There are many reasons that Canada ended up with a federal system. Throughout the first half of the nineteenth century, Britain's Canadian colonies edged toward political union. The 1841 union of Upper and Lower Canada (now Ontario and Québec, respectively) was the first step. As the population of Upper Canada grew in relation to that of Lower Canada, Upper Canadians demanded more political influence. Meanwhile, Lower Canada steadfastly insisted on non-interference with the French, Catholic way of life. As political deadlocks developed, tensions mounted and the experiment of joining the two Canadas failed.

Sir John A. Macdonald played a leading role in resolving the situation by establishing a federal union in 1867. Each of the British colonies in North America saw advantages for itself in the union. The leaders from Upper Canada looked forward to further economic expansion and development. Those from Lower Canada were willing to consider a federal union if their language and culture could be protected by law. The sparsely populated Maritime colonies of Nova Scotia and New Brunswick were perhaps the most reluctant, but they were attracted by economic advantages of union such as a new transcontinental railway and potential subsidies from a future federal government.

Conferences in Québec and Charlottetown and protracted negotiations culminated in an agreement to form the Dominion of Canada, a *federal* system or **federation** in which powers were divided between the federal and provincial legislatures.[2] Confederation was finalized in 1867. As it turned out, *confederation* was a confusing term. A **confederation** is a form of political organization that very loosely unites strong provincial or state units under a weak government. That was not the case here. We still refer to the *Confederation Agreement* and the *Fathers of*

federation: a form of political organization in which the activities of government are divided between regional governments and a central government in such a way that each level of government has activities on which it makes final decisions.

confederation: A form of political organization that very loosely unites strong provincial or state units under a weak central government.

Confederation, but the authors of the agreement wanted Canada to be a centralized *federation* with a strong central government (see Figure 4.1). One of the key provisions of the Constitution was an agreement on provincial representation in the House of Commons and Senate. Despite contemporary foolishness on the topic, there would not have been an agreement if the provinces had not been allowed regional equality in an appointed Senate.

THE FEDERAL–PROVINCIAL DIVISION OF POWERS

The need for a "federal bargain" to divide powers between the central and the regional governments was urgent in the nineteenth century. The colonists were used to rule by local governments, and transportation and communication among the provinces were difficult. Sir George-Étienne Cartier and other French-Canadian leaders demanded a degree of exemption from central government authority, so some independence had to be granted to the local entities. While Sir John A. Macdonald would actually have preferred a British-style unitary form of government, the federal principle was accepted as a necessary compromise. It maintained the unity of the political system while protecting the interests of provinces and language groups.[3]

The 10 provincial constitutions follow the federal pattern. In each of the provinces, the Queen is represented by a lieutenant-governor appointed by Governor-in-Council on the advice of the prime minister. The lieutenant-governors act on the advice, and with the assistance, of the prime minister's ministry or executive council, which is responsible to the legislature. They resign office under circumstances similar to their counterparts in the federal government. Provincial legislatures are elected for a maximum of five years and, unlike the federal Parliament, which has two Houses, the provincial legislatures today are all unicameral.

The three northern territories remain under the constitutional authority of the federal government. Several federal statutes—the *Yukon Act*, *Northwest Territories Act*, and *Nunavut Act*, along with the *Government Organization Act* and *Interpretation Act*—provide their legal structures, and the *Canadian Charter of Rights and Freedoms* also provides a degree of independent legitimacy in Sections 3 and 30 by referring to the legislative assemblies of the territories. In political terms, the first two territories to be established (Yukon and Northwest Territories) were given fully elected assemblies; responsible executives, called councils; and a form of delegated responsibility for most matters under provincial jurisdiction. The commissioners, appointed by the minister of Aboriginal Affairs and Northern Development, act as quasi-lieutenant-governors under the authority of the minister. Nunavut, the newest territory carved out of Northwest Territories, gained official status only on April 1, 1999, and now has the same form of government as Northwest Territories.

In early Canadian history, provincial constitutional power appeared relatively insignificant. The Constitution awarded most authority to the federal government, giving it three centralizing constitutional powers:

1. In extreme circumstances, the national government could use its power of **disallowance**—the power to disallow provincial legislation, even though the subject matter of the legislation was assigned to the provinces by the *British*

disallowance: The power to disallow provincial legislation, even though the subject matter of the legislation was assigned to the provinces by the *BNA Act*.

North America Act, 1867 (*BNA Act*). This power of disallowance was employed 112 times after Confederation, but it has not been used since 1943.

2. The federal government also had the power of reservation. **Reservation** refers to the constitutional ability of lieutenant-governors to reserve provincial legislation for federal approval. Reservation was employed quite often: Some 70 bills were reserved before the practice was discontinued in 1961.[4]

3. The federal government may have had the power of **veto**—the power to block legislation or to block a constitutional amendment by use of the royal prerogative. Since this power was never exercised, however, it is presumed to have atrophied.

reservation: The constitutional ability of lieutenant-governors to reserve provincial legislation for federal approval.

veto: The power to block legislation or to block a constitutional amendment.

These three powers were so centralizing that some experts refer to the early period of Canadian history as one of *quasi-federalism*—having a federal appearance (i.e., divided jurisdictions) but a unitary reality (i.e., no divided authority) because there was no significant power in the subunits. However, it is very unlikely that such extreme federal powers as disallowance or reservation will ever be contemplated again in Canada, except perhaps in a circumstance as grave as the secession of a province from the federal union. Today, Canada is certainly not a quasi-federal state.

The Constitution also gave the federal government more powers than the provinces in another way. The Fathers of Confederation regarded the American Civil War as an example of what could happen if a central government did not have strong authority. They therefore included in the Constitution a **residual clause** (the "Peace, Order, and good Government" clause) to allow the federal government to legislate in any matter not specifically assigned to the provinces. **Section 91** of the Constitution specifies the areas belonging to the federal government. It also contains the residual clause. Section 91 states:

residual clause: A clause in the Constitution that allows the federal government to legislate in any matter not specifically assigned to the provinces.

Section 91: A section of the Constitution that specifies the areas belonging exclusively to the federal government. It also contains a residual clause.

> It shall be lawful for the Queen, by and with the Advice and Consent of the Senate and the House of Commons, to make Laws for the Peace, Order, and good Government of Canada, in relation to all matters not coming within the Classes of Subjects by this Act assigned exclusively to the Legislatures of the Provinces . . .

In addition to granting this sweeping authority, Section 91 specifies 29 items as belonging exclusively to the federal government, including trade, commerce, banking, credit, currency, taxation, navigation, citizenship, and defence. **Section 92** of the Constitution, on the other hand, outlines 16 specific areas of provincial jurisdiction, including direct taxation, hospitals, prisons, property, and civil rights. These latter, provincial subjects were of only limited and local concern in 1867 but later became much more important than the Fathers of Confederation could have foreseen.

Section 92: A section of the Constitution that delineates 16 specific areas of provincial jurisdiction, including direct taxation, hospitals, prisons, property, and civil rights.

Issues over the Division of Powers

While the *BNA Act* was a centralist document, it is important to note that some of its terms were not defined precisely, so that they changed meanings over time. These omissions enabled both federal and provincial authorities to interpret them to their own advantage after Confederation. The contest continues even now. For example, Section 93 gave power over education to the provinces, but today it is debatable whether education, a provincial responsibility, encompasses or should encompass cultural matters, broadcasting, occupational training, and research.

The conflict over the division of powers is evident in the field of natural resources. The *BNA Act* clearly assigned "ownership" of resources to the provinces. However, it gave the federal government a major voice in the sales of resources by allowing it to control interprovincial and international trade. Thus, today, the provinces control oil because it is under the ground, but oil wells are in the hands of private or public companies and the Parliament of Canada exercises some authority over oil through taxation and jurisdictional powers.

The federal government was also given specific power to interfere in provincial jurisdictions. Through the **declaratory power** (*BNA Act*, Section 92.10(a)), the federal government is allowed to assume jurisdiction over any "work" considered to be for the benefit of Canada as a whole. The power was exercised 470 times before 1961. In the 1920s, for example, Parliament placed every grain elevator under federal control but did not assume ownership. Federal control over uranium exploration is a more recent example. The provinces have often contested the use of the declaratory power, but the courts have backed the federal position.

Clearly, the Constitution has proven inadequate in clarifying the use of power in many jurisdictions. Today, very few areas of policy are handled exclusively by one level of government. The only exclusively federal areas appear to be defence, veterans' affairs, the postal system, and monetary policy. The only exclusively provincial areas are municipal institutions, elementary and secondary education, and some areas of law related to property and other non-criminal matters.[5]

In all other areas, both levels of government engage in activities in the same fields. Sometimes the process is harmonious, as for example when the federal government allows the provinces to regulate interprovincial highway transportation. In other areas, such as external trade, workforce training, communications, language, and culture, the two levels are in constant conflict.

Another aspect of the constitutional division of powers that continues to be controversial is the field of **concurrent powers**. Concurrent powers are those shared by the Parliament of Canada and the provincial legislatures. Section 95 of the *BNA Act* called for concurrent powers in agriculture and immigration. However, de facto concurrent powers have also arisen in other fields because of the federal government's control of *spending power*. Just because the federal government has little or no legal jurisdiction over particular matters such as education, health, consumer protection, and the environment, this does not prohibit Ottawa from spending money in these areas and therefore influencing policy. The provinces have great difficulty refusing such "gifts." Scientific research, recreational activities, tourism, and protection of the environment are handled today as if they were areas of concurrent jurisdiction, although they are not mentioned in the Constitution as concurrent powers.

Conflicts over jurisdictional boundaries are to be expected in federal systems. Flexible or woolly clauses are particularly troublesome. In Canada, persistent arguments have arisen because some matters in the provincial sphere, such as "property and civil rights," have become more significant over the years. At the same time, the "Peace, Order, and good Government" clause grants the federal

declaratory power: Allows the federal government to assume jurisdiction over any "work" considered to be for the benefit of Canada as a whole (e.g., uranium exploration).

concurrent powers: Power shared between the Parliament of Canada and the provincial legislatures.

government authority in all fields in the case of an emergency. As social and economic policies have evolved, this federal power has increasingly conflicted with specific provincial powers.

SHIFTING PATTERNS OF CANADIAN FEDERALISM
From 1867 to the Late 1950s

In the new Canadian administration of 1867, the central government was meant to be predominant. The federal government was the beneficiary of the residual "Peace, Order, and good Government" clause. The limited jurisdiction of the provinces indicated their subordinate position in the federation. Over time, however, this relationship has been interpreted in different ways by courts, causing different patterns of federalism.

The relative power of the provinces grew during the latter part of the nineteenth century, when a consistent pattern of judgments by the Judicial Committee of the Privy Council (JCPC) favoured provincial over federal rights.[6] Forceful provincial leaders demanded the erosion of central government powers to the point that the JCPC interpreted the *BNA Act* more like an international treaty than the constitution of a new country.[7]

This situation did not last long, however. Under the *BNA Act*, the provinces had jurisdiction over such matters as education, health, and social welfare, which originally required very little expenditure. However, as the demand for social services grew in the twentieth century, the provinces found themselves starved for funds since the other provisions of the Act made it virtually impossible for them to raise revenue. To help the provinces financially, the federal government offered them various grants on condition that the money be spent in a specified manner. The provinces resented this intrusion but had little option but to accept the money.

The Great Depression in the 1930s deepened the dependency of the provinces on the federal government. The necessity to prepare Canada for war in 1914 and again in 1939 also tended to centralize power in Ottawa. Except perhaps in Québec, where there was considerable opposition to the two world wars—especially to conscription—the federal government came to embody patriotism and loyalty for most Canadians, who endowed it with enormous prestige and symbolic influence.

The centralization of power continued into the second postwar era, but there were early signs that the provinces would eventually seek to regain their lost ground. New ideas about decentralization began to circulate as early as 1937, with the recommendations of the Royal Commission on Dominion–Provincial Relations, known as the Rowell–Sirois Commission.[8] This commission was set up to investigate the reasons for the near-bankruptcy of the provinces and recommend ways to revitalize the federation. It came out strongly against the existing grants procedure. It also recommended that Ottawa take over such expensive responsibilities as unemployment insurance and pensions and generally seek to equalize the financial resources of the provinces.

In the early days of Confederation, then, there was not much need for formal federal–provincial consultations, and the meetings that did occur were of an ad hoc nature. However, over time, economic policies that aimed at full employment, growth, and trade liberalization and a wide range of social policies necessitated a dramatic increase in intergovernmental relations. New departments or offices were established within the federal and provincial governments to deal with these issues.

Intergovernmental relations immediately after World War II were reasonably harmonious. It was a period of "cooperative federalism," albeit with a decidedly federal predominance. Economic times were good, and federal–provincial relations primarily concerned social programs that did not necessarily involve regional conflict. Bureaucrats tended to resolve problems before they reached the political agenda.

The 1960s to the Early 2000s

By the 1960s, the provinces needed financial relief. At the same time, important social changes were occurring in Québec and Western Canada.

Throughout the decade, a new, confident French-Canadian elite led an assault on Ottawa's "paternalism." Ottawa responded by expanding what were referred to as *shared-cost programs* or *conditional grants* (discussed below), which were awarded to the provinces on *condition* that they were spent in a certain way. However, these programs were often seen as distorting provincial spending priorities. Québec politicians insisted on the right to "opt out" of certain programs so that they could go their own way. Ottawa was unable to muster a coherent or effective response to meet this challenge.

A simmering sense of grievance against Ottawa also began to emerge in the western provinces during this period. Made confident by enormous resource revenues, Alberta and British Columbia in particular sought greater political clout within the federation to match their wealth. While they were not sympathetic to the cultural and linguistic aspirations of the Québécois, the western provinces shared with them a degree of hostility toward what they perceived as paternalism of the federal government and favouritism toward Central Canada.

The 1960s and 1970s were characterized by less cooperation and more confrontation between the two levels of government. Economic downturns and an increased concern for the jurisdictional integrity of the provinces changed the nature of federal–provincial relations. The term coined to describe this relationship was *executive federalism*. Intergovernmental talks shifted from public servants behind closed doors to open discussions among politicians, often in the full glare of publicity. At First Ministers' conferences, federal and provincial leaders met to hammer out deals, often under the scrutiny of television cameras. Some of the most important of these meetings were referred to as constitutional conferences.

These public meetings became an opportunity for the provinces to express publicly discontent and resistance to federal authority. Premiers appealed to each other and also directly to their electorates. Soon, the 10 premiers began to meet separately from First Ministers' conferences and to approach the final bargaining table as a *unified* group to oppose the federal government. Ottawa was no longer able to dominate its partners in the federation.

There is little question that the era of executive federalism was characterized by decentralization and intergovernmental conflict. Some commentators, for example, argued that the increase in intergovernmental specialists made federal–provincial conflicts more difficult to solve.[9] Competing representatives at each level of government tended to promote their own narrow interests, thereby impeding compromise.

In the 1980s, federal–provincial relations reached a new level of hostility. Discussions about the mechanics and institutional arrangements for consultation between Ottawa and the provincial capitals shifted to major constitutional discord. The 1982 patriation of the Constitution gave rise to continual wrangling between the federal government and Québec. Negotiations and deals—from the Meech Lake Accord to the Charlottetown Accord—dominated federalism. The cozy centralization of the postwar period and the pendulum swings between federal and provincial power that followed it were over. In their place was upheaval over the very nature and future of Canadian federalism, and especially the role of Québec in it (see Chapters 3 and 5).

MONEY AND FEDERALISM

This short overview of Canadian federalism shows that obtaining and spending money have been, and remain, crucial aspects of federal–provincial relations. Four general problems were identified early by J.C. Strick as being at the root of federal–provincial financial arguments.[10] They continue today.

The first and most obvious problem is that there has always been a fundamental incongruence between jurisdictional responsibilities and sources of revenue. To create a highly centralized federal system, at Confederation the federal government was awarded the most significant revenue sources. It was entitled to raise money "by any mode or system of taxation" while the provinces were limited to direct taxation. As we have noted, however, provincial expenditures mushroomed, and the provinces needed more revenues. This became a constant source of tension and conflict.

The second problem stems from the fact that provincial wealth has always differed widely. In the early years of Confederation, relatively prosperous provinces like Ontario and Québec were fortunate in having strong tax bases that gave them the ability to raise adequate funds to provide social services. Poorer and relatively depressed provinces like those in the Maritimes, however, were unable to obtain sufficient tax revenue. Increasing provincial taxes there would only lower individual incomes and undermine economic growth. Over time, this relative ability to obtain high tax revenues has shifted from province to province—recently, for example, from Ontario to Alberta during periods of high energy prices.

The third problem results from the joint occupancy of tax fields. As we have seen, the *Constitution Act* gave the provinces control of direct taxation only. **Direct taxes** are collected directly by the government, and include individual income tax, corporate income tax, and succession duties. The federal government, on the other hand, was authorized to tax in any manner. It could collect its own direct taxes in competition with the provinces. It could also levy indirect taxes. **Indirect taxes**, including customs and sales tax, are collected by other persons or institutions and passed along to the government. Eventually, the provinces obtained the right to

direct taxes: Taxes that are collected directly by the government, such as individual income tax, corporate income tax, and succession duties.

indirect taxes: Taxes that are not collected by the government, but by other persons or institutions and passed along to the government (e.g., sales tax).

collect indirect taxes as well, and then both levels of government began to levy taxes on the same sources. The competition for revenue sources became yet another contentious aspect of federal–provincial fiscal relations.

The fourth problem relates to fiscal policy. It was always feared that without close cooperation between federal and provincial taxation and spending policies, the overall economy could not be controlled effectively. If, for example, the federal government sought to cut taxes to stimulate the economy at the same time as the provinces decided to increase taxes, the federal initiative would be negated. Without a degree of cooperation, federal and provincial policies automatically would work at cross-purposes.

These four issues have been handled differently at different times since Confederation. Essentially, Ottawa collected income taxes for itself and all provinces based on the federal tax rates, except in the province of Québec. More recently, all provinces with the exception of Québec continue to allow the federal Canada Revenue Agency to collect their taxes, but all now have separated their tax rules from the federal rates. With the exception of Ontario, Québec, and Alberta, all provinces also have tax collection arrangements with the federal government for corporate income taxes.

Key Concepts: Conditional Grants, Unconditional Grants, and Spending Power

Methods for transferring funds from the federal government to the provinces have evolved over the years from relatively simple grants to complex financial arrangements. To understand these arrangements, it is necessary to have a grasp of some basic vocabulary, including *conditional grants*, *unconditional grants*, and the *federal spending power*.

conditional grants: Funds given by the federal government to provincial governments on the condition that they are spent in a certain way.

Conditional grants are funds given by the federal government to provincial governments on the condition that they are spent in a specific way. The first conditional grants in Canada were paid out for agricultural instruction in 1912. Larger-scale grants were offered in 1927 to help the provinces finance old-age pensions and help to alleviate the financial problems of the 1930s. After World War II, increased spending on health and welfare necessitated another major expansion in the field of conditional grants.

spending power: Refers to the federal government's blanket authority to spend money for any purpose in any field, even if it has no legal jurisdiction over the area.

shared-cost programs: So-called "50-cent dollar" programs in which the federal government pays 50 percent of costs.

The federal government was able to act in these fields, which were under provincial jurisdiction, because of its spending power. **Spending power** refers to the federal government's blanket authority to spend money for any purpose in any field, even if it has no legal jurisdiction over the area. In most conditional grants programs, Ottawa offered to pay half of the costs of a specific program, with the provinces paying the rest. These were **shared-cost programs** in which the federal government paid 50 percent of the costs. They were an attractive proposition for some provinces; they also encouraged provincial legislatures to spend their resources on programs chosen by the federal government. Sometimes, provincial leaders might have preferred to spend the money on other programs, but there was no way to shift resources unless Ottawa agreed.

In 1964, as a result of criticism of shared-cost programs, the federal government began to allow provinces to opt out and still receive an equivalent sum of money by way of a federal tax withdrawal or some other means. Only Québec took up this offer. It developed its own hospital and old-age pension schemes, highlighting its claim to "special status" within Confederation.

As the financial health of all provinces improved, it was inevitable that they would seek a revision of these fiscal arrangements. In 1977, led by Québec, and to some extent Alberta and Ontario, the provinces won the struggle to end the relatively restrictive conditional grants system. Ottawa increasingly offered **unconditional grants**—money that was not designated for any specific policy field so the provinces could spend it in any way they wished. This shift from conditional to unconditional grants illustrates the decentralization of the federal system during the period. Such unconditional grants began to be regarded as essential because of the unequal distribution of resources in the country. They became the norm and were even included as equalization principles in the new constitution in 1982.

unconditional grants: Money from the federal government that the provinces can spend in any way they wish since it is not designated for any specific policy field.

Key Funding Mechanisms

Over the years, Established Programs Financing (EPF) and equalization payments were put in place using conditional and/or unconditional grants. (See Table 4.1.)

Equalization We have noted how the differing economic prosperity of the provinces has posed a continuing problem in federal–provincial relations. In 1867, the financial gap between the provinces was already wide; it has been growing ever since. A primary objective of fiscal policy since World War II has been to narrow this gap and to provide a degree of economic stabilization. The main mechanism for accomplishing this has been, and continues to be, the provision of equalization payments to the provinces.

Equalization payments are unconditional transfer payments to the provinces from the federal government, calculated on the fiscal capacity (the ability to generate tax revenue) of each province in comparison to the others. A "standard" tax yield is worked out and provinces that fall below it receive transfers from the federal government to bring them up to the standard yield. They were put into effect in 1957 and enshrined in the Constitution in 1982. They are designed to ensure that the provinces can offer reasonably similar public services in areas such as health care, welfare, and education without excessive levels of taxation.

equalization payments: Unconditional transfer payments to the provinces from the federal government, calculated according to the ability of each province to raise revenue.

Table 4.1 Basic Federal–Provincial Financing in Canada

Grants	Unconditional	Traditional Conditional	New Conditional Block
Programs	Equalization	Canada Assistance Plan (CAP) Established Program Financing (EPF)	Canada Health Transfer (CHT) (funding for health) Canada Social Transfer (CST) (funding for education, social assistance, etc.)
Funding Mechanisms	Based on revenue sources	Proportion of actual expenditures	Each a combination of cash and tax points

The pool of funds for equalization rises and falls with the performance of the national economy. Provinces that fall below a given standard are considered "have-not" provinces and given equalization payments. In 2007–2008, all provinces except Alberta, British Columbia, and Ontario were in this "have-not" category and received equalization funds. As of 2015, six provinces are considered "have-not" provinces and receive equalization payments—Nova Scotia, New Brunswick, Prince Edward Island, Québec, Ontario, and Manitoba.

In terms of funding per capita provincial government expenditures, equalization payments have proven successful, but they have not brought the "have-not" provinces up to the level of the "have" provinces. The provinces may be relatively equal in terms of providing government services, but interprovincial and inter-regional disparities remain.

Equalization payments remain unconditional (a province may spend the money any way it chooses); payments are made to the less prosperous provinces and, as a province's fiscal capacity improves, the equalization payments decline.

Also, under this present system, the three northern territories are handled differently than the 10 provinces. Their special challenges include small communities; extreme population increases; and high costs of public services such as hospitals, schools, social services, and infrastructure. The Territorial Formula Financing (TFF) makes up more than two-thirds of government revenues in Yukon and Northwest Territories and more than three-quarters of the revenue of Nunavut (see Table 4.2).

Established Programs Financing (EPF)

block grant: A grant of one large sum of money from the federal government to the provinces to be spent in certain policy fields.

The most significant, comprehensive innovation came in 1977 to 1982, when the federal government offered the provinces a hybrid **block grant** (a grant of one large sum of money from the federal government to the provinces) earmarked for health and post-secondary education.[11] This block

Table 4.2 Federal Support to Provinces and Territories (in millions of dollars)*

Major Transfers	2012–13	2013–14	2014–15	2015–16
Canada Health Transfer	28 596	30 283	32 114	34 026
Canada Social Transfer	11 859	12 215	12 582	12 959
Equalization	15 423	16 105	16 669	17 341
Offshore Offset Payments	443	350	196	116
Territorial Formula Financing	3111	3288	3469	3561
Other Payments	680	56		
Total Federal Support	60 085	62 297	65 030	68 004

*In 2015–16, provinces and territories will receive $68 billion through major transfers—an increase of $3 billion from the previous year.

Source: Adapted from Department of Finance Canada, "Federal Support to Provinces and Territories," accessed at http://www.fin.gc.ca/fedprov/mtp-eng.asp.

grant program, called **Established Programs Financing (EPF)**, was essentially conditional in nature. The federal monies had to be spent in the general fields of health and education as outlined, but within these broad parameters the provinces were largely free to make their own policy choices.

Established Programs Financing (EPF): A federal block grant program that is essentially conditional in nature.

The EPF provided two types of funding for provincial expenditures on health care and post-secondary education—a tax transfer of personal and corporate income tax points and a cash transfer. While the federal government interpreted the Act as giving autonomy to the provinces, the legislation also placed some of the most expensive areas of social services squarely in the laps of the provincial governments. From the provinces' point of view, the federal government, which got them into these expensive fields in the first place, was simply preparing to disengage itself as costs began to rise.

FISCAL ARRANGEMENTS IN FLUX

The next major negotiations over the renewal of federal–provincial relations came in 1982. The federal government sought to correct what it perceived to be two fundamental problems. First, it saw a growing fiscal imbalance between the two levels of government; while the federal government's deficit increased, there was an overall surplus in provincial revenues. Second, the federal government wanted to maintain what it called a proper "political balance." It argued that its contributions to provincial government services were not sufficiently visible, and this hindered proper government accountability for taxes and expenditures and prevented taxpayers from recognizing that the federal government was responsible for much of the assistance provided.

The provinces, on the other hand, generally favoured maintaining the status quo. They argued that the federal deficit was not due to federal transfers to the provinces but rather to federal policies of indexation, tax expenditures, the subsidization of oil and gas prices, and interest rate policies. The provinces also noted that the overall provincial revenue surplus was the result of the resource wealth of a few provinces and did not reflect the overall fiscal capacity of the provinces as a whole. The "have-not" provinces were especially concerned with the future of the equalization program. The wealthier provinces, for their part, sought to protect the money they received from the EPF.

In spite of severe opposition, the federal government remained determined to reduce its transfers to the provinces. After months of inconclusive bargaining, it enacted fiscal arrangements in the EPF that continued until the fiscal year 1996–97, but some technical changes were made that had the effect of transferring an increasing share of the burden of these programs to the provinces.

Changes were also made in the method of calculating equalization payments. The federal government proposed Ontario as the standard for determining eligibility for equalization payments, thereby ensuring the province's continued exclusion from receiving such grants. However, the poorer provinces (and Ontario) objected to having the amount of money they received be contingent on Ontario's economic performance, especially in light of that province's economic stagnation during those years. Ottawa therefore dropped the so-called "Ontario standard," replacing it with a formula based on the average revenue of five provinces.

Canada Assistance Plan (CAP):
A program by which the federal government helps to finance welfare and other provincial social services.

Transfers from the federal government to the provincial and territorial governments remained mostly in the EPF; the equalization program; and the **Canada Assistance Plan (CAP)**, a shared-cost program (established in 1966) by which the federal government helps to finance welfare and other provincial social services. Under the CAP's terms, the federal government paid 50 percent of the costs of provincial and municipal programs in welfare, daycare, child welfare services, and homemakers' assistance. The basic restriction on federal funding for the CAP was that the provincial social assistance programs had to be based on "need." Programs would therefore vary widely across the country (see Table 4.1).

The New Systems during Contested Federalism

In 1995, federal finance minister Paul Martin announced that a major shift in the funding of provincial transfers would take effect in 1996. The EPF and the CAP would be folded into a new block grant system called the Canada Health and Social Transfer (CHST). The federal Liberals defended the new CHST on the grounds that it would simultaneously eliminate federal authority over provincial spending and reduce overall costs. However, at the same time, the federal government maintained that it would continue to apply its laws in the *Canada Health Act* and the CAP rules concerning residency requirements.

This new federal approach was established on the principle that its transfers would not be based on provincial costs but rather on a combination of cash payments and tax points that reduced the total federal funds for social programs. The reduction was approved by those who advocate more decentralization and censured by those who feared it would lead to a reduction in national standards in the fields of health, education, and welfare. However, as soon as the federal deficit reached zero in 1997, finance minister Paul Martin announced that he would put a floor on the reduction of the CHST transfer reductions. The federal Liberal government said that it would give even more money if there was a new agreement on the Canadian social union. This led to the Canada Child Tax Benefit and the new Universal Child Care Benefit (UCCB) program, which continue today.

The result was another compromise. *A Framework to Improve the Social Union for Canadians* was endorsed by nine premiers and the prime minister. Only Québec declined to sign the document. Under the proposal, the federal government agreed to collaborate with the provinces on any future Canada-wide initiatives in fields such as health care, post-secondary education, and social assistance (see Close-Up 4.1). Ottawa also agreed to provide one year's notice for any future funding changes, and promised to consult the provinces on any direct payments to individuals. Most important, once Ottawa and any six provinces agreed on objectives, new programs in fields such as home care or pharmacare could be set up by the federal government as long as each province could work out the details of its own program. If a province already had a program in place that met the objectives of the policy, it would still receive federal funds. In other words, the federal government in effect allowed provincial constraints on its spending power and in return received provincial acceptance for its willingness to compromise and undertake consultation.[12]

This agreement was applauded by Saskatchewan premier Roy Romanow as "80 percent of the solution to Canadian unity," and by Ontario premier Mike

Funding for Colleges and Universities

Because education is a provincial responsibility, the federal role has simply been to provide transfers to the provinces. At first, payments were earmarked directly for post-secondary education, but later the funds came with no strings attached. That meant the federal government spent billions of dollars on post-secondary education but got little credit and no influence on policy, except through the Canada Student Loans Program.

As of 2004, the federal government began to grant funds to the provinces as part of the Canada Social Transfer. It continued the Canada Millennium Scholarship Fund of up to $3 billion, with money going to students on the basis of both merit and need. The federal government also increased funding for university research with such programs as the Canada Foundation for Innovation, Canada Research Chairs, and the Canadian Institutes of Health Research.

Is this use of federal money in post-secondary education justified, or should it be left to the provinces to decide how to allocate funds in this area? What kind of transfer of money to students would you and your fellow students prefer? Direct or via the university?

Harris as capping a "tremendous day."[13] But Québec premier Lucien Bouchard would not sign the agreement under which, he claimed, "six provinces and the federal government could trigger a new program, define national objectives, devise a framework for accountability, and then Québec, to get compensation for its part of the program, would have to abide by the national objectives."[14] Premier Bouchard asked that Québec be compensated without having to give any commitment to national objectives. It was classic Canadian federalism.

Paul Martin, the finance minister, summarized the government's position:

> Provinces will now be able to design more innovative social programs that respond to the needs of people today rather than to inflexible rules. However, flexibility does not mean a free-for-all.[15]

Despite this justification, however, there is little doubt that the Liberal government decided to loosen its control over provincial financing in order to reduce the pressure on its finances while also placating nationalist tendencies in the province of Québec (see Figure 4.2). In light of the massive debt and the continuing separatist challenge in Québec, the Liberal government decentralized the country to the largest degree possible without amending the Constitution. It was a major step in the method of distributing federal transfers to the provinces.

Key Issues: Health and Social Programs

The twenty-first century has witnessed an explosion in health care costs. An aging population, advanced technologies, and new demands have driven the costs to new heights. With such large sums of money involved, and the public's desire for even more health care funding, it is not surprising that, to a very large extent, federal–provincial financial relations have become health care relations.

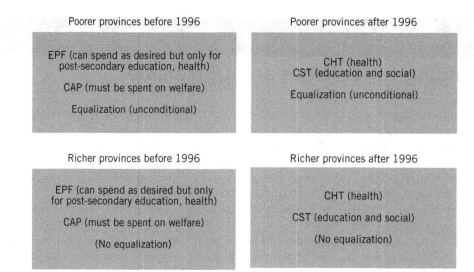

Figure 4.2 Basic Federal Financing for "Richer and Poorer" Provinces before and after 1996

The constant squabbling between the federal and provincial governments over health care costs and rules led to the federal Parliament passing the *Canada Health Act* in 1984. This Act is at the heart of provincial complaints. It penalizes provinces that do not meet the conditions in the Act, including accessibility, comprehensiveness, portability, proper administration, and universality. Much of the discussion is only public posturing, but the provinces maintain that the federal government does not give them enough money for the increased costs of health care and have begun to experiment with forms of private health care. Some provinces have allowed private, for-profit clinics to perform surgical procedures and these private clinics have charged *facility fees*.

In an effort to end the long-festering issue of health care funding, the 2003 First Ministers' conference reached an accord on health care renewal. That agreement saw the federal government contribute $34.8 billion for health over the next five years, and a further $2 billion was added in 2004, making the federal contribution $36.8 billion, or about 40 percent of the total health care costs in the country. In 2004, the federal government divided the CHST into two parts: the Canada Health Transfer (CHT) and the Canada Social Transfer (CST), thus separating health care costs from those of other social programs.

The policy debate continues. In September 2004, the federal government, 10 provinces, and three territories agreed to a new 10-year plan to sustain the health care system. The first ministers agreed to such items as universality, accessibility, and portability, but added the notion of jurisdictional flexibility. The primary controversies continued over the amount of funds the federal government should make available to the provinces, privatization, primary and home care, long waiting times, and prescription drugs. As part of this new 10-year plan, the federal government agreed to provide an extra $18 billion over the first six years for health care and guaranteed a 6 percent annual increase after that until 2015. Not all commentators were pleased with the results. Then senator Michael Kirby, for example, concluded that, "what it does is put the patient—the health-care system—on life support, but it does not put it on the road to full recovery."[16]

The federal government's demands for national targets on waiting times and an increase in home care were partially met. The first ministers could not agree on a national data collection system, but each jurisdiction agreed to establish comparable indicators and benchmarks for medically accepted wait times, starting with cancer and heart treatments, diagnostic imaging procedures, joint replacements, and sight restoration. The ministers also agreed to increase the amount of funds for short-term acute home care, short-term acute community mental health home care, and end-of-life care.

To bring Québec on board for the new health care arrangement, the government agreed to a side deal with Premier Jean Charest. The written agreement exempted Québec from some of the promises made by other provinces.[17] Québec said it would reform its own home care services in its own way. It agreed to set its own benchmarks for waiting times and establish indicators that would be comparable with the other provinces. For many years, Québec has had a separate pension plan and has been allowed to opt out of some federal–provincial social programs. However, this agreement's explicit assertion of the principle of *asymmetrical federalism* (i.e., different rules for different provinces) was unique, and gave a more explicit legitimacy to the practice. The federal intergovernmental affairs minister declared that other provinces could come to a one-to-one agreement with the federal government in the future, and that this offer was *not* limited only to Québec.

The subsequent federal government continued the basic framework for the CHT and CST transfer, but made some changes to provide more transparency and predictability in the process. The CST was extended to 2013–14, putting it in line with the long-term plan for equalization, territorial funding, and the CHT. The funds allocated to the various components of CST—namely, post-secondary education, social programs, and support for children—were itemized to improve transparency. Moreover, as the CHT had already received a commitment of 5 percent annual growth until 2013–14, the CST was given a 3 percent growth assurance until the same date.

As Table 4.2 shows, the funding for all federal–provincial programs is now in place until 2016. They indicate an immense federal commitment to provincial and territorial expenditures. In 2015-16, the commitment is for $68 billion in federal tax dollars to be handed over to the provinces and territories. Despite the constant and obvious politicking, Prime Minister Stephen Harper once again changed the formula and maintained that after fiscal year 2016–17, health transfers would be based on the rise in the gross domestic product (GDP), with a floor of 3 percent.

Are we at the beginning of yet another new era in federalism? Is such an explicit acknowledgment of asymmetrical federalism and its flexibility the sign of a new cooperative federal government, the recognition of past practices, or the federal government caving in to provincial demands? All of these assertions have been made by politicians and commentators.

Liberals and Prime Minister Justin Trudeau On victory in the 2015 general election, the Liberal government promised a new approach to federal–provincial relations. There have not been any federal–provincial conferences for some years and

Trudeau began his tenure by inviting the premiers to attend a climate change conference in Paris as one of his first gestures in office. During the campaign itself, the Liberals promised to borrow $10 billion annually to pay for a huge new investment in federal and provincial infrastructure programmes. The government also began to negotiate with the provinces, led by Ontario, for the development of a new pensions policy for Canada.

The signs of new co-operation between Ottawa and the provinces was underway. But the fiscal arrangements between them looked less than rosy bearing in mind the difficulties in the economy. With resource sales limited and the economy only barely chugging by, there are likely to be new calls for federal money from the provinces and perhaps even a shift in which provinces are treated as "have not" provinces. New forms of equalization payments may be required as well as federal funds for new pensions arrangements with the provinces. It may take more than one Liberal government to return the country to greater federal–provincial co-operation and by then new governments may have arisen in some of the provinces. Such political re-balancing has often happened in Canadian history. Sunny fall days are often followed by dark, wintery nights.

Discussion Questions

1. What are some of the factors that account for the major shifts in the pattern of federalism in Canada since 1867?

2. Are conditional or unconditional transfer programs more effective? Do equalization payments improve the overall level of equality in the country?

3. Are shared-cost programs an ideal form of government cooperation, or are they an intrusion into areas of provincial jurisdiction by the central government?

4. Should Canadians have the option of private health care?

5. How did Stephen Harper's Conservatives change the federal government's approach to federalism?

6. Is the Trudeau approach similar?

Chapter 5

Québec Nationalism and
Aboriginal Peoples

Equality and Justice

Learning Objectives

After reading this chapter, you should be able to

1   Explain the grievances that underlie Québec nationalism.

2   Discuss the merits and demerits of the federal government's response to the
    Québec referendum of 1995 and the implications for another separatist challenge.

3   Explain the legal basis of Aboriginal rights and the "nation to nation" concept
    held by members of the First Nations.

4   Outline the types of land claims under dispute across the country and why they
    are taking so long to settle.

5   Explain the intersection of Aboriginal land claims and resource development
    and how this impacts on other Canadians.

In this chapter, we consider the claims of two different groups of Canadians who have
fought, and continue to fight, for better treatment within Canada. Are their demands
merely political posturing, or do they reflect more serious issues of justice and equality?

To answer this, we focus on the background and contemporary arguments of
Québec nationalism and the rights and aspirations of Aboriginal peoples. The claims
and grievances of these two groups represent some of the most serious conflicts
within Canada, and both raise issues of justice and equality.

We begin by addressing the question of nationalism and the separatist movement
in Québec. French Canadians were one of the founding peoples of Canada, and were
given certain rights and privileges as part of the original bargain. Yet separatists in
Québec view the federal bargain as obsolete and inadequate to meet the aspirations
of their society. In recent decades, this powerful nationalist group created the most
serious challenge that Canada has ever faced. In 1995, the country came close to
breaking apart. Concessions were made, but although the separatist challenge has
diminished over the last decade, it still simmers below the surface. Today's calm rests
in a fragile status quo that could erupt again to break up the country.

The second group under consideration here consists of Canada's Aboriginal peoples. These descendants of Canada's original inhabitants also sought, and sometimes

signed, agreements to protect their rights. However, they were powerless when those rights were ignored and agreements were broken. What would equality and justice be for them today? We saw in Chapter 2 that their culture and way of life have been severely compromised. What has become of their rights to land and resources? How can their interests be reconciled with those of other Canadians in a modern world?

The Canadian federal structure has proved remarkably resilient in meeting its various challenges since Confederation in 1867, but the claims of these two groups are far from resolved.

NATIONALISM

Nationalism is at the root of Québec separatism. It is a phenomenon that has appeared in many forms in different states over the centuries. Political leaders have used it to justify economic expansionism, protectionism, and imperialism. As an ideology, it has been employed to promote the supremacy of particular nations or peoples, it has justified quests for emancipation from colonial rule, and it has been an integrative force in newly independent multiracial or tribal societies in the developing world.[1] It also has been savagely attacked. Albert Einstein called nationalism "an infantile sickness of tribal societies ... the measles of the human race."[2]

In many cases, political leaders have used nationalism to integrate the members of an existing or future state. However, nationalism can also be a divisive force. Territorially concentrated ethnic minorities sometimes seek increased autonomy or even total independence. The breakdown of the former Yugoslavia into multiple republics and then the violent fragmentation of one of them, Bosnia, is just one example.

Disputes about nationalism abound, largely because of disagreements about definitions and explanations. The term is used colloquially to mean "love of country," but that is not precise enough. Some experts see nationalism as anti-colonialism and believe that it differs fundamentally depending on whether it is in established or developing states. Others contend that it can appear only in modern, developed political systems because it is a product of modernity that originated in the Industrial Revolution in Europe.

Most authors, however, believe that nationalism is closely associated with ethnicity. Some even see it as the political manifestation of ethnicity, although not all organized ethnic activity should be labelled as nationalism.[3] Many ethnic demands, such as those for minority language education or ethnically oriented television programs, do not challenge the integrity of the existing state and may be quite easily accommodated.

There are a great many theories about the causes of nationalism and its consequences. Several factors are generally thought to give rise to it. Clearly, ethnicity alone is not responsible, nor is regionalism—although they often coincide with nationalism. Nationalist movements encompass some of the following features:

- Common ethnicity
- A common grievance or threat
- Common territory
- Motivational leadership

- Great emotional intensity
- A common goal (sometimes for a separate state)

In this volume, **nationalism** is defined as the collective action of a politically conscious ethnic group (or nation) in pursuit of increased territorial autonomy or sovereignty. Examples of contemporary nationalist movements may be found in many advanced industrial societies: the Scots and Welsh in the United Kingdom; Bretons and Corsicans in France; Flemings and Walloons in Belgium; the Chechens in Russia; and, of course, the Québécois in Canada. In each case, the ethnic minorities have reduced any previous commitment they may have had to the larger state and have acted collectively to develop political parties, nationalist and cultural organizations, and sometimes even terrorist groups in order to pursue fundamental changes to the territorial boundaries and sovereignty of the state.

nationalism: The collective action of a politically conscious ethnic group (or nation) in pursuit of increased territorial autonomy or sovereignty.

Roots of Québec Nationalism: Early French–English Conflicts

After the British conquest in 1760, the Roman Catholic Church exercised a powerful influence on its French-speaking parishioners. It successfully encouraged them to remain socially separate from the English and maintain an essentially agrarian society. French Canadians generally remained aloof from political affairs, and even after Confederation in 1867, the English minority within Québec dominated urban and political economic life. By that time, the French were a minority in Canada. Two major conflicts set the tone for French–English relations.

The Manitoba School Issue The ethnic conflicts that periodically erupted after Confederation had their roots in the linguistic and educational rights of the provinces. One of the first and most enduring occurred in Manitoba. That province, with its large French-speaking community, was created in 1870 on the same basis as Québec, with rights to Roman Catholic schools and bilingual education. By 1885, however, French-speaking Métis in the West were being swamped by English-speaking settlers. To protest land losses, they rallied around Métis leader Louis Riel, who led a rebellion against the government.

English Canadians saw Riel as a traitor or a madman and sent troops to quell the disturbance. Riel was defeated and executed. French Canadians grieved for Riel as a patriot who died to preserve the "Frenchness" of his people. The ethnic groups were thus polarized, and only five years after the rebellion the government of Manitoba established a non-sectarian educational system in which Roman Catholic schools no longer received provincial aid and French could no longer be used in the secondary schools.

Two decisions of the British Judicial Committee of the Privy Council (JCPC) upheld the Manitoba law but also confirmed that the federal government had the power to restore school privileges. The situation posed a unique problem for French Canadians. Their church and the federal government urged them to support overturning the Manitoba legislation, but that required agreeing with the federal disallowance of provincial legislation, and French Québec was against the principle of federal veto power.

The federal Conservative government introduced remedial legislation in 1896, but, under pressure, it had to be withdrawn. A bizarre election ensued in which Manitoba francophones supported the Roman Catholic Church and the federal Conservative Party in demanding federal disallowance of the Manitoba law. Québec francophones, on the other hand, supported the Liberal Party, which demanded provincial autonomy and opposed the federal use of the disallowance power. Ironically, the Liberals were also supported by anti-French and anti-Catholic forces. The Liberals won in 1896, and thus Québec francophones in effect stopped the legislation that would have protected French-Canadian interests in Manitoba.

The Conscription Issue Ethnic division appeared in another guise in the conscription crises of both World War I and World War II. The 1917 federal election on the conscription issue divided the country along ethnic and linguistic lines: Every riding in which French was the majority language voted against the government and conscription. There were insufficient French votes to prevent conscription, but fortunately the war ended before the conscription law could be implemented, and the issue died.

However, the repercussions for Robert Borden's Conservative government, which had supported conscription, were severe. In the federal election campaign that followed the conscription bill, the Conservatives and English-speaking Liberals united to run Union candidates. They won the election but captured only three seats in Québec. In the first postwar election, in 1921, the Liberals formed the government, this time winning all Québec seats. Provincially as well as federally, the Conservatives were severely defeated and lost the confidence of French Canadians.

In 1942, during World War II, the conscription issue arose again and the federal government called a plebiscite to settle the issue. The campaign was bitter. French-speaking Québec voted against conscription by a huge majority, while English-speaking Canada was overwhelmingly in favour of it. The pro-conscription forces narrowly won, but Liberal Prime Minister William Lyon Mackenzie King postponed the imposition of conscription. The delay minimized the crisis because the war ended before the conscripts were sent into battle overseas. However, the apparent impotence of the French in face of an English majority decision on a topic of life or death helped to fuel new bursts of Québec nationalism.

Language Issues: Past and Present

Canada's Confederation was essentially a bargain between the French and English in British North America to create one strong political unit that would protect the rights and assist the advancement of two culturally diverse peoples. On this basis, linguistic duality was embedded in the *British North America Act, 1867* (*BNA Act*). It has had both positive and negative repercussions for Canadians, provoking divisive social and political tensions but, at the same time, enriching the experience of being Canadian. Today, as ever more immigrants arrive, French is competing with non-official languages in terms of mother tongue. Nearly 20 percent of Canadians claim a non-official language as mother tongue compared to 21.3 percent who claim the French language (see Table 5.1).

Table 5.1 Mother Tongue* in Canada and Québec, Percentages, 2011

	English	French	Non-Official Languages	English and French	Other Combinations
Canada	56.9	21.3	19.8**	0.4	1.5
Québec	7.7	78.1	12.3	0.8	1.2

*Mother tongue refers to the first language learned at home in childhood and still understood by the individual at the time of the census.

**Only 6.2 percent spoke a language other than English or French as their sole home language.

Source: Statistics Canada, Language Highlight Tables, 2011 Census, Catalogue no. 98-314-WE2011002, Table 1, released October 24, 2012.

Although the Confederation arrangement gave constitutional protection to both English and French languages in the federal Parliament and the legislature of Québec, in the other provinces there was no such protection. The practice until the 1940s was for English-speaking Canadians, wherever they were in the majority, to deprive French-speaking minorities of public school facilities in their native language, and to refuse them the use of their language in government institutions. Even within the federal government, where the *BNA Act* had stated the right of both groups to function in debates, records, journals, and courts in their own language, government employees were mostly unilingual English. Later reforms reversed these trends, but they left a legacy of fear and distrust.

The legal basis for language regulation in Canada is divided across three jurisdictions: the Constitution, federal law, and provincial law.

a) The Constitution establishes the framework for rules about language usage and development. In 1867, the *BNA Act* specified that Parliament and the Québec National Assembly were to function in both French and English. Much later, in 1982, the *Canadian Charter of Rights and Freedoms* enshrined English and French as the two official languages of Canada for matters pertaining to Parliament. Minority language rights were enshrined in Section 23 of the Charter, which stipulates that citizens of Canada whose first language is that of the French or English minority of the province in which they reside, or who have received their instruction in one of these languages in Canada, have the right to have their children educated in that language wherever numbers warrant.[4]

b) Within these parameters, the federal government creates language policies. In 1963, the Liberal government declared Canadian federal institutions to be officially bilingual, and in 1969 it passed the *Official Languages Act*. This Act, updated in 1988, has two parts: It regulates bilingualism in federal governmental organizations and federally regulated institutions such as banks and airlines, and it provides a national framework for promoting the two official languages. For example, it gives Canadians the right to be served by federal institutions in the official language of their choice where "significant demand" exists, allows federal employees the right to work in the official language of their choice, and establishes that there should be an equitable distribution of English and French Canadians in the public service.

The passage of the 1982 *Canadian Charter of Rights and Freedoms* expanded the basis for legal challenges against governments that do not uphold the provisions concerning language. Since it came into effect, many cases have been brought to the Supreme Court of Canada to challenge provincial governments and force them to accommodate language minorities in their laws and schools.

c) Provincial assemblies, too, can legislate language policies. However, such language legislation has often been restrictive and controversial. In Québec, the provincial government maintains an *Office québécois de la langue française*, which enforces the *Charte de la langue française*. This Charter makes French the official language of the province and the normal language of communications, business, and the workplace. New Brunswick enacted its first Official Languages Act in 1969, making the province officially bilingual.

In Québec, the fear that French language and culture is in decline in Canada, or may soon be, is widespread and is used by Québec nationalists to rally support. Québec's fertility rate is lower than that for the rest of Canada, which, as we have seen, is not adequate to sustain the current population level. Therefore, Québec sees a need to attract, hold, and integrate immigrants into the French culture and language. Motivated by these demographic concerns, Québec authorities in the 1960s began to assert and protect the province's distinctive character through legislation concerning language within its jurisdiction.

> *Bilingualism, in spite of widespread belief, is not quite synonymous with hell.*
>
> Keith Spicer, official languages commissioner, 1976

official bilingualism: As outlined in the *Official Languages Act,* it ensures the legal equality of English and French languages in the Parliament and courts of Canada and protects the rights of French-speaking minorities in different provinces. It ensures a level of government services in both languages across the country and gives both language groups the right to communicate with the federal government in the official language of their choice.

Language policy in Canada has become highly politicized. It is a magnet for intolerance, often based on misinformation and misunderstanding. **Official bilingualism** in Canada, as outlined in the *Official Languages Act,* describes the policies, constitutional provisions, and laws that ensure legal equality of English and French languages in the Parliament and courts of Canada, protect the linguistic rights of English- and French-speaking minorities across the country, and ensure a level of government services in both languages. It does not mean that all Canadians must speak both French and English. It means that Canadians have the right to communicate with their governments in the official language of their choice. It is based on the belief that a highly bilingual public service could be expected to increase sensitivity, tolerance, and respect between the two language communities.

Ironically, while bilingualism has reached nearly 43 percent in Québec, it is no longer considered a goal there. Rather, many French-speaking Québeckers aspire to be recognized as a "distinct society" with unique rights, to enable them to protect their distinctiveness and make Québec as unilingually French as possible. Meanwhile, in 2012, 72 percent of Canadians said that they favour bilingualism for all of Canada, a 16 percent increase since 2003.

Since Québec's population is growing more slowly than the national average, its demographic weight within Canada is declining, largely due to lower fertility

Table 5.2 Percentage of Population by Knowledge* of Official Languages, Canada and Québec (Census 2011)

	English Only	French Only	Bilingual English/ French	Neither English/ French
Québec	4.7	51.8	42.6	1.0
All of Canada	68.1	12.6	17.5	1.8

*Refers to the ability to conduct conversation in English only, in French only, in both English and French, or in neither English nor French.

Source: Statistics Canada, 2011 Census, Catalogue no. 89-314-XWE2011002, Table 2.

among francophones, immigration from countries where the mother tongue is neither English nor French, and geographical mobility of francophones toward English or English-speaking provinces. Given current demographic trends, Canadians should expect Québec francophones to continue their struggle to preserve the pre-eminence of the French language and culture within their province, using whatever tools are available to them (see Table 5.2).

MODERN NATIONALISM IN QUÉBEC

Québec francophones started to demand fundamental change in the late 1950s and 1960s. What began as a "Quiet Revolution" eventually blossomed into an outright challenge to Canadian federalism and the very existence of the Canadian state.

Québec increased political pressure on the federal government throughout the 1960s. The Front de libération du Québec (FLQ) represented the most extreme separatists. It initiated violent activities that culminated in the October Crisis of 1970, in which a British diplomat was taken hostage and the Québec minister of labour, Pierre Laporte, was kidnapped and murdered. In response, the federal government invoked the *War Measures Act* for the first and only time during peacetime. The basic freedoms of Canadians, mostly French-speaking Canadians, were compromised. Hundreds of Québeckers were arrested. When the crisis atmosphere faded, it left many Canadians uncertain that the crisis had warranted such a large-scale repression.[5]

As Québec nationalism grew in the 1960s and 1970s, Québécois intellectuals became increasingly divided. Prime Minister Pierre Elliott Trudeau offered the vision of a bicultural and bilingual federal state, but with no special status for Québec. He became the major spokesman for Henri Bourassa–style nationalism: one state that would be both bicultural and bilingual.

The Québec Referendum, 1980

There have been four "successful" nationalist organizations with aspirations for Québec independence.[6] The most recent was launched in 1968, when former provincial Cabinet minister René Lévesque formed the Parti Québécois (PQ). This party brought nationalists together under a new umbrella organization to fight for separation.

In the 1976 provincial election, Lévesque offered to hold a referendum on the right to negotiate sovereignty-association and promised a second referendum for Québeckers to ratify the eventual results of the negotiations. The PQ gained control of the government in Québec, but the ensuing May 1980 referendum on sovereignty-association was a disaster for Premier Lévesque. The vote required Québec residents to choose between *Oui* (for the Québec government to negotiate sovereignty-association) and *Non* (for it not to negotiate). This mild resolution was defeated by almost 6 out of 10 votes, partially because Prime Minister Trudeau promised "renewed federalism" as an alternative.

The threat of independence did not die with this vote, however. PQ strategists believed that Québec had both the people and the resources necessary to form an independent state.

Constitutional Patriation (1982) and Its Aftermath

The separatist flame was reignited in 1982 when Premier Lévesque refused to sign the amendment package to patriate the Constitution from the United Kingdom, and the federal government and the other nine provinces forged ahead without Québec's approval. Doing so broke a political impasse but handed the separatists an emotional weapon. The country, Lévesque said, had separated from Québec.

Before the next provincial election, however, Lévesque died and the party developed major internal splits. In 1988, the PQ elected as leader Jacques Parizeau, an arch-nationalist who revived the *indépandantiste* spirit. In 1990, following the advice of Parizeau, the party declared

> . . .we must break the iron collar of a federal system that serves us badly, that will always subordinate our national interests to those of another majority. . . . If others have become sovereign why not us?[7]

When the Meech Lake Accord failed to produce the reforms that Québec politicians wanted in 1990 (see Chapter 3), Lucien Bouchard (former minister of environment in Prime Minister Brian Mulroney's Cabinet) and others from Québec left their respective parties to form a separatist group in the House of Commons: the Bloc Québécois (BQ). As we saw in Chapter 3, the federal government continued its efforts to build a constitutional agreement that would bring Québec on board. This eventually resulted in an omnibus proposal called the Charlottetown Accord, which was put before the Canadian people for approval in a referendum held in October 1992. When the proposal was massively rejected, Québec nationalists resumed their call for separation.

In the general election of October 25, 1993, the BQ won 54 seats, enough to become Her Majesty's Loyal Opposition in the House of Commons. The BQ's next stated goal was to combine with the PQ in a campaign to separate Québec from Canada. This became more probable when the PQ, under Jacques Parizeau, won the 1994 provincial election and promised a referendum on sovereignty by the end of 1995.

The Québec Referendum, 1995

Two elections—the federal election of 1993 that gave the BQ 54 seats, and the Québec election of September 1994 that brought the PQ to power—set the stage for a dramatic separatist offensive. The Québec election gave the PQ of Jacques Parizeau 44.8 percent of the vote and 77 seats.

The PQ had campaigned for sovereignty, contending that Canada could be broken up without creating excessive problems. It formed a temporary alliance with the BQ and l'Action démocratique du Québec (ADQ). Then, on June 12, 1995, the three party leaders joined to ask Québeckers to support independence for Québec, along with political and economic association with Canada, if the Yes side won a referendum. It was a move designed to appeal to nationalist voters who did not want outright secession. If negotiations succeeded, they said, a treaty would be put in place that included a customs union, mobility of people, capital and services, a monetary policy, and citizenship. Deals could be struck on topics such as enhanced trade, common transportation, defence, and environmental and fiscal policies. If negotiations with Canada failed, they said, Québec would become an independent country anyway, while maintaining the use of Canadian currency and Canadian passports.

The thrust of this deal was posed as a question for the Québec population to vote on in a referendum on October 30, 1995. It required those who supported the sovereignist option to vote Yes, and those who did not support it to vote No. The question, as illustrated in Figure 5.1, was highly criticized for being ambiguous and misleading.

The Cree and the Inuit in northern Québec, meanwhile, held separate referendums. Both groups voted massively against the sovereignist proposal, and their leaders expressed a desire to remain in Canada no matter what the outcome of the imminent Québec referendum.

In a massive voter turnout of more than 93 percent, Québeckers voted narrowly (50.6 percent to 49.4 percent) to reject the sovereignty proposal. The close finish encouraged Premier Parizeau to adopt a confrontational tone. He said that Québeckers had not really lost the referendum because more than 60 percent of

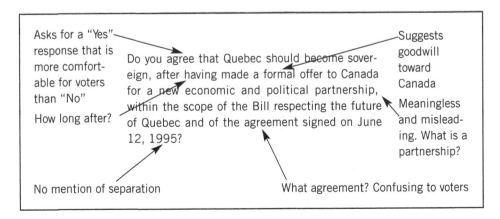

Figure 5.1 The Québec Referendum Question, October 30, 1995

francophones had voted for independence. "It's true that we were beaten, but by whom? Money and ethnic votes." He also spoke of the "temptation for revenge."[8] In doing so, he isolated and insulted many people in Québec and in the rest of Canada.

At the time, anglophones and allophones (residents whose mother tongue or home language is neither French nor English) made up about 19 percent of Québec's population, but more than 80 percent of them lived in Montréal and its suburbs. This numerical strength clearly acted as a powerful counterweight to the franco-phone vote of the area, which was roughly evenly split. Outside Montréal, with the exception of a handful of ridings along the Ontario boundary and the U.S. border, the anglophone population constituted less than 2 or 3 percent of the population. Therefore, the polarization of the Yes and No votes was clearly related to ethnic-ity, but other forces also seem to have been at play. The division was typical of urban–rural splits in which recession-ridden rural areas felt isolated from what they perceived as the political power, economic clout, and good life of big cities like Montréal.

Leaders for the Yes forces made it clear that the issue of Québec separatism was not resolved, and another referendum would be held in the near future. Within days of the referendum, however, Jacques Parizeau resigned as premier and was replaced by Lucien Bouchard, who gave up his seat in the House of Commons. Given how close the vote was, Prime Minister Jean Chrétien came forward with new and con-troversial ideas for reforming the Constitution.

Federal Post-Referendum Response

On October 24, six days before the 1995 Québec referendum, a desperate prime minister, Jean Chrétien, had promised that he was open to change, including consti-tutional change, and would fight for the concept of a distinct society for Québec. He therefore put forward new measures to appease Québec: Plan A and Plan B.

Plan A Plan A was essentially a reconciliation effort—a plan to sell a majority of Québeckers on the success of Canada and the benefits of staying in the federal union. The steps included:

1. An overhaul of the Cabinet, to bring in two potential star candidates from Québec, Stéphane Dion and Pierre Pettigrew.

2. Efforts to meet the distinct society and veto promises. Within weeks of the ref-erendum, the House of Commons passed a resolution recognizing Québec as a distinct society and another one concerning the veto. A statutory (but not consti-tutional) veto approved by Parliament in 1996 affirmed that any further consti-tutional changes approved by Parliament would require consent from Ontario, Québec, and British Columbia, as well as two of the four Atlantic provinces and two of the Prairie provinces.

3. Decentralization measures to show that the government was flexible concerning Québec's desires. Among them, powers were devolved to the provinces in areas such as forestry, mining, recreation, tourism, and social housing.

4. A campaign to extol the virtues of being a Canadian. This included initiatives such as setting up the Canadian Unity Information Office (CUIO), which was

intended to counter the negative image of Canada that the separatists had propagated during the referendum. The CUIO claimed that separatist leaders had distorted history and used emotive words such as *conquered*, *rejected*, and *humiliated* to unfairly describe relations with the rest of Canada.[9]

Plan B Plan B was a plan to clarify rational, logical terms for secession—without using harsh federal threats about the risks of partition.

Prime Minister Chrétien said that Québec would never be able to leave Canada unilaterally, even if a majority of Québeckers voted Yes in a referendum. The law must be respected. The rest of Canada would have to approve the terms of separation through a constitutional amendment.

In September 1996, the federal government asked for a Supreme Court ruling on the legality of unilateral secession by Québec. The feds sought a ruling to the effect that a unilateral declaration of independence by Québec would be illegal.

Ottawa's Questions and the Supreme Court's Answers Concerning Unilateral Secession

The Supreme Court's rulings on the issue of unilateral secession were woolly and controversial. Clearly aiming for a political compromise, the Court responded to the government's questions as follows:

Question 1: *Under the Constitution of Canada, can the National Assembly, legislature, or government of Québec effect the secession of Québec from Canada unilaterally?*

Ruling: A regular constitutional amendment would be required for separation from Canada to be constitutionally valid. However, the Court added, "Nor, however, can the reverse proposition be accepted: the continued existence and operation of the constitutional order could not be indifferent to a clear expression of a clear majority of Québeckers that they no longer wish to remain in Canada."

The Court judgment went on to practically demand that "negotiations" take place if there is a "demonstrated majority support for Québec secession."

Question 2: *Does international law give the National Assembly, legislature, or government of Québec the right to effect the secession of Québec from Canada unilaterally?*

In this regard, is there a right to self-determination under international law that would give the National Assembly, legislature, or government of Québec the right to effect the secession of Québec from Canada unilaterally?

Ruling: In the circumstances, the National Assembly, the legislature, or the government of Québec does not enjoy a right at international law to effect the secession of Québec from Canada unilaterally.

Question 3: *In the event of a conflict between domestic and international law on the right of the National Assembly, legislature, or government of Québec to effect the secession of Québec from Canada unilaterally, which would take precedence in Canada?*

Ruling: In view of the answers to Questions 1 and 2, the Court said that this third question did not need to be answered.

In response to the ongoing charge that the federal government was not proactive enough, the Chrétien government tabled Bill C-20 in December 1999. This legislation, the *Clarity Act*, sets out the rules by which the government and Parliament of Canada would analyze any future separatist referendum. It concludes that the government will

Clarity Act: Legislation in 1999 that set out the rules by which the government and Parliament of Canada would react to any future separatist referendum. It concludes that the government will not enter into any negotiations over separation with a province unless the House of Commons determines that (1) the referendum question is "clear" and (2) a "clear" expression of will has been obtained by a "clear" majority of the population.

not enter into any negotiations with a province over separation unless the House of Commons determines both that the referendum question is "clear" and that a "clear" expression of will has been obtained by a "clear" majority of the population.

The *Clarity Act* is bizarre legislation, as few states make such direct provisions for their own destruction. On the other hand, the Liberal government defended the Act as necessary to spell out precisely how a future referendum in Québec would be handled by the federal government and Parliament. The PQ government in Québec immediately tabled a competing bill in the National Assembly, claiming that only the Québec people can decide on the legal status of their province and that a 50-percent-plus-one vote would be considered enough for a referendum victory.

Despite the posturing, neither bill was constitutionalized, and both can be changed by any future legislature. The constitutional amendment process remains intact; the secession of a province from Canada would require resolutions to be passed in the federal Parliament and all 10 legislative assemblies. There is no easy way to achieve lasting political change without overcoming this high obstacle.

The call for formal constitutional recognition of Québec as a "nation" remained a trigger for conflict. This was clear in September 2006, when Liberal federal leadership candidate Michael Ignatieff called for "ratification of a new Constitution" that would recognize Québec as a nation. The BQ took the opportunity to ask the House of Commons to recognize Québec as a nation. Prime Minister Stephen Harper responded:

> Do the Québécois form a nation within Canada? The answer is yes. Do the Québécois form an independent nation? The answer is no and it will always be no.[10]

However, the exchange precipitated the prime minister to move the following resolution through the House of Commons:

> The Québécois form a nation within a united Canada.

This was not a constitutional change, nor was it a prelude to one. Supporters argued that the resolution clarified the situation because it did not say that Québec is a nation, which would have implications of statehood, but rather that the "Québécois form a nation within a united Canada." They maintained that the resolution would clarify the issue and prevent federalists from being backed into a corner by separatists' demands. Opponents of the resolution feared that the move would "bolster the separatists' argument that they are not being recognized and strengthen their resolve to form an independent society."[11]

The referendum raised several issues that need to be clarified in the event of another referendum on separation in Québec or elsewhere on topics such as the dollar, passports, sharing the country's debt, and what would happen to the constitution and the rule of law.

Is the Constitution Merely a Red Herring?

In the future, could a small majority in one province effectively deprive millions of citizens of their country? If they could, that would render the Constitution meaningless. During the referendum, many argued that if Québec voted to separate, the Constitution would be irrelevant. Clearly, however, since secession would destroy fundamental institutions such as the monarchy, the governor general, and lieutenant-governors, a change of such magnitude would require the application of the most rigid constitutional amendment rule—the unanimous consent of all provinces of Canada plus a majority of members of both Houses of Parliament. Provincial politicians have no authority to make a unilateral declaration of independence, as they are elected only to govern over classes of subjects mentioned in the Constitution and secession is not one of them.

It is clear, therefore, that a **unilateral declaration of independence (UDI)** (in which a province declares its independence outside of the law) by Québec would be unconstitutional. The Canadian Constitution provides no rules about the right of a province to secede from Canada. Nowhere in the list of jurisdictional powers does a province have the right to separate from Canada. The courts therefore could be called on by the federal government or by private interests to contest the validity of the referendum—or any decision to declare a UDI. The federal government and the courts have no justification or legal obligation to pay any attention to a UDI. Thus, constitutionally speaking, if a UDI were declared, political legitimacy and power would remain with the federal government and the provinces.

unilateral declaration of independence (UDI): A declaration of independence by a province outside constitutional law.

Two arguments are fundamental. Without the guidance of a constitution, there would be chaos. Politicians become dictators and the political system becomes authoritarian when there is no legal framework. If Québec were to vote Yes in a future referendum, the federal government would be required to adhere to the Constitution. Without adherence to the Constitution, there would not be any authoritative body to deal with Québec or any process of law or deliberation about the future of Québec should it decide to separate. Whose law would apply to those Québeckers who want to remain Canadians and pay taxes to Ottawa? What courts would determine the status of the Cree and Inuit who do not want to belong to a new Québec?

Those who stress the significance of the Constitution understand that "the will of the people" is important and that a national election or referendum may be required if Québec ever does vote to separate from Canada. However, without the Constitution, how could democracy be actualized? What would constitute a fair and just process? Answers to these questions cannot be determined outside the Constitution. To say that the legal issue is irrelevant is tantamount to saying that a small majority in one province could effectively deprive millions of citizens of their country.

Nationalism and Self-Determination

The issue of Québec independence raises questions about the right of people to self-determination and statehood. International law is not conclusive on this point. In fact, two principles clash: International law recognizes both self-determination and the inviolability of borders.

Self-Determination In international law, the right of self-determination extends only to those circumstances in which people are experiencing foreign or alien domination, or are subject to discriminatory regimes.[12] Neither of these situations applies in Québec. Citizens there have democratic rights in any part of Canada. As Jean Chrétien forcefully put it, "In international law, Québec cannot separate from Canada without Canada's consent."

However, new states have often been recognized even when the parent country did not consent. For example, in December 1991, Canada rushed to recognize Ukraine before there was any thought of Russian consent. It was a political decision. Canadian leaders did not even wait for other countries in the United Nations to make similar declarations. On the other hand, the Canadian government did the opposite in the cases of Slovenia and Croatia. It waited to see what decision other countries would make before recognizing these two new states.

Borders If Québec did unilaterally declare independence, then what territory could it claim? Using the same logic as expressed above, it could claim only the territory and people over whom it could maintain effective control. If two rival governments contest a territory, political (not legal) justifications finally resolve the issue. Borders have to be adjusted to conform to the reality of who has the power and legitimacy in the land.

Aboriginal peoples would have the legal justification and power to stay within Canada even if there were a Yes victory in a referendum. The Constitution makes it clear in Section 91(24) that "Indians and their lands" come under the federal authority, and Section 35(1) protects Aboriginal rights and treaties that were made with Canada. At the very least, the federal government would have a moral duty to help those Canadians who did not wish to stay in Québec—including Aboriginals and possibly Canadians in the western part of the province, near Ottawa.

Québec's Major Grievances

Shared grievances are a vital ingredient of nationalism. According to former Québec premier Bernard Landry, Québeckers are victims of discrimination in Canada based on economic maldistribution. In other words, Québeckers do not get their fair share of federal spending. In 2001, Landry's argument was rebutted by Stéphane Dion, then minister of intergovernmental affairs in Jean Chrétien's Liberal government. He put forward the following checklist. The facts are based on 1998 data, which Dion pointed out were entirely representative of what happens every year.[13]

- Québeckers received 24.2 percent of total federal spending. Since Québec's population represents 24.2 percent of the Canadian population, the redistribution is eminently fair. Obviously, Québec does not get 24.2 percent of every item in the federal budget, but it does get that much overall.

- Québec contributed 20.6 percent of federal revenues. Its contribution to Canada's gross domestic product (GDP) is 21.8 percent. "This shows that Québec is contributing in accordance with the size of its economy and receiving in accordance with the size of its population."

- Québeckers receive 21.2 percent of federal research and development (R&D) spending. This cannot be considered lower than its population share because it does not include spending undertaken in the National Capital Region (NCR). Québec's share of federal R&D spending outside the NCR is 26.8 percent.

- Québec suppliers receive federal spending on goods and services roughly equivalent to the size of Québec's economy within Canada.

- The portion of federal public servants in Canada who work in Québec is 23.1 percent. The number would be higher, but the Québec government assumes some responsibilities (such as policing) that most other provinces leave to the federal government.

After the 1995 referendum, discussion on and overt support for the separatist and sovereignist options faded. Figure 5.2 shows the trajectory of sovereignist support in Québec.

In both the 2004 and 2006 federal elections, the BQ received considerably more support than the Liberals in Québec, encouraging PQ leaders to again publicly speculate on the date of the next referendum. However, in the Québec provincial election in 2007, André Boisclair led the PQ to a dismal third-place showing. In 2008, the PQ lost to the Liberals again. In 2012, the PQ won once again under the leadership of Pauline Marois. She revived separatist slogans, but to no avail. In 2014, the PQ came second to the Liberals with its lowest seat total (30) since 1989 and its smallest share of the popular vote since its founding election in 1970. Marois lost her seat, and Pierre Karl Peladeau became leader. Federally, as well, separatism fared badly. The BQ fell to four members in 2011 and lost its official party status. By the 2015 election, it was nearly extinct.

Recent relations between Québec City and Ottawa have been good, in large part because of the concessions that Québec has received and the fact that Stephen Harper's Conservative government needed to win seats in Québec if it was to maintain a majority. Meanwhile, Liberal premier Phillippe Couillard has noted a changing culture in Québec:

> Young people are more interested in the values of openness, confidence, inclusion than the values that are about mistrust and exclusion...[14]

Québec sovereignty, deprived of charismatic leadership and emotive issues or perceived injustices, has, for the time at least, fallen dormant. However, this does not

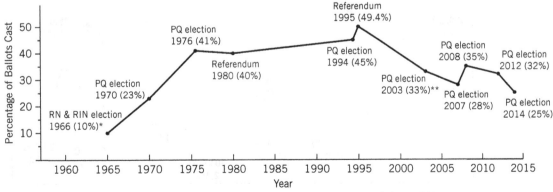

*Ralliement Nationale (RN) and Ralliement pour l'Indépendance Nationale (RIN) and Parti Québécois (PQ) percentage votes.

** The anti-separatist Liberal Party led by Jean Charest won the 2003 election with a majority, and was re-elected in 2007 with a minority.

Figure 5.2 Support for Separatism in Québec as Expressed in Key Provincial Elections and Referendums

mean that nationalism is dead in Québec. The situation is typically volatile. Support for sovereignty has held at around 40 percent of the population since the 1960s.

THE RIGHTS OF ABORIGINAL PEOPLES

We saw in Chapter 2 that Canada's Native peoples are located unevenly throughout the country (see Figure 5.3). As a whole, they are disproportionately affected by serious social and economic problems. They make up just over 4 percent of the population but constitute 23 percent of the prison population. As well, they are much worse off than other Canadians in every measure of social welfare, including suicide rates, infant mortality data, percentage unemployed, percentage living in homes below standard repair, and households below the poverty line. Many are trying to adhere to the old ways of their ancestors but their communities are mired in problems related to drugs, alcohol, and welfare. To help their people, Native leaders are seeking justice in terms of their Aboriginal rights and ownership of the land of their ancestors. This is increasingly bringing them into conflict with other Canadians.

Aboriginal rights: Historic rights (mostly in the form of land claims) of various groups of Aboriginals, based on Aboriginal occupancy and use of North American land before Europeans arrived.

Aboriginal rights are based on Aboriginal peoples' occupancy and use of North American land before Europeans arrived. Traditional Aboriginal societies were based primarily on hunting and gathering and, to a minor extent, agriculture. To a large extent this relationship to the land defines Aboriginal culture and economy. Aboriginal peoples consider that land was put here by the Creator for the use of *all*

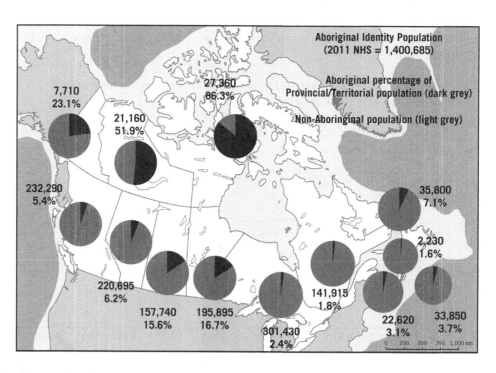

Figure 5.3 Aboriginal Percentage of Provincial/Territorial Population

Source: Aboriginal Demographics from the 2011 National Household Survey CIDM: 5242964 - Aboriginal Identity Population. Courtesy of Aboriginal Affairs and Northern Development Canada. CIDM: 5242964.

people and therefore, in Aboriginal culture, land belongs to everyone living today and to the unborn to come. It is not "owned" by anyone.

We noted in Chapter 2 that, to some extent, politically, Aboriginal peoples still occupy a dependent, semi-colonial position in relation to the federal and provincial governments. Proposals to end Indian status and repeal the *Indian Act* have been called for by Native peoples struggling for greater recognition of their traditional rights, settlement of land claims, and the power to manage their own lands and affairs. Former grand chief of the Assembly of First Nations Georges Erasmus put the case this way: "we want to have a relationship with this country that is nation to nation" as expressed in the "two-row wampum" analogy of the Mohawks.

> The two-row wampum is an agreement whereby two nations coexist and travel the River of Life in peace and friendship. . . . Legally, it means that each of the two nations retains its own respective laws.[15]

The British Royal Proclamation of 1763 recognized the rights of the Indian nations and provided that those rights could not be taken away without due process (i.e., a negotiated treaty). These obligations were passed on to Canada through the Constitution. **Section 35** of the *Constitution Act, 1982* recognizes and affirms the existing rights and treaty rights of the Aboriginal peoples. It gives the federal government exclusive jurisdiction over Indians and lands reserved for Indians (although today many non-status Indians, Métis, and Inuit are also subject to provincial laws). Section 35(3) affirms that "treaty rights" include "land claims agreements" now and in the future.

Section 35: Section 35 of the *Constitution Act, 1982* recognizes and affirms the existing rights and treaty rights of Aboriginal peoples, including land claims agreements now and in the future.

The Canadian Constitution therefore recognizes Aboriginal and treaty rights, and the *Canadian Charter of Rights and Freedoms* (Section 25) protects them in that Aboriginal or treaty rights cannot be abrogated by anything in the Charter. This means that these treaty rights are recognized and even protected without specifying exactly what they are. It is generally agreed, however, that they include rights to hunt and fish, harvest food, and have access to and occupy land to conduct these activities. Courts have ruled that, where no previous treaty or land claims agreements are in place surrendering such rights, governments are bound by the Constitution to protect or compensate Aboriginal peoples before they can sell the land or grant interest in it to third parties.

There is also a vague, general consensus that Aboriginal peoples should be able to enjoy certain rights of self-government (seen, for example, in policing on reserves), but it is such a complicated topic that courts have not ruled whether Aboriginal self-government, like territorial rights, is in fact an Aboriginal right.

Land Claims and Other Land Issues

Over the years, treaties were signed giving North American Indians reserves in exchange for land. However, many of them were so blatantly unfair to the Indians that they are being challenged in courts. In cases where reserves are inadequate for the resource needs of the Aboriginal communities, courts have recognized that an expanded land base is required for the people to become economically self-sufficient. When no treaties were signed, Aboriginal peoples, particularly the Métis, were left without land rights.

Aboriginal title: An Aboriginal claim to land on the basis of traditional occupancy even when no treaty has been signed.

Aboriginal title—the claim to land on the basis of traditional occupancy even when no treaty has been signed—has been tested in the courts. In the 1973 *Calder* case, the Supreme Court affirmed the principle that the historic occupation of land by Aboriginal peoples gives rise to legal rights.[16] Soon afterwards, the federal government established the Office of Native Claims within the Department of Indian and Northern Affairs and announced that it would negotiate Aboriginal title even when no treaties existed. This offer later even included claims where treaties had been signed but were considered unjust.

However, First Nations criticized the process of negotiating title as lacking impartiality because some claims they thought should have been considered were being ignored. A 1990 clash in the town of Oka, Québec, over such a Mohawk claim led to the creation of the Indian Specific Claims Commission (ISCC) to review specific claims rejected by the government. In 1996, the Royal Commission on Aboriginal Peoples submitted a report urging the establishment of an independent tribunal with authority to adjudicate specific claims and issue binding decisions to replace the ISCC. As discussed below, this was acted on in 2002.

We have seen that Section 35(3) of the *Constitution Act, 1982* clarifies that "treaty rights" include rights that already exist by way of land claims agreements or that may be acquired in the future. This means that land claims agreements are constitutionalized and cannot be changed at will by governments after they have been completed. There are therefore two kinds of land claims currently in process: **comprehensive claims**, dealing with cases of Aboriginal title not covered by treaty or other legal means, and **specific claims**, dealing with challenges to existing treaties.

comprehensive claim: A land claim dealing with cases of Aboriginal title not covered by treaty or other legal means.

specific claim: An Aboriginal land claim dealing with challenges to existing treaties.

In the North, where the *federal* government has legal jurisdiction over the land, claims have moved relatively quickly. By 1993, Canada's entire North above the 60th parallel was covered by final agreements or agreements in principle about land claims. The territory of Nunavut, inhabited almost solely by Inuit, won full government institutions equal to other territories or provinces. In Yukon, several First Nations signed self-government and final land claims agreements with the federal and territorial governments. However, further south, where provincial governments are in control of public lands, progress is complicated by provincial jurisdiction, natural resource companies, and non-Aboriginal settlements on disputed land. Claims have moved slowly. The main settlements to date have occurred in the North, Québec, and British Columbia.

Meanwhile, the Supreme Court has clarified aspects of land claims settlements, fishing, and Métis rights to speed up claims resolution. In 1997, for example, it ordered that oral history evidence be admissible in certain court cases. It also clarified that a group must establish its exclusive occupation of the land in question at the time the Crown asserted sovereignty. In 2002, the Supreme Court ruled that if Aboriginal peoples can prove that their forebears honestly believed that they had reserve lands set aside for them, but in fact did not, they still might have a legal case for their claim.

Roughly half of the more than 600 status-Indian bands have not yet resolved their traditional territorial disputes with the Canadian government. They claim outstanding Aboriginal rights over, and title to, traditional lands, and assert historic rights over roughly half of the country. In British Columbia, for example, overlapping claims by bands cover almost the entire provincial land mass.[17] In 2002, to help speed up the process of specific claims, a new claims commission was set up with the power to grant awards of up to $7 million.

Despite this commission, cases still drag on for years and the confrontation between Aboriginal peoples and other Canadians is sometimes severe. In early 2006, for example, a land dispute developed between Henco Industries and Six Nations Indians over a 40-hectare tract of land in Caledonia, near Hamilton, Ontario. A group of Aboriginal protesters seized an unfinished housing development, saying that the land on which it was being built had been taken from them by the Crown 200 years ago. Violent clashes between First Nations members and local residents erupted. The federal government was forced to become involved, and about a year later it gave the Ontario government more than $26 million to help cover the massive costs related to the dispute. In June 2008, Prime Minister Harper set up a new impartial Specific Claims Tribunal (SCT) to speed up the processing of more than 800 backlogged cases.

Since current claims take about 13 years to resolve treaty issues that date back more than a century, few people would disagree that the process should be speeded up. Unless that happens, First Nations protests can be expected to continue. Since the authority of the SCT is limited to dealing with certain specific claims and to awarding compensation, and does not extend to declaring ownership or title of lands, it remains to be seen whether delays in the resolution of valid claims will change. Indian leaders are particularly concerned with resolving ownership issues in order to be able to control their own resources and development and have a chance to improve their immense social problems. Between 2011 and 2014, 61 claims were submitted to the SCT, 49 of which were ongoing in 2015.[18]

Issues over Resource Development on Disputed Aboriginal Lands

With land claims unresolved, disputes over natural resources on these lands are increasing. Currently, developing Alberta's oil sands is a central pillar of the Canadian economy. The federal and provincial governments both need revenue from the oil sands, but Alberta is landlocked and needs pipelines to export its product. A proposed Northern Gateway pipeline by Enbridge would cut through traditional territories of First Nations in Alberta and British Columbia (see Figure 5.4). Kinder Morgan also proposed a Trans Mountain project to twin an existing line to transport oil products through British Columbia, thereby tripling the transportation capacity of oil from bituminous sands to export markets. However, Aboriginal groups fear spills as bitumen passes through their traditional land and waters and have challenged in the courts the right of these companies to build pipelines.

The Aboriginal position was strengthened in 2014 by two landmark Supreme Court decisions that defined Aboriginal title to land. In the **Tsilhqot'in decision** in British Columbia, the court established title for the Tsilhqot'in for part of their land. It ruled that their title confers the exclusive right to control the land (680 square miles) that their band had historically occupied, so that any activity such as resource development, including clear-cut logging, mining, or pipelines to carry

Tsilhqot'in decision: A 2014 landmark Supreme Court decision that awarded the Tsilhqot'in of British Columbia the right to bar mining and commercial logging from their territory.

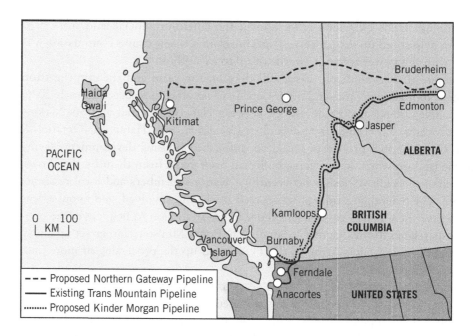

Figure 5.4 Location of Proposed Pipelines

Source: Based on Northern Gateway Pipeline (Enbridge) and the Trans Mountain Pipeline (Kinder Morgan). Trans Mountain Expansion Project, December 2013.

oil, must have *consent* of the relevant and specific nation. (Formerly, only "consultation and accommodation" were required.)[19] In other words, Aboriginal peoples have the right to bar from their territory mining and commercial logging that does not have their approval. Governments may still infringe on title in certain circumstances, but litigation and justification are required. Major resource projects, including the proposed pipelines from Alberta to the coast, received a serious setback with this court decision.

In the **Keewatin decision** of July 2014, the Supreme Court rejected a claim from the Grassy Narrows First Nation band arguing that Ontario required approval from the federal government before issuing a logging permit on their land. The band argued that an agreement they had signed 141 years earlier required Ontario to get the federal government's approval before issuing the logging permit. The Court said that those seeking a development permit on treaty lands in Ontario do not need approval from Ottawa, just from Ontario, but that the Ontario government must consult with Aboriginal peoples and accommodate their needs before proceeding.[20] This case has implications for much of Western Canada, where Aboriginal treaties also were signed by the "Dominion" government before current provincial boundaries were established.

Since these two 2014 Supreme Court rulings, several First Nations in British Columbia have pledged to block the proposed federal government–backed Enbridge Northern Gateway pipeline and have filed separate lawsuits in the Federal Court of Appeal. About half of the 50 First Nations along the pipeline route have not yet backed it. The anti-pipeline First Nations are supported by a large environmental lobby in British Columbia. As a result, although the federal government issued a license for Enbridge in 2014, allowing them to proceed with the Northern Gateway pipeline, the British Columbia government has yet to sign off on it.

Kayakers in Vancouver protest the Northern Gateway pipeline.

Enbridge continues to sweeten the offer to First Nations along the pipeline's proposed route, offering to procure materials from Native-owned suppliers as well as providing job training, jobs, and many of protections against leaks and other problems. However, court cases could take years to resolve. Enbridge appears to be banking on the clause in the Supreme Court decision that states that infringement will be allowed after reasonable accommodations have been judged to have been made. Aboriginal and civic opposition is also high to the Kinder Morgan Trans Mountain pipeline expansion proposal.

Self-Government

Aboriginal self-government is another broad, contentious, and ongoing issue. Attempts to achieve constitutional recognition for self-government failed with the collapse of the Charlottetown Accord (see Chapter 3). According to some Aboriginal leaders, such rights should not even be defined in documents such as the Constitution because they are "inherent rights." Courts have never ruled whether there is an Aboriginal right to self-government. In fact, there is not even agreement about what self-government means. For some, it means a level of government roughly equivalent to a municipality within a province. For others, it means that the First Nations should constitute an independent "third" order of government.

Under self-government, as conceived by recent federal governments, First Nations would remain subject to almost all federal and provincial laws and their powers would be only slightly greater than those of Canadian villages, towns, or cities. However, some Native leaders maintain that they cannot accept any imposition on the *inherent right* of their people to govern themselves.[21] They consider that their right to govern themselves is a pre-existing, continuing, natural right given to them by the Great Creator. It cannot be given or taken away by any government. They reason that they have never given up their right to self-government, and it has never been extinguished by any legislation (because such power could not exist). They are supported to some extent by courts and international law, which affirm that Aboriginal rights may be extinguished only by treaty or conquest, or by an explicit act of the Parliament of Canada.

The federal *Indian Act* has long provided for limited local government on reserves through band councils. However, their jurisdictions are very narrow, and some communities want them to be much wider. Essentially, groups that desire self-government want control over areas such as the use of their land, community development, economic development, education, policing, and so on. They have no interest in broader concerns such as foreign affairs, defence, or banking. However, many policy areas, such as health care and education, are under provincial or territorial jurisdiction, and agreements about funding and sharing of interests must be reached not only with the federal authorities but also with these governments.

However, progress also has been made on the community-based aspects of self-government. Aboriginal peoples now control 80 percent of their program funding from the Department of Aboriginal Affairs and Northern Development, and Aboriginal authorities increasingly deliver many services, such as police, education, child welfare, and so on. Some provinces are allowing Aboriginal peoples to police their own reserves and have their own justices of the peace and correction services. Once they are achieved, the only way to protect self-government agreements is to complete them as *Section 35 treaties*, as is done with land claims, so that they have constitutional protection and can be amended only if both or all parties to the agreement give their consent. In some cases, the federal government and some provincial governments have moved piecemeal to negotiate self-government agreements with some Aboriginal peoples who have expressed such a desire.

First Nations' self-government agreements in Yukon (1993 and 1995) were the first to be ratified.[22] and that process has become a model for the negotiation of other self-government and comprehensive claims. The Nisga'a and Labrador Inuit Association (LIA) agreements that followed were built on, and added to, the Yukon model. These model agreements allowed the new government of Yukon a wide range of legislative powers that very few Aboriginal governments are in a position to finance from their own revenue sources. Consequently, many politicians both federally and provincially are wary of the implications of self-government agreements. Yukon First Nations are still involved with several legal battles with the territorial and federal governments, claiming that these governments have not lived up to various aspects of the self-government agreement. Similarly, in the Northwest Territories, land, resources, and government matters are still being negotiated with different Aboriginal groups.

As early as 1976, a land claims agreement between the Inuit Tapirisat and the federal government considered dividing the Northwest Territories to provide a separate territory and government for the Inuit. Such an agreement was completed in 1992 and ratified in Nunavut in a referendum. In 1999, the self-governing region of Nunavut was created, comprising a major portion of northern Ontario and most of the Canadian Arctic Archipelago, an area the size of Western Europe. It represents 14 Inuit communities and a public service responsible for matters such as education and health. It has a Legislative Assembly as well as representation in Canada's Parliament. Both Ottawa and Québec City retain all legal powers in the region.

EQUALITY AND JUSTICE

Aboriginal peoples consider themselves as equal and parallel nations within Canada—as nations within a nation. They want to deal directly with the Crown as the highest political authority. French-Canadian nationalists also see themselves as a nation within Canada, and believe that Quebec is not merely a province like the others.

They seek special status in several respects, and many French-Canadian nationalists even seek to escape the bonds of Canada and set up their own state. Aboriginal peoples also seek justice within Canada for past wrongs, and want ownership and control of their lands and resources as well as a form of self-government. However, their aspirations often conflict with the dreams and aspirations of other Canadians.

These are serious challenges for Canada's future, and it is at least questionable whether our federal institutions and leaders are up to the task.

Discussion Questions

1. Is the French language threatened in Québec? What factors would make this situation better or worse if Québec formed an independent country?

2. What are some of the main issues raised and left unresolved by the 1995 Québec sovereignty referendum campaign and its outcome?

3. How and why has the government plan to build pipelines from Alberta through British Columbia been thwarted?

4. What are the main claims of Aboriginal peoples and Québec separatists to equality and justice? Are they justified? How should the Government of Canada respond?

Chapter 6

The Executive

Ceremony and Leadership

Learning Objectives

After reading this chapter, you should be able to

1 Identify the three main components of the formal executive and describe the role of each.

2 Describe the position and importance of the prime minister and Cabinet in the political process.

3 Compare governmental politics in minority and majority governments.

4 Describe the four central administrative agencies and differentiate their roles in the political system.

5 Compare the relative strengths and weaknesses of the Canadian executive to that of the United States.

6 Account for prime ministerial "greatness" or "failure"?

executive: A broad term that refers to the institutions, personnel, and behaviour of governmental power. In modern times, executives are the organizational centre of political systems.

In politics, **executive** is a broad term that refers to the institutions, personnel, and behaviour of governmental power. In modern times, executives are the organizational centre of political systems.[1] Governments have expanded over the years, taking on new functions, and as their responsibilities have increased, executives have become more important. The executive branch of government has two main categories of tasks: one is performing ceremonial duties, the other is providing political leadership.

Canada's constitutional heritage from Britain includes an executive with two parts. Each part is assigned one of the two key executive tasks. The *formal executive*, composed of the Crown, monarchy, and governor general, performs largely ceremonial functions. The *political executive*, composed of the prime minister, ministry, and Cabinet, is concerned with leadership and the realities of power in contemporary Canadian politics. A large network of committees and central agencies supports the political executive.

In this chapter, we examine the respective roles of the formal and political branches of the executive in Canada. Power resides with the political branch but, as we shall see, it is difficult to locate and measure with certainty. In fact, what exactly is political power, and who exercises it? Political power is an abstract commodity that changes in response to issues, problems, and personalities, which come and go. It is dramatically affected by majority or minority government circumstances. There were three consecutive minority governments before the Conservative Party of Canada's majority victory in 2011. In 2015 the Trudeau Liberal victory provided the second majority government in a row.

Much important information about how the executive operates is shrouded in mystery. Parliamentary traditions and legal devices, such as the *Security of Information Act*, shield the executive from penetrating scrutiny. In spite of this, a significant amount is known about the executive in Canada. We conclude the chapter by assessing the ongoing debate about the role and power of the position.

THE FORMAL EXECUTIVE

The Canadian Constitution established a government based on the British model. Canada was to be governed by a parliamentary system with British historical traditions and procedures and by a constitutional monarch represented by an appointed governor general. Aside from the physical absence of the monarch, the main difference from Britain was that there was to be a division of legislative powers among the provincial and federal authorities in recognition of the diversity of the country.

The Crown and Monarch

Government functions in Canada are carried out in the name of the Crown. The term **Crown** refers to the composite symbol of the institutions of the state. The Crown assumes a variety of duties and responsibilities. For example, it may be involved in court proceedings, and government property is held in the name of the Crown.

The reigning **monarch**, currently Queen Elizabeth II, is the personal embodiment of the Crown. **Prerogative authority**, or the powers of a monarch or a monarch's representatives that have not been bypassed by constitutional or statute law, can be traced to the period of authoritarian rule in Great Britain when the Crown possessed wide discretionary authority. As we shall see, prerogative authority has been eroded to include only a very few reserve powers. Although the monarchy is personified in an individual, individual peculiarities must be separated from institutional strengths. Individuals come and go, but the Crown is permanent. It provides history, tradition, and an institutional framework that can promote political stability as long as the institution is held to be legitimate by a large majority of the people.

Although Parliament and the political executive govern in the name of the Crown, the powers of the monarch are severely limited. Even the ability of a king or queen to stay on the throne is no longer a right but subject to acceptance by British ministers and Parliament. The functions of the monarch are largely ceremonial and strictly non-partisan. The monarch reigns but does not govern. Queen Elizabeth II carries out ceremonial responsibilities that generate mass support for government. She makes royal tours and acts as the symbolic head of the Commonwealth, of which Canada is a member.

The Governor General and Lieutenant-Governors

Since the monarch was not based permanently in Canada, a representative, the governor general, was appointed by the British government. Section 9 of the *Constitution*

Crown: Refers to the composite symbol of the institutions of the state. The Crown assumes a variety of duties and responsibilities; for example, it may be involved in court proceedings.

monarch: The monarch, currently Queen Elizabeth II, is the personal embodiment of the Crown.

prerogative authority: Powers of a monarch (or his or her representatives) that have not been bypassed by constitutional or statute law.

Act, 1867 states that the "Executive Government and Authority of and over Canada . . . is vested in the Queen." This principle is fleshed out in the **letters patent**—the prerogative instruments defining the office of the governor general—that the sovereign makes applicable to each governor general through a commission of appointment. As Canada matured, the nature of this appointment changed. By the *Letters Patent, 1947*, the sovereign affirmed that all powers delegated to the governor general were to be exercised "on the advice of his Canadian ministers" as they affect Canada.

Today, the **governor general** is the representative of the monarch, appointed by Her Majesty on the recommendation of the Canadian prime minister and Cabinet. There have been two significant changes concerning the role of the governor general. The first is that, since 1952, the governor general has been Canadian. The second is that the post has become politicized—a candidate may be chosen by a prime minister primarily for his or her personal characteristics. In 1952, Vincent Massey became the first Canadian to hold the position. It has become customary to alternate the position between English- and French-speaking Canadians. In 2005, Prime Minister Paul Martin appointed Michaëlle Jean, a Haitian-born Canadian, to be governor general, and in 2010 Prime Minister Stephen Harper chose David Johnston and then reappointed him until September 2017 (see Table 6.1).

The governor general resides in Rideau Hall in Ottawa and has a second residence in Québec City. The tenure of office is usually five years, but the officially recognized term is six years, which has occasionally been extended to seven. The title *right honourable* is assigned for life and *excellency* for the period in office. In the event of death, incapacity, removal, or absence of the governor general, the chief justice of the Supreme Court, Canada's leading judge, may carry out all duties of the office. The governor general is ceremonial commander-in-chief of the armed forces and is charged with swearing in Cabinet ministers and commissioning high state officials. The official duties include purely ceremonial functions such as conferring the Order of Canada awards or reviewing troops. As chancellor of the Order of Canada and the Order of Military Merit, the governor general administers the Canadian system of honours.

Table 6.1 Canadian Governors General, 1952–2015

Governors General	Year Appointed
Vincent Massey	1952
Georges Vanier	1959
Roland Michener	1967
Jules Léger	1974
Edward Schreyer	1979
Jeanne Sauvé	1984
Ramon Hnatyshyn	1990
Roméo LeBlanc	1994
Adrienne Clarkson	1999
Michaëlle Jean	2005
David Johnston	2010

Even the term *Governor-in-Council* refers to Cabinet acting in the name of the Crown, not a meeting of the governor general with government officials.

The governor general is a primary symbol of the state. As such, a function of the position is to socialize Canadians into acceptance of authority through emotional attachment to an authority figure. In performing the Queen's "dignified" roles in Canada, however, the governor general has little practical input into the political process. As for political duties, the governor general is bound to act on practically every piece of advice received by his or her ministers, but a few specific functions are left to the governor general alone. The most important of these stem from the prerogative powers left to the monarch. The letters patent provide the governor general with all powers of the Queen "in respect of summoning, proroguing or dissolving the Parliament of Canada."[2]

Only a prime minister can ask for, and obtain, a dissolution of Parliament. However, a governor general did once refuse such a request. This incident was the famous King–Byng Affair in 1926. Governor General Lord Byng declined Liberal prime minister William Lyon Mackenzie King's request for a dissolution and an election. Instead, he called on Conservative leader Arthur Meighen to form a new administration. It was a controversial move, and in an ensuing election the Liberals won. This event set a precedent that governors general should follow the advice of their prime ministers about the dissolution of Parliament.

Governor General David Johnston.

The Canadian Press/Adrian Wyld

Another issue about the prorogation power arose after the 2008 election of Stephen Harper. The new government was short of a majority, so when the opportunity arose the Liberals and New Democratic Party (with Bloc Québécois support) offered to form a coalition government. The prime minister delayed a scheduled non-confidence vote on the budget statement by asking Governor General Michaëlle Jean to prorogue Parliament to avoid the issue. While some political commentators disapproved, the governor general rightly approved the request.[3] Parliament was prorogued and a new session called, giving no opportunity to vote for a Liberal-led coalition. The desire for a coalition quickly faded and Prime Minister Harper later called a general election in 2011, which he won decisively.

Perhaps the governor general's most important power is appointing the prime minister. In cases where a party leader holds a clear majority of the seats in the House of Commons, the governor general merely selects the obvious candidate for that position. However, if no leader has the support of a majority in the House of Commons, the governor general may be forced to use discretion and select the prime minister, albeit with caution and perhaps danger.

In 31 of the 42 elections since Confederation, one of the two major parties obtained an absolute majority of the seats in the House, so the governor general was not required to exercise personal discretion. In the 11 remaining cases, the governor general chose as prime minister the leader of the party that appeared to control the largest number of seats in the House of Commons—even when his party did not constitute a majority (see below).

Perhaps more significant than these formal constitutional powers is the governor general's informal ability to advise ministers. The governor general usually meets regularly with the prime minister and receives Cabinet minutes and therefore has a degree of access that is denied to most ordinary individuals. As head of state, he or she holds the right to be consulted and the right to encourage or warn political leaders.

The monarch has a representative in each province as well as in Ottawa. **Lieutenant-governors** are appointed by the Governor-in-Council (see below) on the advice of the prime minister. Each lieutenant-governor acts on the advice and with the assistance of the provincial ministry or executive council, which is responsible to the legislature and resigns office under circumstances similar to those for the federal government.

Although the Constitution makes it clear that the governor general is the country's formal executive, the powers and prerogatives of the position are in fact severely limited. Only in extraordinary situations has a governor general attempted to interfere even indirectly in the political process. Executive power, though carried out in the name of the governor general, resides elsewhere in the political structure.

lieutenant-governor: Appointed by the Governor-in-Council on the advice of the prime minister to represent the monarch in each province.

THE POLITICAL EXECUTIVE

Following the British model of government, the Constitution does not list the prime minister or even Cabinet among its institutions. All that the 1867 Act dictates is that there be an appointed Privy Council to advise the governor general on his or her responsibilities. However, through tradition and convention the prime minister chairs the Cabinet, which acts in the name of the Council.

The Prime Minister

The prime minister is unquestionably the central figure in Canadian politics. The basis of the prime minister's power and authority is leadership of a party that commands at least a plurality, and often a majority, of the seats in the House of Commons. The prime minister, above all else, is an elected member of Parliament, who has been chosen national leader of the party at a leadership convention. Today, convention demands that the prime minister be a member of the House of Commons either before or shortly after *investiture* (when the title is assumed).

As leader of the party that has been victorious at the polls, the prime minister is able to claim that the "right" to govern is based on a popular mandate. The link with the people through an election gives enormous legitimacy and authorizes the pursuit of programs and policies until the next election. This legitimacy is important in controlling the party and dealing with the bureaucracy and the press. As leader of the party and holder of a mandate, the prime minister needs, and normally can command, obedience and support from Cabinet ministers and backbenchers alike. However, in a minority government, the prime minister's power can be limited.

Canada's Prime Ministers

Canada has had 23 prime ministers since 1867 (see Table 6.2)—10 Liberal and 13 Conservative. All but Kim Campbell, who became prime minister for a few months in 1993, have been male. Joe Clark was the youngest in Canadian history at the age of 39. Justin Trudeau was 44 at his appointment. Every prime minister since

Table 6.2 The Prime Ministers of Canada

Name	Party	Tenure
Sir John A. Macdonald	Lib.-Con.	July 1867–Nov. 1873
Alexander Mackenzie	Lib.	Nov. 1873–Oct. 1878
Sir John A. Macdonald	Con.	Oct. 1878–June 1891
Sir John Abbott	Con.	June 1891–Nov. 1892
Sir John Thompson	Con.	Nov. 1892–Dec. 1894
Sir Mackenzie Bowell	Con.	Dec. 1894–Apr. 1896
Sir Charles Tupper	Con.	Apr. 1896–July 1896
Sir Wilfrid Laurier	Lib.	July 1896–Oct. 1911
Sir Robert Borden	Con.	Oct. 1911–July 1920
Arthur Meighen	Con.	July 1920–Dec. 1921
W.L. Mackenzie King	Lib.	Dec. 1921–June 1926
Arthur Meighen	Con.	June 1926–Sept. 1926
W.L. Mackenzie King	Lib.	Sept. 1926–Aug. 1930
R.B. Bennett	Con.	Aug. 1930–Oct. 1935
W.L. Mackenzie King	Lib.	Oct. 1935–Nov. 1948
Louis St. Laurent	Lib.	Nov. 1948–June 1957
John Diefenbaker	Con.	June 1957–Apr. 1963
Lester B. Pearson	Lib.	Apr. 1963–Apr. 1968
Pierre Elliott Trudeau	Lib.	Apr. 1968–June 1979
Joseph Clark	Con.	June 1979–March 1980
Pierre Elliott Trudeau	Lib.	March 1980–June 1984
John Turner	Lib.	June 1984–Sept. 1984
Brian Mulroney	Con.	Sept. 1984–June 1993
Kim Campbell	Con.	June 1993–Nov. 1993
Jean Chrétien	Lib.	Nov. 1993–Dec. 2003
Paul Martin, Jr.	Lib.	Dec. 2003–Jan. 2006
Stephen Harper	Con.	Jan. 2006– Oct. 2015
Justin Trudeau	Lib.	Oct. 2015–

World War I has been a university graduate. Eight prime ministers have come from Québec, six each from Ontario and the West, and three from the Maritimes.[4] Three provinces—Prince Edward Island, Newfoundland and Labrador, and New Brunswick—have never produced a prime minister. All Liberal prime ministers have come from Ontario or Québec (John Turner was elected in British Columbia but lived in Ontario).

The tenure of Canadian prime ministers has varied enormously. Unlike U.S. presidents, who may serve only two terms, Canadian prime ministers retain power as long as the public and House of Commons support them. In fact, prime ministers in Canada have averaged longer in office than those of almost all Anglo-American and continental European countries.

Among the 23 Canadian prime ministers, the shortest careers were those of Sir Charles Tupper (69 days), John Turner (80 days), and Kim Campbell (133 days). At the other extreme, four individuals held the office of prime minister for about half of Canada's history since Confederation (72 of 148 years, as of 2015): William Lyon Mackenzie King (22 years), Sir John A. Macdonald (20 years), Pierre Elliott Trudeau (15 years), and Sir Wilfrid Laurier (15 years). Laurier enjoyed the longest continuous term of any prime minister. In 2000, Jean Chrétien won a third consecutive majority government—a feat last accomplished by Mackenzie King. Stephen Harper also won three elections in a row—two minority victories and a majority government.

How are prime ministers' terms ended? Few retire entirely of their own choice; their careers are usually terminated following defeat in a general election, as Stephen Harper was in 2015. Only Macdonald, King, Meighen, and Pierre Trudeau managed to stay on as leader and win another general election after their parties had been defeated. Macdonald and Sir John Thompson died in office. Jean Chrétien was forced out by party pressures.

Winning elections is a primary preoccupation for prime ministers.

Gary Clement/National Post

Getting rid of a prime minister, even via the electoral route, is difficult. Prime ministers have been defeated in about one-third of all elections, whereas in around two-thirds of elections prime ministers were returned to the House of Commons—but about half the time with a reduced majority.

Powers of the Office The office of prime minister is prestigious and pre-eminent. Its powers include the following:

- The prime minister and Cabinet together control the making and signing of treaties and the conduct of international relations, including the declaration of war and peace.

- The prime minister's power to dissolve Parliament continues despite Bill C-16, which declares that Parliament will last for a fixed term of four years unless the government is defeated in the House of Commons. In 2008, Prime Minister Harper simply obtained the governor general's consent to use her prerogative to call an election. This prerogative had not been eliminated by the legislation. Normally, Parliament is dissolved only when the prime minister believes that the party has a good chance of victory at the polls. The power of dissolution can also be used to impose solidarity on a Cabinet or caucus. It is a potent weapon, helping to maintain the stability of the Cabinet system. Today, the prime minister still holds this power, but with less flexibility. If defeated in the Commons, the prime minister must ask the governor general for dissolution and an election. If not defeated, the dissolution and election are triggered by a fixed-date mechanism unless the prime minister asks the governor general to act earlier.

- The prime minister controls the organization of government. On appointment, nearly every prime minister puts in place a revised organizational structure to streamline or modernize the government. Cabinet structures are modified, portfolios limited, renamed or combined, bureaucratic agencies abolished, Crown corporations created, and Royal Commissions appointed—all on the initiative of the prime minister.

- The prime minister chairs the Cabinet and is the key figure in the Cabinet committee system. However, no prime minister can deal personally with all of the matters needing attention, and therefore he or she delegates authority and responsibility to Cabinet members.

- The prime minister controls appointments. Among them are the members of the ministry (which, as we shall see, includes all ministers and ministers of state, whether in Cabinet or not) and usually chosen from the parliamentary caucus. (See Justin Trudeau's adjustments later in this chapter.) A number of criteria may guide the prime minister's choice of ministers, including the desirability of having regional and ethnic representation. As we will see, an effort is generally made to have at least one minister from every province, and significant representation from the largest ethnic groups in the country.

- The prime minister, in consultation with his or her ministers, is also responsible for appointing parliamentary secretaries. Parliamentary secretaries aid ministers in their duties but have no statutory authority. Usually ministers agree beforehand to the appointment, but on occasion the prime minister may make an appointment without any consultation.

- In addition to choosing the members of the executive, the prime minister also appoints senators, judges, and the senior staff of the public service, among others. Legally, the prime minister's appointments are mere recommendations forwarded to the governor general for formal approval. However, a modern prime minister's appointees are never rejected. In fact, as we have seen, the prime minister chooses the governor general. Through these placements, the prime minister's influence is felt throughout the governmental structure. An appointment may be made as a reward for favours or services rendered to the prime minister or the party. Positions may also be withheld as a punishment for some misdemeanour.

- The prime minister and Cabinet have inordinate power in Parliament as their program is introduced in the Speech from the Throne, and also because legislation that raises or spends money must constitutionally originate with a Cabinet minister.

The Prime Minister and Government

The prime minister and his or her personally selected ministers form the government. Together, the ministers formulate policy and direct administrative operations for as long as they are supported by the House of Commons. Once they no longer receive such support, they are replaced or Parliament is dissolved and elections are called. There is no doubt that executive power belongs to the prime minister and government.

Executive and legislative powers are fused or combined in Canada as they are elsewhere in British parliamentary systems. Canadians vote for members of the House of Commons, including the prime minister, and almost all members of the government emerge from this elected body. Ministers are therefore members of both the legislature and the executive.

Historical Origins The modern Cabinet originated in Britain in the Middle Ages. It began with the Privy Council, a group chosen by the monarch to give advice on state business. During the eighteenth century, these advisers gradually became more powerful vis-à-vis the monarch.

Queen's Privy Council for Canada: A body established at Confederation in the Constitution to assist and advise the governor general. Today, the body is largely ceremonial and members are nominated by the prime minister and appointed for life.

At Confederation, the Constitution established a **Queen's Privy Council for Canada** to assist and advise the governor general. Today, it is a largely ceremonial body whose members are nominated by the prime minister and appointed for life. The members include current and former ministers of the Crown, as well as a few other politically prominent individuals.[5] The Cabinet, which is composed only of current ministers of the Crown, constitutes the real executive power in Canada but acts in the name of the Privy Council. The authority of the prime minister and ministers rests not in the written Constitution but on custom and convention. As members of the Privy Council, its members have the right to the title *honourable* and *privy councillor* for life, while the prime minister is designated as *right honourable*.

Cabinet and Ministry

Size is an important factor in setting up political executives—the bigger they are, the more unwieldy they become. During the 1984–1993 Progressive Conservative (PC) governments, the number of ministers reached a record high. At one point, Brian Mulroney named 40 ministers. The next prime minister, Kim Campbell, reduced the number to 24, but Stephen Harper enlarged it again to 26, and Justin Trudeau appointed 30 ministers.

When Jean Chrétien became head of government in November 1993, he created two types of ministers—appointing 30 to the ministry but including only 22 of them in his cabinet. Paul Martin continued this new system, appointing 31 ministers (full members of Cabinet) and 8 ministers of state in his first government. In 2011, Stephen Harper appointed 26 ministers and 13 ministers of state. Justin Trudeau has reverted to the traditional style of appointing only full ministers to his Cabinet. Since the 1970s, each minister has been sent a so-called **ministerial mandate letter**, which

ministerial mandate letter: Letter that explains what the prime minister expects the minister to accomplish in his or her department.

explains what the prime minister expects the minister to accomplish during his or her tenure. In 2015, Trudeau broke with tradition and made all these letters public.

The **ministry** is now composed of all ministers who are appointed by the prime minister. The **Cabinet** consists of all ministers, no matter how powerful or weak. It acts in the name of the Privy Council. No **ministers of state** were appointed by Prime Minister Trudeau. Some members of Parliament (MPs) are also chosen to be **parliamentary secretaries** to help ministers—one for each minister and the prime minister. Their responsibilities are assigned by their ministers and they are sometimes considered to be the government's "B Team," waiting for an opportunity to join the Cabinet.

As we have noted, ministers are nearly always chosen from the House of Commons. In some historical periods, a few have been appointed from the Senate, particularly when the governing party lacked elected representatives from a particular region—as the PCs did from Québec in 1979 and the Liberals did from the West in 1980–1984. Only rarely and temporarily have Cabinet positions gone to persons outside of Parliament. For example, a diplomat, Lester Pearson, was appointed secretary of state for external affairs in 1948 and subsequently won a seat in a by-election. More recently, Stephen Harper selected a newly appointed senator—his 2006 campaign co-chair, Michael Fortier—to be minister of public works. Fortier resigned his Senate position, ran for the House in 2008, and was defeated.

Cabinet Composition

The relationship between distribution of Cabinet ministers and provincial population has been relatively constant since Confederation. There is usually a Cabinet member from each province, with the largest urban regions receiving extra members. As a general rule, Ontario has had slightly more members in Cabinet than any other province, with Québec second. For example, because of his large 2004 victory in Ontario, and the Liberals' much smaller representation from the rest of the country, Paul Martin chose 16 ministers from Ontario, only 8 from Québec, and 8 from the West.

By contrast, Stephen Harper's first Cabinet was novel. He broke the traditional regional composition of Cabinet by including 12 ministers from the West, 10 from Ontario, 6 from Québec, and only 3 from the Atlantic provinces. In 2008, he continued the practice with 15 ministers from the West, 13 from Ontario, and only 5 from Québec.

The composition of the 2011 Harper ministry followed these principles closely. Every province except Newfoundland and Labrador received one or more ministers, and membership was reasonably representative of the provinces in basic proportion to their population, with the evident distortion of Quebec. The new government members were highly educated and professionally trained, however they still did not form a social or economic cross-section of Canadians.

The 2015 Cabinet of Justin Trudeau broke recent patterns in many fields. The shape of Cabinet returned to a traditional structure as every minister was made a member of Cabinet. No ministers of state or junior ministers were appointed. Eighteen parliamentary rookies were included in the new group.

The composition also showed new types of membership. Every province and region was represented in Cabinet. Women were given equal representation (15 of 30 ministers), and language, ethnicity, and visible minorities (including the disabled) were recognized. As the new prime minister put it: "The Cabinet looks like Canada."

ministry: may be larger than Cabinet. It is composed of all ministers who are appointed by the prime minister. It may consist of both full Ministers of the Crown and ministers of state.

Cabinet: The collective body of ministers appointed by the prime minister, which acts in the name of the Privy Council.

minister of state: Like a full Cabinet minister, a minister of state is sworn to the Privy Council and bound by the rules of collective responsibility, but is only allowed to attend meetings of Cabinet on request, and his or her salary and staff allotments are lower than that of full Cabinet ministers. None were appointed by Trudeau.

parliamentary secretary: An MP who aids a minister in his or her duties but has no statutory authority.

New Justice Minister Jody Wilson-Raybould, for example, was chief of the Assembly of First Nations and a member of the We Wai Kai Nation in British Columbia.

The prime minister also chose to put intergovernmental affairs under his own responsibility and to appoint a rookie female, former Afghanistan refugee, as Minister of Democratic Institutions under his own portfolio.

The composition of Cabinet also depends on how many seats the government controls in the House of Commons. Most elections have produced a **majority government**—one based on the support of a single party in the House of Commons. Only once has a Canadian **coalition government** been formed from more than one party. On other occasions (11 times since 1867), Canadians elected a **minority government** (i.e., the governing party had less than a majority of the members of the House of Commons). Prime ministers of minority governments have to select policies very carefully to ensure that a majority of House members will support the government. Even with such precautions, minority governments have tended to be quite unstable and to pass less legislation than governments with majority control of the House.

Ethnicity is also a significant factor in Cabinet composition in Canada. The two founding ethnic groups are usually represented in approximate proportion to their population size. Of the total number of Cabinet ministers serving between 1867 and 1965, for example, 28 percent were French Canadians, a figure that was remarkably close to the French-Canadian percentage of the population.[6] Prime ministers generally appoint a chief lieutenant from the opposite official ethnic group. Sometimes they are made deputy prime minister, but neither Stephen Harper nor Justin Trudeau appointed a deputy prime minister.

Obviously, the distribution of seats that the government has obtained throughout the country is also an important factor in many Cabinet assignments. In the case of the Liberals, the Department of Finance traditionally went to an Ontarian. However, in 1980, Pierre Trudeau appointed a French Canadian to that post to bolster Québec strength in Cabinet, and when the Liberals returned to power in 1993, Jean Chrétien nominated a bilingual anglophone from Québec, Paul Martin (who served as finance minister until 2002). Martin chose a westerner, Ralph Goodale, as his finance minister upon becoming prime minister, while Stephen Harper returned to tradition by appointing his finance minister from Ontario in 2006, 2008, and in 2011. Justin Trudeau also appointed his finance minister from Ontario in 2015.

The Tories gave Canada its first female prime minister, Kim Campbell, and Jean Chrétien countered in 1993 by appointing Sheila Copps as the first female deputy prime minister. Paul Martin made Anne McLellan his deputy prime minister.[7] Justin Trudeau was the only prime minister to make gender a principle of Cabinet formation.

Cabinet Conventions Cabinet is bound by two important conventions: collective and individual responsibility. **Collective ministerial responsibility** means that, as a group, ministers are supposed to be held accountable to Parliament for their government's actions. Cabinet deliberations are held in secret, individual opinions are not publicly voiced, and ministers are not supposed to speak or act except in the name of the entire Cabinet. They may speak about policy only after it has been agreed to in private by their colleagues. This convention allows ministers to be frank in private but support the government in public.

majority government: A government based on the support of only one party in the House of Commons.

coalition government: A government formed from more than one party.

minority government: A government in which the governing party has less than a majority of the members of the House of Commons.

collective ministerial responsibility: A standard for the federal Cabinet; as a group, ministers are supposed to be held accountable to Parliament for their government's actions.

Each minister's personal responsibility is referred to as **individual ministerial responsibility**. However, the minister's ability to act is critically circumscribed by the "mandate letter" he or she receives from the prime minister, which outlines the leader's explicit policy expectations. Moreover, as heads of departments, ministers receive confidential advice from public servants, make decisions, and then are held accountable for those decisions in Parliament and by the populace. In other words, public servants forgo public praise in order to avoid public blame. Ministers accept credit but also any criticism that may be forthcoming. While they may delegate authority to their officials, they remain at the apex for appeals of administrative decisions and must be involved in initiating and defending new policies.

In practice, however, it is nearly impossible to follow these two conventions at all times. Where is the line to be drawn between ministerial and departmental responsibility? Ministers do not even know the details of most of the decisions that are carried out in their names. The main check on ministerial responsibility is the free and open debate that takes place inside and outside of Parliament. The minister is judged in the department, in Cabinet, in Parliament, before the media, and on the hustings. In these functions, ministers are aided by a paid "political" or "exempt" staff of advisers and experts.

Cabinet Organization All new prime ministers change the organization of Cabinet. Jean Chrétien reduced Cabinet size from earlier governments and created an inner and outer ministry system. He dropped Priorities and Planning, a formerly powerful committee under both Pierre Trudeau and Brian Mulroney, and had Cabinet as a whole assume the former committee's function. As well, Chrétien established five new committees: Economic Union, Social Union, Special Committee of Council, Treasury Board, and Government Communications.

The 2004 Paul Martin government retained the distinction between ministry and Cabinet begun by Chrétien. Martin appointed 39 members to the ministry—31 Cabinet ministers and 8 ministers of state—and set up a brand new system of committees. He did not restore the Priorities and Planning Committee but gave its functions to the whole Cabinet and set up eight Cabinet committees, reinstating the role of an Operations Committee as used by Mulroney.

The system used in Stephen Harper's 2011 government went back to earlier formulations. Cabinet met about once a month. Priorities and Planning was the major committee. It met weekly and was chaired by the prime minister. It included the chairs of other committees and a number of political heavyweights. It provided strategic direction on priorities and expenditure management, as well as ratifying committee recommendations. The Operations Committee controlled the day-to-day coordination of government priorities. It looked after issues management, legislation, House planning, and communications. Social Affairs integrated policy development in health care, justice, training and skills development, culture, and immigration. Economic Prosperity considered economics, natural resources, fisheries, agriculture, and regional development topics. Foreign Affairs and Security handled foreign issues, defence, and national security (see Figure 6.1).

Lastly, the **Treasury Board** is the only committee of Cabinet named in the Constitution. Chaired by the president of the Treasury Board, it has legal responsibility for the authorization of expenditures and is the committee that allocates resources

individual ministerial responsibility: Refers to the personal responsibility of each minister. As heads of departments, ministers receive confidential advice from public servants, make important decisions, and then are held accountable for those decisions in Parliament and by the populace.

Treasury Board: A central coordinating agency that is constitutionally a committee of the Privy Council.

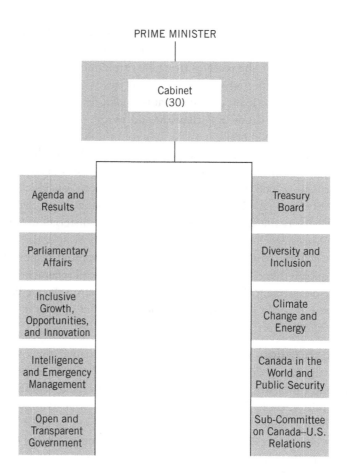

Figure 6.1 Cabinet in the 2015 Liberal Government

within the government. It is the only committee that does not position itself into a circle for policy deliberations but sits like a jury, facing any petitioners and acting as a tribunal. In recent years it has also become responsible for accountability and ethics.

Prime Minister Trudeau has also changed Cabinet organization. The 30 ministers are assigned to 10 committees. Instead of Priorities and Planning, the lead committee is now called Agenda and Results. It is chaired by the PM and consists of 6 men and 4 women. The other committees are Parliamentary Affairs; Inclusive Growth, Opportunities, and Innovation; Diversity and Inclusion; Canada in the World and Public Security (with a sub-committee on Canada–U.S. relations); Intelligence and Emergency Management; Open and Transparent Government; Climate Change and Energy; and Treasury Board.

Cabinet Functions Cabinet performs many functions as part of the political executive:

1. It is the organization in which major decisions are made or ratified. Ministers act collectively in Cabinet to develop policy, approve draft legislation, manage the country's finances, and adopt **orders-in-council**—decisions that carry legal force rendered by Cabinet under the auspices of the Privy Council. Technically

orders-in-council: Decisions rendered by Cabinet under the auspices of the Privy Council that carry legal force.

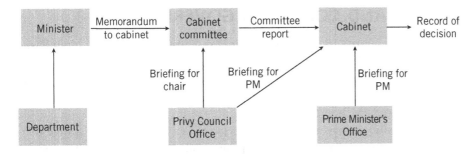

Figure 6.2 The Formal Cabinet Policy Process

speaking, a *Cabinet directive* is an agreement arrived at in council with the governor general absent. However, as we have seen, the governor general is obliged by convention to grant formal approval to virtually every Cabinet decision or bill approved by Parliament. The formal executive authority of the governor general, carried out on the advice and consultation of the Cabinet, is referred to as a decision of the **Governor-in-Council**.

Ministers bring policies to Cabinet for resolution. (The formal process for approval of a document by Cabinet is illustrated in Figure 6.2.) A **Memorandum to Cabinet (MC)** begins the process. Every such document is numbered and awarded a security classification. The minister's memorandum is forwarded to the Privy Council Office, which distributes it to Cabinet members. It is then discussed by the appropriate Cabinet committee and forwarded to Cabinet for final determination. As Figure 6.2 indicates, the Privy Council Office briefs the prime minister, as does the Prime Minister's Office. Following this series of actions, Cabinet gives final approval or disapproval in a record of decision. Of course, private communications dramatically increase the complexity of such decisions.

2. Cabinet, led by the Cabinet Committee on Parliamentary Affairs and the House leader, plans the business of Parliament, making decisions about timetables for legislation and choosing major government speakers.

3. Cabinet members are responsible for the operation of departments of the public service and for bringing departmental initiatives to Cabinet for approval. Public policy derives from a multitude of sources, but it is the individual minister who puts the final stamp of approval on departmental initiatives. A minister needs the expertise and the information that comes from his department's permanent contact with interest groups. However, only a minister may carry forward departmental requests to the Cabinet.

4. Cabinet provides political leadership for the party in power.

Cabinet Staff Individual ministers are supported by their departments and political appointees. Each minister's political office employs at the minister's discretion an executive assistant, special assistants, a private secretary, and other support personnel. Ministers may second (temporarily transfer) departmental employees to their offices and hire policy and communications advisers under contract. They hire political aides on an individual basis largely to perform partisan tasks. Aides are not subject to the same regulations as other public servants and hence are called "exempt staff."

Governor-in-Council: The formal executive authority of the governor general applied on the decision of the Cabinet.

Memorandum to Cabinet (MC): A document, signed by a minister, that begins the process of Cabinet decision making.

MINORITY AND COALITION GOVERNMENTS

If no party has a majority of members of the House of Commons, a Cabinet based on a minority of members may be set up. As we have seen, a minority government is one that emerges from an election with less than a majority of members of the House of Commons. A majority government, by contrast, is based on a majority of the governing party's MPs in the House.

Constitutionally, the governor general accepts the view of the current prime minister about who to appoint as the incoming prime minister. If the party of the current prime minister has the largest number of seats, or nearly the same number as the second placed party, he or she will stay in place. If beaten, however, the prime minister will ask the governor general to call on another party leader who has a chance of commanding support from the House of Commons to become the new prime minister. Of Canada's 42 general elections, 11 have resulted in no party winning an absolute majority in the House of Commons. The percentage of minority governments has increased in the post–World War II period along with the rise of the multi-party system.

In many other democratic countries, particularly in Europe, multi-party legislatures with no single party controlling a majority of members of the legislature set up coalition governments, with the administration formed by more than one party. States such as Austria, Switzerland, and the Netherlands have continual coalition governments and still manage a high degree of government coherence in law-making because of long-established norms and practices that enable coalitions to hold together despite party differences and pressures.

Only once in Canadian history, during World War I, has there been a coalition government (although the country's first prime minister, Sir John A. Macdonald, achieved Confederation based on a combination of Liberals and Conservatives). Eleven minority governments have been elected (see Table 6.3)— two of which were

Table 6.3 Canada's Minority Governments								
	Liberal	Conservatives	Progressive	Labour	Social Credit	CCF/ NDP	Crediste	Bloc	Ind.
1921	117	50	64	3	—	—	—	—	1
1925*	101	116	24	2	—	—	—	—	2
1957	107	112	—	—	19	25	—	—	2
1962	100	116	—	—	30	19	—	—	—
1963	129	95	—	—	24	17	—	—	—
1965	131	97	—	—	5	21	9	—	2
1972	109	107	—	—	—	31	15	—	—
1979	114	136	—	—	—	26	6	—	—
2004	135	99	—	—	—	19	—	54	1
2006	103	124	—	—	—	29	—	51	1
2008	77	143	—	—	—	37	—	49	2

*Two minority governments were formed following this election—first Liberal, then Conservative.

Source: Elections Canada, www.elections.ca.

formed in the 1926 Parliament making it 12 minority governments in total. Minority governments have usually (but not always) been short-lived and tended to pass less legislation than majority governments (we do not attempt to assess the quality of the bills). Most minority governments were defeated by a vote of non-confidence in the government, forcing a dissolution and election.

Problems With Minority Governments

The number of seats held usually determines which party forms the government. On rare occasions, parties with fewer seats in the House than their opponents have managed to govern—witness Mackenzie King's Liberals in 1925 (they had 101 seats compared to 116 for the Conservatives—the so-called King–Byng case is discussed earlier in the chapter). In minority situations, minor parties often have more influence on policy than their support in the country warrants. To remain in office, both Pearson and Trudeau had to make major concessions to the NDP; more recently, on many occasions Harper was forced to compromise with the Bloc Québécois (BQ), Liberals, and NDP.

Parliament is a more exciting and less predictable place during minority governments. Historically, social policy has undergone dramatic changes in such situations. Minority governments under both Pearson and Trudeau passed important social legislation. With the support of the NDP, these governments passed the Canada Pension Plan, the Canada Assistance Plan, the Guaranteed Income Supplement for seniors, and medicare. It is unclear whether the Liberals would have passed these measures without the prodding of the NDP. As well, in the case of a minority government an early election is almost certain to be called. However, minor parties generally find that their number of seats decreases after minority Parliaments, so they tend to be cautious about trying to provoke an early election.

The most recent tumultuous effects of minority government were evident from 2006 to 2008. At times, the opposition amended legislation, while at other times the government taunted the opposition to amend or defeat its legislation and force an election. Interparty relations seem ridiculous, as each party vied for significance in the policy process. The unintended consequences of the new fixed-election law also weakened the government in many ways, and in 2008 Prime Minister Harper simply evaded the impact of the law by asking the governor general to dissolve Parliament early.

A minority situation affects what types of tactics are used by leaders of all parties. Prime ministers need to keep both their own backbenchers and opposition parties satisfied. The tactics for this have included reducing the length of sessions, avoiding controversial legislation to postpone the date of defeat, making deals and compromises with other parties, and setting up liaison systems with opposition parties to solicit their views. The government usually attempts to play off one minor party against another, using a "divide and rule" strategy. On occasion, prime ministers have even given patronage, contracts, and employment to members of opposition parties in order to sustain themselves.

Opposition parties, too, adopt new strategies and tactics during minority Parliaments. They must appear responsible and not be seen to oppose the government *just* for partisan reasons. On the other hand, they cannot be seen to be pandering to the government. They understand that the lack of an overall majority still allows the prime minister much leverage in the process and an easy ability to claim that the opposition parties are undermining good and strong government.

In 2008, the three opposition parties became so frustrated with the Harper minority government's budget (one item of which would have taken away their party subsidies) that they proposed to set up a coalition government to replace the Conservatives. The strategy required the defeat of a major piece of legislation in the House, then the setting up of a Liberal–NDP coalition with the explicit backing of the BQ, and finally the selection of Stéphane Dion as prime minister. The Tories prorogued Parliament rather than face a vote in the House, and thus outmanoeuvred the opposition. Before Parliament met again in January to discuss the 2009 budget, distrust of the coalition idea had set in throughout the country. Stéphane Dion resigned as leader of the Liberal Party and was replaced by Michael Ignatieff. In 2011, such policy and process tangles came to an end when Stephen Harper won his first majority government (one of his first actions was to remove the quarterly allowances for qualifying political parties).

CENTRAL AGENCIES

The Cabinet is assisted by four central coordinating and support agencies: the Prime Minister's Office, the Privy Council Office, the Treasury Board, and the Department of Finance. The first two report directly to the prime minister; the other two have their own ministers.

The Prime Minister's Office

Prime Minister's Office (PMO): One of four central agencies assisting Cabinet. This is the political office of the prime minister and members are appointed directly by him or her.

Of the various executive support agencies, the **Prime Minister's Office (PMO)** is the most overtly political. The upper echelon of the PMO is composed of the personal appointees of the prime minister. It is the largest and most important of the "exempt" staffs and only rarely does it employ public servants. Its organization and importance are the sole prerogative of the prime minister.

The PMO performs many roles. It takes a major role in drafting the Speech from the Throne, the government's program as outlined at the beginning of each session of Parliament. However, perhaps its most crucial task is monitoring political developments and their implications for the prime minister. In concert with the Privy Council Office, the PMO provides the prime minister with a range of technical and political advice that may not be available from the non-partisan bureaucratic structures. It develops policy suggestions to boost the political fortunes of the prime minister and the governing party. In addition, the PMO carries out considerable public relations work. It gathers survey data on the popularity of the prime minister and political initiatives, helps to prepare press conferences, and deals with the media generally. Other related responsibilities include answering the prime minister's mail, coordinating his or her daily appointment schedule, and finding candidates for nominations and awards.

The Privy Council Office

Privy Council Office (PCO): The main public service organization supporting the Cabinet and prime minister.

The main organization supporting the Cabinet and prime minister is the **Privy Council Office (PCO)**. It is the prime minister's department and Cabinet's secretariat. Today, it supports the prime minister and ministers in the prime minister's portfolio—the leader of the government in the House of Commons, the minister of intergovernmental affairs (in this case the prime minister), the minister of democratic institutions—and Cabinet as a whole. In recent years there have been no appointments of a deputy prime minister and the role of president of the Privy Council has been, to some extent, downgraded and assigned to a minister with another portfolio.

The top position in the PCO is held by the **clerk of the Privy Council**. This post, which has existed since 1867, is mentioned in the Constitution. It was combined with the function of secretary to the Cabinet in 1940. The individual who holds this position (currently Janice Charette) is at the top of Canada's civil service. The clerk meets regularly with the prime minister and the chief of staff in the PMO and is in charge of coordinating Cabinet activities. The clerk's staffers set agendas, take the minutes of Cabinet meetings, and convey Cabinet decisions to the bureaucracy. However, the role and stature of the clerk depend to a great extent on his or her rapport with the prime minister.

clerk of the Privy Council: The head of the Privy Council Office (PCO) and the whole civil service.

The PCO performs some of the same functions as the PMO but is staffed by career bureaucrats seconded from various government departments. It has responsibility for the development and coordination of overall government policy. Although the top-ranking staffers of the PCO are appointed by the prime minister on the advice of the clerk, there is normally little emphasis on partisan politics. The PCO must, however, be politically sensitive. Under all recent prime ministers, the PCO, like the PMO, has flourished in size and scope of responsibility, but it has only rarely included political appointees.

The PCO possesses an impressive research capability and acts as the "eyes and ears" of the Cabinet in coordinating the numerous governmental departments and agencies. With a staff of about 500, the PCO is divided into several principal units. While structures and powers ebb and flow with the styles and organization of different prime ministers, the most influential tend to include plans, operations, intergovernmental affairs, machinery of government, foreign affairs, senior personnel, and security and intelligence. Each of these divisions has its own staff and is responsible for advising the prime minister, the plenary Cabinet, and the various Cabinet committees on matters of national policy.

The relationship between Cabinet ministers and officers of the PCO is for the most part cordial and constructive. The staff of the Privy Council may be more expert than the ministers on specific matters of policy, but in the end it is the elected ministers who make the decisions. In principle, the PCO exists to offer ministers objective advice and suggest policy alternatives since the weight of public and political responsibility is not on its shoulders.

Issues that concern both the federal government and the provinces are periodically negotiated and adjusted through federal–provincial conferences. These meetings, especially constitutional revisions, necessitate intensive planning and preparation on the part of federal officials. A central agency—the Federal–Provincial Relations Office (FPRO)—was established in 1974 within the PCO to deal with these issues. It became a separate department under the prime minister in 1975. Until 1993, it functioned independently of the PCO while reporting directly to the prime minister. As part of the 1993 government restructuring, it was subsumed once again inside the PCO while reporting to the minister responsible for intergovernmental affairs.

The PCO now carries out the traditional FPRO responsibilities to help coordinate Ottawa's interaction with the provinces and anticipate provincial reactions. In particular, it has a special mandate to monitor events in Québec and prepare scenarios for action vis-à-vis its government and the issue of independence. It also has ongoing special duties in the areas of Aboriginal rights, the infrastructure program, constitutional planning, and security analysis.

The Treasury Board

The third central coordinating agency is the Treasury Board, which, as we have noted, is constitutionally a committee of the Privy Council. In 1966, the staff of the Treasury Board was removed from the jurisdiction of the Department of Finance, and the unit was elevated to the legal status of a separate government department. The Treasury Board and its secretariat are headed by a Cabinet minister—the president of the Treasury Board. The Treasury Board itself includes six Cabinet ministers, one of whom is always the minister of finance. Aided by its secretariat, the Treasury Board is charged with two broad areas of responsibility: review of government expenditures and personnel management.

Responsibility for the review of expenditures means that the annual budgets of all government departments are screened and approved by the Treasury Board. It monitors all requests for money, evaluates them, and provides an overall budget in keeping with the priorities and objectives expressed by the prime minister and Cabinet. There is continuous consultation and negotiation between the Treasury Board and the spokespeople for all Cabinet portfolios, as each department attempts to maximize its share of the government's budget. The Treasury Board assesses these requests and makes recommendations.

Treasury's second major responsibility is to manage civil service personnel. It exerts control over salaries and job classifications across the civil service, following the merit principle. Motivating the Treasury Board above all else is the goal of effective use of human resources.

Treasury Board secretariat (TBS): An administrative unit of government with a highly qualified staff to assist the six Cabinet members of the Treasury Board.

To assist the Cabinet members of the Treasury Board, there is a highly qualified staff—the **Treasury Board secretariat (TBS)**—headed by a secretary to the Treasury Board. The staff of the TBS includes some of the brightest and most efficient members of the public service. Its economists, statisticians, and efficiency experts analyze departmental budgets. Since 2003, there has also been a controller general in the department.

The Department of Finance

Department of Finance: One of four central coordinating agencies of the executive, it analyzes policies and the impact of government activity on the economy.

The fourth central coordinating agency is the **Department of Finance**. While it is legally a regular government department, by virtue of its subject matter it is one of the most politically sensitive. Its authority is assigned under the *Financial Administration Act*. Finance shares some of the general concerns of the Treasury Board, but its chief preoccupation is analyzing taxation policy and the impact of government activity on the economy. It engages in long-range economic forecasting and suggests ways to maximize the performance of the economy. It also provides the Cabinet with information about the performance of the economy. On the basis of these facts, Cabinet, led by the minister of finance, establishes priorities. Public servants employed by the Department of Finance analyze four areas: taxation policy, economic development and government finance, fiscal policy and economic analysis, and international trade and finance.

The first major responsibility, *taxation policy*, is handled in cooperation with the Canada Revenue Agency. Specialists analyze existing tax measures from the perspective of the business community. A personal income tax unit examines proposals relating to personal taxation, deferred income plans such as retirement savings plans, and trusts and partnerships. Other tax units attempt to determine the effects of taxation and the distribution of income on the long-term growth of the economy and on the behaviour of individuals and corporations. Finally, the Department of Finance maintains an international tax policy unit, which negotiates tax treaties with foreign countries and examines the effects of foreign taxation on the Canadian economy.

With respect to its second responsibility, *economic development*, the department seeks to devise policies and strategies to encourage the overall growth of the Canadian economy. Finance is also involved in providing government loans to promote economic development and in negotiating financial guarantees to Crown corporations.

The third responsibility is *fiscal policy and economic analysis*. The department monitors indicators of the overall economic conditions of the country and prepares forecasts used in the development of the annual government budget. This involves establishing the annual fiscal framework and maintaining a close link with the Treasury Board secretariat.

The fourth concern of the Department of Finance is *international trade*. It investigates and reports on proposals concerning the Canadian customs tariff and its relation to the General Agreement on Tariffs and Trade (GATT) and various bilateral trade agreements, such as the North American Free Trade Agreement with Mexico and the United States. It also makes recommendations on international trade policy. The department maintains a liaison with international financial organizations and, of course, seeks to promote export development. The international finance section is also concerned with topics such as the balance of payments and foreign exchange.

Finance maintains a relatively high profile among government departments. The minister of finance presents the government's budget to Parliament and is inevitably the object of criticism or praise by the press and the opposition parties. The budgetary process is discussed in detail in Chapters 8.

POLITICAL EXECUTIVES: CANADA AND THE UNITED STATES COMPARED

Because it follows Britain's parliamentary model, Canada's executive differs from that of the United States in a number of ways. First, the U.S. president embodies the formal as well as the political executive—he or she is head of government and head of state. The president is also commander-in-chief of the armed forces. In Canada, although wars are fought in the name of the Queen, the role of governor general as head of the armed forces is purely ceremonial and the government controls the military.

The Constitution of the United States is based on the premise that a concentration of power is undesirable and that law-making and implementation should be separated by preventing the overlap of key personnel. Thus, the United States has three separate and equal branches of government: President, Congress, and the Courts. This presidential–congressional system of checks and balances creates an atmosphere of public political bargaining not found in Canada. For example, in the United States, the executive must rely on both houses of Congress to authorize funds to implement policy, and the Senate must confirm presidential appointments to cabinet, the diplomatic service, federal courts, and other boards and commissions.

The prime minister of Canada is simultaneously a member of the legislature and the executive. By contrast, the U.S. president is not allowed to serve in Congress but is elected directly by the people. The U.S. presidential form of government, therefore, provides a clear separation of executive and legislative powers. Canada's does not.

Whereas in the United States an individual may not hold a post in Congress and an executive position at the same time, precisely the opposite is true in Canada. All members of Cabinet, not just the prime minister, must be either elected to the House of Commons or appointed to the Senate. This *fusion* of powers creates, at least in theory, a government that is more coherent and responsive to the will of the people. The Canadian executive, backed by a parliamentary majority, can be assured of legislative support on most of the bills and programs it wishes to enact. It will of course be held accountable by the people at the next election, but during the interim it is relatively free to pursue its agenda. The executive in the United States is much more restricted, especially if different parties control the presidency and Congress.

In contrast to the Canadian model, the U.S. executive can also frustrate Congress—for instance, Congress is dependent on the president to implement its laws, and the executive often controls the information needed to formulate effective policies in Congress. On the other hand, Congress can, and often does, reject executive proposals, an exceedingly rare event in Canada except during minority Parliaments when such behaviour could cause the government to fall and necessitate a new election.

DOES THE PRIME MINISTER HAVE TOO MUCH POWER?

Some observers of politics in Canada find that the political executive has overstepped its proper authority, inviting grave consequences for responsible government and the parliamentary system. In a classic article, Denis Smith suggested that Parliament has surrendered its important roles of providing a forum for serious public debate and developing public policy.[8] According to Smith, a great deal ultimately depends on the prime minister, who appoints and dismisses his or her ministers at will. Although Cabinet may include some unusually powerful and prestigious figures, the decisions that Cabinet reaches ultimately depend on the prime minister. Cabinet policy becomes government policy, and backbenchers have little choice but to vote in obedience to the party and their prime minister.

There is considerable force to this argument, especially during majority governments. Changes in procedural rules and the expanding jurisdiction of the central coordinating agencies have helped to lessen the effectiveness of Parliament in its role of scrutiny and deliberation. House rules permit the government to pass legislation with a minimum of delay or modification. Opposition parties are rarely able to thoroughly scrutinize and effectively criticize the details of government policy.

This exceptional policy-making authority of the prime minister is generally resented by ministers, middle and upper echelons of the civil service, and members of Parliament, and distrusted by the press and opposition. While the descriptions of flagrant abuse of power may be overstated, the potential for abuse has been very real. The power of the prime minister and his staff has become enormous and pervasive. A prime minister with a majority government can shape the direction and content of policy, and, except in extraordinary situations, can count on dominating the political process until the next election.

In minority situations, however, prime ministers are considerably weaker. They must bargain with opposition members and also their own backbenchers to maintain the confidence of the House. Otherwise, they may be forced to call an election when they do not want to. Their legislative priorities may have to be significantly altered to accommodate others and get their votes.

Clearly, there are powers and advantages in the position of prime minister but, especially in minority situations, there are many limitations on those powers. Prime ministerial power is not exercised in isolation. The Cabinet and caucus must avoid policies that invoke hostile reactions from Parliament and the public. Care must be taken to hold the Cabinet together, to direct a complex government machine, and to secure adequate support for government.

Prime ministers obtain much of their strength from holding their team together. This requires conciliation, tact, and, only rarely, force. Pearson was a deft chairman-of-the-board type of leader; King was a master electioneer. Mulroney and Chrétien combined both talents. The skills required are so varied that no prime minister can be said to have had all of them. Paul Martin, with his very tenuous minority mandate, was dubbed "Mr. Dithers" because of his shifting priorities as he tried to hold his government together. Stephen Harper has been accused of being dictatorial with his Cabinet and staff.

Canada does *not* have prime ministerial government, but a majority prime minister is certainly in a powerful position. A minority government weakens a prime minister, particularly if members of Parliament are willing and able to combine their votes to pass non-confidence motions. Stephen Harper was known for keeping tight control during his minority governments, a remarkable feat in such precarious governing situations.

Assessing Prime Ministers: Greatness or Mediocracy

Canadians are less likely than American, British, or French publics to assess their leaders in terms of greatness. Debates about the "great man" theory of government are often criticized in this country, where the modest Canadian approach is to attribute success to broad economic and political forces that shape the environment and therefore leadership. Certainly, political leaders are influenced by these forces, but great leaders surmount them and still make lasting policy contributions.

Most Canadian leaders have been successful, some even outstanding. But how successful? Many considerations are important in assessing prime ministers.[9]

Political leaders have different abilities and idiosyncrasies. Some are able to use the outstanding abilities of those around them. Others show character and talent even when individuals and institutions around them are weak.

There is a reigning belief among Canadian political scientists and journalists that, overall, prime ministers are too powerful, but there is much nonsense and little common sense about this topic. That prime ministers lead the country from "the centre" is not a proper criticism, although given the way that academics and journalists pander to this conclusion one would assume it had been proven beyond debate. It has not. Where should prime ministers lead from—from a hodgepodge of ideas from Cabinet ministers whose combined talent is often lacking, from central agencies or government departments, from Parliament in its wisdom, or perhaps even from small towns?

There are two distinct ingredients for the success of a prime minister: One is *durability* and the other is the *ability to get important things done*. Durability indicates an ability to maintain a strong base, while not getting bogged down with trivia. In terms of longevity, Conservative Prime Minister Sir John A. Macdonald held office for 20 years, and Liberal Prime Minister William Lyon Mackenzie King served for 22. Both were skilled in seducing, cajoling, and manipulating colleagues in Cabinet and Parliament, as well as voters, to support their policies. Macdonald kept dispirited leaders together long enough to create the new state of Canada. King, an eccentric consumed with thoughts of his dead mother, his three dogs, and communicating with the "great beyond," helped to bring in the welfare state. His perseverance was key in allowing him to achieve great accomplishments. Other leaders also have fared fairly well on this indicator. Liberal prime ministers Pierre Trudeau and Sir Wilfrid Laurier both governed for a decade and a half. Jean Chrétien won three consecutive majority governments, a feat no other leader of either major party has accomplished.

A second factor in judging greatness is whether leaders manage to deliver important services to the country. This brings a large number of variables into play and is certain to raise issues about ideology and the state of the economy at the time. Some stresses come from specific problems, and others from the constant need to adjust political power, especially in a federation. Perhaps all 22 prime ministers should receive some credit for this. Pierre Trudeau was responsible for bringing the *Canada Health Act* to fruition; Brian Mulroney negotiated the Canada–U.S. free trade deal.

The interaction between leaders and their times is crucial. Greatness is often related to the mix of historical ingredients that leaders encounter—the opportunities or dangers of their age. Leaders who govern in times of crisis have to face factors beyond their immediate control. In this sense, John A. Macdonald should be judged highly, as he used his talents to manipulate and seduce colonists from various territories to join together in a new country, Canada. While he did not have a war to fight, he made use of the tinder of his time to ignite the passion that created the new state. In addition to his domestic accomplishments, King held the country together during World War II, and Conservative Sir Robert Borden led the country during World War I, but the fact that the homeland was never directly attacked reduced their opportunity for supreme leadership. Perhaps, in this regard, Pierre Elliott Trudeau could be given credit for facing down a significant domestic rebellion from separatists in Québec.

Stephen Harper did not have to face a significant crisis at home or abroad, but he has proven to be more than adequate as prime minister. He was one of the longest-lasting prime ministers. He re-engaged the West in Canadian politics, and avoided a separatist crisis in Québec. Time will tell if his record will indicate that he deserves to be ranked among the country's great prime ministers. Judgment of his policy contributions cannot be made without the test of time.

Discussion Questions

1. Where does political power lie in the Canadian system? With the prime minister? With Cabinet? With Parliament? With the people of Canada? Does it matter if there is a minority or majority government?

2. Who were the two longest-lasting prime ministers in Canadian history? Why do you think they were so successful?

3. Does the Prime Minister's Office or the Privy Council Office have too much control over the prime minister? Explain your response.

4. Does the prime minister have too much power? Why or why not? Why did Stephen Harper become so significant in the politics of Canada? Can the same arguments be made about Justin Trudeau?

Chapter 7

Parliament

The Public Arena of Politics

Learning Objectives

After reading this chapter, you should be able to

1 Name three major functions of the Canadian legislature in general, and discuss the distinct functions of the House of Commons and the Senate in particular.

2 Describe the major stages in the life cycle of a Parliament and the three major items of business for each session.

3 Describe how politicians interact in Parliament, both within their party and with other parties.

4 Name the kinds of committees in the House of Commons and describe what they do.

5 Distinguish between non-financial and money bills and trace the path that each must follow in order to become law.

6 Analyze alternative Senate reform proposals.

The Parliament of Canada is the main arena of politics in the country; when it is in session, the issues, parties, events, personalities, and even scandals that are part of political life become the focus of national media. It is here that the public game of power politics is played. With journalists as their guide, Canadians become spectators in the clash of ideas and events that could ultimately affect their lives.

In this chapter, we examine the origin and functions of the Canadian Parliament and explain how it operates. Elections decide which party controls Parliament and therefore determines who runs the executive. Members of Parliament (MPs) and senators discuss, debate, and argue over the virtues and justice of laws and how they affect all Canadians. They use Parliament as a forum for tabling their ideas about who should "get what, when, and how" in Canada. It is perhaps no wonder that reform of Parliament, especially of the Senate, is so often hotly debated.

THE PARLIAMENT OF CANADA

The Parliament of Canada, established by the *Constitution Act, 1867*, was shaped by Britain's Westminster model. It legally includes three bodies: the House of Commons, the Senate, and the Crown. As the embodiment of the Crown, the monarch plays a formal role in the Canadian legislative process through the governor general. To become law, legislation must pass through these three bodies. The **legislature**—the branch of government that makes or amends laws—is **bicameral**; that is, it is composed of two Houses. It has an elected lower House of representatives (the House of Commons) and an appointed upper House (the Senate). The parliamentary *executive*—the prime minister and Cabinet—is based in the lower House and is responsible to it. The executive directs parliamentary business, while an institutionalized opposition is charged with criticizing government.

Canada is a **parliamentary democracy** in that Parliament exercises power on behalf of the public and may be called the "repository of popular sovereignty." In a parliamentary system, the political executive receives its power to govern from the legislature. The prime minister and Cabinet are accountable to Parliament and may govern only as long as they retain the "confidence" of the majority of the House of Commons. We have seen that this is called *responsible government*. Canada's system is also a *representative democracy* in which citizens choose individual MPs to represent them in making national policies.

The Origins of Canada's Parliament

All countries have some means of discussing common problems and to decide what, if any, action should be taken to resolve them. The Canadian Constitution established Parliament as the main institution for this purpose.

In Britain, the idea of parliament can be traced back to the medieval council that the king used to summon for advice. This gathering, over time, was called "parliament" from the Old French, meaning "discussion." As centuries passed, political power gradually shifted from the monarch to Parliament. By the eighteenth century, senior advisers or ministers sat in the Commons (rather than the upper House); by the nineteenth century, they required the support of the Commons, not just the king, to retain office. In this way, executive power came to be centred in Parliament.

Canadians borrowed the blueprint for their Parliament from Britain and adapted it. From the early stages, Canadians concentrated on making the governor and the executive council responsible to the elected assembly. At Confederation in 1867, Canada joined the world of states as a representative, parliamentary democracy. It established an adversarial system of party politics with a clear dichotomy between government and opposition. It also established a code of procedures to govern the behaviour of members and adopted norms of behaviour to counteract potential hostility arising from the partisan nature of the House.

From the beginning, Canada's lower House, the House of Commons, was an *elected* assembly while the upper House was *appointed*. The idea of an appointed upper House was considered appropriate for two reasons. The first was that the founders believed that "men of wisdom and good stock" would be among the best qualified to watch out for the public interest. They also thought that such a body could help to protect provincial rights. Indeed, Confederation would not have been achieved without an agreement on the appointed upper House. This is often overlooked in contemporary debates about Senate reform.

The Senate has survived as an institution from the country's origin. Concepts of equality have made obsolete the original desire to confine the upper House exclusively to "men of wisdom and good stock." As well, the Senate has not been able to develop an acceptable role as a legitimate protector of provincial interests. The allotment of senators did, however, provide the less populous provinces a large degree of influence in Parliament. Ontario and Québec received 24 senators each, while Nova Scotia, New Brunswick, and Prince Edward Island were awarded a combined 24. As other provinces were formed, their rights to representation in the Senate were established on the same principle.

The Functions of Canada's Parliament

As the vehicle for representative democracy, Parliament provides a forum for members to debate major political issues of the day. The debate is relayed to the public by the mass media, informing and also openly responding to public opinion.

Like many other legislatures, the Canadian institution has three major functions:

- It has *policy-making functions*, including the passage of legislation (a lengthy process outlined below).

- It has *representational functions* since it is responsible for expressing the interests and opinions of the electorate and dealing with the problems of constituents.

- It has *system-maintenance functions* that contribute to the working and legitimacy of other parts of the political system and the state itself.

The Canadian legislature performs a host of other services as well. It legitimates the activities and policies of the government, it regularly participates in the recruitment and socialization of future members of the government; it aids in the regulation and management of conflict; and it may serve to integrate and achieve consensus among rival political elites. The two Houses of Parliament each have specialized functions, which we explore below.

The Life Cycle of Parliament

The term *Parliament* is used in different ways. Its general usage is, as we have seen, to describe a certain *type* of legislature. However the term *Parliament* is also used to refer to the House of Commons *building* in Ottawa, and it is also used in a very specific way to identify a particular government from the time of its election to the formation of the next government. Parliaments in this latter sense are labelled by consecutive numbers, which change after each general election. For example, the 338 MPs returned in the 2015 general election collectively form the forty-second Parliament.

All Parliaments pass through the same life cycle, but their lifespans vary and each is unique in significant ways. In each Parliament, there may be one or a number of **sessions**, or working periods when Parliament is open for business. The number of sessions depends on the wishes of the government of the day and on the length of the Parliament—that is, on how much time elapses between general elections. The Constitution requires Parliament to meet at least once a year.

Generally, a session of Parliament includes three major events concerning the business of Parliament: a Speech from the Throne, the presentation of a budget, and

session: Working period when Parliament is open for business.

the tabling of the estimates. Every session begins with the governor general summoning the MPs and senators to Parliament at the request of the prime minister. Members of both Houses come together in the Senate chamber, with great pomp and ceremony, to hear the governor general deliver the **Speech from the Throne**, which outlines the government's proposed legislative program for the forthcoming session. The first Speech from the Throne in a new Parliament tends to be a reiteration of campaign promises, as was the December 4, 2015 Speech from the Throne which reiterated Liberal promises on tax cuts, infrastructure spending, the environment, and aboriginal issues (see Chapter 11). After the speech is read, members return to their respective chambers to commence business. In the Commons, a debate on the Throne Speech usually occupies the first few days of the session; afterwards, the normal timetable of the House comes into effect. In total, six days may be used to debate the Speech. A break taken by the House within a session is called an **adjournment, or a recess.**

The second feature of parliamentary sessions is the budget. Delivered by the minister of finance, the **budget** document is primarily concerned with setting out where the revenue will come from to carry out the government's program. It generally includes tax changes to raise revenue and is kept secret until it is unveiled in a dramatic, public presentation. Tax changes go into effect immediately, although the legislation for them is necessarily drawn up later. A four-day **budget debate** (not necessarily on consecutive days) follows the presentation of the budget. The debate can be dramatic, because it provides the opposition with an opportunity to try to defeat the government. Such a defeat does not happen to governments that have a majority of members in the House of Commons. Minority governments fare differently. In 2005, with only a minority, Paul Martin's government barely survived a vote on the budget. The Stephen Harper minority governments that followed also needed to finesse their way through budget votes, but after his 2011 majority Harper was able to call the shots with little parliamentary input.

Tabling the **estimates**—the government's spending proposals for the next fiscal year—is the third major item of business for each session. Apart from these three events, every session is devoted largely to debating the political issues of the day.

When the government wants to end a session of Parliament, it closes it. Closing a session is called **prorogation**. Prorogation of one session is often immediately followed by the summoning of the next. Unless there is prior agreement, any legislation that has not successfully completed all stages of the process automatically dies when Parliament is prorogued; if the government is still committed to an unpassed bill, it must begin the entire process again in the next session. Sessions used to last a year or less, but in recent years they have been longer. The first session of the thirty-second Parliament lasted a record three years and eight months.

In 2006, Parliament passed Bill C-16, which fixed election dates for every four years unless an earlier dissolution was forced on the federal government or the prime minister requested the governor general to use his or her prerogative to dissolve Parliament. **Dissolution** is the name given to the ending of a particular Parliament. It necessitates an election on either the third Monday in the fourth calendar year following polling day for the last general election, or at a time when the government has been defeated in the House or when the governor general has approved a dissolution, as occurred in 2008.[1] The forty-second general election followed the rules of Bill C-16 and was called for October 19, 2015.

Speech from the Throne: Delivered by the governor general, it outlines the government's proposed legislative program for the forthcoming session.

adjournment (recess): A break period taken by the House of Commons within a session.

budget: A document that primarily sets out the revenue and expenditures required to carry out the government's program.

budget debate: The four-day (not necessarily consecutive) debate that follows the presentation of the budget.

estimates: The government's spending proposals for the next fiscal year.

prorogation: Closing a session of Parliament. Formally, this is done by the governor general on the advice of the prime minister.

dissolution: The end of a particular Parliament, which occurs at the request of a prime minister who seeks a new mandate, or whose government has been defeated in the House of Commons.

THE HOUSE OF COMMONS

Today, the House of Commons has 338 MPs, distributed among the provinces and territories by a formula that adheres to the principle that each should be represented in proportion to its population. Rules concerning how many MPs are elected and how the constituency boundaries are determined are discussed in Chapter 11.

The Functions of the House of Commons

The House of Commons has several distinct functions:

- As a representative institution, it is supposed to reflect the ideas and wishes of Canadians. On the other hand, it is also expected to lead and educate the public.
- It provides the government with the authority to govern.
- It supervises the work of the Cabinet. Motions of confidence and non-confidence determine which party will form the government.
- It passes laws, imposes taxes, and authorizes government expenditures.
- It provides a forum to legitimize decisions that are taken by the government under existing statutes or regulations.
- It provides a forum for backbenchers to initiate ideas and, to a limited extent, even legislation, through Question Period, parliamentary debates, and private members' bills.
- It is a forum for extended debates on political questions that expose the advantages and disadvantages of different courses of action.
- It acts as a critic or watchdog to keep the government accountable.
- It provides an alternate government in the form of the Official Opposition party.
- It provides a training ground for future leaders.

Members of Parliament

Each MP is elected to the House of Commons (usually on a party "label") in a single-member constituency. They constitute a visible link between the public and the federal government. In Canada, many have short careers in Parliament, and often find the switch back to private life difficult both financially and psychologically.

backbenchers: MPs on the government side who are not ministers or on the opposition side who are not designated party critics.

The position of MP has many facets. The basic work of **backbenchers**—those on the government side who are not ministers or on the opposition side who are not designated as party critics—is of two types: parliamentary and constituency. In Parliament, the job is basically to support the party leadership and attend plenary sessions of the House of Commons to debate and vote on legislation. Apart from this, MPs also serve on parliamentary committees and are members of parliamentary caucuses. They also have large caseloads of constituency duties to perform. For many, the constituencies they represent are far from Ottawa, and it takes considerable time and effort to act as representatives. They take up constituent problems with ministers, public servants, or representatives of government agencies. They may also inform constituents about legislation and issues that are being discussed in Parliament. In summary, MPs choose many different roles to play in the House.

For their efforts, MPs in 2015 received a salary of $167 400, benefits and pensions, an office budget of around $300 000, travel allowances (return trips between Ottawa and their respective ridings for themselves and a named person), and free telephone and mail services.

Theoretically, almost any adult Canadian with residency in the country can run for Parliament and be elected as an MP. In practice, however, it is not so simple. Campaigns are expensive and usually require a significant personal investment of money and time. A good education is necessary to understand and communicate issues to the public, and it is helpful to have an alternative source of income for security in such a tenuous job. To be victorious, one also must be affiliated with, and win a candidacy for, a political party. Independents without a party label are rarely elected.

MPs do not represent a cross-section of the population. Those with British and French backgrounds predominate, as do those with law degrees. Most MPs come from urban areas because the majority of ridings are clustered around larger city-centres. Most are middle-aged males. No women were elected as MPs in Canada until 1921, and the numbers of female MPs did not reach double digits until 1979 (see Close-Up 7.1).

Rules of the House

The procedures for the daily activities in the Commons are set out in the Standing Orders. The **Standing Orders** contain the rules of the House, which are of a general

Standing Orders: Contain the rules of the House of Commons that are of a general nature and more or less permanent.

nature, impartial and technically amendable. Although the rules prevent any particular party from receiving partisan treatment, they do allow the government to monopolize the time of the House and for the most part to set its agenda. The rules of debate also favour the government. Individual members, as we shall see, are guaranteed some time to put forward bills, but this is minimal.

Procedural rules have been designed to reduce antagonism in the House of Commons by limiting the direct personal interaction of the members. For example, verbal confrontations during debate are constrained by the requirement that no member may speak officially without recognition by the speaker and that all statements must be addressed to the chair. This means that members do not speak directly to one another or even of one another, inasmuch as individuals are referred to not by name but through more impersonal titles, such as "the prime minister," "the leader of the Opposition" or "the honourable member for constituency X."

There is even a list of terms deemed to constitute "unparliamentary language." It is not permitted, for example, to use expressions that cast doubt on the legitimacy of a member's birth, nor to allege that a speech has been inspired by intoxicating substances. On December 8, 1994, the speaker ruled that "mean-spirited" terms constituted unparliamentary language and could not be used in the House. Members have been suspended from the House for suggesting that another member was lying and then refusing to withdraw the accusation.

Other rules that help to reduce antagonism include the principle that, once recognized by the speaker, every MP has the right to speak for a specific length of time without interruption if the speech remains relevant to the motion before the House. Rules also protect certain persons (especially the royal family and the governor general) from explicit attacks in the Commons.

The House of Commons also enjoys collective privileges, which enable it to conduct its business in an orderly fashion. The House has the power to preserve order and discipline in its proceedings and to punish those who are guilty of making libellous statements concerning it or its members. It has the power to refuse a seat to a person who has been duly elected and can expel any member of the House.

Although this basic code of civility is enforced, members of both Houses enjoy special privileges regarding freedom of speech that other Canadians do not. This is because **parliamentary privilege** enables members to express themselves freely and without intimidation. This rule, adapted from British tradition, grants members freedom of speech, so that they cannot be prosecuted in court for anything they have said in Parliament. As well, they cannot be intimidated, nor can they be arrested for certain minor offences for a period before, during, and after a parliamentary session.

parliamentary privilege: A House of Commons rule that enables MPs to express themselves freely and without intimidation.

Organization and Officers of the House of Commons

The seating plan of the Canadian House of Commons follows the British model in which the government and opposition face one another with the government to the speaker's right and the opposition to the left. The leaders of the two major parties confront each other surrounded by their lieutenants and backed by their backbenchers. The smaller parties also take their place on the opposition side of the House. This face-to-face positioning physically separates the government from the opposition and reinforces the sense of political identity and party cohesion on both sides of the Commons (see Figure 7.1).

In the central area of the chamber, between the two main rivals, sit the officials of the House. The **speaker of the House of Commons**, who sits at one end, is officially an impartial arbiter elected by the whole House. She or he is not permitted to vote (voting takes place when a "division" is called), except for casting the deciding vote in the event of a tie, when the speaker is required to support the government of the day.

speaker of the House of Commons: A member of Parliament elected to act as an impartial arbiter of the whole House.

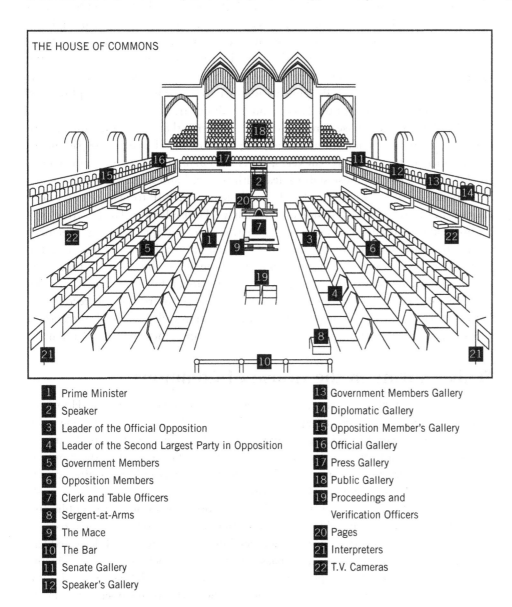

THE HOUSE OF COMMONS

1 Prime Minister	13 Government Members Gallery
2 Speaker	14 Diplomatic Gallery
3 Leader of the Official Opposition	15 Opposition Member's Gallery
4 Leader of the Second Largest Party in Opposition	16 Official Gallery
5 Government Members	17 Press Gallery
6 Opposition Members	18 Public Gallery
7 Clerk and Table Officers	19 Proceedings and Verification Officers
8 Sergent-at-Arms	20 Pages
9 The Mace	21 Interpreters
10 The Bar	22 T.V. Cameras
11 Senate Gallery	
12 Speaker's Gallery	

Figure 7.1 General Seating Plan of the House of Commons

Source: From Who's Who in the House. Guide to the Canadian House of Commons. Library of Parliament. Available at http://www.parl.gc.ca/About/Parliament/GuideToHoC/who-e.htm. Reprinted with permission.

Since September 1986, the speaker has been elected by secret ballot in a vote of all members of the House. A Liberal, Peter Milliken, was elected as speaker in 2001 and re-elected in 2004 and 2006. After Milliken resigned, Andrew Scheer, the 32-year-old Conservative member for Regina-Qu'Appelle, was elected speaker after six rounds of balloting. In 2015, for the first time, a preferential ballot was used and Geoff Regan, Liberal MP for Halifax, was elected Speaker of the House of Commons.

The speaker is in charge of the administration of the House, overseeing staffing with secretaries, clerks, and so on. As well, the speaker is jointly responsible, with the *Board of Internal Economy* (a body composed of the speaker and deputy speaker of the House, two members of the Privy Council, the leader of the Official Opposition or a designee, and four other members—two from the government caucus and two from the opposition benches), for the economic management of the House, and prepares and steers through the House the annual estimates of the cost of running the Commons. The speaker is aided by a deputy speaker (who is also elected by fellow MPs at the beginning of each Parliament) and by two senior permanent employees of the Commons—the clerk of the House and an administrator.

clerk of the House: An official responsible for ensuring that relevant documents are printed and circulated and for advising the speaker of the House on the parliamentary business of the day.

The **clerk of the House** is responsible for ensuring that relevant documents are printed and circulated and for advising the speaker of the House on the parliamentary business of the day. In recent years, the *House administrator*, a senior bureaucrat, has been added to the House staff to deal with financial and management issues.

House leader: An MP designated by the leader of each party in the House of Commons to manage party conduct in the House.

The leader of each party in the House designates an MP to manage party conduct in the House; this MP is known as the party's **House leader**. The government's House leader is usually a member of Cabinet, responsible for obtaining agreement among the parties in setting the timetable for the House. House leaders have the authority to negotiate the list of speakers and manage other administrative functions.

In addition to these individuals, there is a professional staff to manage day-to-day activities of the House. The staff includes translators, transcribers who record verbatim the House of Commons debates in a publication called *Hansard*, secretaries, security personnel, maintenance staff, and research staff at the Library of Parliament.

Daily Routine in the House of Commons

The timetable of *plenary meetings* (meetings of the full House) in the House of Commons varies slightly from day to day. The House has a five-day working week that may be increased by adding evening sittings. Members meet in the House of Commons four mornings and every afternoon during the week while the House is sitting. Wednesday morning is reserved for caucus meetings and Friday afternoon is usually relegated to private members' business.

Each day, after a brief prayer,[2] the Commons opens its doors to the public and according to the day's timetable proceeds to one of several considerations: routine business, government orders, private members' business, or review of delegated legislation. Routine business may encompass a host of items, including announcements and questions of privilege; reports from interparliamentary delegations and committees; documents and government papers for the notice of members; statements by ministers regarding government policy; the introduction and first reading of Commons bills and the first reading of public bills that originated in the Senate; government notices of motions to be introduced later; and other motions, particularly those requesting concurrence in committee reports and those pertaining to special arrangements for the sittings and proceedings of the House.

Much of the time of plenary sessions is consumed by the **Orders of the Day,** the procedure under which the House deals with the public business placed before it. Orders are the prime means by which the House of Commons formulates instructions in the form of motions. They guide the speaker and other members and direct the officers of the House to pursue particular courses of action. The greater part of this period is devoted to government business in the form of the Throne Speech debate, motions dealing with the passage of bills, and the referral of legislation, estimates, and investigatory tasks to standing and special committees. *Resolutions* are another form that motions can take. With the exception of constitutional resolutions, resolutions are not binding on anyone but are simply expressions of *opinion* of the Commons. *Orders*, as we have seen, express the *will* of the Commons and are binding.

Not all of the House's business is instigated by the government. Private members may put forward bills and motions. Historically, these bills and motions were placed in a lottery or draw. The first 30 items chosen were placed in an "order of precedence" for 15 bills and 15 motions. Today, at the beginning of each session of Parliament, the names of all MPs who are neither ministers nor parliamentary secretaries are listed and a draw is held to determine the "order of precedence"—that is, which members' bills will come up for debate and deliberation. This process is a way to manage time, but it is also based on "chance," culls out many items, and prevents most items from being considered at all. Private members' bills that actually became law include such gems as recognition of the beaver as an official symbol and hockey as the national sport of Canada.

To assure that the opposition voices in the House of Commons are heard, certain sitting days during a session are reserved for *opposition* business, when the opposition has a chance to lead major debates on government policy. At the start of the session, the House is permitted six days to debate the address in reply to the Speech from the Throne. A further four days are allocated for the budget debate. As well, the opposition parties have about 20 **Opposition Days** (or **Supply Days**) on which to debate their motions. These are spread unevenly over the three supply periods of the session. Opposition Days provide time for opposition parties to mount attacks on government policies, to propose alternative policies, and to introduce motions of non-confidence in the government. In practice, these days are more a symbolic recognition of the opposition's right to criticize the government than a forum for policy initiation.

The most publicized and entertaining aspect of work in the House is the daily **Oral Question Period**—a 45-minute period held five days a week that provides a forum for the opposition parties to embarrass the government, criticize its policies, and force discussion on selected issues. The government is subjected each day to relentless questioning by the opposition parties. Ministers are not given prior notice of what issues will be discussed and the speaker allocates questions roughly proportionate to party membership in the House.

However, there are rules that make it difficult for serious, sustained attacks by the opposition. The speaker calls on members to speak following lists supplied by the party whips. Supplementary questions are permitted in Question Period, but no

Orders of the Day: The procedures under which the House of Commons deals with the public business placed before it. Orders guide the speaker and direct the officers of the House to pursue particular courses of action.

Opposition Days (Supply Days): Days on which opposition motions can be debated (20 per session).

Oral Question Period: A 45-minute period held in Parliament five days a week that provides a forum for the opposition parties to try to embarrass the government, criticize its policies, and force discussion on selected issues.

formal debate is allowed. As a result, ministers can often avoid the main substance of a question. In fact, MPs used to joke that Question Period got its name because questions are asked—but answers are never given. Government backbenchers also use up some of the valuable time that Question Period provides by asking their ministers questions about "minor" constituency interests or making "friendly" queries to give their ministers the floor on topics they wish to discuss. The opposition's use of Question Period is thwarted in yet another way. When there is more than one opposition party, the unstructured attack on the government often loses its effect. Frequently, Question Period degenerates into a torrent of verbal abuse.

In spite of these difficulties, well-directed opposition tactics can still make the daily Question Period an important occasion for calling the executive to account for its actions, allowing effective participation by backbenchers and providing an opportunity for the public to see responsible government at work. In recent years, considerable effort has gone into preparing questions that might provide a favourable "clip" for the evening news. After the period, reporters generally flock around politicians who use the most colourful language or blunt delivery. The media are constantly judging performance and conveying their conclusions to the public.

Question Period, like all plenary sessions, has been televised since 1977, giving MPs a public outlet for their messages. Government MPs know that this daily ritual represents the "public face" of their government. Cabinet ministers prepare diligently. The usual routine is for key staffers to meet with the House leader early each day to anticipate questions that might arise. About an hour before Question Period, ministers and parliamentary secretaries may meet with the House leader to go through possible questions and responses.

The House is usually not well attended except for Question Period or for important divisions. This is because plenary sessions of the House of Commons are only a part of the total workload and MPs are often busy elsewhere—such as in committee.

COMMITTEES IN THE HOUSE OF COMMONS

Much of the work carried on by the House of Commons is in committee. There are four basic kinds of committees:

committee of the whole: A committee of the House in which all MPs sit in the chamber as one large committee chaired by the deputy speaker or the deputy chair of committees.

1. In **committee of the whole**, all MPs sit in the chamber in one large committee chaired by the deputy speaker or the deputy chair of committees, using committee rules rather than House procedures. This committee is currently used much less than in previous years; it is reserved mainly for money bills or, on rare occasions, to expedite passage of other legislation. The **ways and means committee** is a committee of the whole. It considers the resolutions that contain the proposals of the minister of finance. Once they are passed, the resolutions are embodied in one or more bills (such as a bill to amend the *Income Tax Act*) and then proceed through the usual legislative stages necessary to pass a public bill.

ways and means committee: A committee of the whole; it considers the resolutions that contain the proposals of the minister of finance.

standing committee: A committee that is relatively permanent for the life of a Parliament.

2. **Standing committees** are relatively permanent committees that may last for the life of a Parliament. In 2014, there were 26 standing committees, each with 10 to 12 members proportional to party standings in the House. They study and report on all matters relating to the mandate, management, and operations of

the department or departments assigned to them—such as agriculture and agri-food, foreign affairs, international trade, national defence, and veterans affairs. Chaired, except in rare circumstances, by a member of the governing party in the House, standing committees focus on program and policy objectives and effectiveness, expenditure plans and the relative success of the department(s), etc. In recent years, the finance committee has been given the responsibility to participate in pre-budget discussions. The committee begins to study the government's financial policies in early September and reports before the end of December—that is, before the annual budget is delivered.

Standing committees may also handle the committee stage of legislation. When the Liberals came to office in 1993, they began to send all bills to standing committees once again. To assist them, standing committees are empowered to form subcommittees and to "send for persons, papers and records" that might be helpful. All individuals appointed by order-in-council may be scrutinized by these committees.

3. Two **joint standing committees** are composed of members of both the House of Commons and the Senate: the joint standing committee on scrutiny of regulations (which studies all delegated legislation by departments, agencies, boards, or other authorities) and the Library of Parliament committee.

joint standing committee: A committee composed of members of both the House of Commons and the Senate.

4. **Legislative committees** may be set up to examine individual, specific bills. They are temporary and do not carry out the functions of standing committees. Legislative committees can be numerous or few depending on the amount of legislation before the House.

legislative committees: Committees that are set up to receive bills for examination.

These four kinds of committees provide MPs with opportunities to make an impact on policy-making. Standing committees are especially important, with three principal areas of operation: detailed consideration of legislation; scrutiny of the financial aspects of government and bureaucracy; and investigation of reports, policy proposals, and other items. Standing committees are also empowered (under Standing Order 111) to judge whether order-in-council appointees have the "competence and qualifications" to do their jobs. If committees are to perform all of these functions well, they need to be well staffed and have the resources to conduct serious investigations.

Despite various reforms over the years, criticisms of the committee system are common.[3] For example, some complain that committees do not enjoy an even workload throughout the year: It is usually very slow at the beginning of a session and very busy in the spring when the major bills usually reach them—right at the same time that they get the spending proposals in the main estimates to scrutinize. Another traditional lament is that after all of the work that goes into them, committee reports are ignored; the government is required to respond to all reports in Parliament, but it is not obliged to adopt the recommendations they contain. In recent years committees have sometimes been used to actually draft a bill. If this process were made permanent, it would be a significant reform of the House of Commons.

PASSING LEGISLATION

We have noted that a key function of the House of Commons is to pass laws. These are presented to the House of Commons as **bills**.

bills: Legislation presented to the House of Commons that may be passed into law. There are two categories of bills: public and private.

Types of Bills

private bill: A bill that confers special power or rights on specific individuals, groups, or corporations rather than on society as a whole.

public bills: Bills that seek to change the law concerning the public as a whole. There are two kinds of public bills: government bills and private members' bills. The vast majority are government bills.

private members' bill: A bill sponsored by an individual MP.

government bill: A bill introduced by the Cabinet as government policy.

money bill: Government bill for raising or spending money.

supply (appropriation) bills: Bills that authorize the spending of money by the government.

ways and means motions: Motions that introduce bills to authorize the raising of money by taxation.

There are two categories of bills: public and private. **Private bills** are bills that confer special power or rights on specific individuals, groups, or corporations rather than on society as a whole. Today, they constitute an extremely small proportion of total legislative activity. **Public bills** seek to change the law concerning the public as a whole. They include such well-known laws as the *Income Tax Act* or the *Canada Health Act*. There are two kinds of public bills: those sponsored by individual MPs, called **private members' bills**, and those introduced by the Cabinet as government policy, called **government bills**. The vast majority of bills passed by the Canadian Parliament are government bills.

Government bills come in two varieties: financial or non-financial. The financial ones are known as **money bills** because they are government bills for raising or spending money. Bills to authorize the spending of money by the government are called **supply (appropriation) bills**. **Ways and means motions** are motions that introduce bills and legislation to authorize the raising of money by taxation. (For the various kinds of bills, see Figure 7.2.) While private members may *introduce* bills that include spending, those bills cannot be *passed* through Parliament without receiving "royal assent" or government agreement at some stage in the process.

How Laws Are Passed

Preparing, introducing, and passing a bill into law is a long process. Besides a lengthy pre-parliamentary process to create policy and legislation (discussed in Chapters 6 and 8), there is also a formal parliamentary stage. To become law through an act or statute, a bill must pass three readings in the House, pass three readings in the Senate, receive royal assent (from the governor general), and (sometimes) be proclaimed by the government.

When a draft bill has been prepared, 48 hours' notice is given and the minister responsible presents it to Parliament. All bills that involve raising or spending public money, as well as most other bills, are introduced first in the House of Commons and then go to the Senate. However, as we shall see, there are some bills that are introduced first in the Senate and then passed through the House of Commons.

The introduction of a bill by the minister is brief; it outlines the purpose of the bill and asks that it be given a *first reading*. The first reading is invariably granted and allows the bill to be printed and numbered (with a C prefix if it originates in the

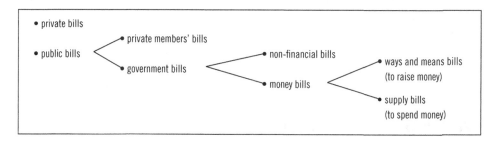

Figure 7.2 Types of Bills

House of Commons, S if in the Senate) and distributed to MPs. Bills are referred to by a combination of a letter and a number. Numbers C-1 to C-200 are reserved for government bills, C-201 to C-1000 for private members' public bills, and C-1001 onward for private members' private bills. The bill is then placed on the **Order Paper**, the schedule of pending parliamentary business.

Order Paper: The schedule of pending parliamentary business.

Second reading is initiated by a motion, again usually by the sponsoring minister. This is the most important stage in a bill's passage. This time, debate on the principle of the bill is allowed so that the House can decide whether there is need for such a bill and whether it is sound. No amendments are accepted at this stage. When debate is finished, bills are sent directly to a House of Commons standing committee. In committee, as we have seen above, the bill concerned is studied in detail by a small group of MPs. The committee may call expert witnesses for advice at this time.

There are a few exceptions to this usual procedure. Bills may be sent directly to a committee *before* second reading. The House can also refer a bill to a special legislative committee set up for the purpose, or to a joint committee (which includes members from the Senate). For supply bills, ways and means motions, and certain other legislation on which the House agrees, the committee stage is undertaken by the committee of the whole. At this stage, the bill receives detailed clause-by-clause consideration and amendments may be moved. The amended bill is then voted on as a whole when it is *reported* back to the House. At the normal report stage, the House has an opportunity to debate and perhaps amend or even block the bill. Unless unanimously agreed otherwise by the House, the third reading then commences. There is often little debate at this time and a final vote is taken on the bill.

If the bill is passed, it must now repeat the whole process in the Senate. Here the passage is normally easier, except when the government party does not control a majority of members in the Senate. First and second readings pass quickly. It is at the committee stage that the major legislative work is done in the Senate. The upper House rarely amends the substance of a bill, but it often improves the details of hastily drafted bills. No Senate changes that cause increased taxation or spending are permitted. As in the House, the final product as revised in committee is then sent back to the Senate for debate, possible further amendment, and acceptance. After the final consideration of the bill by the Senate and the third reading vote, the House of Commons is informed whether the Senate has rejected, amended, or passed the bill.

If, as rarely happens, a bill is defeated by the Senate, it must begin the entire process again from the start. If the Senate amends a bill, it must be returned to the lower House for reconsideration. Usually Senate amendments deal with minor details, not the substance of the bill, so they are readily disposed of by the responsible minister. Once this is achieved, the bill is ready for its final stage.

Finally, the bill is sent for **royal assent**. The governor general, sitting in the Senate chambers before the assembled members of both Houses, puts the final seal of approval on the bill. The function may also be carried out by the governor general or his or her advisers by written confirmation. The bill thereby becomes an act of the Parliament of Canada, and henceforth is law—unless it contains a requirement for formal government proclamation at a later date. **Proclamation** involves proclaiming, publishing, or declaring under the Great Seal a statute that thereby becomes law. The entire process is shown in Figure 7.3.

royal assent: When the governor general, sitting in the Senate chambers before the assembled members of both Houses, puts the final seal of approval on legislation.

proclamation: Involves proclaiming, publishing, or declaring under the Great Seal a statute that thereby becomes law.

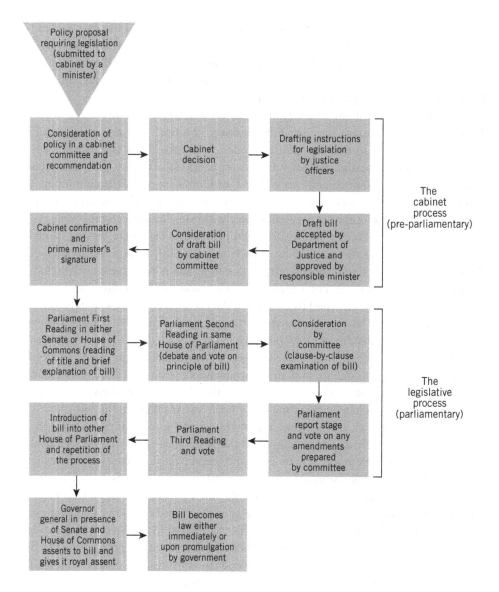

Figure 7.3 How a Government Bill Becomes Law

We have said that there are some unique conditions that apply to money bills (bills to raise or spend money). Ways and means bills originate in the budget speech delivered by the minister of finance. This speech outlines the government's economic policy and summarizes the changes that will subsequently appear in tax legislation. Supply bills are debated by standing committees. Once the estimates are examined, appropriation bills are passed quickly, authorizing the money for the government's spending proposals. Money bills therefore follow the same general process as other bills, with five important differences:

1. They must originate in the House of Commons.
2. Ways and means bills are considered by the committee of the whole as "motions" before they go through the normal legislative process as taxation bills.

3. Supply (the process by which Parliament approves the government's projected annual expenditures) has two phases. The estimates (proposals to spend) are tabled along with a royal recommendation (i.e., Crown agreement) in the House and then referred to standing committees.

4. There are significant limitations on the Senate's ability to amend such bills.

5. They take longer than other bills because many aspects of them invoke extensive partisan debate.

PARTIES IN PARLIAMENT

There are two important aspects to party behaviour in Parliament. One is behaviour within the parties themselves; the other is the relationships among the parties. We consider each of these in turn.

Inside Parliamentary Parties

Almost all MPs belong to a political party. This fact has a profound effect on legislative politics in both Houses. The government relies on its backbenchers to remain loyal in order to pass its legislative proposals and even to stay in office. The opposition parties rally their troops in order to present a coherent attack on the government. In both cases, this requires individual members to compromise their own short-term interests for the unity of their party. In fact, the electorate does not tend to reward rebellious MPs at the polls.[4]

Party leaders, especially in government, have a number of penalties that they can use to ensure **party discipline**—that is, to ensure that the party remains united. Individuals may be coerced in a number of ways. They may lose their positions on parliamentary committees, as several Liberals did when they rebelled against their government's gun control legislation in June 1995. They may be threatened with being suspended from caucus meetings or even expelled from the party. As well as these "sticks," party leaders also have a number of "carrots" to keep their backbenchers in line. These include such rewards as promotion to Cabinet minister, parliamentary secretary, or committee chair; appointment to the Senate; or one of numerous positions in public corporations and Crown agencies. Obviously, these rewards are more available to the government than to opposition parties.

To enforce party discipline, the House leader for each party is assisted by a chief whip and assistant whips. **Whips** are MPs assigned by the party leaders to help maintain party cohesion. They keep in touch with the members, informing them of their duties in the House and on committees. On the whole, unity is maintained more often by party and leader loyalty than by the whips' ability to apply sanctions. From time to time party leaders have tried to relax the rules of party discipline—usually to their chagrin.

Each party in Parliament forms its own group or **party caucus**. Every Wednesday morning when Parliament is in session, all members of the House of Commons and any senators (but no longer Liberal senators) meet in their respective party groups. Caucus meetings are held in private so that members can speak frankly without the press reporting division within the parties.

party discipline: The ability of the leaders of a parliamentary party to ensure that its members function as a cohesive group.

whip: An MP assigned by each party leader to help maintain party cohesion.

party caucus: A group formed by each party in Parliament. Every Wednesday morning when Parliament is in session, all members of the House of Commons, and in some parties all senators, meet in their respective party groups.

In the governing party, caucus is often consulted only after policies have been decided by Cabinet, and members are expected to support these decisions. However, members are often shown the principles of forthcoming legislation despite government denial. Indeed, governments rarely act in the face of clear caucus opposition. While a major function of the government caucus is to ensure party unity—and opposition leaders also strive to achieve this—opposition caucuses usually have more latitude because, in opposition, there is less of a distinction between leaders and backbenchers. Since opposition MPs do not have as much to lose as their government counterparts, they tend to express their points of view more freely. In any case, a strong degree of party cohesion in the House of Commons is an integral part of representative and responsible government.

It is often argued that MPs should be free to vote according to their conscience, or in accordance with the views of their constituency. Otherwise, the argument goes, they are just "trained seals." The former Canadian Alliance party, in particular, advocated that MPs should accurately represent their constituents' views when they vote in Parliament. The Alliance went so far as to promote devices such as **recall** in which constituents would have been able to vote to recall their MPs if they did not vote as instructed.[5] None ever became law.

Just what constitutes the appropriate relations between MPs and their constituents has been debated for more than two centuries. It is not possible for a member to represent constituents perfectly on every issue because there is no way of determining what constituents want on every topic. Constituents usually do not even know themselves what they want, nor do they often care about issues that do not affect their personal lives. On the other hand, in theory, complete independence for an MP would not be democratic in that the government would not be responsive to its citizens.

It appears that the best solution to this dilemma is to elect MPs wisely and then allow them to exercise their best judgment about what is needed as circumstances arise. Members of the House will listen to their constituents if they want to be re-elected, and voters will respect that their MPs should have some leeway because of party cohesion, personal values, and other circumstances. Members are not puppets but neither are they fully independent. Subjecting them to act according to public opinion polls or recall procedures would be cumbersome, expensive, and threatening to the democratic process.

Relations among Parties in Parliament

The parliamentary system enhances adversarial politics: It is the function of the opposition parties to criticize. This presents a challenge for the Official Opposition, which seeks to provide effective criticism but does not want to be perceived as mainly negative and lacking ideas. Other parties are too affected. The Bloc Québécois (BQ), for example, finds it particularly difficult to appear positive while putting forth its ideas for the secession of Québec from Canada.

The parliamentary system also creates a challenge for the government. It has to get bills passed, and yet it must allow the opposition time to criticize. To assist it, the parliamentary rules are loaded in the government's favour. Before the opening of

recall: A device to promote public participation by forcing a new election whereby constituents can recall an MP who does not vote or act as they want.

the thirty-fifth Parliament, it was popular for MPs to claim that the new Parliament would no longer engage in destructive bickering but would be a model of dignity and decorum with no "whimpering and snivelling" from the opposition.[6] Initially, this was true; then, fewer than nine weeks into the session, the rankerous atmosphere in the House resumed its usual pattern of insults and accusations. Such behaviour reached a crescendo during the Liberal minority government in 2005 and continued with the Conservative minority governments that followed.

The adversarial nature of the parliamentary system requires strong party cohesion in the House if there is to be representative and responsible government. The government needs unified support from its backbenchers to retain office and realize its policy goals. At the same time, opposition parties must be cohesive in order to mobilize all of their resources to criticize the government and portray themselves as viable alternatives.

Both government and opposition have developed ways to balance the adversarial nature of the parliamentary system and allow Parliament to work. Opposition members guard their right to criticize government policy, but they also recognize the government's responsibility to carry on the business of governing and sometimes even support it to that end. Similarly, the government must recognize the right of the opposition to criticize, without allowing it to obstruct. As we have seen, there are many *formal* provisions recognizing the right of opposition parties to oppose—through budget and Throne Speech debates and also Supply Days (in which the opposition parties may choose the topics for debate). There is *informal* co-operation between the two adversaries as well. The government House leader and party whips try to foster a spirit of cooperation by accommodating their counterparts' needs concerning the disposal of parliamentary time.

On occasion, however, cooperation breaks down, especially during minority governments when the opposition parties want to bring the government down, or during majority governments when the government attempts to ram through a bill with what the opposition regards as "unseemly haste" or is confronted with what it views as "obstruction" by the opposition. In a majority situation, the government always has the upper hand. It may resort to **closure** (Standing Order 57), a measure to terminate debate. Closure requires that all outstanding discussion and divisions on a particular stage of a bill must be completed within the next sitting day. A less harsh alternative to closure is **time allocation**, in which debate in the House is limited by a pre-arranged allocation of time for a particular bill or its various stages (Standing Order 78 (1, 2 and 3)). A balance of power is maintained between government and opposition by rules that become more complex procedurally as they require less interparty co-operation.[7]

Governments usually resort to closure and time allocation with the greatest reluctance because of procedural complexity and negative ramifications. The Progressive Conservatives (PCs) under Brian Mulroney and the Liberals under Jean Chrétien used this device with a reckless lack of concern for parliamentary traditions, but Stephen Harper surpassed both of them in its use.

In an adversarial parliamentary situation, a majority government has the advantage in that it controls the parliamentary timetable and access to departmental information as well as closure and time allocation. Still, the opposition also has ways to

closure: A measure to terminate debate in the House.

time allocation: A device to limit debate in the House.

combat what it sees as abuse of the parliamentary process. One of the most important avenues is the media. Television broadcasts of Question Period and major debates provide an audience for opposition criticism, and give opposition leaders and their "teams" countrywide exposure. They are able to criticize government policy and also present themselves as alternative leaders. Opposition parties also receive public funding for their caucus research groups, and to some extent this helps to make up for the government's monopoly of bureaucratic information.

In minority situations, governments lose the upper hand. Government leaders have to be more creative and resourceful to stay in power. During the minority Liberal government of 2004, the Conservatives and BQ battered the Liberals relentlessly in Question Period and in the media. When it came to the crucial May 2005 budget vote that could have brought down the government, however, Prime Minister Paul Martin managed to keep his Liberals in power by making a deal with Jack Layton, leader of the New Democratic Party (NDP), to rewrite the budget in exchange for the NDP's support. When the numbers to pass the budget were still lacking, the Liberals wooed Belinda Stronach, co-founder and former leadership candidate of the new Conservative Party, to cross the floor to join Martin and the Liberals just in time for the crucial budget vote. She immediately joined the Cabinet and became the lead minister on the Gomery Commission. The House was tied at 152 to 152. The speaker's vote broke the tie, and the Liberals clung to power, but the situation remained tenuous. The government could neither count on control of the House in the future nor be certain how the committees might act, since the opposition parties maintained a majority in them.

Minority governments are exciting; the government's tenure is perilous and the Official Opposition's ambition whetted. However, no other occasion in modern Canadian history has approached the shenanigans, procedural bickering, and outright horse-trading of the 2004–2005 minority situation. Major government bills were amended by the opposition; committees were often unable to function efficiently or effectively; and the three opposition parties adopted Machiavellian strategies and tactics, sometimes joining to defeat government proposals and sometimes dividing to prevent the defeat of the government and a new election. The 2006 minority Harper government promised parliamentary reform, and in 2007 the minister for democratic reform commissioned papers, public opinion surveys, and public consultations across the country on both House and Senate reform. The 2011 election of a Conservative majority reversed the situation to the extent that many Canadians believed that Prime Minister Harper was too powerful in controlling the House, but many commentators would have preferred more shenanigans. The 2015 election brought a new situation (see Figure 7.4).

THE SENATE

The Senate, or upper House of the Parliament of Canada, is housed in the east wing of the centre block of the Parliament buildings. As of early 2016, the Conservative party had 45 seats, Liberals 28, Independents 10, and Vacant 22.

Senators are appointed by the governor general on the advice of the prime minister. Since 1999, the membership of the Senate has been fixed at 105, representing seven areas of Canada, each according to a set number: Ontario (24), Québec (24), the three

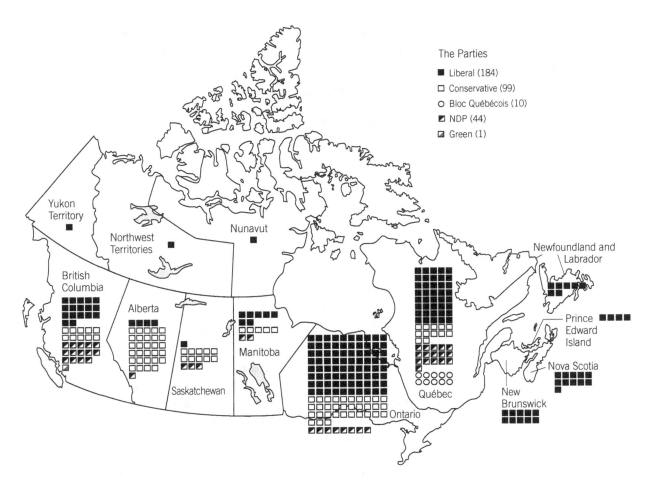

Figure 7.4 Seats by Province and Party Following the General Election, October 2015

Source: Elections Canada, www.elections.ca.

Maritime provinces (24—10 each from New Brunswick and Nova Scotia, 4 from Prince Edward Island), 6 each for the four western provinces (24), Newfoundland and Labrador (6), Yukon (1), Northwest Territories (1), and Nunavut (1). There is also a provision (Section 26 of the Constitution) allowing four or eight more members to be appointed when it becomes necessary to break a deadlock between the Senate and the House of Commons. Prime Minister Mulroney used this provision for the first and only time in Canadian history in 1990, adding eight additional senators and temporarily increasing their number to 112 in order to pass the goods and services tax (GST) legislation.

The prime minister and Cabinet are responsible to the House of Commons because it is the elected representative body. They are not responsible to the Senate, however. If a government were defeated in a vote in the House, it might have to resign or call an election. If a government bill were defeated in the Senate, the government could remain in power. The fact that it is an appointed rather than an elected body has other repercussions for the Senate. The Constitution awards the Senate almost equal power with the House of Commons, but in reality the upper House is relatively inconsequential. Only very rarely does it try to exercise any kind of control over the Commons. Because it is appointed, the Senate lacks the legitimacy that elections bestow, and over time it has become relatively insignificant in passing legislation.

The Functions of the Senate

The modern Canadian Senate fulfills many of the formal roles assigned to second chambers only imperfectly. It is neither a straightforward champion of a particular economic class nor a sanctuary for aging politicians, although it is often criticized along these lines, and is the constant focus of reform proposals.

The Senate performs several important functions:

- Senators can introduce legislation, except for bills dealing with the raising or spending of money, and they are required to vote on legislation which originates in the House of Commons.

- On occasions when the government of the day does not have sufficient elected representatives from a region, ministers may be named from the Senate to ensure regional or linguistic balance in Cabinet.[8]

- The Senate can delay the passage of constitutional amendments—even those that would abolish the Senate—for up to 180 days.

- As when it was established, the Senate still provides some protection for provincial rights—for example, it assures Québec a set number of senators even if the population of that province falls in relation to others. However, the Senate is not always a strong representative of provincial rights; provinces and regions depend mostly on Cabinet and provincial governments to stand up for their particular interests.

- Senators continue to be appointed along party lines and can be of service to the country. The Senate reviews all legislation that is passed in the House of Commons—providing "sober second thought" in order to refine the legislation and prevent errors. Because senators are appointed rather than elected and do not need party or electoral approval, they can criticize freely without the fear of electoral repercussions. Most of the review work occurs in committee deliberations and is arguably the Senate's most significant contribution.

  A major policy change occurred in 2014 when Justin Trudeau, leader of the Liberal Party, stopped Liberal Senators from attending the party's parliamentary caucus, declaring that they could not be organizers, fundraisers, or activists for Liberal election campaigns. They formed an independent Liberal Senate caucus instead. As the government, the Liberals will have to find new methods to control the Senate—perhaps even giving out new forms of patronage.

After legislation has received three readings in the House of Commons, it is referred to the Senate, where it goes through the same process again. Because the legislation has been debated and decided on by elected representatives in the House of Commons, senators normally approve bills that reach them, but they often refine the language and other details. To do more than that would raise comments about the propriety of an appointed body thwarting the will of elected representatives.[9]

On rare occasions, the Senate has rejected government legislation. For example, under Prime Minister Mulroney's tenure from 1984 to 1988, when there were more

Liberals than Conservatives in the Senate, there were many clashes between the two chambers. The Senate interfered with and delayed several bills. It tried to amend the Meech Lake Accord, unemployment insurance payments, and the GST. It even succeeded in rejecting an abortion bill after a free vote was called. While technically this was the first senatorial veto in three decades, it did not truly represent a rebellion against the government.

In the thirty-fifth Parliament, the PCs held a majority of seats in the Senate for a time even though they had only two MPs in the House. It was enough to delay the passage of Bill C-22, the cancellation of the Pearson Airport development legislation. In the thirty-sixth Parliament, the Liberals once more had a majority in the Senate and legislation passed smoothly.

The most important incidence of the Senate blocking the elected House occurred in 1988 when Liberal senators, at the request of John Turner, prevented the passage of free trade legislation. When the trade bill reached second reading in the Senate, Liberal senators abstained and allowed it to go to the foreign affairs committee. The Liberal-dominated committee deliberately provoked the PC government by setting up an extensive program of hearings. Because of this Senate obstruction, the government was forced to call a general election for November 20, 1988—an election for which the Senate had helped to set the date and the agenda.

The thirty-ninth Parliament provided the Liberal-dominated Senate with many more opportunities to defeat Conservative government legislation, but the senators did not do so for fear that it would provoke more proposals to reform or even abolish the upper House. Instead, the Liberal senators often delayed legislation or stalled it in committee before finally agreeing to pass it. By 2011, the Conservatives were in a much stronger position with a large majority of members in both the House and the Senate.

The Senators

The qualifications for senators have changed since Confederation in 1867. Initially, they were all males who held the position for life. Today they may be male or female, and those appointed after 1965 must retire by age 75. Other rules require senators to be Canadian citizens over 30 years of age, own at least $4000 in property, and be residents of the respective provinces they represent. No one can hold a seat in the Senate and the House of Commons at the same time. Many senators are politicians or party workers who have been rewarded with the political appointment for their partisan activities. Others are Canadians who have made an outstanding contribution in other ways.

Carine Wilson became the first woman senator in 1930 after the British Judicial Committee of the Privy Council ended a long constitutional wrangle by declaring that women were "persons" under the relevant sections of the *British North America Act*. Since then, appointments of women and leading figures from minority groups have increased, and in recent years about a third of senatorial positions have been filled by women.

In 2015, senators earned $142 400. Their perks included offices, secretarial help, mailing privileges, free telephone service, and so on. It is rare for a senator to be fired, but it is possible: if a senator fails to attend two consecutive sessions, loses

Canadian citizenship, ceases to meet the residence and property qualifications, is adjudged bankrupt, or is convicted of a criminal offence. In 1997, Senator Andrew Thompson was penalized by his peers in an unprecedented manner when he was suspended because of his poor attendance record, even though he had not violated any rules of the Senate or the Constitution. Major charges of senatorial corruption arose during the third Harper government, and penalties were levied.

Rules of the Senate

Like the lower House, the Senate is organized into government and opposition ranks, and although senators historically vote across party lines more than members of the House of Commons, they do vote with their parties on most occasions. The Senate is not, therefore, the independent and non-partisan counterweight to the Commons that its founders may have envisaged. Almost all senators have declared loyalties to a political party and highly political career backgrounds.

Many senators hold positions with private companies, are connected to other people who have holdings in corporations, or are connected with law firms that represent clients who do business with the government. For this reason, they have been called the "lobby from within" and have reaped considerable public condemnation for informal conflicts of interest. This is an ongoing problem because the guidelines to regulate senators' behaviour are inadequate (see Chapter 13).

Organization and Officers of the Senate

The Senate has two senior officers: the government leader and the speaker. Historically, the government Senate leader was appointed by the prime minister to represent and speak for senators in Cabinet and, conversely, to be the voice of the Cabinet in the Senate. Only rarely have there been senators in Cabinet other than the government leader. In 2013, Prime Minister Harper declined to appoint the new government leader in the Senate to a position in Cabinet, breaking a long tradition linking the Senate to the government. The speaker of the Senate, unlike the elected House speaker, is appointed by the governor general on the recommendation of the prime minister for the term of the Parliament. The duties of this position are similar to those of the speaker of the House of Commons.

Senate Reform

Triple-E Senate: A proposal that the Senate be elected, effective, and equal in its representation of all provinces.

Because of perceived problems of legitimacy and the relative failure of the Senate to represent provincial interests in Parliament, there have been many proposals over the years to reform and even abolish it. Indeed, calls for Senate reform have been made since at least 1893. A hundred years later, in the 1990s, a Western initiative for a new **Triple-E Senate** called for the Senate to be *elected*, *effective*, and *equal* in its representation of all provinces. The smaller provinces, of course, supported the idea of having an equal number of senators from each province, regardless of size or population base. Larger provinces, on the other hand, tended to support the idea of a "Double-E" Senate—one that would be elected and effective in its functioning but whose membership would continue to be based on some principle of representation by population. Detailed proposals to create a modified Triple-E Senate were embodied in the Charlottetown Accord in 1992, but it was soundly defeated (see Chapter 3).

Until an accepted constitutional amendment reform can be achieved, the Senate will maintain its role as a usually co-operative but sometimes cantankerous part of the legislative process. The problem for the Senate is simple—if it does little, it is accused of being a "rubber stamp," but if it acts decisively, it is reprimanded for blocking "the will of the people."

These days, abolishing the Senate or instituting other far-reaching reforms is almost impossible; instead, initiatives should be concentrated on creating an institution that is valued for its symbolic contribution to Canadian unity and the federal system and for the minor but important role it plays in the legislative process. It is time to settle for reforming the Senate *within* the existing Constitution.

Senate Reform Proposals on Consultations and Tenure Early in its mandate, the Harper minority government announced that it was "pursuing comprehensive Senate reform" and that, "pending the pursuit of a constitutional amendment under subsection 38(1) of the *Constitution Act, 1982*, for direct election to the Senate," it wanted to create a method to ascertain the preferences of electors for Senate appointments and to reduce the tenure of senators. In other words, frustration with the rigidity of the Constitution led the Conservative government to propose legislation—Bill C-43—that would have allowed the voters of each province to be consulted with respect to their preferences for Senate appointments at the time of a general election. The bill also specified the mechanism and method of voting and the system of counting votes in these public consultations.

A second bill would have limited the tenure of new senators to eight years. There was some dispute among scholars over the constitutionality of this proposed legislation. The majority of members of the Special Senate Committee on Senate Reform concluded that Parliament could "proceed to amend the *Constitution Act, 1867*, acting under the authority of Section 44 of the *Constitution Act, 1982*, without resorting to the complex amending formula in Section 38(1) of the Act." Presumably, they thought that since prime ministers may consult or take advice from whomever they wish before making any appointment to the Senate, this would have been a reasonable constitutional change.

The Constitution says only that the governor general will summon to the Senate those named by the prime minister, subject to minor qualifications (Section 24). The constitutional issues concern whether the Supreme Court can, or should, have a say about this consultative process. A 1980 judgment by the Supreme Court had ruled that alterations to the Senate that would affect the "fundamental features, or essential characteristics" given to the Senate as a means of ensuring regional and provincial representation in the federal legislative process could not be made by Parliament alone. However, this case did not provide a proper precedent as it was bypassed by the constitutional patriation of 1982.

Would these two reform bills have met the major objectives for reform of the Senate? On the whole, they appeared to meet the criterion for increased legitimacy, as they would have increased democratic participation and accountability. Legislative effectiveness, on the other hand, would have remained undiminished, but one could

Responding to criticisms of senators in the Auditor General's Report.

argue that the more legitimate senators become, the more weight they would have in the legislative process. As the number of senators for each province could not be adjusted, the criterion of enhancing regional and provincial influence would not be met, however. There are arguments for reassigning the number of senators inside the federation generally, but the process still would require a constitutional amendment. At a minimum, the current regional representation would not have been weakened by this formula.

These piecemeal reforms might have moved the country further along the road to democratic reform. Canada does, after all, have a reputation as the only major federal system in the world with a wholly appointed upper House with no public consultation in the selection of its members. The major drawback of Bills C-43 and S-4 was that they were ordinary legislation (i.e., not "constitutionalized") and therefore could easily have been amended or repealed in the future. At any rate, both bills simply died on the order paper and eventually the government decided to send its Senate reform ideas to the Supreme Court to test their legality.

Reform issues arose again in 2013 when questions of corruption and illegal behaviour erupted in the Senate. Three Conservative Senators—Patrick Brazeau,

Mike Duffy, and Pamela Wallin—and one Liberal, Mac Harb, were accused of various expenses scandals. Meanwhile, the Auditor General investigated the expenses of all senators and came to some strong accusatory conclusions. The dates of the cases encouraged the government to do two things: send its ideas about senatorial reform to the Supreme Court (allowing the justices to sort out the contradictions) and hold the general election on its normal date on October 19, 2015. These cases are discussed in Chapter 13 on ethics.

The Senate and the Supreme Court Reference Case, 2014

After attempting both procedural and political approaches to Senate reform, the Harper government finally decided to ask the Supreme Court for its opinion on the constitutionality of several reform proposals. Under Section 53 of the *Supreme Court Act*, the government asked for a judgment on the following questions:

1. Is it within the legislative authority of Parliament acting under Section 44 of the *Constitution Act, 1982* to make amendments to Section 29 of the *Constitution Act, 1867* providing for term limits on senators' tenure?

2. Is it within the legislative authority of Parliament acting under Section 91 of the *Constitution Act, 1867* or Section 44 of the *Constitution Act, 1982* to enact legislation that provides a means of consulting people about their preferences for potential nominees for appointment to the Senate?

3. Is it within the legislative authority of Parliament acting under Section 91 of the *Constitution Act, 1867* or Section 44 of the *Constitution Act, 1982* to allow provinces to find a means of consulting people about their preferences for potential nominees for the appointment to the Senate?

4. Is it within the legislative authority of the Parliament acting under Section 44 of the *Constitution Act, 1982* to repeal the property qualifications for senators?

5. Can an amendment to the Constitution to abolish the Senate be accomplished using the general amending procedure of Section 38 of the *Constitution Act, 1982* by:

   a) Simply abolishing the Senate.

   b) Amending or appealing all references to the Senate in the Constitution.

   c) Abolishing all Senate powers and eliminating the representation of the provinces.

The eight acting justices unanimously ruled in April 2014 that none of Harper's proposals met the constitutional test. None could be implemented unilaterally by Parliament. Changing senatorial terms would require the agreement of at least seven provinces and 50 percent of the population, as would both types of consultation mechanisms. The property qualifications would require the agreement of each pertinent province. And last but not least, abolition of the Senate itself would require the consent of all 10 provinces and, of course, the Parliament of Canada.

Prime Minister Harper declared Senate reform dead. He would not attempt to convince provincial premiers of the validity of his cause and would no longer campaign on the issue. He also left 22 vacancies in the Senate. In January 2014, the Liberals under Justin Trudeau made a half-hearted reform advance by kicking their senators out of the official Liberal caucus.

After the 2015 election, Prime Minister Trudeau promised that there would be a new process for selecting senators. According to the plan, a non-partisan panel of distinguished Canadians would be appointed. This panel would confer with a similar provincial panel. These two groups would send a shortlist of possible senators to the prime minister who would make the final selection, and the new senators would sit as Independents in the upper chamber. NDP leader Tom Mulcair said that, he would continue to campaign vigorously for the abolition of the Senate. This remains an unresolved, contentious issue in Canadian politics.

Discussion Questions

1. Is Question Period a noisy, undisciplined waste of time? Simulate a Question Period, formulating questions and answers.

2. Is the procedure of passing a bill into law too time consuming and cumbersome? Why or why not?

3. Should there be strict party discipline or should MPs be allowed to vote as they wish?

4. Has Prime Minister Stephen Harper "weakened" the role of backbenchers and "muzzled" parliamentary journalists?

5. Should the Senate be abolished or reformed? Given what you have learned about how to achieve a constitutional amendment, do you think that major changes to the Senate are likely to be achieved? Have recent proposals adequately addressed this issue?

Chapter 8

Public Administration

Democracy, Bureaucracy, and Public Policy

Learning Objectives

After reading this chapter, you should be able to

1   Name the basic organizations found in the Canadian federal bureaucracy, describe their basic structures, and explain what they do.

2   Describe how the public service has changed over time in terms of size, recruitment, and composition.

3   Draw three important distinctions between the political role of the executive and the administrative functions of public servants.

4   Describe the process of drawing up a government budget, including both the expenditure and the revenue processes.

5   Name and evaluate three important ways in which politicians keep the power of unelected civil servants in check.

All modern states possess an extensive public administration, using civilians, soldiers, police, and prison guards to uphold the interests of the state. Public administrators are, if you wish, the groundskeepers and Zamboni drivers for the political players! They collect taxes, inspect agricultural products, and provide health care and police services, to name just a few of their contributions.

As the modern state developed, its activities became extensive in scope, complex in organization, and expensive to run. It took on new functions and responsibilities, including economic tasks previously associated with the private sector. The shift in government responsibilities was particularly evident in liberal democracies after the two world wars. This chapter examines the structures and employees of the bureaucracy and assesses what it accomplishes.

ADMINISTRATION, BUREAUCRACY, AND BUREAUCRATS

As the modern state expanded, it adopted a specific form of government administration often known as *bureaucracy*. The term *bureaucracy* originated as a satirical combination of the French word *bureau* ("desk") and the Greek word *kratein* ("to rule"). In 1745, a French physiocrat first used the term *bureaucracy* to describe the

bureaucracy: Refers to a form of government organization based on the premise that it should be structured to provide as much efficiency as possible and that this is best achieved through a hierarchically structured decision-making process that minimizes arbitrary decision making.

eighteenth-century Prussian system of administration, but in its more modern meaning **bureaucracy** refers to a form of government organization based on the premise that government should be as efficient as possible, and that this is best achieved through a hierarchically structured decision-making process that minimizes arbitrary decision making.

The term *bureaucracy* is often used negatively, associated with inefficiency, red tape, and even lazy, overpaid employees. Much of this criticism is explained by the fact that it is easy to blame a large, faceless organization. In the technical sense, bureaucracy has nothing to do with such negative values. Rather, it refers to a hierarchically organized institution that divides work so as to allow the orders of superiors to be communicated effectively to subordinates. Even in this neutral sense, however, a bureaucracy can be criticized, particularly for not being flexible enough to handle the administrative requirements of a complex, modern society.

public servants (bureaucrats): Tenured state officials involved in advising government ministers and implementing policies.

In Canada, the Constitution makes the elected executive of the federal government responsible for formulating policies. However, politicians and ministers come and go, while administrators remain to carry out the goals and purposes of their political masters. **Public servants** (or **bureaucrats**) are tenured state officials involved in advising government ministers and implementing policies. Fifty years ago they were a highly respected, elite group who saw public service as a duty and a privilege. Today, there has been a public backlash against bureaucracy and public servants, which goes along with cynicism about politicians and diminished expectations about what governments can do. However, Canadians are generally better served by their public service than they realize.

Bureaucracy and Democracy

The emergence of democratic forms of government forced the development of many specific characteristics of the modern bureaucracy. As the idea of alternation of power between competing parties became accepted as an important component of British parliamentary democracy, it became necessary to separate the bureaucracy from the political executive. The bureaucracy was freed to exercise rational administration without needless political influence, and individual public servants became protected from arbitrary dismissal on political grounds, as long as they maintained partisan neutrality.

Liberal democracy also brought demands for the substitution of *merit* for patronage in the recruitment and promotion of public servants. Appointments to administrative office traditionally had been made on the basis of family and "old school" networks, or as a reward for political services rendered. The democratization of the public service brought a merit system involving open competition.

Thus, a neutral, professional public service based on the organizational principles of modern bureaucracy emerged alongside, and partly as a consequence of, the development of liberal democracy. Yet a fundamental contradiction exists in the coexistence of bureaucracy and democracy. While easy in theory, it is difficult in practice to separate the political and administrative dimensions of government action. The bureaucracy may not be overtly political, but bureaucrats do influence the formation of public policy in a number of ways, therefore usurping some of the power of their political masters.

For example, Cabinet ministers rarely hold their positions long enough to acquire a high degree of expertise in the affairs of their respective ministries. Governments often change hands at general elections, and periodic Cabinet shuffles move ministers from department to department. Each time a minister is put in charge of a new department, it takes a while to learn a new policy field. Since the average departmental tenure of Canadian Cabinet ministers has been short, they tend to spend considerable time in office simply learning the workings of their departments.

During minority governments, Cabinet ministers are required to share policymaking with leaders of opposition parties and thus find it more difficult than usual to provide coherent advice to the public service about the direction in which they wish to take the country.

In contrast, the relative permanence of public servants allows them to develop expertise and practical knowledge on which politicians can draw. Consequently, if, as Max Weber maintained, "knowledge is power,"[1] then the bureaucracy in a complex, technical society may have a great deal of political power. It can screen the data made available to its political masters and influence the direction of government policy.

The relative security and access to information enjoyed by bureaucrats may influence the policy process in a number of other ways as well. Bureaucratic tenure permits public servants to develop a relatively long-term view of policy formulation compared to politicians, who must remain more responsive to short-term shifts in public opinion. Administrative personnel who have close links with interest groups may also be in a better position than politicians to identify public demands and how to cope with them.

Furthermore, the bureaucracy sometimes acts as an "interest group" in its own right. Policy proposals generated within the bureaucracy may influence the government's choice among competing alternatives. Here again, bureaucrats may be in a better position than politicians to recommend fine-tuning or wholesale changes in existing policies. Finally, even after the government has made a political choice, a high degree of discretion has to be left to public servants with regard to policy implementation.

Public servants, then, are linked to politicians through their mutual concern for making public policies. "Policies" are categorized in at least three different ways, as (1) the intentions of politicians; (2) the actions of governments; and (3) the impact of government on individuals and society. In other words, **policy** is the broad framework within which decisions are taken and action (or inaction) is pursued by governments.[2]

policy: The broad framework within which decisions are taken and action (or inaction) is pursued by governments.

Developing public policies involves a complex process of interaction between politicians and public servants. However, in general terms, these policies emerge from the impact of historical, geographical, and socio-economic conditions on mass political behaviour, elite behaviour, and governmental institutions. Canada witnessed an enormous growth in policy activity after World War I and II as governments defined the country's problems, outlined the goals to be achieved, and chose the means of solving the problems. It has grown ever since.

STRUCTURES OF FEDERAL BUREAUCRACY

Canadians frequently come into contact with some structures within the federal bureaucracy—*government departments* and *Crown corporations*. Few citizens escape encounters— some pleasant, others less so—with institutions such as the Canada Revenue Agency, which collects taxes and customs duties. Most Canadians have contact with Crown corporations every day—for example, when they watch CBC Television or listen to CBC Radio. However, government departments and Crown corporations that interact directly with the public are merely the most visible tip of the administrative iceberg.

It is possible to classify *central agencies* as a third type of bureaucratic structure. (Recall that we discussed central agencies in Chapter 6, along with the political executive of Canada.) With the exception of the Prime Minister's Office (PMO), these agencies are staffed almost exclusively by career public servants appointed under the aegis of the Public Service Commission of Canada. They are all formally headed by a Cabinet minister and in all structural and legal respects closely resemble the standard departmental form of organization. For the purposes of this discussion, however, central agencies are viewed as a unique subcategory of government departments.

Federal Government Departments

government department: An administrative unit of government that is headed by a Cabinet minister and largely responsible for the administration of a range of programs serving the public.

deputy minister (DM): The administrative and managerial head of each department or ministry—its senior public servant.

assistant deputy minister (ADM): One of two or more individuals who heads a branch or bureau and reports directly to the deputy minister (DM).

Government departments are administrative units of a government, each of which is headed by a Cabinet minister, and they are largely responsible for the administration of a range of programs serving the public (see Close-Up 8.1). While the minister is politically responsible for the activities of the department and for formulating general policy, the administrative and managerial head of each department or ministry is the **deputy minister (DM)**—its senior public servant.[3] Departments, on the whole, obtain their funding through the standard appropriation acts of Parliament.

The deputy minister is at the apex of a pyramidal structure of authority and organizational agencies. Two or more **assistant deputy ministers (ADMs)**, heading branches or bureaus, report directly to the DM. Below the ADMs are directorates or branches, each run by a director general or director. These directorates are composed of divisions, headed by directors or divisional chiefs; the divisions are further broken down into sections, offices, and units. The number of senior officials, and the range of subunits and employees for which they are responsible, differ according to the type of department. The exact titles of departmental subunits and their respective senior officials vary from department to department.

Close-Up 8.1

Departmental Names Reflect Values and Biases

The names of federal departments often reflect the values and biases of the government. This is particularly evident in the department dealing with immigration. Since Confederation, it has been called:

- Canadian Immigration and Quarantine Services (1867–92)
- Immigration Branch, Department of the Interior (1892–1917)
- Department of Immigration and Colonization (1917–36)
- Immigration Branch, Department of Mines and Resources (1936–50)

- Department of Citizenship and Immigration (1950–66)
- Department of Manpower and Immigration (1966–77)
- Canada Employment and Immigration Commission (1977–93)
- Immigration divided between Department of Public Security and Department of Human Resources (1993)
- Department of Citizenship and Immigration (1993 to 2015)
- Immigration, Refugees and Citizenship (2015–)

Each new government may change the organization of departments, but this requires legislation and may be slow to develop. After the terrorist attacks in the United States on September 11, 2001, a new Department of Public Safety and Emergency Preparedness was created, which gave the new minister wider control than the former solicitor general had possessed. The department, now called Public Safety, currently includes the Royal Canadian Mounted Police (RCMP), the Canadian Security Intelligence Service (CSIS), Correctional Service Canada, Parole Board of Canada, and Canada Border Services Agency.

The Department of Foreign Affairs and International Trade (DFAIT) was split into two departments—Foreign Affairs and International Trade—and then recombined again as Foreign Affairs and Trade, and recently became Foreign Affairs, Trade and Development (DFATD). In 2015 its name changed to Global Affairs, but the new minister, Stephane Dion, kept his title as minister of foreign affairs. Other examples include Aboriginal Affairs and Northern Development which became Indigenous and Northern Affairs after the election of the new government in 2015 (see Table 8.1).

Table 8.1 Departmental and Central Agency Structure of the Public Service, 2015

Departments

Agriculture and Agri-Food

Canadian Heritage

Environment and Climate Change

Finance

Fisheries and Oceans

Global Affairs

Health

Human Resources and Skills Development

Immigration Refugees and Citizenship

Indigenous and Northern Affairs

Innovation, Science, and Economic Development

Justice

National Defence

Natural Resources

Public Safety

Public Services and Procurement

Transport

Veterans Affairs

Central Agencies

Finance

Prime Minister's Office

Privy Council Office

Treasury Board Secretariat

Government Agencies

The second organizational form in the federal bureaucracy is the agency. **Agencies** include a wide variety of types of organizations that are non-departmental in structure, including Crown corporations, regulatory agencies, administrative tribunals, and advisory bodies. Advisory bodies are primarily involved in the process of policy formulation, while Crown corporations are structured like private corporations and are charged directly with attaining government policy objectives—through public ownership, regulation of the private sector, and so on.

Depending on the definition employed, there are approximately 400 federal agencies. A number of characteristics distinguish agencies from government departments. Agencies are not directly responsible *to* a minister but usually report to Parliament *through* a designated minister. The degree of supervision and accountability of agencies varies, but is much less than with departments. The Public Service Commission, Treasury Board, and departments set the rules and recruit the personnel of departments, but not of agencies. Departments have deputy ministers as administrative heads, while agencies vary widely in the nature of their management. They usually have boards of directors, led by chairs, commissioners, or directors.

Crown Corporations A **Crown corporation** is a semi-autonomous agency of government organized in a corporate form to perform a task or group of related tasks in the national interest. They operate at "arm's length" from the government.

The variety of Crown corporations is immense. The Bank of Canada regulates the money supply, the Royal Canadian Mint prints money, and Canada Mortgage and Housing Corporation guarantees housing loans. The best-known transportation corporation is Via Rail. Atomic Energy of Canada, Business Development Bank of Canada, Export Development Canada, and Farm Credit Canada are among those that foster economic development. Canada Post and the CBC aid national integration.

In recent years, the government has privatized many Crown corporations. Corporations that could operate in a purely competitive business environment were the first to go. Among those no longer with the government are the well-known Air Canada, Canada Ports Corporation, Eldorado Nuclear, Northern Transportation Company, Polymer Corporation, Teleglobe Canada and Petro-Canada. Public ownership is criticized by neo-conservatives, who view any government intervention as an infringement on the free market economy. Thus, while it is improbable that privatization will be carried as far as it is in some countries, it seems certain that new forms of public ownership will be much less common in the future.

Regulatory Agencies Agencies also include regulatory organizations. **Regulation** is making government rules that are intended to change the economic behaviour of individuals in the private sector. Among other functions, regulatory agencies may be required to influence private or corporate behaviour with respect to prices and tariffs, supply, market entry and conditions of service, product content, and methods of production. Furthermore, some agencies have quasi-legislative powers that permit them to formulate general rules; an example is Canadian-content regulations applied by the Canadian Radio-television and Telecommunications Commission (CRTC). Most agencies also enjoy investigative powers, allowing them to undertake research and pursue inquiries within their field of competence.

Members of independent regulatory agencies are appointed by the Governor-in-Council, usually for terms of 5 to 10 years. On the whole, they are patronage appointments. Most agencies are subject to ministerial directives, but ministers usually are unwilling to infringe on the traditional arm's-length relationship. Regulatory bodies are required to submit their budgets to the Treasury Board for review (and usually, also, to the auditor general) and to present annual reports to Parliament.

Advisory Bodies Federal departments and some agencies are designed to deal primarily with the implementation and administration of government policies. **Advisory bodies** are agencies whose activities are closely related to the formulation of public policies. Advisory bodies include Royal Commissions, government and departmental task forces, and advisory councils.[4]

advisory bodies: Federal organizations whose activities are closely related to the formulation of public policies. They include Royal Commissions, government and departmental task forces, and advisory councils.

Royal Commissions and task forces are set up by the executive for public policy advice. They are generally mandated by the government to investigate an area of critical public concern and recommend a suitable course of action. Typical issues have included the economy (the Macdonald Royal Commission on the Economic Union and Development Prospects for Canada), cultural policy (the Applebaum-Hébert Federal Cultural Policy Review Committee), Aboriginal peoples (the Royal Commission on Aboriginal Issues), human reproduction (the Royal Commission on New Reproductive Technologies), and health care (Commission on the Future of Health Care in Canada). More politically contentious have been commissions of enquiry into topics such as the Sponsorship Program (Gomery) and the attack on Air India Flight 182.

Royal Commissions: Widely employed as sources of public policy advice to the executive. They are generally set up by the government to investigate an area of critical public concern and to recommend suitable courses of action.

These temporary bodies inform the public about serious national problems and at the same time provide an informed basis for future policy-making by the government. They generally solicit outside views through public hearings at which individuals, groups, and organizations are invited to submit briefs. They also initiate programs of directed and commissioned research. Most of the time they have no direct policy impact, although they may contribute to the debate of issues.

PUBLIC SERVANTS AND POLICY-MAKING

Although both politicians and public servants are engaged in making policies, three important distinctions can be drawn between the political role of the executive and the administrative functions of public servants in this process.

First, the members of the political executive are partisan, while the public service is neutral. Second is the difference of tenure: on the whole, political leaders come and go while public servants enjoy relatively permanent positions. Third, public servants are supposed to administer the policies of government, while the political executives make them.

In theory, therefore, public servants make the plans of politicians feasible. In reality, however, the roles of politicians and public servants are considerably blurred. The idea that public servants only *administer* the policies set by politicians is severely disputed. Few scholars today would agree that executive, legislative, and judicial functions can be neatly assigned to a particular structure of government—let alone that civil servants are limited to implementing the laws. The public service is involved in many forms of government activity, since it is part of the consultation, deliberation, legislative, and administrative processes.

What control does Cabinet have over the administrative process to ensure that policies, once made, are actually implemented? The major principle of government organization in Canada—and the primary link between the bureaucracy and Parliament—is the doctrine of individual **ministerial responsibility**.

Civil servants are supposed to be non-partisan, objective, and anonymous, shielded from the glare of public attention and from the partisan political arena by their minister, in order to safeguard their neutrality and ensure their ability to serve whichever government is in power. In the event of a serious error in the formulation or administration of policy within a department, therefore, convention dictates that the minister, rather than the officials, be held responsible. If the minister cannot account to the satisfaction of Parliament, convention dictates that the minister should resign.

However, there are severe limitations to this doctrine of individual ministerial responsibility (as we saw in Chapter 6).[5] The sole responsibility of ministers for the operations of their departments is often sacrificed in favour of another principle, the *collective* responsibility of the Cabinet to Parliament. As long as a minister retains the confidence and support of the prime minister, resignation is extremely unlikely (unless political expediency interferes). As well, ministers are not held responsible for administrative matters occurring *before* their current appointments. Thus, when questions are raised in the House, a new minister is able to hide behind this convention, saying that the events took place *prior* to his or her appointment.

Perhaps it is reasonable that ministers should not be held responsible to the point of resignation for the administrative errors of public servants. The relative impermanence of Cabinet ministers and their multi-functional roles make it impossible for them to be involved extensively in their departments. Ministers are expected to focus primarily on policy matters. For this reason, one observer argues, it is "unrealistic to expect a minister to accept personal responsibility for all the acts of his departmental officials. Why should a minister 'carry the can' when he has little or no knowledge of its contents?"[6]

The role of the deputy minister is crucial to effective administration and the coordination and direction of policy implementation. Certain financial and managerial responsibilities of the DM are laid down by the *Financial Administration Act* and the *Public Service Employment Act*, or are delegated to the DM by the Treasury Board and the Public Service Commission. Otherwise, the DM possesses only whatever power the minister chooses to delegate, and that is a personal decision.

The main function of the DM, apart from managing the department, is to act as the minister's chief source of non-partisan advice on public policy. The problem for the DM is how to initiate policy proposals and studies without appearing to undermine the ultimate policy-making responsibility of the minister.

Deputy ministers are appointed by the Governor-in-Council on the recommendation of the prime minister. Their office is held "during pleasure," which means that they can be dismissed or transferred at any time without assigned cause, and they are not protected by the provisions of the *Public Service Employment Act*. This insecurity of tenure naturally creates further ambiguity about the DM's role. Deputies who advise against ministerial decisions risk being dismissed. However, if they become identified with programs that are unpopular with the opposition, they risk losing their jobs when the government changes hands.

In spite of these insecurities, the political neutrality and relative permanence of senior public servants is a safeguard against political patronage and partisan bureaucracy and a source of continuity in administration.

THE PUBLIC SERVICE

While the word *bureaucracy* refers to the structures and principles of organization in the administrative arm of government, **public service** is the collective term in Canada for the personnel employed in those structures. Like other political institutions, the public service of Canada has undergone many profound changes. It has evolved from a loosely organized, patronage-based service, where most people were recruited on the basis of political connections, into a modern, professionalized bureaucracy appointed on the principle of merit. It has changed from a predominantly anglophone and almost exclusively male preserve into an equal opportunity employer that reflects Canada's ethnic and linguistic diversity, and has introduced effective affirmative action programs designed to promote the participation of women, visible minorities, persons with disabilities, and Native peoples.

public service: The collective term in Canada for the personnel employed in the administrative arm of government.

The hierarchical system fosters a definitive chain of responsibility. Within each department, a descending order of command is evident. This chain of command, which ultimately begins with a government minister, protects against the arbitrary assumption of power by individuals within the bureaucracy. Bureaucratic "red tape" in the guise of standard forms and triplicate copies is, in fact, a necessary part of the process of horizontal and vertical communication among employees and departments. Given the immense number of people involved and the diversity of their duties, it is easy to appreciate why the bureaucracy's primary goal of efficiency is sometimes difficult to achieve.

Who Works in the Public Service?

The federal government is a major employer. Its public servants provide myriad public services such as collecting taxes, delivering the mail, and issuing passports. Approximately one out of every four Canadian workers is paid in the public sector, including federal, provincial, and local governments. Despite Prime Minister Stephen Harper's effort to reduce the size of the bureaucracy, in 2013 the federal government employed approximately 400 000 people spread throughout the country in the public service, military, corporations, agencies, enterprises, and RCMP.[7] Of these employees, more than half were under the auspices of the Treasury Board (263 000 in 2013) and the remainder work for separate government agencies, National Defence, the RCMP, and smaller government entities.

Entrance into the public service carries no restrictions by age, race, sex, religion, colour, national or ethnic origin, marital status, or disability. Recruitment is carried out across the country on the basis of merit. Entrance exams determine the applicant's capabilities and job placement. Recruitment programs are sponsored by the Public Service Commission (PSC). The *Public Service Reform Act, 1992* confirmed that the PSC is to continue basing its employment practices on merit.

To a large extent, however, the bureaucracy is expected to be representative of the society it serves. Over the past four decades, there has been an increased sensitivity to the under-representation of francophones, women, Aboriginal peoples, people with disabilities, and other historically disadvantaged groups in the bureaucracy. At the same time, accessible university education has helped to enhance opportunities in the civil service for individuals from middle- and lower-class backgrounds. In 2013, the public service included 55 percent women (45 percent of the executive class), with about 71 percent claiming English as their first official language and 29 percent claiming French. Over the past 30 years the number of women in the public service has grown by more than 11 percent.

In 1989, the government set up *Public Service 2000* in an attempt to reorganize the public service to make it more service oriented and reduce morale problems caused by fiscal restraint. This new set of proposals to streamline public service practices was incorporated into 1992's *Public Service Reform Act*, which constituted the first major amendments to staffing legislation in 25 years. It provided for more flexible staffing arrangements and mandated the PSC to initiate employment equity programs while retaining the merit principle.

The reform of human resources management in the public service continued with the *Public Service Modernization Act*, passed in November 2003. This Act, fully in place by 2005, left the PSC as guardian of the merit principle, but allowed much more delegation of hiring to deputy heads. In theory, this increased the ability of departments and agencies to hire the right people but still keep the merit principle in place. The Public Service Agency is the lead agency in human resources, which administers training, language education, and the new Canada School of Public Service.

BUDGETS, DEFICITS, AND DEBTS

In recent years, there has been considerable debate about the dire state of the federal government's finances. The Canadian government spends a large amount of taxpayers' money. Projections for 2015–16 show that the government raised $290 billion in revenue but had $263 billion in program expenditures and paid $26 billion in debt-servicing charges on its $692 billion debt. As a percentage of gross domestic product (GDP), interest payments on the public debt now consume 1.3 percent. The 2015 Conservative government took a novel approach to the national debt. Joe Oliver, the minister of finance, claimed that the annual budget now showed a surplus of $1.4 billion—a major success for his party—but this figure quickly became controversial.

budget: A document that primarily sets out the revenue and expenditures required to carry out the government's program.

expenditure process: Brings together the estimated spending requirements of all government departments and agencies for the next fiscal year.

revenue process: Concerns the means by which funds are to be raised—by taxation and other measures.

The **budget**, or management of the overall revenue and expenditures of the government on an annual basis, entails two separate processes. The first, the **expenditure process**, brings together the estimated spending requirements of all government departments and agencies for the next fiscal year (see Close-Up 8.2). It takes place under the watchful eye of the Treasury Board, a Cabinet committee, and its secretariat. These estimates are subsequently submitted to Parliament and its committees for scrutiny and approval via supply (appropriations) bills (which grant the government permission to spend or disburse public funds).

The second process, the **revenue process**, concerns how funds are to be raised—by taxation and other measures. It is largely the responsibility of the Department of

Key Financial Terms

Deficit: The annual amount by which government spending exceeds revenues.

Surplus: The annual amount by which government revenues exceed spending.

Debt: The accumulation of annual deficits less surpluses since Confederation.

Finance and Canada Revenue Agency. Its parliamentary focal point is the Budget Speech delivered by the minister of finance.

The Canadian budget does not contain all of the detailed proposals for spending—these estimates are tabled separately. This runs contrary to the budgetary practices of some political systems (which are not British parliamentary in origin) and to those of private businesses, where budgets present detailed targets for both spending and revenues. The budget and its proposals are released only after lengthy preparation. Preliminary discussions are held in the Department of Finance to fix an approximate level of expenditures for the fiscal year and an estimate of revenues expected from existing taxes. From these two estimates—expenditure and revenue—emerges a surplus or a deficit (see Table 8.2).

Essentially, governments have four strategies for cutting deficits and reducing debts: decreasing expenditures, increasing taxes, reducing interest rates (in order to reduce payments on the public debt), and increasing productivity. Since ministers have little control in the latter two areas due to Canada's dependence on foreign capital and the country's position in the global economy, the choice is normally between cutting expenditures and raising taxes.

Table 8.2 Federal Government Budgets for 2015–2017 in Billions of Dollars

	2015–16	2016-17
Revenue Outlook (where government money comes from)		
Total budgeting revenues in billions of dollars	290.3	302.4
Expenditure Outlook (where government money is spent)		
Program spending	263.2	274.3
Public debt charges	25.7	26.4
Total expenses	288.9	300.7
Projected Surplus	1.4	1.7
Net public debt	692.0	693.4
Net public debt as percent of GDP	30.8	29.3

Note: Totals may differ due to rounding.

Source: Adapted from general tables in *Budget Plan, 2015* (Ottawa, 2015).

The minister of finance receives an analysis of the economic situation and outlook from departmental officials. These are supplemented by information from the governor of the Bank of Canada on general economic conditions, the climate in the money markets, monetary policy, and the market's capacity to absorb government bonds. Analysis of this information indicates what the appropriate budget surplus or deficit could be and, if necessary, the size of deficit to be financed. This helps the government to formulate overall fiscal strategy.

Departmental officials advise the minister of tax loopholes that could be closed, possible tax reform proposals, and changes that might be made in customs and tariffs. From these discussions, a pattern of taxation policy emerges. The costs of tax reduction and the revenues from projected tax raises are calculated and compared with the estimates and the desired fiscal stance. When the appropriate balance is achieved, the road is then clear to begin drafting the Budget Speech. Historically, finance ministers have presented the budget at the last possible moment before budget day, but in recent years, there has been a tendency to undertake more lengthy consultation both outside and inside Cabinet. Since 1994, the finance minister has held pre-budget conferences across the country, and the Commons finance committee has also toured the country and reported to the minister before the budget is delivered.

The address and the debate are regulated by the Standing Orders of the House of Commons. The Budget Speech is often delivered in the evening, after the markets have closed. The speech reviews the fiscal plan, the state of the national economy, and the financial operations of the government over the past fiscal year. It also provides a forecast of spending requirements for the year ahead, taking into account the estimates. At the end of the Budget Speech, the minister tables the "ways and

Gary Clement/National Post

Election budgets are traditionally full of gifts; the 2015 budget increased benefits for children.

means" motions (the ways and means of raising money), which become the taxation or excise legislation.

Budget making is particularly difficult in minority governments. Both Paul Martin and Stephen Harper had to make budgetary compromises with opposition parties. These compromises were lauded by those who approved the bargaining skill of opposition parties such as the New Democratic Party (NDP), but were highly criticized by those who believed that the government budget should be sacrosanct and not be subject to partisan pressures in the House of Commons.

DEMOCRATIC CONTROL OF THE BUREAUCRACY

Bureaucracy, we have said, is an organizational form ideally suited to provide an efficient means of achieving a given objective. In a parliamentary democracy such as Canada, selecting policy objectives ought to be the task of the political executive, which is responsible through Parliament to the people. The bureaucracy, in theory, should implement these goals efficiently and effectively.

However, the distinctions between the work of administrators and politicians are not clear. Public servants enjoy relative permanence in their jobs and have immense organizational resources. This gives them considerable influence in the policy-making process. They also have discretionary power in many areas of policy implementation, especially where Parliament has delegated decision-making authority to government departments, agencies, and tribunals. How, then, do politicians keep these unelected bureaucrats in check? There are three important ways: through strengthened parliamentary committees, the reports of the auditor general, and freedom of information legislation.

Parliamentary Committees

Several House of Commons reforms over the last two decades have attempted to reduce government dependence on the bureaucracy for information and policy advice. Parliamentary committees have become more effective, and their reports generally present a view of government policy that differs from that of the public service, but much more could be done to enhance the role of members of Parliament (MPs) in committee. As well, opposition parties now receive research funds to help them make policy input or, at least, develop more informed criticism of existing policy-making and implementation. More research assistance for individual MPs is vital to enable them to question bureaucratic decisions effectively.

Monitoring Agencies

The number of independent agencies of Parliament that monitor government activities continues to grow. They now include an auditor general, an information commissioner, a privacy commissioner, a commissioner of official languages, a conflict of interest and ethics commissioner, a lobbying commissioner, a chief electoral officer, a Parliament budget officer (some of which are controversial), and even a public sector integrity commissioner.

auditor general: An official charged with making a public appraisal of the effectiveness of both public spending and accounting practices to Parliament and, in particular, to the Public Accounts Committee.

The Auditor General The **auditor general** provides a critical appraisal of both public spending and accounting practices to Parliament and the Public Accounts Committee. The auditor is directly responsible to Parliament (not to the executive), and his or her reports on government spending trigger major debates in the House of Commons and the press about mistakes, inefficiencies, and corruption in government policy-making.[8]

Since 1977, the Auditor General's Office (AGO) has had the power to carry out "value for money" audits that assess policy and the substance of spending decisions. It "has become concerned not only with whether federal funds are properly accounted for, but how they are being managed, at what cost, to what end and with what effectiveness."[9] It was the report of Auditor General Sheila Fraser that uncovered the Québec sponsorship scandal that severely weakened the federal Liberals in the 2004 election and afterwards. The increasing size and costs of the AGO prompted one expert to conclude that the AGO itself should be subjected to a value-for-money, comprehensive audit.

Parliamentary and administrative reforms to the expenditure budget process in light of these reports have enhanced the potential for democratic control. As well, the development of multi-year fiscal plans provides a broader, longer-range context for the evaluation of both spending plans and individual estimates. Both of these reforms illustrate the important role of the auditor general and explain why the auditor is often in conflict with the minister of finance.

Freedom of Information In 1983, the federal government took an important step toward providing more open government when it formally promulgated the *Access to Information Act*. With a number of controversial exceptions, Canadians now have the right to obtain or examine records that were previously kept secret by federal government institutions. At stake, in many cases, is the individual's right to know why certain government decisions were taken, or to determine whether these decisions were fairly arrived at or mistakes were made (see Close-Up 8.3). If the government refuses to disclose information on a request, a preliminary appeal can be made to an information commissioner. Ultimate recourse, however, is via the Federal Court—an expensive procedure in which the judicial process replaces Parliament as the primary mechanism for ensuring bureaucratic accountability.

Close-Up 8.3

The Right to Privacy

In its 2000 annual report, Canada's then privacy commissioner, Bruce Phillips, revealed that as many as 2000 pieces of information on almost every citizen were stored by the Department of Human Resources Development.* The huge database was compiled from information such as income tax returns, child tax benefit statements, welfare files, disability and job records, among others. The privacy commissioner and others maintained that the *Privacy Act* is inadequate in preventing the misuse of this information.

Should the laws be reformed to provide penalties for unauthorized access, careless storing, or misuse of these data?

*The Globe and Mail, May 18, 2000.

The *Access to Information Act* is intended to make government more accountable and open and to reverse any public image of public servants scheming to hide blunders or corruption from unsuspecting citizens. Still, some observers are skeptical of the value of the Act in its present form. The late Donald Rowat argued that some of the exceptions to access "go against the whole spirit of a freedom of information act by absolutely prohibiting certain types of records from being released, thus turning these exemptions into an extension of the *Official Secrets Act*."[10] He also noted a long list of subjects on which discretionary exemptions can be made by bureaucrats, which may well "limit the accountability of the government to Parliament."

In the final analysis, public confidence in the Act depends on how well the mechanics of releasing information work and on whether information that should be released is actually made public. This, in turn, will depend on the extent to which the Cabinet and the bureaucracy comply with the spirit as well as the letter of the new law. So far, there are mixed results.

The Ombudsman and Other Proposals For many years, there has been a debate about whether to create a position of federal **ombudsman**, an independent officer who would be responsible to Parliament for the investigation of citizens' complaints against the bureaucracy. Although an ombudsman might provide an additional mechanism of overall surveillance of the bureaucracy, it should be noted that Canada already has a number of specialized ombudsman-like officers, including the commissioner of official languages, a privacy commissioner, a correctional investigator for penitentiary services, and others, all of whom act as watchdogs over specific aspects of bureaucratic activity.

> **ombudsman:** A (proposed) independent officer responsible to Parliament for the investigation of citizens' complaints against the bureaucracy.

Other non-parliamentary means of controlling the bureaucracy's role in policy-making have been suggested. The judicial process, for example, could play a greater role in protecting citizens against arbitrary bureaucratic decisions. However, although there has been an increase in court challenges to bureaucratic decisions since the *Canadian Charter of Rights and Freedoms* was implemented, we agree with the conclusion drawn by one opponent of judicial review of the bureaucracy:

> It would be wrong to abandon democratic processes working through Parliament to check bureaucratic power in favour of a more elitist approach based upon courts, lawyers and tribunals as the primary mechanisms for safeguarding the rights of individuals.[11]

Are More Reforms Needed?

The perceived lack of accountability of Crown corporations to Parliament is one of the major problems that remains in controlling the bureaucracy. Reports of public enterprises and regulatory agencies are automatically referred to standing committees, but inadequate auditing provisions and difficulties in imposing ministerial responsibility for these semi-autonomous agencies hinder effective parliamentary control. With this exception, the mechanisms for parliamentary control of the bureaucracy are largely in place. The key question is whether MPs have the resources, inclination, or time to ensure government accountability.

Discussion Questions

1. Should public servants be chosen for their professional qualifications? Why or why not?

2. Are politicians the masters of public servants? Should ministers be forced to take responsibility for mistakes made by public servants?

3. What are the four major strategies that can be used to reduce a deficit or cut the country's debt? Why is this such a difficult task for governments?

4. How does a minority government situation affect the functioning (effectiveness and efficiency) of the bureaucracy? Consider the contentious issue of budget amendments during minority governments as part of your answer.

5. Are democratic controls of the Canadian bureaucracy satisfactory? What additional reforms would you make?

Chapter 9

The Administration of Justice and Human Rights

Courts, Police, Prisons, Public Security, and Terrorism

Learning Objectives

After reading this chapter, you should be able to

1 Differentiate between the types of law used in the Canadian legal system.

2 Describe the basic organization of the court system in Canada.

3 Trace the changing role of the Supreme Court since Confederation.

4 Discuss how the *Canadian Charter of Rights and Freedoms* has influenced judges, politicians, Canadian citizens, and police.

5 Describe the organizational arrangements for policing and prisons in Canada.

6 Assess the Canadian government's continuing response to terrorism in terms of strengthening Canada's security arrangements, and explore whether civil liberties have been adequately maintained in this age of insecurity.

Sports matches require referees to ensure that rules are followed and that appropriate penalties are dispensed when they are broken. This is also true in other aspects of life. Canada, like all modern states, maintains an extensive system of laws, courts, police, and prisons. The institutions of law and order allow the government to exercise authority in disputes between and among individuals and institutions. As we have seen, the general rules for politics in Canada are established in the Constitution. More specific laws to manage societal conflict are made by legislatures and governments and are then delegated to other bodies. Judges and juries are commissioned to act, under the laws of the country, as referees or umpires to settle disputes with authoritative, impartial decisions.

Without exception, national governments maintain a military organization or a very powerful police force—for external security, for suppressing internal disorder, and for managing large-scale natural disasters and other crises. While the military is discussed in Chapter 12, courts that interpret the law, as well as the police and the administrative justice officials who enforce it, are examined here. This includes the prison or corrections system as the final recourse for individuals who do not comply with the law as interpreted by the courts. First, we examine the role and organization of courts in Canada's legal system, including the impact of the *Canadian Charter of Rights and Freedoms*. Second, we examine the role and organization of policing and the prison system—the ultimate sanction of the state. Finally, since security has taken on increased importance in recent years, the last section discusses and critiques the new arrangements for security that the Canadian government has put in place to counter political terrorism.

THE LEGAL SYSTEM

In Chapter 3, we discussed the constitutional rules affecting the Canadian legal system. We saw that the "rule of law" means that citizens, no matter what their transgressions, should not be denied due process of law and that this regularizes the relationship between citizens and their governments. No individual or institution is above the law, no one is exempted from it, and all are equal before it. No government or administrative official or even member of the royal family has any power beyond that awarded by law.

The Canadian legal system is derived from British and, to a lesser extent, French and American models. The complex arrangements are underpinned by the Constitution and constitutional precedents, as well as by the laws and regulations emanating from the federal Parliament, the 10 provincial legislatures and 3 territories, and local governments. The courts rely heavily on the Canadian equivalent of English common law and the Civil Code of Québec to guide their decision making.

The courts are the guardians of the rule of law and as such should be beyond partisan influence. In Canada, judges are protected from the arbitrary whims of politicians. Judges of the highest courts, the most important provincial courts, and the provincial courts of appeal are removable only by an address to the governor general by both Houses of Parliament. No higher-court judge has ever been removed in this fashion. This tradition of the independence of the judiciary is particularly significant in constitutional development because the Supreme Court interprets the written Constitution and therefore defines the limits of federal and provincial power as well as the applicability of the *Canadian Charter of Rights and Freedoms*. As a further precaution against undue influence on judges, the Canadian Constitution provides that almost all courts are established by the provincial legislatures, but that all judges from the county courts up (except courts of probate in Nova Scotia and New Brunswick) are appointed by the federal government.

The Constitution is an important part of the legal system. As we saw in Chapter 3, it is a body of fundamental rules, written and unwritten, that underlie all other laws. When disputes that require legal decisions occur, resolution normally requires enforcing the basic rules of the political game. These include rules about federal and provincial jurisdictions and the relationships between individuals or groups and governments. Cases that involve these aspects of law may end up at the Supreme Court for resolution. As we will see, the 1982 *Canadian Charter of Rights and Freedoms* has greatly enhanced the judiciary's role in settling political disputes. Many aspects of these decisions are highly political.

Courts as Arenas for Solving Disputes

Laws and regulations that concern politics and social life are, of necessity, extremely general and abstract because they apply to a multitude of differing situations. Their meaning and relevance has to be interpreted in each specific case. Judges and juries are constantly interpreting and reinterpreting the law and shaping its direction. They not only apply the law but also make new law with their judgments.

In Canada, when disputes cannot be solved among individuals or between individuals and the state, the courts regulate the conflict. An adversarial system pits lawyers against one another, or against the state's prosecutors, in courts. Judges and juries determine the outcome of cases. The judgments themselves may then add to the development of case law and the common law tradition of the country.

Canadian law is divided into two categories: civil law and criminal law. The federal structure basically gives jurisdiction over civil law to the provinces and over criminal law to the federal Parliament.

Civil law regulates relations between or among private individuals and corporations. It is concerned mainly with disputes over property and commercial contracts. Judges and juries follow laws based on provincial authority in the fields of property and civil rights, and render decisions about the amount of damages and payments. Civil law also includes topics such as torts, wills, company law, and family law.

Criminal law pits the individual against the state. Unlike civil law, criminal law comes under federal authority in Canada. It is listed in Clause 91 of the Constitution and includes crimes such as theft, assault, and murder. Since the "administration of justice" is a provincial power in Clause 92, however, police and Crown attorneys, working for the provincial attorneys general, normally lead the prosecution against wrongdoers. The judges, acting on the conclusions of juries, make decisions about what penalties (if any) to impose. These may take the form of fines or prison sentences.

civil law: Regulates relations between or among private individuals and corporations. It is concerned mainly with disputes over property and commercial contracts.

criminal law: Pits individuals charged with criminal offences against the state. Unlike civil law, criminal law comes under federal authority in Canada.

The Organization of the Court System

The basic, unitary structure of the court system in Canada is that of a pyramid with a very wide base and a narrow tip, with the Supreme Court of Canada at the top. The judiciary makes decisions when there are disputes over the law. Whether the law is civil or criminal, judges deliberate in courts.

The Fathers of Confederation did not establish the Supreme Court in the Constitution but left Parliament to propose and establish it through legislation. Section 101 of the Constitution gave the Parliament of Canada the authority to create a Supreme Court and other courts. The **Supreme Court of Canada** is Canada's highest court for civil, criminal, and constitutional cases. It was established by the *Dominion Act* in 1875 as a general court of appeal for Canada. At the time, it was not the final court of appeal, as that power still rested in Britain with the Judicial Committee of the Privy Council (JCPC). It wasn't until 1949 that the Supreme Court became Canada's final court of appeal.

Supreme Court of Canada: Canada's highest court for civil, criminal, and constitutional cases.

Today, a chief justice and eight *puisne* judges—judges of slightly lesser rank—serve on the Supreme Court (see Close-Up 9.1). Three of the nine must come from the civil law tradition; in practice, that means from from Québec. All are appointed by the Governor-in-Council[1] and have to retire at age 75. Beverly McLachlin is the first woman to be Chief Justice of Canada. By 2015, seven of the nine judges had been appointed by Prime Minister Stephen Harper, a lasting legacy for his governments.

Immediately below the Supreme Court in the judicial pyramid are the provincial superior or supreme courts. Each province has a superior or supreme court of general jurisdiction, which is charged with administering all laws in force in Canada, whether

Supreme Court of Canada Judges, 2015

Chief Justice: Beverley McLachlin
Judges:
  Mr. Justice Russell Brown
  Madam Justice Suzanne Côté
  Mr. Justice Thomas Cromwell

  Mr. Justice Clément Gascon
  Madam Justice Andromache Karakatsanis
  Mr. Justice Michael Moldaver
  Madam Justice Rosalie Silberman Abella
  Mr. Justice Richard Wagner

enacted by Parliament, provincial legislatures, or municipalities. They are usually divided into trial and appeal divisions; some may also have county or district courts of both civil and criminal jurisdiction. Article 96 of the Constitution stipulates that appointment to these superior district and county courts is made by the governor general—in practice, by the federal Cabinet. In other words, while each province determines how many judges it will need in these courts, Ottawa determines who will be appointed and how they will be paid. All provinces also have courts that are staffed by judges appointed by the province and that deal with lesser criminal and other matters. These provincial courts include magistrate, family, and juvenile courts. The appeal divisions of the provincial supreme or superior courts hear appeals from the lower courts and from certain provincial administrative tribunals (see Figure 9.1).

As the highest court in the land, the Supreme Court's decisions are binding on all courts below it. The Supreme Court deals primarily with cases that have already been appealed at least once in the lower courts. In these situations, the task of the Court is to render "an authoritative settlement of a question of law of importance to the whole nation."[2] On rather rare but important occasions, it also deals with questions referred to it directly by the federal government—as with the 1997 questions on Québec

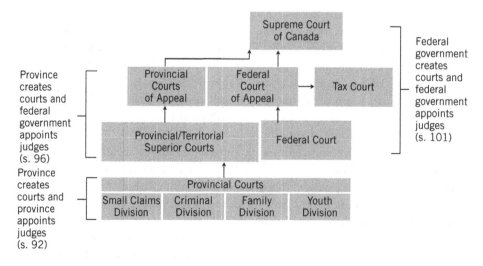

Figure 9.1 The Basic Canadian Court System

independence and, more recently, the reform of the Senate in 2014. These are called "reference" cases.

Canada's Supreme Court is not required to hear all appeals. It is highly selective, concentrating on questions that it considers are of fundamental importance to Canada. It shapes the direction of the law by applying general rules to the specific circumstances—rules that then get passed down to other courts as principles. It should be remembered as well that, as a general court of appeal, the Supreme Court of Canada has a right to the final say in all areas of law for the country. This combination of selectivity and breadth makes the Supreme Court extremely powerful. Since the adoption of the Charter of Rights, the Supreme Court has become the final arbiter "not only of the division of power between governments but also of the line between the powers of both levels of government and the rights and freedoms of citizens."[3]

Below the Supreme Court of Canada but separate from the provincial court structure is the **Federal Court of Canada**. This court was established by Parliament in 1971 to settle claims by or against the federal government on matters relating to maritime law, copyright, patent and trademark law, and federal taxation statutes, and to undertake a supervisory role related to decisions of tribunals and inferior bodies established by federal law. The Federal Court has both a trial and an appeal division. Decisions of the Federal Court of Appeal can be appealed to the Supreme Court of Canada when the amount of money involved in the matter exceeds a set amount. Otherwise, an appeal to the Supreme Court requires either the intervention of the Supreme Court itself or the agreement of the Federal Court of Appeal. If the dispute is interprovincial or federal–provincial in nature, the route of appeal to the Supreme Court is automatically open. There are a few other specialized federal courts, such as the Tax Court of Canada, whose decisions are also subject to review by the Federal Court.

Federal Court of Canada:
Established by Parliament in 1971 to settle claims by or against the federal government on matters relating to maritime law, copyright, patent and trademark law, and federal taxation statutes, and to undertake a supervisory role related to the decisions of tribunals and inferior bodies established by federal law.

Canada's judicial system is highly integrated. The Constitution does not even mention a purely federal judicial power. Instead, it integrates the court system with federally appointed judges in provincial superior and intermediate courts. Thus, despite the fact that Section 92(14) of the Constitution authorizes the provinces to control the "administration of justice," the federal government appoints the most important judges in each province. Canada is the only federation to have this high level of judicial integration. Parliament established the Supreme Court of Canada as a "general court of appeal" rather than one that is limited to federal law and constitutional law. Another integrating feature of the judicial system is that while Parliament has exclusive jurisdiction in the area of criminal law, the provincial legislatures have powers to establish courts of criminal jurisdiction. This means that federal law is administered in provincially established courts, by federally appointed judges.

Some constitutional experts note that there has been a tendency, in recent years, to move away from the integrated model to a system of "dual courts." This is because more provincial and federal courts have been established and staffed by their respective levels of government. The federal government, therefore, is increasingly dependent on judges appointed and paid by the provinces to administer federal laws, so it

Supreme Court of Canada/Philippe Landreville

The Right Honourable Chief Justice of Canada, Beverley McLachlin, P.C.

tends to establish federal trial courts for cases involving federal laws. This combination of events suggests movement in the direction of federalizing Canada's judicial structure. The merits of such a move are debatable, in particular because the unitary court system was designed to apply the law equally to all Canadians, regardless of region.

Aboriginal justice constitutes a special problem for Canadian law. There is general agreement that the justice system does not work well for Aboriginal peoples. Many experts believe that each Aboriginal community in Canada should develop its own justice system to conform to its traditions and cultures. This process is already under way, especially in the North. In 1999, for example, a new kind of court, the Nunavut Court of Justice, was created in the Far North. It combines the power of a superior trial court and territorial court, so the same judge can hear all cases that arise in the territory. Moreover, "sentencing circles" originated in the Yukon Territorial Court in the 1990s and are now used in many parts of the country in cases involving Aboriginal offenders and victims. As a general principle, however, some commentators are still wary of creating many separate justice systems on specific areas of land across Canada.

The Changing Role of the Supreme Court: Positive or Negative?

In its early years, the Supreme Court of Canada was a subordinate, secondary institution. Not until appeal to the Judicial Committee of the Privy Council was abolished in 1949 did the Supreme Court of Canada assume the leadership of the judicial system. The next major evolutionary change came in 1974 when the Supreme Court of Canada's jurisdiction was changed, allowing it to control its own agenda. Finally, the 1982 patriation of the Constitution, with its *Canadian Charter of Rights and Freedoms*, heralded a new and expanded role for all courts in Canada.

In a landmark decision in 1981, the Supreme Court judges ruled in the Patriation Reference case that Prime Minister Pierre Trudeau's government could legally patriate and amend the Constitution unilaterally, while warning that to do so would violate an established "constitutional convention." This ruling on a question of "constitutional convention" was unique in that it reached beyond the law, into the realm of politics. It amounted to a legal green light combined with a political red light. Under the circumstances, Trudeau chose to return to the constitutional bargaining table with the provincial premiers to seek compromise before proceeding with patriation.

The *Constitution Act, 1982* greatly increased the political importance of the Supreme Court of Canada, mainly because of the *Canadian Charter of Rights and Freedoms*. Under the Charter, the Supreme Court of Canada can overrule legislation and executive acts of government not only on the grounds that they violate the federal division of powers but also on the grounds that they violate the fundamental rights and freedoms of citizens. The consequences of this development are discussed in the next section on the Charter, but here it is important to remind ourselves that the Canadian judiciary has gradually become more powerful.

The mandate of judges has remained constant—to respect the laws governing the disputes they arbitrate and to contribute to the development of those laws while acting, and being seen to act, with independence and impartiality. Increasingly, however, judges are perceived by some as "politicians" who promote change in public policy. As Canadians have become more conscious of judicial power, they are scrutinizing more closely the judiciary's claims of impartiality.[4]

The appointment procedure in particular has become the object of public debate. Since the Supreme Court was not established by the Constitution, but by federal legislation, there is no reference in the Constitution to either its composition or the method by which judges are to be appointed. Reform proposals include that potential government appointees to the Supreme Court should be confirmed by parliamentary hearings, or that the prime minister should choose nominees from a short list drawn up by a nominating committee with wide representation. The only mention of the Supreme Court in the *Constitution Act* concerns the amending formula—which requires the agreement of Parliament and all of the provincial legislatures to change the composition of the Supreme Court, and the agreement of Parliament and two-thirds of the provinces (representing 50 percent of the population) for any other constitutional change to the Court. Another reform proposal is that the Supreme Court be established in the Constitution so that it will not have to depend on federal legislation for its existence and so that its composition or method of appointment cannot be changed easily.

The Impact of Charter Decisions on Human Rights: Positive or Negative?

In Chapter 3, we discussed why Canadians entrenched the *Canadian Charter of Rights and Freedoms* in the Constitution and what fundamental rights were protected as a result. Here we are concerned with what impact the Charter has had on the politicians who make laws, the judges who interpret them, the police who enforce them, and the Canadians who live under them. The Charter has had a profound influence on all four groups.

Influence on Governments The fact that the Supreme Court now is able to use the Charter to strike down government-made laws has made governments much more cautious in drafting legislation. On the other hand, having the Charter has allowed governments to escape from responsibility by leaving their legislation vague, so that the tough, unpopular decisions must be made by the courts. Of course, the courts ought to be careful not to be too far ahead of, or behind, public opinion or they may lose the confidence of Canadians. As discussed in Chapter 3, legislators in some cases can override a court decision by using the Charter's Section 33 "notwithstanding" clause, but to do so could trigger a public backlash if the public did not agree.

Influence on Judges and Lawyers When the Charter came into effect in 1982, Supreme Court judges found their new powers and responsibilities awesome because of the novel, abstract principles and the lack of familiar paths. One Supreme Court judge asked,

> What is liberty? What should be the limits to it? We all know what we think ourselves. But when it comes to defining liberty, each and every state restriction exists in a proper context. There is no way to escape these problems. . . .[5]

The early court cases indicated that the judges would base their decisions on new considerations. In the *Southam* case, for example, Chief Justice Brian Dickson "traced the right to security from unreasonable searches back to the common law concept of trespass and its application by English judges in the 1700s to make an Englishman's home his castle." Next, he "followed the evolution of this private property interest into a wider concern with personal privacy as a fundamental value of a liberal society."[6]

It was also clear from the beginning that the nine justices of the Supreme Court would play a powerful political role when the Charter came into effect. They quickly began to overturn legislation that they considered conflicted with rights guaranteed in the Charter. In many cases, they have made decisions on social policy matters that used to be in the exclusive domain of politicians. In January 1988, for example, the Supreme Court declared in the *Morgentaler* case that the federal abortion law, which restricted access to therapeutic abortions, did not conform to the Charter, and struck it down. Despite parliamentary efforts to regain control of abortion policy, the Supreme Court's judgment remains in place with little likelihood of further legislation because of the controversial nature of the subject.

Many other highly publicized public policy issues decided by the Supreme Court have involved Charter decisions on fundamental freedoms. These include cases concerning union rights, language legislation, pornography, freedom of the press, street prostitution, the right to die, and same-sex marriage, to cite only a few examples.

The relative importance of the courts increased even more in 1985, when the Charter's equality provisions took effect. These provisions immediately established a new, burgeoning area of litigation. In fact, a question soon arose as to whether the courts had the authority to determine what constitutes "equality" without Parliament having an opportunity to respond legislatively. The necessity to draw a line between acceptable and unacceptable forms of discrimination in an attempt to achieve equality is now one of the most difficult tasks under the Charter. In 1988, for example, the Federal Court decided that a section of the *Unemployment Insurance Act* discriminated against "natural" fathers because it denied them paternity leave benefits. Eventually, the federal government agreed and extended the benefits to fathers as well as to mothers. Clearly, this type of ruling affects the balance of power between Parliament and the courts.

> "We are talking about inserting equality into life which is not equal."
> Mr. Justice Antonio Lamer[7]

Does the Charter confer too much power on lawyers and judges? It does enable unelected judges to strike down measures enacted by elected politicians. On the surface, this looks unjust; however, one should not equate democracy with the "raw will of the majority." The Charter assigns the courts the responsibility to ensure that the claims of minorities and those without influence be heard. Ultimately, elected officials do have the final say because the Charter provides that the equality rights provisions are subject to the legislative override provision (the "notwithstanding" clause) that can be used if legislatures disagree fundamentally with the courts.

Influence on Police Another controversial area of Charter politics concerns the police. The Charter has made it increasingly difficult for police to build effective cases against criminals. Some applaud that difficulty; others see it as aiding criminals.

Section 24(2) of the Charter states that a court shall exclude from the proceedings evidence obtained in a manner that infringed on or denied any guaranteed right or freedom. Canadian judges have proven willing to dismiss illegally obtained evidence because it might "bring the administration of justice into disrepute." Until 1982, illegally obtained evidence was accepted in Canadian courts. After the Charter came into effect, the courts began to rule that much of this evidence was inadmissible.

Influence on the Rights of Citizens As for Canadians in general, the Charter has given them the ability to challenge laws that they perceive to be unjust—that is, those thought to impinge on basic rights of freedom and equality. However, changes made to the law by the Supreme Court also created new problems for Canadians. For example, in 1992, the Supreme Court changed Canada's obscenity law. It tossed out the old test of obscenity, based on the vague and arbitrary notion of "community standards," and replaced it with a "harm-based" test. Material would be judged obscene if it portrayed sexual violence or degrading and dehumanizing acts, or contained the sexual depiction of children. Within a short time, the new law had become the moral underpinning for prosecutions of the "wrong" people—peaceable gay and lesbian artists and bookstores. Many felt that Canada Customs and the police pushed the interpretation too far, and that the new test of obscenity was just as vague and subjective as the old one.

Also on the negative side for many Canadians is a feeling that Charter interpretations are shifting values toward those of the United States. Some critics of the Charter believe that Canadian values that emphasized tradition, order, and historical continuity are being replaced by American values that stress individual interests above those of the collectivity. Constitutional experts R.I. Cheffins and P.A. Johnson, for example, express the fear that the Charter "will bring an essentially counter-revolutionary, non-rationalist communitarian society into direct collision with individual-focused legal rights based upon Charter arguments."[8] Doing so, they maintain, gradually will accelerate the Americanization of Canada.

Legal equality, including protection from discrimination, is the starting point for any move toward greater equality of opportunity. Since the Charter, women's groups have organized effectively to have the courts examine issues such as child care, harassment, and violence. Lesbian, gay, bisexual, and transgender (LGBT) rights activists have also made effective cases. The Supreme Court rulings have indicated that while the Constitution explicitly promises equality to individuals, it also applies to disadvantaged groups such as women and minorities (see Close-Up 9.2). However, critics ask why Canada prohibits discrimination only on the basis of sex, national or ethnic origin, race, age, colour, religion, or disability, when other characteristics such as character and ability are also acquired by chance.

Equality and Legal Cases Since the Charter of Rights and Freedoms

In the first equality case before the Supreme Court after the Charter, a white, Oxford-educated, male U.S. citizen, Mark Andrews, argued that he had been discriminated against when British Columbia's law society would not allow him to become a lawyer because he was not a Canadian citizen. He won his case. The Supreme Court argued

The Supreme Court and Sex: Privacy and the Presumption of Innocence

In 1997, Parliament amended the *Criminal Code* to outline the strict conditions under which a court could disclose medical, counseling, or therapeutic records held by the Crown or a third party relating to a complainant in a sexual assault case. There were many challenges to this law by lawyers who argued that unless they had access to these records, their clients' right to a fair and full defence would be thwarted.

Two principles clash here: the accused's right to a fair trial and the complainant's right to privacy. In November 1999, the Supreme Court ruled by a vote of seven to one

that the rape shield law was constitutional. This means that judges continue to have the power to block defendants from obtaining such records. The sole dissenting judge, Justice Antonio Lamer, said that the onus should be on the Crown to explain why such disclosure would be unwarranted.

What do you think? Should the law privilege the privacy of the alleged sexual assault victim over the rights of the accused to a fair trial? Or, is this law reasonable given the heinous nature of the crime? Should the courts be allowed to make the final decision in such cases?

that equality rights protections in Section 15 of the Charter were intended to protect the disadvantaged, and that Mark Andrews was a member of a disadvantaged group (non-citizens). As such, he was the victim of illegal discrimination.

The Mark Andrews decision set a precedent for women and minorities in subsequent decisions where, in essence, the Court was being asked to lead social change, or to give official recognition to changes that already had taken place. In May 1995, the Supreme Court announced three such significant decisions concerning the equality rights section of the Charter. In all three cases, the question concerned what constituted discrimination. The first decision was scrutinized by supporters of women's rights; the other two concerned those who supported same-sex and common law couples.

In the first case, *The Queen v. Suzanne Thibaudeau*, a divorced woman in Québec argued that the fact that she (and not her former husband) had to pay tax on support payments for their two children meant that she was being discriminated against. The Court disagreed five to two. It found that there was no discrimination, that the government had already taken this kind of situation into account in taxing divorced parents, and that the rules reduced the tax burden of the couple and had the result of increasing the available overall resources that could be used for the benefit of the children. The decision created a dilemma for the federal government. If it retained a system that taxed the recipients of child support, it would face continued agitation from lobbyists claiming the system was unfair to women. If it changed the rules to shift the tax to the parent making the support payment, it would anger others. It decided to legislate in favour of the parent who receives child support.

The second case, *The Queen v. Egan*, concerned a homosexual couple from British Columbia. James Egan, a pensioner, applied for a spousal pension for his male partner (the law at the time allowed spouses of some pensioners to receive an allowance). Mr. Egan's request was turned down, and he appealed to the Supreme Court on the basis that he had been discriminated against because of the definition of "spouse" in the *Old Age Security Act*. Again the Court disagreed. Even though it unanimously found that homosexuals are covered by the equality provisions of the Charter and cannot be discriminated against on the grounds of sexual orientation, a majority of judges argued that Parliament had set up spousal pensions to benefit aged, needy married couples and that marriage is by nature heterosexual. Marriage is "fundamental to the stability and well-being of the family," the Court stated in its decision, so the government was not discriminating in this case, but making a political choice. Under Section 1, the Court concluded, the Constitution stipulates that governments may violate constitutional rights when it is "reasonable" to do so in a free and democratic society.

The judges were seriously divided in the Egan case, five to four. The majority stressed the traditional family structure and opposed extending to same-sex couples government benefits that were originally designed for traditional families. The four other judges took a broader view of the contemporary family. They said that legislatures should treat different family structures, including same-sex couples, roughly the same. Two of the dissenting judges even wrote, "This distinction amounts to clear denial of equal benefit of the law." The "swing vote" was that of John Sopinka, who agreed that discrimination existed in this case but said he was willing to defer to Parliament on the matter. He added that "equating same-sex couples with heterosexual couples . . . is still generally regarded as a novel concept."[9] In other words, despite its negative conclusion, the Court agreed that "sexual orientation" was analogous to the enumerated categories of equal rights protections in the Charter.

Lesbian and gay activists saw the Court's recognition of sexual orientation benefits as a *victory* for gay rights, even though the specific case about pensions had been lost. The decision had been only one vote away from a win, and there was speculation that in future cases Mr. Justice Sopinka might be swayed, or a new judge might change the composition and orientation of the Court. The ruling put pressure on the federal government to move faster on gay rights legislation if it wanted to avoid a spate of lawsuits. In 1996, the federal Parliament amended the human rights legislation to add "sexual orientation" to the Act.

The third case, *John Miron et al. v. Richard Trudel et al.*, proved a clear victory for John Miron and Jocelyne Vallière, a common law Ontario couple with two children. Mr. Miron had been injured in a car accident while travelling with an uninsured driver. He would have been covered under provincial law by Ms. Vallière's insurance policy, but only if the couple were married. The Court decided five to four that Ontario's provincial policy constituted unjustifiable discrimination against common law couples because it required insurance companies to provide benefits only to married couples. The ruling went on to argue that common law couples were a historically disadvantaged group that was entitled to constitutional protection under the law. This decision required federal and provincial governments to examine a wide array of other laws to ensure that they comply with this particular ruling.

In another round of Charter equality cases after 1997, the Supreme Court came even closer to establishing the full effect of equality rights in the Charter. In *Eaton v. Brant Board of Education*, the Court ruled that an Ontario school could place a child in a special education class as long as the child did not suffer adverse effects. In *Eldridge v. British Columbia*, the Court drew the same distinction when it ruled that the British Columbia Medical Services Commission violated the Charter when it failed to provide sign language interpreters, causing a child to suffer adverse effects. According to the Court, equal access to medical treatment requires the provision of sign language interpreters in hospitals. Lastly, in *Benner v. Canada*, the Court ruled that the *Citizenship Act* violated equality rights because a man seeking citizenship required a security check if his mother was a Canadian citizen but did not require one if his father was.

Marriage Rights The equality case that provoked the most publicity and political controversy involved the *Vriend v. Alberta* decision of April 1998. In that case, the Supreme Court concluded that gays and lesbians had to be granted the same protection of their sexual orientation under Section 15(1) of the Charter as other people were given under the Alberta *Individual Rights Protection Act* (IRPA). The decision was remarkable because it was based on the ruling that a legislative "omission" could bear judicial disapproval on the same basis as a legislature's positive act.[10] In other words, the Court ruled not on what was *in* the Act but on what had been *omitted* from it. The Court decided, in effect, that sexual orientation had to be "read into" the IRPA. This decision is often taken as evidence of a new dynamic interaction between courts and governments in Canada. After this decision, all provincial human rights rules were amended to include sexual orientation in their equal rights codes.

On the political front, then Progressive Conservative premier of Alberta, Ralph Klein, hinted that he might invoke the notwithstanding clause to overrule the Supreme Court's judgment on the sexual orientation ruling, but he backed off when the expected public approval did not emerge. While social conservatives tried to force the premier to nullify the Court ruling on homosexuals, Klein demurred, declaring, "It's like that train. You can't stop it, you have to deal with it."[11] In other words, politicians and others have to put up with Supreme Court rulings on equality whether they like them or not.

There are several problems with this. The Court could require citizens to show that an instance of alleged discrimination is unfair, or it could require governments to justify differing forms of treatment. Prohibitive costs and poor public financing for test cases may make litigants reluctant to challenge governments in court for alleged discrimination. Another issue is deciding how to prove discrimination. Mr. Justice Lamer commented, "What the courts will want is up in the air. Will we need statistical evidence? How will we get at the records we need?"[12] Furthermore, should the courts determine what constitutes equality without giving Parliament and provincial legislatures an opportunity to respond legislatively?

Although equality rights have become a fast-growing area of Charter litigation, it is still too early to determine how far the Supreme Court will expand rights for women, the disabled, and others. But there is a "consistent trend towards a liberal judicial philosophy," according to Professor Frederick Vaughan, an astute commentator on judicial trends in Canada.[13]

The controversial issue of same-sex marriage reached its zenith at the beginning of the twenty-first century. On June 10, 2003, the Ontario Court of Appeal ruled in *Halpern v. Canada* that the opposite-gender requirement for marriage is unconstitutional and directed that marriage in the province of Ontario be open to same-sex couples. Similar decisions by the British Columbia Court of Appeal and the Québec

Superior Court also effectively allowed same-sex couples to marry. After the high courts of six provinces and one territory ruled that the traditional definition of marriage as a union between a man and woman was discriminatory and perhaps unconstitutional, the prime minister announced that Ottawa would not appeal the decisions and that the federal government would draft legislation to legally recognize the union of same-sex couples, while recognizing the freedom of churches and religious organizations to not perform marriages that are against their beliefs. In September 2003, the House of Commons rejected by a vote of 137–132 an opposition motion reaffirming the traditional definition of marriage. Prime Minister Jean Chrétien requested a ruling from the Supreme Court as to whether traditional marriage laws were discriminatory and violated the *Canadian Charter of Rights and Freedoms*. In December 2004, the Supreme Court gave the go-ahead for the federal government to introduce legislation redefining marriage across the country to include same-sex couples. It also ruled that the Parliament had exclusive authority over the definition of marriage.

In 2005, despite the Liberals' tenuous minority government situation, Prime Minister Paul Martin promised to press ahead with legislation. Opposition lobbies, including the Canadian Conference of Catholic Bishops, vowed to fight any legislation in favour of equal marriage, while gay rights groups expressed their enthusiasm for legislation that would make Canada the third country, after Belgium and the Netherlands, to permit gays and lesbians to marry. In June 2005, the House of Commons voted to extend marriage rights to gay and lesbian couples throughout Canada.

Clearly, the nine justices of the Supreme Court of Canada play a very powerful political role today. They can overturn legislation that they decide conflicts with rights guaranteed in the Charter, and they can have a major say on social policy matters such as marriage, union rights, and abortion that used to be in the exclusive domain of politicians. The controversies that began with the introduction of the Charter continue. Depending on the issue, both pro- and anti-factions can point to disappointing judgments and unfulfilled expectations. However, a definitive verdict on the value of the Charter will not be clear until much more time has passed. The power of the courts and legislatures is still open for future problems and decisions (see Table 9.1).

Politics and the Supreme Court

R.I. Cheffins and P.A. Johnson argue that the Charter is "centralizing, legalizing and Americanizing."[14] By centralizing, they mean that it provides a common national standard for the protection of civil liberties and engenders national debates that transcend federal–provincial or regional differences. By legalizing, they mean that policy issues are now handled in a more legalistic manner. By Americanizing, they are referring to Canada's political system becoming more like that of the United States. Another commentator, Peter Russell, has summed up the legalizing and politicizing effect of the Charter this way: It tends "to judicialize politics and to politicize the judiciary."[15]

Critics of the Charter insist that it inhibits rather than fosters progressive social change. They maintain that by framing the agenda for debate, the courts can limit social reform. The rights protected under the Charter, they claim, are a reflection of middle-class preoccupations; no basic entitlement is included for a decent level of

Table 9.1 Decisive Decisions by the Courts on Charter Cases

1984	Skapinker: Ontario law did not violate "mobility rights."
1985	Singh: Provided refugees the right to a full and oral hearing because of "fundamental justice."
1985	Big M Drug Mart: Struck down the *Lord's Day Act* on Sunday shopping as a violation of "freedom of religion."
1986	Oakes: Established guidelines for interpreting the "reasonable limits" clause.
1988	Morgentaler: Outlawed *Criminal Code* restrictions on abortion employing the "security of the person" clause.
1990	Keegstra: Determined that "freedom of expression" does not apply to disseminating hate literature.
1992	Butler: Limited "freedom of expression" in relation to pornography.
1993	Rodriguez: Concluded that "security of the person" does not include the right to assisted suicide.
1995	Egan: Determined that "equality rights" included sexual orientation.
2003	Halpern: Ontario Court of Appeal ruled that same-sex marriage was legal and constitutional.
2004	Reference: Supreme Court ruled that federal legislation redefining marriage to include same-sex couples would be constitutional.

education, housing, nutrition, or health care. However, Section 36 of the Charter does enshrine the commitment of both federal and provincial governments to provide "essential public services of reasonable quality to all Canadians." As well, although it does not protect present social and economic arrangements, the Charter identifies and protects the political and legal rights essential to those who promote social change.

It is unfortunate, but true, that the political majority at times overlooks minority rights. The Charter assigns courts the responsibility to ensure that the claims of minorities and those without influence are considered. Ultimately, of course, elected politicians can have the final say, because the Charter provides that equality rights are subject to the legislative override provision (the "notwithstanding" clause) if legislatures disagree fundamentally with the courts. This, of course, is not the case for democratic and majority rights.

However, the Charter also has a clearly positive side. Judges have taken the stand that citizens should be allowed to ask courts to declare laws unconstitutional when there is a potential infringement of their rights—that is, they do not have to wait until their rights are actually violated. As a result, many laws that threatened to deprive individuals of basic rights have been struck down. Supreme Court Justice Lamer commented that governments have been more careful in drafting laws since 1982.[16] This was evident in 1986, when a parliamentary subcommittee presented 85 recommendations for making federal law conform to the Charter. Part of that list, including discrimination against homosexuals in the federal jurisdiction, was acted on quickly and outlawed.

We conclude that Canadian judicial tradition will continue to influence the conduct of judges when they assess Charter implications, especially in issues of equality. While the opportunity for a more active, interventionist, and perhaps more creative role for the judiciary now exists, this will not come about suddenly. There will be a gradual but constant evolution in the power of the Supreme Court. Clearly, the Charter and the Supreme Court's judgments based on it have become an important Canadian symbol and a significant part of the policy process, a balance to both executive and legislative power.

POLICE FORCES: ENFORCERS OF LAW AND GOVERNMENT

Police enforce the country's laws and maintain order. They also carry out innumerable functions for society, such as detecting crime and protecting life and property, as well as such mundane activities as imposing parking fines, directing traffic, and providing emergency health care. Their activities with respect to domestic disputes, gambling, marijuana smoking, prostitution, pornography, protest demonstrations, and violent acts evoke support from many citizens but derision from others.

The manner in which the police carry out their functions is controversial. There are a large number of laws, regulations, and ordinances, and some would like all of them to be enforced equally by the police, but that is not practical. In choosing which issues to pursue, the police exercise a high degree of discretion. In fact, it may not always be possible to enforce unpopular laws, and since the police must count on public support, some specialists argue that it is counterproductive for the police to enforce unwanted laws. Other citizens contend that it is not up to the police but to politicians to make laws, and those laws should all be enforced equally, regardless of their popularity. The best-known example of the questionable use of police to enforce an unpopular law occurred during the Winnipeg General Strike of 1919. However, the current enforcement of controversial laws about marijuana, cigarette taxes, gun controls, and terrorists may run as close seconds.

Organization of Policing

Canada's police system is highly complex. It is governed by a maze of laws and regulations, making generalization difficult if not perilous. Federalism, provincial police acts, and financing agreements between different governments all complicate the situation. Some things are clear, however. All police forces are responsible to one or all levels of government—municipal, provincial, and federal. In 2014, there were 68 896 police officers across the country. Policing in Canada costs about $14 billion a year, with municipal policing responsible for most of the costs, provincial policing costs running about half that, and federal policing costs about half that again.[17]

There are three standard organizational arrangements for policing in Canada: federal (Royal Canadian Mounted Police [RCMP]), provincial (Ontario Provincial Police [OPP], Sûreté du Québec [SQ], Royal Newfoundland Constabulary, and the seven other provinces and three territories that are policed by the RCMP on contract), and municipal (see Table 9.2).

Table 9.2 Canadian Police Organization*	
Level of Government	**Police Organization**
Federal	Royal Canadian Mounted Police (RCMP)
Provincial	Ontario: Ontario Provincial Police (OPP)
	Québec: Sûreté du Québec
	Newfoundland and Labrador: Royal Newfoundland Constabulary (shared with RCMP)
	Seven provinces and three territories (RCMP on contract)
Municipal	Municipal police force unless there is a contract for RCMP or provincial police to provide this service for the municipality

*Other public police functions are carried out by Canadian Security Intelligence Service (CSIS), Canada Border Services Agency, CN Police, CP Police, Military Police, Ports Canada, and federal and provincial department officials in fields such as income tax, customs and excise, fisheries, wildlife, and terrorism.

Royal Canadian Mounted Police (RCMP): The police force responsible for enforcing federal statutes; it is also under contract to many provinces and municipalities, and polices the territories to enforce criminal and provincial law.

The **Royal Canadian Mounted Police (RCMP)** was created in 1920 out of the North-West Mounted Police, which had been established in 1873 to enforce Canadian law in the western prairies. The RCMP is responsible to a commissioner (with the rank of a deputy minister) who reports to the minister of public safety. The department is scrutinized by the House of Commons Committee on Public Safety and National Security. The RCMP is responsible for enforcing all federal statutes. As well, it is under contract to every province except Ontario and Québec, and to more than 100 municipalities, to enforce criminal and provincial law. It also polices the territories. The RCMP maintains forensic labs, identification services, the Canadian Police Information Centre, and the Canadian Police College in Ottawa for the advanced education of all police in Canada.

Two provinces (Ontario and Québec) have their own province-wide forces—the **Ontario Provincial Police (OPP)** and the **Sûreté du Québec (SQ)**. In Newfoundland and Labrador, the **Royal Newfoundland Constabulary** shares responsibilities with the RCMP. The seven other provinces and three territories contract the RCMP to carry out functions in their areas. Besides these special provincial arrangements, specific policing powers throughout the country are also given to the Canada Border Services Agency, Canadian National Railways, Canadian Pacific Railways, and Ports Canada. Each city and sizable town is also required to have police to maintain law and order. They contract the police from the RCMP or OPP, receive them automatically (as in Québec), or set up their own forces.

Ontario Provincial Police (OPP): Ontario's province-wide police force.

Sûreté du Québec (SQ): Québec's province-wide police force.

Royal Newfoundland Constabulary: The Newfoundland and Labrador police force that shares policing responsibilities with the RCMP.

Aboriginal policing follows several models. Some communities contract with the RCMP or provincial forces to police their territories. Others have their own police forces with their own codes of conduct, answerable to their own police commissions. Still others are in transition, policed by a mixture of RCMP, provincial police, and their own officers until they are ready to police themselves.

In addition to the RCMP and these other forces, the minister for public safety and emergency preparedness is responsible for the **Canadian Security Intelligence Service (CSIS)**, an intelligence gathering institution. Its operations are governed by the 1984 *Canadian Security Intelligence Service Act*. This Act removed the security function from the RCMP (where it had been lodged since 1920) and established CSIS as a separate unit. The *Canadian Security Intelligence Service Act* defined the functions of CSIS, putting it in charge of threats to Canadian security such as espionage, sabotage, terrorism, and foreign-inspired activities. CSIS also continues to do security screenings for appointments to the federal public service. Other intelligence gathering agencies exist inside the Departments of Global Affairs; National Defence; and Immigration, Refugees and Citizenship.

Many Canadians do not accept that a government agency should maintain a constant watch on their daily lives because they believe that such activities run counter to individual liberties. No democracy finds it easy to handle secretive organizations. The problem with supervising CSIS very closely is that the more public scrutiny there is, the less secret and thus the less effective CSIS may become. To ensure that Canada's "snooping" institutions are democratically controlled, the *Canadian Security Intelligence Service Act* set up an external review committee, the **Security Intelligence Review Committee**, to monitor the activities of CSIS. It reports to Parliament annually and the information is public. Presently, this process is inadequate in terms of parliamentary oversight and reforms are urgently required.

CSIS continues to have its detractors. Many members of the police community believe that it should have been left inside the RCMP and not "civilianized." In fact, the RCMP and CSIS have clashed over such subjects as data handling. Some contend that with the end of the Cold War, Canada does not need a secret service. Others think that the terrorist threat means that the role of CSIS should be expanded, as it was in recent legislation by the Conservative government.

Who does CSIS spy on? It can investigate anyone who presents a threat to "national security," and the controversial 2015 *Anti-terrorism Act* allows it to take action to disrupt terrorist organizations. CSIS manages only domestic security. It has relied on about 50 mostly "liaison" officers to collect foreign intelligence in about 30 countries, but depends largely on friendly help from the American Central Intelligence Agency (CIA) and the UK's MI6 (Military Intelligence, Section 6) for most of its external information. Parliament continues to debate whether the CSIS mandate should be broadened to include espionage abroad or whether an entirely new service should be created. The 2015 *Anti-terrorism Act* clearly assigns new powers to CSIS (see below).

Canadian Security Intelligence Service (CSIS): An intelligence gathering institution. Its operations, headed by a director, are governed by the 1984 *Canadian Security Intelligence Service Act*.

Security Intelligence Review Committee: An external review committee that monitors the activities of the Canadian Security Intelligence Service (CSIS).

THE PRISON SYSTEM: FINAL RECOURSE

The corrections, or prison, system is the ultimate sanction of the state against citizens who fail to adhere to peaceful and lawful activities. The system is the final proof that, even in democratic societies, the state retains the ultimate recourse to the use of coercion against its citizens. Issues about prisons in democracies are hidden from view by political parties and politicians who are reluctant to regard the prison system as an important instrument of public policy. However, although prisons are often overlooked, they are an essential part of the institutions of democracy.

Organization of Prisons

Correctional services are divided along federal lines. For adults, the *Criminal Code of Canada* makes the federal government responsible for all offenders sentenced to prison for two or more years, and provincial governments responsible for lesser sentences.[18] For youths, the provinces have authority over offenders of any law, including laws covered by the federal *Youth Criminal Justice Act* (YCJA).

The **minister of public safety** is responsible for the Correctional Service of Canada and the National Parole Board (as well as CSIS, the RCMP, the Canada Border Services Agency, and other organizations). **Corrections Canada** consists of government officials responsible for inmates in federal prisons and for parolees. The Parole Board has the authority to grant or revoke paroles for prisoners and advises the minister on pardons. Each province has its own laws and rules governing prisons, and friction with federal authorities is as routine as in other institutions that cross federal–provincial jurisdictions. Canada abolished capital punishment in 1976, and in 2014 there were 139 337 prisoners in federal or provincial/territorial institutions. It costs Canada about $4.6 billion a year to run the corrections system as a whole.

Prisons serve a number of purposes that are often contradictory. A list of penitentiary functions includes the somewhat contradictory purposes of punishing wrongdoers, deterring criminal behaviour, safeguarding society by depriving criminals of their freedom, and rehabilitating prisoners so that they can be successfully reintroduced into society with appropriate skills and behaviour.

Despite the fact that political scientists generally overlook the role of corrections in Canadian society, prisons are highly political institutions. Debates about prisons abound. Many citizens want prison expenditures reduced. But how? Some propose to privatize prisons while others seek to reduce prison sentences by making use of other forms of punishment, such as heavy fines and home confinement. Others complain that early release schemes put violent criminals back on the streets. Prisoners complain about brutality by prison guards. Corrections guards counter that prison populations are unstable and difficult to administer.

There is no agreement on how to control violent prisoners without repression and detention. Prison inmates include an extremely high proportion of disadvantaged individuals, especially Aboriginal people. Are the prisons capable of correcting Aboriginal behaviour that is the result of decades of intolerable government neglect? Should Aboriginal peoples have their own justice system and methods of punishment?

The prison system is vital to the political system. The Canadian democratic system could not function without law and order, but its application is always controversial and political. Unfortunately, it is a topic that is often overlooked in Canadian political science textbooks.

CIVIL LIBERTIES, TERRORISM, AND SECURITY POLICY

The events of September 11, 2001, followed by the American "war on terrorism" and violent terrorist events at home, made it imperative for Canadian leaders to consider the level of security in Canada. **Terrorism** is defined as "the systematic use of violence or threat of violence against citizens and/or states to obtain political concessions for a designated enemy."[19] Terrorists attack vulnerable targets in free and open

minister of public safety: Cabinet minister responsible for the Correctional Service of Canada and the National Parole Board (as well as CSIS, the RCMP, and other areas).

Corrections Canada: Government officials responsible for inmates in federal prisons and for parolees.

terrorism: The systematic use of violence or threat of violence against citizens and/or states to obtain political concessions for a designated enemy.

societies, attempting to cause a siege mentality by provoking a fear of unusual and suspicious people and behaviour. The dilemma for democrats is that their response to terrorist threats may turn citizens against other citizens, destroying the freedom and openness democracy requires. As governments pursue more and more security for citizens at home, civil liberties are, to an ever larger degree, reduced. The issue comes down to how democratic states can subdue virulent terrorism without surrendering the freedoms of their own country. What costs are acceptable in this struggle? What balance should be achieved between security and legal rights?

In Canada, terrorism has historically been handled as a criminal matter, not as a matter of international relations. That has changed. Before September 11, 2001, the main issue concerned immigrants and security. The most pertinent example was the process by which non-Canadians could be tried and deported as dangerous to the country.

The controversial national **security certificate process**, which was part of the *Immigration and Refugee Protection Act*, was the regulation used to jail non-Canadians (foreign nationals or permanent residents) judged to be a threat to national security and then, if necessary, to deport them. Before September 11, 2001, about two dozen foreign nationals had been named as dangerous to Canada, and several were added later. In this program, two Cabinet ministers signed a certificate labelling a non-Canadian citizen a threat to national security. The government then attempted to show a judge that it had acted reasonably in doing so. A first hearing was held in secret; the named person was not present and had no legal representation. At that stage, the judge cross-examined the state's witnesses. In a second hearing, the case was opened up to allow the defendant to be present, but still without counsel. It was argued that this system was unfair because although the judge could question the government witnesses, he or she was not equipped to do a proper cross-examination. Civil libertarians claimed that the system contravened the *Canadian Charter of Rights and Freedoms* and made it possible for the security service to send the named individuals to countries where they could be jailed or tortured.

On February 23, 2007, the Supreme Court suspended for a year the provisions of the Act that prevented a fair hearing, and said that a new law must be written that complies with the Charter. In other words, it concluded that in the search for a balance between security and rights, the Constitution should not be "a suicide pact" but at the same time the law also should not undermine Canadian individual and collective rights. Secret hearings violate those rights, as named individuals should be allowed to know the case against them and be able to mount a proper defence. Legislation was passed in 2007 to replace the security certificate process. Special counsels with security clearance could be appointed to act on behalf of the accused.

security certificate process: A regulation that was used to jail non-Canadians (foreign nationals or permanent residents) thought to be a threat to national security and then, if necessary, to deport them to a foreign country.

Terrorism in Canada

Recently, politicians have made many other changes to Canadian laws and procedures in the security field. After September 11, 2001, the Canadian government declared that it needed to pass *anti-terrorism legislation* that would allow officials to identify, prosecute, convict, and punish terrorist groups. It needed new definitions and stronger investigative tools for security agencies. The *Criminal Code* was therefore amended to include two new anti-terrorist conventions of the United Nations—suppression of terrorist financing and terrorist bombings—as well as new definitions and procedures for handling terrorists. Legislation was written and passed to accomplish these tasks. The new law applies to both citizens and non-citizens and therefore is quite different from the security certificate process discussed above.

When the government introduced its new anti-terrorism bills, the bills were vehemently opposed by opposition groups and civil libertarians. The first was passed as omnibus bill C-36 in December 2001. It increased the powers of police and law enforcement agencies to fight terrorism by amending the *Criminal Code* and other statutes. It gave new powers of investigation and detention to law enforcement officers and made it a criminal offence to knowingly aid a banned organization. Among the 55 groups then banned in Canada were al Qaeda, Hamas, the Islamic State, Lebanon's Hezbollah, Abu Sayyaf (viewed as an al Qaeda affiliate and based in the Philippines), the Palestinian radical group Abu Nidal, and the Sendero Luminoso (or Shining Path), a Maoist organization in Peru. A changing list of terrorist organizations is posted at www.publicsafety.gc.ca and needs to be examined regularly for updates and deletions.

The second bill (Bill C-42) was delayed and had not passed before prorogation in September 2002. It gave broad declaratory powers to Cabinet, and many believed that it went too far in allowing the government to create new regulations without parliamentary oversight. After considerable controversy, the bill was eventually passed as C-55 in February 2004 and called the *Public Safety Act*. This Act permits ministers and officials to make emergency decisions on aviation security and other emergency issues for up to 72 hours after a relevant event takes place.

In the meantime, in September 2003, the government announced that a new organization—the **Department of Public Safety** (known for a while as the Department of Public Safety and Emergency Preparedness)—would be set up to monitor national security, crisis management, emergency preparedness, border functions, corrections, policing, and crime prevention. It subsumed the old departments of the solicitor general, including the RCMP, CSIS, Border Services Agency, Corrections, and the Parole Board, and a new Cabinet committee on security, public health, and emergencies was set up to deal with emergency health situations such as pandemics. A new position of national security adviser to the prime minister was established in the Privy Council Office.

The government published its first National Security Policy (NSP), titled *Securing an Open Society*, in April 2004. It outlined the government's strategy for addressing emergencies and terrorism. Declaring that the safety and security of Canadian citizens was its highest priority, it set up an intergovernmental forum on emergencies, a round table on security for ethnocultural and religious communities, and a National Security Advisory Council. The NSP addressed questions concerning intelligence, emergency management, public health, transportation, border issues, and international security.

In the comprehensive new anti-terrorism legislation, "terrorist activity" is defined as action inside or outside Canada that is "an offence under one of the ten UN anti-terrorist conventions and protocols" or action "taken or threatened for political, religious or ideological purposes and [that] threatens the public or national security by killing, seriously harming or endangering a person, causing substantial property damage that is likely to seriously harm people or by interfering or disrupting an essential service, facility or system."

Department of Public Safety: An organization set up by the federal government in 2003 to monitor national security, crisis management, emergency preparedness, border functions, corrections, policing, and crime prevention.

The legislation forced people with information relevant to an investigation to appear before a judge and supply that information (i.e., investigative hearings), allowed for people who had committed no crimes to be arrested (i.e., preventive arrest), and allowed information to be kept secret from accused individuals. Clearly, the details threatened a possible assault on individual rights and liberties. For that reason, Parliament insisted that the legislation include a sunset clause of three years.

On March 1, 2007, the government's anti-terrorism act came back to Parliament, where it was stripped of two of its clauses—those on extraordinary "investigative hearings" that had compelled testimony and on "preventative arrest" that had allowed security services to detain terror suspects without charges being placed. Despite government arguments to the contrary, the clauses were killed by the Opposition in a vote of 159 to 124.

Over time, Canada has experienced many significant issues of domestic terrorism (anarchist, anti-Semitic, environmental, nationalists, Sons of Freedom) and international terrorism (Cuban, Sikh, and Khalistan). The most recent violent expressions have been Islamist (see Table 9.3).

The Canadian government has taken several steps to improve security. On June 18, 2007, it put into effect a Canadian "no-fly list" based on a list prepared by the Canada Border Services Agency, the RCMP, and CSIS of some 2000 people "reasonably suspected" of being a threat to the safety of commercial aircraft, passengers, or crew. The names include suspected terrorists or those linked to outlawed terrorist groups as well as individuals convicted of serious crimes. While citizens may appeal having their names on the list, they have no legally enforceable right to have their names removed, no right to an oral hearing, no right to receive written reasons for their names being placed on the list, and no right to compensation for any damages caused to them or their businesses. Canada's federal and provincial privacy commissioners have expressed serious concerns about the policy and have suggested that it may contravene the Charter.

Before a formal no-fly list existed, there was an informal government list of suspected terrorists. The best-known example of this list being used was the case of Maher Arar.

Table 9.3 Examples of Recent Islamic Terrorism in Canada	
1999	Ahmed Ressam, the "Millennium Bomber," attempted to bomb Los Angeles International Airport. Ressam was an Algerian citizen who for some time had claimed refugee status in Canada.
2006	Ontario plot by 18 Canadian-born terrorists (the "Toronto 18") inspired by al Qaeda to storm Parliament and behead the prime minister. Several participants were convicted on terrorism charges.
2014	Saint-Jean-sur-Richelieu ramming incident in which a recent Muslim convert, Martin Couture-Rouleau killed a warrant officer.
2014	Michael Zehaf-Bibeau, a self-convert to Islam, killed Cpl. Nathan Cirillo at the National War Memorial in Ottawa and tried to attack Parliament. He was killed on the premises.

A joint Canadian–Syrian citizen and software engineer living in Ottawa, Arar was detained in 2002 during a stopover at New York's JFK Airport and sent by U.S. security agents to Syria. In Syria, he was held without charge, abused, and tortured until 2005. Later, Arar was exonerated of all charges by a Canadian judicial inquiry headed by Justice Dennis O'Connor. Justice O'Connor concluded, "I am able to say categorically that there is no evidence that Mr. Arar has committed any offense or that his activities constitute a threat to Canadian security." The judge recommended a complete overhaul of the RCMP civilian review process because it had erroneously put an Islamic extremist label on Arar. Eventually, it was disclosed that both the RCMP and CSIS had worked with the CIA on the case, and had even suggested that torture might be used on Arar.

In another notable case, Omar Khadr, a 15-year-old Canadian citizen, was captured in 2002 on a battleground in Afghanistan and incarcerated at the U.S. Guantanamo Bay detention camp. He was the first person since 1945 to be prosecuted for war crimes while still a minor. In 2010, he pleaded guilty for his actions during the war. The Supreme Court of Canada agreed that his Canadian rights had been violated, but would not advise the Canadian government on what action it should take.

In 2012, Khadr was repatriated to Canada to serve the remainder of his sentence in a Canadian prison. While his lawyers insisted that Khadr should originally have been tried as a juvenile, the Canadian government continued to hold him in custody. On May 7, 2015, Khadr, by then 28 years old, was freed on bail and allowed to give interviews. The case continues but, on behalf of his government, former Prime Minister Harper declared that he was unapologetic about Khadr's imprisonment.

In the meantime, in 2015, a new *Anti-terrorism Act* (Bill C-51) was passed by Parliament to help law enforcement and national security agencies prevent the promotion of terrorism, interfere with terrorist radicalization and recruitment efforts, and disrupt planned terrorist attacks. The New Democratic Party (NDP) voted against the legislation but the Liberals voted for it while arguing that a sunset clause should be added to the bill so it could be revisited at another date. The Act was criticized by Canadian academics as being too broad. According to them, the legislation generates major issues for Canada's privacy and freedom of speech laws. It is "a dangerous piece of legislation" that provides new, enhanced policing powers to CSIS and allows the courts to preauthorize the violation of Canadian law. The legitimacy of Bill C-51 is now before the courts as legislation that would allow judges the power to permit government agencies to violate the Constitution.

The Communications Security Establishment

Communications Security Establishment (CSE): Established in 1949 as part of the National Research Council to intercept the communications of clandestine organizations.

Communications are another aspect of security. The **Communications Security Establishment (CSE)** was established in 1949 as part of the National Research Council to intercept the communications of clandestine organizations. It was transferred to the Department of National Defence in 1975 and put under the authority of the minister of defence. During the Cold War, the CSE gathered secret information on the Soviet Union. It now provides secret data on security, especially terrorism, to the whole government. It collects foreign intelligence for the day-to-day assessment of foreign intentions and capabilities and shares information with the United States,

UK, Australia, and New Zealand. Since the December 2001 anti-terrorism law came into effect, the CSE also intercepts the communications of "legitimate" governments if those communications enter or depart Canada.

A commissioner of the CSE reviews the legality of CSE actions; submits an annual report to Parliament via the minister of defence; and also provides confidential, classified reviews of the organization. This watchdog function is vital, as the CSE must act within the law and not infringe on privacy or other rights included in the *Canadian Charter of Rights and Freedoms*. Since these classified reports are not tabled in Parliament, a House of Commons committee should be given authority to see them. However, since members of Parliament (MPs) are not sworn members of the Privy Council, this will be difficult unless a new system of "swearing in" some committee members can be instituted.

Discussion Questions

1. What are the advantages and disadvantages of an "integrated" court system? Should the provinces be more involved in the appointment of some judges?

2. In what respects has the impact of the *Canadian Charter of Rights and Freedoms* been positive? Negative? About marriage? About same-sex marriage? About women?

3. If you committed a criminal offence in Ontario, what police force would be involved? In Québec? In Newfoundland and Labrador? Does this mean that individuals who break the law are treated differently across Canada?

4. What should be the goals of prisons? Should Aboriginal peoples have their own justice system and methods of punishment?

5. Do the post–September 11, 2001, policies of the federal governments provide an adequate balance of security and protection of individual rights given the level of terrorist threats today?

6. How closely should CSIS be monitored? Explain your answer.

Chapter 10
Parties and Interest Groups

Teams in the Game

Learning Objectives

After reading this chapter, you should be able to

1   Distinguish between political parties and interest groups and identify several functions that each performs in the political process.

2   Describe how the Canadian party system has changed over time.

3   Explain the general structure of Canadian parties and how they are organized and financed.

4   Describe the process of electing party leaders.

5   Identify the three main target areas of interest groups and the kinds of tactics they employ to influence public policy.

In democracies, politics and government determine who decides how scarce resources and power will be divided. Since politics is essentially a "team game," parties and interest groups are key participants in the decision process. How they function depends on the nature of the political system in which they operate.

In Canada, parties help to organize both the electorate and the government. They organize the electorate by providing a means for ordinary citizens to participate in political discussions. They recruit candidates for elections, organize campaigns, educate the electorate about issues, help individual voters to get their names on polling lists, and generally stimulate voter participation. Parties organize the government by providing a degree of policy direction and supplying party leaders as potential prime ministers and Cabinet ministers. The winning party fuses the executive and legislative branches of government, establishing the foundation of Cabinet government.

Parties are valuable in other ways as well. They articulate, or express, interests in our society, providing a non-violent outlet for debate, dissent, and pressure for change. They shape the opposition and legitimize the individuals and institutions that control political power. Parties also can be a unifying force in that they appeal to and cut across classes, regions, interests, and ethnic groups. They thus encourage cooperation and compromise by providing national symbols, heroes, and villains.

Interest groups, too, influence how scarce resources are divided. In Canada, they organize to petition and influence governments. Like parties, they operate in and help to mould the federal political system. Interest groups represent a host of interests as varied as business, agriculture, medical doctors, and even public interests such as a clean environment. Examples that students might be familiar with include the Brewers Association of Canada, which attempts to prevent the importation of inexpensive foreign beer, and the Canadian Federation of Students, which fights for lower university fees for students, but there are thousands more of these groups.

In this chapter, we examine the respective roles of parties and interest groups in the Canadian political system. We also trace the developments and changes in the parties and party system up to and beyond the October 19, 2015 Liberal victory and majority government.

PARTIES AND PARTY SYSTEMS

Political parties are organizations designed to secure the power of the state for their leaders. Unlike interest groups, political parties seek to form a government in order to realize their policies or programs. In democratic systems, this is achieved through open competition in the electoral process. In Canada, once a party exists, it may apply to be registered under the *Canada Elections Act*. If it meets all of the legal requirements (such as having at least 250 members who are electors), it will be registered. Once that is achieved, the party must endorse one or more confirmed candidates in a general election or by-election. One of the significant benefits of being registered is that the party's name may appear on the ballot, along with the name of the party's candidate in that electoral district. Registered parties are also eligible for certain financial and advertising benefits.

The relationship among parties in a political system is called the **party system**. To compare the various party systems around the world, a number of classifications have been devised. For example, democratic systems have been distinguished by whether or not they are competitive. **Competitive party systems** allow parties to compete for and have access to legislative power. Some competitive systems are *one-party dominant systems* in which a single party regularly wins almost every election, even though opposition parties function freely. Other competitive systems are *two-party systems* in which two major parties dominate and others have only minor political strength. Still other competitive systems are *multi-party systems* in which popular support is regularly divided among several parties so that the largest party must generally form a coalition with one or more other parties to form a government.

Parties and the Party System in Canada

The Canadian party system is competitive, but in terms of the number of parties, it has changed radically over time. Until the rise of third parties in 1921, when the Progressives from Western Canada won 23 percent of the federal vote, the Canadian party system developed along the lines of a classic two-party system. From 1921 to 1993, particularly after the New Democratic Party (NDP) appeared in 1961, third parties fairly consistently captured roughly a quarter of the national vote. The Liberals, Conservatives, and NDP consistently took more than 90 percent of the vote. Until 1993, therefore, the Canadian system fell somewhere between a two-party and a multi-party system. Because of this, Canada was often facetiously said to have a "two-and-a-half-party system."

political party: An organization designed to obtain the power of the state and perhaps form a government.

party system: The relationships among parties in a political system.

competitive party system: A system that allows parties to compete for, and have access to, legislative power.

The 1993 election created what is generally seen as Canada's fourth party system. Many factors contributed to the implosion of the old system—high voter cynicism, declining public confidence in representative institutions, a desire for more direct participation, rejection of consensus politics, and strong regional political interests.[1] The existing parties failed to accommodate these forces in society, and two new parties with strong regional bases filled the vacuum. A five-party "pizza Parliament" was elected, shifting the party system further toward the multi-party end of the spectrum. The new Bloc Québécois (BQ), which ran candidates only in Québec, won enough seats in Québec alone to form the Official Opposition in Parliament. In the West, the Reform Party won just two seats fewer than the BQ. In 2004, following the amalgamation of the Canadian Alliance and the Progressive Conservatives (PCs), the number of parties in Parliament was reduced to four. When the Green Party was elected in 2011 this number grew back to five, where it remains. The large majority victory of the Liberal Party in 2015 showed how the party system is still adjusting.

Other key features of the Canadian party system are that it is both *federal* and highly *regional*. The federal structure means that the oldest parties have both federal and provincial organizations. They are not, for the most part, well integrated. The federal structure also encourages the development of new parties at the provincial level. Some remain unique to one or a few provinces and never move into the federal system, while others do enter the federal contest but never come close to winning power. The BQ, for example, has no intention of extending its electoral base outside Québec.

The regional character of the party system is strong and tends to weaken the ability of parties to create governments that are representative of the entire country. To win an election, Canadian parties must obtain substantial support from at least two and perhaps three of five main regions: the Atlantic provinces, Québec, Ontario, the Prairies, and British Columbia. When severe regional imbalances occur in a party system, parties are limited in their ability to integrate interests across the country. When imbalances occur on a regular basis, it encourages the growth of regional parties as a protest against exclusion from the system. This in turn encourages viewpoints that are parochial rather than national and makes Canada more difficult to govern.

Before 1984, general elections increasingly produced governments with great regional distortions. From 1921 to 1984 and 1993 to 2006, Western Canada was mildly or severely under-represented in almost *all* government caucuses. Conversely, Québec was highly overrepresented in all Liberal government caucuses during the same period. The 2008 and 2011 elections produced relatively regionally balanced Conservative governments, and the 2015 election produced a relatively regionally balanced Liberal government.

Over the twentieth century, the Liberal Party increasingly became based in Central Canada. Ontario has the largest number of seats in the House and has tended historically to divide its votes between the two old parties. However, in 1984, the Liberal Party lost its hold there and also did poorly in every other province. On return to power in 1993, for the first time in many years, the Liberals held the Maritimes and Ontario, but did poorly in Québec (a new development) and the West (a typical result). The party's losses were due to two new regionally based parties, the separatist BQ, which surged in Québec, and the Western-based Reform Party. In 1997, the Liberals almost lost their majority in the House of Commons when the

Maritimes joined Québec and the West in the opposition camp. In 2000, the Liberals gained a few seats but remained largely locked out of Western Canada.

In 2004, the Liberals took 75 seats in Ontario and only 21 in Québec, giving them a minority government. In 2006, the Conservatives picked up 40 seats in Ontario and 10 in Québec, and it was their turn to form a minority government. In 2008, the Conservatives consolidated their position by taking 51 seats in Ontario and 10 in Québec for another minority government. Their 2011 majority win was assured by Ontario, which gave them 73 seats compared to only 11 for the Liberals and 22 for the NDP. At the same time, the BQ vote in Québec collapsed, and the NDP made a dramatic breakthrough in Québec and also did well in Ontario.

Western Canada has followed a quite different pattern. The PCs, generally strong in the West and excluded from Québec, produced governments with strong national mandates in 1958 under John Diefenbaker and in 1984 and 1988 under Brian Mulroney. However, after its devastating loss in the 1993 election—in which it was reduced to two seats in the House of Commons—the PCs struggled even to exist.

The Reform and Alliance parties that formed in the West in 1987 and 2000, respectively, tried to capture the conservative voice, but were largely restricted to that region. In 2003, the remnant PCs joined with the Canadian Alliance to form the Conservative Party of Canada (CPC). In the 2004 election, the new party still did poorly outside of the West. Then it won a minority government in 2006, largely because it did marginally better in both Ontario and Québec; in 2008, it made more gains in Ontario and British Columbia; in 2011, the CPC finally won a majority, largely due to increased support in Ontario. Cut off from their traditional support in Ontario and Québec, the Liberals dropped to third place, their worst-ever result.

Historically, parties have not been able to win a majority in the House of Commons without substantial support from Québec. This is largely because, with rare exceptions, Québec has voted relatively solidly for one party. In the twentieth century, that party was most often the Liberals, but in 1993 that changed. In that election, as in 1997 and again in 2000, 2004, 2006, and 2008, the separatist BQ took most of the votes in the province. In 2011, Québec abandoned the BQ and elected 59 New Democrats. The BQ was reduced to 4 seats and the Liberals and Conservatives to 7 and 5, respectively. The Atlantic provinces are a relatively secure bastion for the Liberals, though they did poorly there in 2011. In 2015, they took every Atlantic seat. British Columbia tends to be divided among Liberals, NDP, and Conservatives, and is also the only province in which the Green Party is a serious contender.

In 2015, the victorious Liberal Party obtained seats in all regions and all provinces (see election results in Chapter 11).

Theories about the Party System

Many ideas have been proposed to explain Canada's changing party system. The most traditional of these has been brokerage theory. **Brokerage theory** maintains that the two oldest parties in Canada have few coherent ideological interests but rather act as brokers of ideas, selecting those that have the widest appeal and the best likelihood of attracting electoral support. Parties are seen as basically pragmatic and

brokerage theory: Maintains that the two oldest parties in Canada have few coherent ideological interests, but rather act as brokers of ideas, selecting those that have the widest appeal and the best likelihood of attracting electoral support.

opportunistic. They act as conciliators, mediators, or brokers among the regions' ethnic and linguistic groups, classes, religions, ages, and genders in Canadian society. They become agents of national integration, reconciling as many interests as possible.

As agents of compromise, parties unite Canadians. However, some political scientists maintain that brokerage activities enable parties to disguise their real ideological interests—protecting the capitalist system by emphasizing ethnic and regional concerns rather than class interests. Both the Liberal and Conservative parties are considered brokerage-type parties.

one-party dominant thesis:
A general theory about Canadian parties, which holds that the Canadian government is normally dominated by one party for long periods of time.

The **one-party dominant thesis** is another traditional theory about Canadian parties.[2] It holds that, since the Canadian government is normally controlled by one party, the system is best characterized as being one-party dominant. Shortly after the beginning of the twentieth century, the Liberals took on the role of the "natural" governing party. The Conservatives were considered to be the "natural" opposition party because they were elected only occasionally when the public wanted an alternative to the Liberals. The general elections from 1993 to 2004 appeared to reconfirm the Liberals in their role as natural governing party, but in 2011 their dominance collapsed. The PCs had reinvented themselves by joining with the Canadian Alliance to create a new Conservative Party. With their 2011 majority win, they became the dominant party, but in 2015 this pattern was shattered once again by a Liberal majority victory.

The NDP has been called the "innovative party"—in reference to the fact that it never came close to power federally but did bring innovative ideas to the political game, particularly in times of minority government. In 2011, when it made a major breakthrough in Québec and became the Official Opposition for the first time, the party's role appeared to be changing. However, in 2015, the NDP dropped back to its traditional role as third party. Possibly, one could call the BQ the "destructive" party, because it seeks the breakup of Canada. The Green Party, which had its first elected member of Parliament (MP) in 2011, is still struggling to be recognized as more than an environmental party. In 2015, it ran nearly a full slate of candidates but won only one seat in Parliament.

POLITICAL PARTIES IN CANADA

In Chapter 2, we discussed the major ideologies that underlie Canadian political parties—liberalism, conservatism, and socialism. We saw that liberal values, based on a belief in a capitalist society, a market economy, and the right to private property, are dominant in Canadian society but not to the absolute exclusion of other perspectives. The main parties from Confederation until 1993—Conservative, Liberal, and New Democratic—reflected three broad ideologies but none ever strayed very far from the liberal opinions of the broader public.

Parties are dynamic institutions that contest for governmental power. They are based on ideologies as well as the interests and opinions of their members. To be successful in elections, party leaders must bring together these ideological foundations with the concerns of their memberships. Leaders must be able to convince large numbers of the general public as well as party militants to support them. In other words, leaders need to balance the principles and views of their membership while courting large numbers of voters who do not have structured or organized ideas about politics.

In the next sections, we outline the history and contemporary fortunes of the five major parties in order to understand the foundations of the current party system and assess its prospects.

The Liberal Party

The nucleus of the original Liberal Party consisted of early reformers: the Parti Rouge (French radicals) in Lower Canada, Clear Grits from Upper Canada, and anti-Confederation Nova Scotians. Alexander Mackenzie was the first leader to bring the party to power, but it achieved little cohesion and was not re-elected.

The philosophical base of the Liberal Party derived from British liberalism. The party was initially denied a foothold in Québec because of the antipathy of the Roman Catholic Church for liberalism in all of its aspects. Then Wilfrid Laurier, a French-speaking Roman Catholic, became leader in 1887. He solidified French support behind the Liberals and created a strong national Liberal Party. He still holds the record for the longest continuous term in office as prime minister (PM)—from 1896 to 1911.

After Laurier, the Liberal Party endured a decade of discontent that climaxed in bitter divisions in Québec over the Conscription Crisis. In 1919, the party elected William Lyon Mackenzie King as party leader. The Liberals won the 1921 election and King rebuilt a strong organization that dominated Canadian government for most of the next six decades. King set a record for total years in power; he was prime minister for 22 years. During his early years in office, King astutely accommodated agrarian protest in the West by forming an alliance with the Progressives. However, as we have seen, that alliance failed and the Liberals lost their support in the West. Louis St. Laurent, who succeeded King, as well as his successors, Lester Pearson (party leader from 1958 to 1968, PM from 1963 to 1968) and Pierre Trudeau (PM from 1968 to 1979 and 1980 to 1984), all failed to acquire support from the West. To varying degrees, however, they were all able to accommodate Québec's interests.

In the spring of 1984, having led his party for more than 16 years with all but 9 months of those as prime minister, Pierre Trudeau resigned. John Turner took over the party leadership and called an election within days. The Liberal Party won only 28 percent of the popular vote in the 1984 election, its worst showing ever. Turner stayed on as party leader, but his caucus was dispirited and fractious over important issues such as the Meech Lake Accord and the Free Trade Agreement with the United States. They lost to Mulroney's PCs again in 1988. Turner resigned and Jean Chrétien became party leader. In 1993, Chrétien became Canada's twentieth prime minister with massive victories in the Maritimes and Ontario as well as moderate support in the other regions.

Over the years, Canadian Liberal leaders have adopted a distinctively pragmatic approach to issues. After World War II, successive Liberal governments introduced important social welfare legislation and assumed more responsibility for directing the Canadian economy. In the late nineteenth century, when the Liberal Party was generally in opposition in Ottawa and in government in the provinces, it was a staunch defender of provincial rights. When it held power in Ottawa, however, the party shifted to espouse strong centralizing policies. Besides the 1984 *Canada Health Act*, bilingualism and a broad commitment to individual and minority rights, both linguistic and legal, were perhaps the most coherently pursued liberal policies under Trudeau, Turner, and Chrétien.

When the Liberal government under Jean Chrétien came to power in 1993, the need for deficit and debt reduction forced it to abandon policy positions that the party had supported for generations. In economic policy, trade, human rights, social programs, and immigration, the party's "conservative" element began to dominate. Despite high standings in the polls, many Liberals began to feel uncomfortable with the general policy direction the party was taking. Party veterans refused to vote the party line on the 1995 budget and other important legislation. The surge to the right continued until after the Liberals won the 1997 election and began to talk about "opening the federal purses" again. With the deficit reduced to zero, Chrétien's ministers began to act on the Liberal campaign promise to divide future surpluses among debt reduction, reduced taxation, and new social programs.

Prime Minister Chrétien called an election for November 2000, only three-and-a-half years into the Liberal government's mandate. By that fall, the government's cuts in program spending, a decline in interest rates, and a growing economy had provided an unexpected budgetary surplus for three consecutive years. When he won his third majority government in a row, Chrétien's electoral instincts appeared flawless. However, before finishing his new mandate, he was outmanoeuvred and

The Canadian Press/Adrian Wyld

Political Profile: Justin Trudeau, leader of the Liberal Party of Canada

Born: 1971
Birthplace: Ottawa, Ontario
Education: BEd, McGill University, UBC
Profession: Teacher
Leader Since: 2013
Leader's Seat: Papineau

forced to resign by Paul Martin and his supporters (who wanted time to consolidate their leadership before calling the next election).

Martin became Liberal leader in late 2003, but in the ensuing 2004 election the Liberals won only enough seats for a minority government. Then, in 2006, they narrowly lost to the Conservatives. That December, Liberals elected Stéphane Dion to lead their disorganized and dispirited party. Following a turbulent post-budget threat to bring down the government, Dion resigned and Michael Ignatieff became interim leader, then leader. In the 2011 election, the Liberals finished in third place, behind the NDP. The party won only 34 seats, the worst showing in its history. Ignatieff lost his seat and resigned. Bob Rae was interim leader until 2008 when Justin Trudeau, son of Pierre Trudeau, won the leadership in a landslide. In 2015, against great odds, he went on to win a massive majority government.

The Conservative Party of Canada

The current Conservative Party of Canada evolved from various combinations of parties over many years.

The oldest party in a country is often the party of established interests, and this is the case in Canada. The Conservative Party originated when John A. Macdonald formed a coalition of pre-Confederation groups. Its goal was to work for Confederation and then a National Policy, which basically meant encouraging national unity and developing the country by means of a national railway, industry, and commerce. At first, the coalition was unstable, but gradually an organized political party was formed. It sought to maintain the British connection and establish relatively high tariffs.

After Macdonald, the party entered its first long period in opposition. Western farmers were wary of the Tories because of their empathy for big business, and French Canadians resented the Tories' strong British affiliations. Negative French attitudes toward the Conservatives were consolidated by two events: the execution of Louis Riel and the Conscription Crisis of 1917 (discussed in Chapter 5). Yet another misfortune for the Conservatives was that they were in power during much of the Great Depression in the 1930s. They also suffered a lengthy leadership vacuum under Arthur Meighen and R.B. Bennett.

Western Canada did not exhibit a strong, single-party tradition in the pre-war period. After World War I, westerners formed the Progressive Party, which allied itself uneasily with the Liberals. In the 1940s, the Conservatives made a breakthrough by winning Progressive support in the West. They chose John Bracken from Manitoba as leader and renamed their party the Progressive Conservatives (PCs).

George Drew became leader of the PCs in 1948, but the party did not win an election until John Diefenbaker, another westerner, won a minority government for them in 1957, followed by a landslide victory the next year. Within a short time, however, Diefenbaker alienated his supporters outside the West. The Conservative defeat in 1963 deepened party factions and eventually forced Diefenbaker to retire. The party entered its second-longest continuous period in opposition. Easterner Robert Stanfield took over the divided party from Diefenbaker. After he lost his third and final campaign in 1974, Joe Clark, a "red Tory," assumed the leadership.

This consolidated Western support, but by then PC support was limited to the Atlantic provinces and rural and small-town Ontario.

Joe Clark's 1979 election victory gave the PCs their first tentative hold on power in 16 years, but just 8 months later their minority government was defeated on a budget vote. Clark accepted the results of the vote as a lack of confidence in the government and advised the governor general to dissolve Parliament. The party was defeated in the ensuing 1980 election and Clark lost the leadership at a bitter convention in 1983. The new leader, Brian Mulroney, forged alliances in Québec and the West and won relatively evenly across the entire country in 1984 and again in 1988. He formed majority governments both times.

Meanwhile, in late 1987 at the time of the first Mulroney government, Preston Manning had founded the Reform Party. The populist party tapped into feelings of economic and political alienation in Alberta in particular and the West in general. It fielded candidates in the 1988 general election but won no seats.

In the spring of 1993, Mulroney was in such disrepute following constitutional reform failures, scandals, and unpopular policies that he resigned. In June 1993, Kim Campbell became party leader and prime minister. However, her tenure was tainted by her predecessor's record and when she led the party into the election that fall, the PC Party fell in ruins. Campbell lost her own seat and the party dropped from 154 MPs to only 2. Two months later, she resigned and Jean Charest became leader of the party. The Progressive Conservatives retained their majority in the Senate, and during the thirty-fifth Parliament their 58 senators kept the party alive and functioning on Parliament Hill.

Reform, meanwhile, had run candidates in all provinces except Québec in 1993. It won 52 seats—not quite enough to become the Official Opposition but enough to displace the NDP and PCs to become the strongest voice of Western interests. However, apart from one seat in Ontario, it had no representation east of Manitoba. By the end of its first session in Parliament, Reform had not climbed higher than 14 percent in public opinion polls.

In the 1997 election, only 20 PCs won seats in the House. Reform, meanwhile, had 60 Western MPs elected. Reform formed the Official Opposition in Parliament and began to assert itself as a national party. Shortly after the election, Charest left federal politics to become leader of the Liberal Party of Québec. Former prime minister Joe Clark took over the remnants of the PC Party again but did not gain a seat in the Commons until late 2000. Manning tried to link the PC and Reform parties together, or at least to run joint candidates for the next election to avoid splitting the anti-Liberal vote, but Clark vigorously objected to any such cooperation. His refusal led to the creation of a new right-of-centre party in early 2000. Manning forced the creation of the Canadian Reform Conservative Alliance (commonly referred to as the Canadian Alliance), which linked dissident Tory groups with Reform/Alliance supporters. In the process, however, he lost the leadership of the party to Stockwell Day.

The Canadian Press/Jonathan Hayward

Political Profile: Stephen Harper, former leader of the Conservative Party of Canada

Born: 1959
Birthplace: Toronto, Ontario
Education: BA and MA, University of Calgary
Profession: Economist; past president, National Citizens Coalition
Leader 2004–2015
Leader's Seat: Calgary Southwest

In the 2000 election, the Alliance still failed to make an electoral breakthrough in Ontario (where it garnered only two seats) or further east (where it won none). The PCs, meanwhile, went into the election with a wide but scattered following that made it difficult to win many ridings. They split the vote with the Alliance Party in several Ontario ridings and won only 12 seats in the House of Commons. Clark consistently refused to compromise his "Progressive Conservative" ideals to form a so-called united right. In 2003, Peter MacKay assumed the PC leadership. He negotiated with Stephen Harper and the Alliance to form a new party, the Conservative Party of Canada, in time to fight the 2004 general election. The union was accomplished at a quasi-national convention held at 27 locations across the country. Ninety percent of Tory delegates and 96 percent of Alliance members voted for the union.

Harper was selected as leader of the new party. The merger was widely depicted as a victory for the Canadian Alliance and a defeat for the "red Tories" of Joe Clark. The amalgamation marked the end of a 40-year struggle over who would control Canada's conservative voice in Parliament. In the 2004 election, the party came in a strong second. In 2006, it defeated the Liberals and formed a minority government. The challenge now was to create a strong, stable base outside of Western Canada. In 2008, when the party won enough seats to form another minority government, it gained 10 more seats in Ontario for a total of 51. In the momentous 2011 election, the Conservatives consolidated their position with 166 of 308 seats, enough to form the first majority government for Stephen Harper. In November 2015, after nearly a decade in office, Stephen Harper resigned as prime minister and leader of the Conservative Party of Canada after a resounding electoral defeat (see Chapter 11). The newly elected caucus appointed Rona Ambrose as interim leader.

The New Democratic Party

In 1961, the New Democratic Party (NDP) was born with the same social-democratic philosophy as its precursor, the Co-operative Commonwealth Federation (CCF). Tommy Douglas, David Lewis, Ed Broadbent, Audrey McLaughlin, Alexa McDonough, Jack Layton, and Tom Mulcair led the party in turn, but until 2011 it was never more than a third party.

In 1993, the party was reduced to nine seats and lost its party status in the House. To a large extent, the Reform Party usurped the NDP role as protest party in the West. The party remained in fourth place after the 2000 election but fell from 21 seats to 13. In January 2003, when Jack Layton was elected party leader, NDP fortunes began to change radically. The party won 19 seats in 2004, not quite enough to hold the balance of power but enough to give it some bargaining power with the Liberal minority government. In 2006, it won 29 seats, almost enough to hold the balance of power with the Conservative minority government. In 2008, it won 37 seats, coming close to its record of 43 in 1988. In 2011, Layton led his party to a momentous victory, winning a record 103 seats, making it the Official Opposition. The win was based on a breakthrough in Québec, where it went into the election with only 1 seat but came out with 59 of 75. Later that year, however, the popular Layton died. He was replaced by Thomas Mulcair in 2012. In 2015, the party was reduced to 41 seats and lost its position as the Official Opposition.

Political Profile: Thomas Mulcair, leader of the New Democratic Party of Canada

Born: 1954
Birthplace: Ottawa, Ontario
Education: BCL, LLB, McGill University
Profession: Lawyer, parliamentarian (first elected provincially 1994, federally 2007)
Leader Since: 2012
Leader's Seat: Outremont

The NDP has played a larger role in Canadian politics than its success at the polls would indicate. Particularly in minority situations, tacit support from the NDP has often been vital for Liberal governments. The party is also considerably stronger at the provincial level than it is federally and has had a handful of premiers elected. Its most dramatic recent provincial win was in May 2015 in Alberta, where it formed the government for the first time.

In general, the NDP platform has been based on diluted democratic socialist goals, advocating policies such as more government regulation of the economy, including more government control of private enterprise, higher taxes for big business and industry, increased social welfare, and protection from U.S. influence in domestic and foreign policy.

The Bloc Québécois

Party leader Lucien Bouchard was a powerful minister in Brian Mulroney's PC government in 1990 when he left the party that had brought him to Ottawa. He and a handful of dissident MPs (some from the PC Party, but two were Liberals) set up a faction in the House of Commons to work for the secession of Québec from Canada. They founded the Bloc Québécois, which became the first separatist party to sit in Parliament. It went into the 1993 election with 8 seats and came out with 54, enough to become Her Majesty's Loyal Opposition in Parliament—by tradition, the government-in-waiting. The BQ, however, sought to dismantle the Canadian federation and make Québec a separate country. It won only 14 percent of the popular vote in Canada but 49 percent in Québec, where it ran all of its candidates.

Following the failed Québec referendum in October 1995, Bouchard left the BQ to lead the Parti Québécois as premier of Québec. In 1996, the reins of the BQ briefly went to Michel Gauthier, then to Gilles Duceppe. Duceppe lacked the charismatic appeal of Bouchard but grew into the job. In the 1997 election, his party won 44 seats in the House of Commons. In 2000, the BQ dropped to 38 seats. Then, in 2004, after a good campaign, the BQ won 54 of Québec's 75 seats. In 2006, it lost seats to the Conservatives, dropping to 51, but in 2008 it held most of its ground and won 49 seats, with 38 percent of the vote in Québec. The 2011 election, in which the NDP surged in Québec, left the BQ close to extinction with only four MPs. Duceppe lost his seat and resigned. Daniel Paillé was briefly leader, but in 2014 he resigned and was replaced by Mario Beaulieu, a divisive choice that reduced the party further by two resignations. Shortly thereafter, Duceppe stepped back into the leadership position and led the party into the 2015 election. The party won 10 seats, not enough for official party status, and Duceppe lost his seat to the NDP incumbent.

The BQ plays only one tune—Québec interests. Its raison d'être is to bring the issue of Québec separation to the House of Commons and thereby assist a separatist Québec government in achieving a Yes vote in a referendum on sovereignty. The volatile situation and the role of the BQ in Québec politics are discussed in Chapter 5.

ZUMA Press, Inc./Alamy Stock Photo

Political Profile: Gilles Duceppe, leader of the Bloc Québécois

Born: 1947
Birthplace: Montréal, Québec
Education: BA, Collège Mont-Saint-Louis
Profession: Orderly, union negotiator
Leader Since: 1997–2011; 2015–
Leader's Seat: Laurier–Sainte-Marie

The Green Party of Canada

The Green Party was founded in 1983. It proclaims its core values as ecological wisdom, social justice, grassroots democracy, and non-violence. Elizabeth May became party leader at a 2006 convention after she won on the first ballot with 65 percent of the votes cast. In 2011, she became the first elected Green MP to sit in the House. In 2013, she was joined by Bruce Hyer, who had left the NDP the previous year to sit as an Independent. In 2015, May was the only Green candidate elected. Most of the party's support is in British Columbia.

Political Profile: Elizabeth May, leader of the Green Party of Canada

Born: 1954
Birthplace: Hartford, Connecticut
Education: LLB, Dalhousie University
Profession: Lawyer, environmental advocate
Leader Since: 2011
Leader's Seat: Saanich–Gulf Islands

PARTY ORGANIZATION

Party Structure

Canadian parties vary in the details of their organization, but they tend to follow the same basic structure. Unlike in some countries, the same political parties compete at both federal and provincial levels of government. However, as we have seen, parties at the two levels often act independently even though they may share the same name. The provincial Liberal Party in Québec has no official affiliation with the federal Liberal Party. On the other hand, a federal party may be closely allied to a provincial party even though it has a different name, as is the case with the Bloc Québécois and the Parti Québécois. A party may restrict itself to either the federal or the provincial level, as the Wildrose does in Alberta.

At the federal level, the traditional parties consist of two wings: the *parliamentary wing*, composed of the party leader and caucus; and a large, three-tier *extra-parliamentary wing*, composed of the national executive, standing committees, a permanent national office, provincial associations, and local constituency associations. The two wings are linked at the upper levels. Both wings are dominated by the party leader.

In the extra-parliamentary party, the **constituency** or *riding* is the locus of the grassroots organization of political parties. Here, a locally elected executive leads the

constituency: A geographical area that elects one MP and is the locus of the local organization of political parties; also known as a *riding*.

party. At this level, convention delegates are elected, candidates for federal elections are chosen, and preparations are made for imminent elections. The dedication of members to this basic unit is vital to party fortunes, but at this level there are few active members and the associations meet only infrequently, so the constituency is relatively weak within the power structure of the party except during elections.

The provincial associations generally coordinate and plan political strategy and activities for implementation at the constituency level. The provincial executive has the ultimate responsibility for all federal constituencies in the province. Sometimes regional organizations exist within the provincial structures. Provincial-level organization may be shared with provincial party counterparts.

The small, permanent national office varies from party to party, but it consists essentially of a small elite that conducts business on behalf of the party as a whole. It generally includes a president, vice-president, and other officers as well as several executive committees. The national offices of the traditional parties function as links between the provincial organizations and the elected members of Parliament. They organize their respective conventions, by-elections, and general elections.

Party Membership

Parties want to increase their membership and finances, so they impose few restrictions on who can join. The separation of federal and provincial organizations even allows individuals to join different parties at different levels. The typical local association of a major party has only moderate numbers of members on the books in an average non-election year, but this mushrooms before an election when members are mobilized to help finance the party, find a candidate and help in the ensuing campaign.[3] Members may seek candidates to run, but sometimes individuals who want to be candidates recruit members to vote for them. This circumstance tends to create "instant members" who join solely to help a specific candidate win the nomination.[4]

Historically, men have been more numerous than women as members of political parties, but this has been slowly changing. Once they have joined, women are "as likely or almost as likely as their male counterparts to participate in party activities."[5] There are few gender differences in either the extent or the form of basic partisan party activities such as attending riding association meetings or contributing funds. However, women are not equally represented in political parties themselves, their campaign offices, or national conventions. Fewer women have participated in federal and provincial politics than in municipal politics, perhaps because of family responsibilities and financial limitations.[6] In recent years, federal parties have taken measures to encourage females to participate and run as candidates. A record number of women was elected in 2011, and again in 2015, but they still make up only 26 percent of MPs. However, Prime Minister Justin Trudeau appointed women as half of his first Cabinet, a landmark in Canadian politics.

Party Leaders

A **party leader** is chosen by party members to fill the pre-eminent role of decision maker, figurehead, and spokesperson in both the parliamentary and the extra-parliamentary branches of the party. A party leader is much more than "first among

party leader: The individual chosen by party members to fill the pre-eminent role of decision maker, figurehead, and spokesperson in both the parliamentary and the extra-parliamentary branches of the party.

equals." The party leader with majority support in the House of Commons is, of course, the prime minister. (The role of the PM is discussed in Chapter 6.) The other leaders are the main focus of media attention for their parties, "ambassadors" who project the ideas and abilities of their respective parties as potential governments.

The **leader of Her Majesty's Loyal Opposition** is the leader of the party with the second-largest number of seats in the House of Commons. The individual in this role spearheads the offensive against the party in power. The functions of the position are not governed by statute, but the role is officially recognized in the procedures of the House of Commons. This party leader has special status at official functions, in parliamentary ceremonies, and even with foreign governments. The job also comes with a host of minor perks, such as a car allowance and an official residence. Within the parliamentary party, the Opposition leader appoints a *shadow Cabinet*, which is a government-in-waiting, and assumes a position inferior to that of the prime minister, who heads the government and public service as well as a political party.

Party Financing

Parties require money for three main purposes: to support research and advisory services for the leader and elected MPs; to maintain a small, permanent staff between elections; and most importantly to fund election campaigns. Party caucuses receive money from the government for the first of these purposes, based on a House of Commons formula. To get such funds, parties must have a minimum of 12 elected members in Parliament. It is difficult for parties to operate effectively without this funding.

To supplement these government funds, parties seek money outside of Parliament. Before 1974, that process was somewhat secretive and based to a large extent on corporate and union donations. Reforms in 2004 brought in a new regime for financing political parties. Corporate and union donations were limited and each party in Parliament was given a quarterly allowance based on the number of votes it had received in the last election. The Harper Conservatives phased out the allowances for parties beginning in 2011 and completely eliminated them by 2015. Corporate and union donations were banned altogether. The logic was that funding ought to be tied to a party's own efforts or the willingness of the voters to contribute.

As of 2015, parties were restricted to raising money through strictly regulated individual donations. Annual limits for donations to each registered party, each registered associations, all nominated contestants and party candidates, and all leadership contestants were set at $1500. Contributions to Independent candidates were also capped at $1500 for the 2015 election. Donations are eligible for a generous tax credit.

Election financing is discussed in detail in the next chapter.

PARTIES AT WORK

The two wings of federal parties, the parliamentary party and the extra-parliamentary party, meet regularly at conventions designed to keep the party in touch with its base. These are designed as policy conventions or leadership conventions, or sometimes both.

Policy Conventions

Roughly every two years, each party holds a convention to elect party officials, debate policy resolutions and constitutional amendments, and raise morale. The policy resolutions have no formal authority and are not binding on the party leadership, but they do constitute important policy guidelines. In all parties, the debates give delegates the opportunity to air their views and communicate their policy concerns to the political wing; they also attract free publicity for the parties. The 2013 party conventions all began preparations for the 2015 election.

Party conventions in the traditional parties are large, widely representative gatherings of several thousand delegates, most of whom have already invested considerable time and energy as executive officers for the party or as members of women's or youth associations. The conventions are not designed to be representative of Canadian society as a whole but to represent that party in society. Delegates are much better educated and economically better off than the general population, and therefore cannot be defended as truly representative in any strict sense. Terms such as *democratic* and *representative* are merely part of the rhetoric used by parties and commentators to generate respect and approval for their party conventions.

Before a policy convention assembles, party associations are invited to send in topic suggestions for consideration. In theory, the resolutions presented to the delegates are debated and passed item by item. However, in fact, a resolutions committee often determines the timetable and success of resolutions.

Party platforms have contributions from both intra- and extra-parliamentary branches of the parties; they are generally what R.M. Dawson called "conspicuously unsatisfactory documents."[7] Of necessity, items must be vague enough to carry wide appeal—examples are social reform or improved education—and so end up reading rather like a list of New Year's resolutions. They must also appeal to regional interests such as maritime rights or economic sectors such as wheat exporters. Party platforms are therefore broadly based documents of compromise that can be used to unite the party nationally. As the three traditional parties have vied for the middle ground, their policy resolutions have often overlapped.

Even after the platform is drawn up and approved by the national convention, it is little more than a guide or, as Mackenzie King was fond of stating, a chart and compass for the party leader to interpret and follow as deemed opportune when steering the ship of state. A grave shortcoming of the pragmatic policy formulation procedures followed by modern Canadian parties is that parochial concerns often dominate at the expense of a national vision. This has discouraged creative thinking about long-term policy solutions to problems, so that parties have been called "political dinosaurs"—that is, having great weight and presence but small brains.

Leadership Conventions and Leadership Reviews

Leadership conventions provide a democratic element to parties and attract a great deal of media attention. Party leadership selection has changed dramatically over the years from a closed, elite system to a very open, broadly based, democratic one.

Modern leadership conventions are called after a leader resigns or dies and sometimes even if he or she does not score sufficiently high on a **leadership review** vote. Rules about when a leadership review will be held differ from party to party.

In practice, Liberal leadership review votes have never called for a leadership convention, but the procedure remains a significant reminder that the leader is responsible to the party. In the Conservative Party, mandatory leadership review now occurs at the first convention following a general election. Since 2003, the NDP has had a similar leadership review mechanism.

Traditional leadership conventions were huge, expensive events. Delegates were chosen and the manner in which this was done had important consequences for the leadership candidates. To be more democratic, parties in recent years abandoned the convention system for electing leaders in favour of "one member, one vote" (OMOV) systems and proportional systems in which each member of the party casts a vote for the leader, and all ballots have equal weight; or a modified version of OMOV where votes are weighed differently to ensure equality among ridings.

Leadership campaign costs have escalated dramatically in recent years. To keep costs low and to discourage candidates from relying on large sums of money from a few donors who hope for future considerations, leadership contestant spending is strictly regulated under the *Canada Elections Act*. New rules limit individual contributions to leadership contestants to $1500. No corporation or other entity may contribute funds to a leadership contestant. This should counter the general criticism that the convention process allows those with the money to walk away with the prize. It is unlikely that parties will abandon conventions because of the media exposure they provide. Nor will they risk returning to earlier models of parliamentary selections that were swift and inexpensive but smacked of undemocratic elitism.

The Conservative Party of Canada
When the Conservative Party of Canada chose Stephen Harper as leader in March 2004, the rules featured a point system in which

- each riding was weighted equally
- each riding was valued at 100 points
- in each riding a preferential ballot (single transferable vote) was used—party members ranked their choices in order of preference. If no candidate received more than 50 percent of the first choices, the ballots were counted again. Candidates with the lowest number of first-place choices were dropped and their ballots went to the second choices
- candidates were assigned points based on their percentage of the vote in the riding (e.g., a candidate winning 29 percent of the vote got 29 points)
- to win, a candidate had to obtain a majority of points across all constituencies

Rather than have delegates attend a convention to choose their leader, Conservative Party members voted across the country, while in Toronto the three

Table 10.1 Leadership Vote, Conservative Party of Canada, 2004

	Tony Clement		Stephen Harper		Belinda Stronach	
	Points	%	Points	%	Points	%
1st Ballot	2887	(9.4%)	17 296	(56.2%)	10 613	(34.5%)

leadership candidates made final presentations that were beamed to the ridings. About 253 000 Conservatives were eligible to vote, and 37 percent did. The results were announced from Toronto.

Stephen Harper won a majority on the first ballot (see Table 10.1), so there was no need to count second choices. Belinda Stronach led in Atlantic Canada and Québec while Harper won in British Columbia, the Prairie provinces, and Ontario.

The Liberal Party The last contested Liberal leadership contest to be decided by convention delegates was in 2006 when Stéphane Dion was elected leader. In 2009, Michael Ignatieff's leadership bid was uncontested. At that convention the Liberal Party adopted a constitutional amendment requiring future leaders to be elected according to a weighted OMOV system in which all party members cast ballots indicating their preference in order for all candidates. The ballots are counted to see if any candidate has achieved 50 percent– plus-one majority. If so, that candidate becomes leader. In 2013, 130 774 Liberals registered to vote. They cast their votes on line and by telephone. Justin Trudeau was elected leader on the first ballot under this new formula (see Table 10.2).

Like the Conservative model, the new formula is based on a preference system model that allocates ballet choices so that the leader must receive 50 percent plus one of the votes cast. Each riding is assigned a total of 100 points, and these points are determined by the percentage of the vote each candidate receives in a riding. The results are then added together for all ridings, and if one person has 50 percent of the points, he or she is the new leader. However, if no one receives 50 percent, the preferences for each riding are redistributed. The person with the lowest percentage of votes is dropped, and his or her preferences are redistributed. This process continues until someone receives 50 percent of the vote. This was not necessary, however, as Trudeau won on the first ballot.

Table 10.2 Leadership Vote, Liberal Party of Canada, 2013

1st Ballot Candidates	Points Won	Percentage
Martin Cauchon	815.86	2.65
Deborah Coyne	214.14	0.70
Martha Hall Findlay	1 760.43	5.72
Karen McCrimmon	210.08	0.68
Joyce Murray	3 130.76	10.16
Justin Trudeau	24 668.71	80.09

Candidate	1st ballot	%	2nd ballot	%	3rd ballot	%	4th ballot	%
Niki Ashton	3 737	5.7						
Jarnail Singh	3 821	5.9						
Paul Dewar	4 883	7.5						
Nathan Cullen	10 671	16.4	12 449	19.9	15 426	24.6		
Brian Topp	13 915	21.4	15 624	25.0	19 822	31.6	25 329	42.8
Thomas Mulcair	19 728	30.3	23 902	38.3	27 488	43.8	33 881	57.2
Total	65 108	100	62 494	100	62,736	100	59,210	100

Table 10.3 Leadership Vote, New Democratic Party of Canada, 2012

The New Democratic Party At its leadership convention in 2003, the NDP also opened the vote to all party members. They devised a complex system that combined member and delegate votes. All party members were eligible to vote, ranking leadership candidates in order of preference. Unions and other interest groups were allotted 25 percent of the vote. Some members voted in advance, over the Internet, and did not attend the convention. The party used a preferential OMOV ballot system. Those who attended the convention were able to vote and cast their preference votes there. The winner needed 50 percent plus one to win on the first ballot. If no candidate received 50 percent plus one, there would be more rounds of voting with the last-place candidate eliminated. Jack Layton won 53 percent on the first ballot.

In March 2012, after the death of Jack Layton, the NDP elected Thomas Mulcair as its leader. Mulcair won with 57.2 percent on the fourth ballot (see Table 10.3). For the first time, no portion of the vote was allotted for labour unions. All votes were treated equally.

The Bloc Québécois The Bloc Québécois, too, has made its leadership selection more democratic. Leader Lucien Bouchard was acclaimed at a party congress in 1991. Five years later, his successor, Michel Gauthier, was elected by fewer than 160 Québeckers in one of the fastest, smallest, and least publicized gatherings to elect an Opposition leader in the postwar era. However, Gilles Duceppe was elected in March 1997 by the entire party membership, using the format of mailed ballots plus a two-day convention. In 2011, after his party's severe electoral losses (including his own seat), Duceppe resigned and Daniel Paillé was elected leader on the second ballot with 61.3 percent of the vote. In 2014, Paillé resigned and Mario Beaulieu became leader on the first ballot with 53.5 percent of the vote. Within months, Beaulieu abandoned the leadership to Gilles Duceppe, a more popular leader.

INTEREST GROUPS AND MOVEMENTS IN CANADA

Many Canadians who want to influence public policy prefer to do so more directly than through party activity. An alternative is to join a group that is organized to influence governments in a specific policy area. Such groups are normally called *interest groups*, *pressure groups*, or, more recently, *advocacy groups*.

Some political scientists prefer the term *advocacy groups* because of the pejorative connotation of the former terms—that all groups that act in the political arena are self-serving.[8] Of course, many groups are engaged primarily in seeking financial or other benefits for their members, but others are engaged in political action because they want to achieve something that they believe is in the public interest, generally an environmental or social cause such as saving endangered species, reducing the causes of global warming, or seeking equality rights. There is a very broad range of such groups and their motivations and contributions to society vary, but they all provide a legitimate and important form of interaction with the government.

We can define an **interest group** as an "organized association, which engages in activity relative to governmental decisions."[9] Interest groups are important to the practice of democratic politics. They also play an important role in the theory of liberal democracy, which holds that the struggle between individual and group self-interest produces the public good. According to **pluralist theory** (a theory that interest groups accept), there are many centres of power in society, and a state's public policy reflects the conflict, cooperation, and compromise of many independent interest groups. Pluralist theory considers interest groups to be relatively active and the state relatively passive in generating public policy. It makes public interest synonymous with competitive self-interest.[10]

Sometimes, informal networks of groups and individuals form broad collective identities to work for social change. They are based on ideas and altruism and have only loose organizational form. They are neither organized interest groups nor political parties. They are **movements**. Movements are tied to ideologies that seek broad social change on issues such as nationalism, nuclear energy, the women's movement, minorities, the environment, animal rights, and nuclear weapons. They often flow across national borders, with international links to groups and individuals who share their vision for social and political change, whereas interest groups are more particularistic and normally reside inside national borders. On occasion, both interest groups and movements may transform themselves into political parties, as is the case with the Green Party.

The structure and behaviour of interest groups and movements are closely related to the political system in which they operate. In modern democracies, interest groups and social movements voice the social and political demands of their members and defend them in society and in the political forum, playing a mediating function between society and government. In authoritarian or communist countries, where citizens have few legal rights to organize associations, unauthorized interest groups sometimes attempt to influence the government by dramatic demonstrations intended to attract international publicity. This was the circumstance at China's Tiananmen Square in 1989 when students demonstrating for democratic reforms were massacred. Of course, in democracies, this may also be the tactic of weak interest groups that have few other avenues to influence the government.

In Canada, interest groups organize legally to petition and cajole the government. They operate in and help to mould the federal political system. Thousands of individuals work in Ottawa and provincial capitals representing interest groups, some of which employ experts such as professional lobbyists, public relations firms, or highly paid lawyers to promote their agendas. Others occasionally send their local officials or CEOs to argue their cases. Many attempt to attract public attention and garner wider support. What they all have in common is the desire to influence government policy, legislation, regulation, or expenditures.

interest group: An organization that engages in activity related to governmental decisions.

pluralist theory: A theory of interest group activity that holds that there are many centres of power in society, and a state's public policy reflects the conflict, cooperation, and compromise of independent interest groups with the government.

movement: An informal network of groups and individuals that works for social change. It is usually founded on an altruistic idea and tends to have only loose organizational form.

However, for all of their importance in the democratic system, there are also problems with interest groups. Who gets to participate in them? Are they just another vehicle for elites to have access to those in political power? Are they able to buy favours at the expense of poorer, less privileged Canadians? Does the public know what different groups are trying to achieve and how they are going about it? Is the government engaged in patronage and pork-barrel activities, giving special favours to some interest groups in return for money or gifts? Are unethical activities such as bribery or blackmail ever involved? Citizens' groups often complain about the influence of big business; business people disparage the persistent pleading of narrowly formed special interest organizations. Some skeptics even harbour the suspicion that interest groups conflict with the basic attributes of democracy because they do not work openly through political parties.

The context of government, whether it is in a majority or minority situation, helps to determine the kind of action that interest groups can take. Minority governments are by nature fragile and vulnerable and can more easily be coerced into acting in favour of groups in order to stay in office.

Some political scientists have argued that Canadian parties have been "in decline," or at least "in transition," as part of a general decline in the role of Parliament.[11] They note that ideological differences between the parties have broken down and other organizations such as interest groups have taken their place. Interest groups have proliferated, the theory goes, because groups prefer to bypass politicians and go directly to more knowledgeable bureaucrats and influential ministers in order to influence policy formulation. In any case, interest groups are flourishing and increasingly sophisticated. They may have even usurped some of the traditional functions of parties.

The Nature of Interest Groups

Some interest groups are relatively transient and issue-oriented while others are institutionalized with many general as well as specific interests.

There are four primary characteristics of interest groups:

1. They have a formal structure of organization
2. They articulate and aggregate interests
3. They act within the political system to influence policy outputs
4. They seek to influence power rather than exercise the responsibility of government themselves—that is, they do not put candidates forward in elections[12]

Like parties, interest groups perform several important functions in liberal democracies:

- They are a major source of communication and mediation between society and government
- They are a means of articulating opinions
- They provide a mechanism for political representation that supplements parties and the electoral process
- They educate governments and keep them in touch with citizens, providing a valuable link between citizens and public policy

- They keep the government in touch with shifts of opinion in society
- They disseminate information by passing on explanations of government policy to their members and to government officials

Interest groups in Canada reflect a wide range of issues and concerns. The Directory of Associations in Canada lists several thousand organizations. Because of the federal political structure of the country, most major interest groups have federated organizations. Both federal and provincial governments, for example, regulate interests in the economic sphere.

While the majority of interest groups are privately funded, a number of them, such as the Consumers' Association of Canada and Pollution Probe, are partially financed by government. Funding began as early as the 1970s to help social groups, such as the National Anti-Poverty Organization, that could not achieve as high a degree of access to government as established groups with good political connections. Groups that receive government money are often criticized because they receive assistance directly through grants and/or contributions, or indirectly through tax breaks, even though they may not reflect the views of the public at large. In the February 1995 budget, Finance Minister Paul Martin announced that the government's approach to interest group funding would change:

> Some groups will continue to be funded. . . . For others in a position to secure financial support from outside government, we will move toward a system based on the provision of matching funds. For still other groups continued funding will not be possible due to our financial situation.[13]

This financial reorganization continued and was enhanced by Conservative governments.

Interest Groups and Lobbying

The political activity of interest groups is known as lobbying. **Lobbying** is activity aimed at securing favourable policy decisions or the appointment of specific government personnel. **Lobbyists** are individuals or organizations who are paid by interest groups to influence government legislation. Governments also hire lobbyists and periodically call on them for advice or research. Lobbyists are useful to governments because their information enables bureaucrats and politicians to develop policies that may gain approval and possibly votes. Lobbying is, in fact, the other side of the patronage coin. The government has many lucrative contracts to give out. Both lobbying and patronage involve the use of political leverage to seek advantage for an individual, group, company, or project. Some interest groups lobby on their own behalf, sending local officials or chief executive officers to argue their cases; others employ experts such as professional lobbyists, public relations firms, or highly paid tax lawyers to promote their interests (see Table 10.4).

Lobbying has a bad reputation in many quarters. There is nothing wrong with lobbying—at least not in principle. People who make decisions about public policy should receive as much information from the various interested parties

lobbying: Activity aimed at securing favourable policy decisions or the appointment of specific government personnel.

lobbyists: Individuals or organizations who are paid by interest groups to influence government legislation.

Table 10.4 Examples of Consultant Lobbying Firms and Their Clients

Firm	Clients
Capital Hill Group	Lockheed Martin; Loews; Canadian Tire
CFN Consultants	Lockheed Martin; Microsoft
Earnscliffe Strategy Group	Petro-Canada; Microsoft; Labatt
Global Public Affairs Inc.	BP Canada; Shell Canada
GPC International	Government of Hong Kong; Labatt
Hill & Knowlton Canada Ltd	Motorola; Dow Chemical; Alcan
Sussex Strategy Group	Molson; Ontario Dental Association; Bell Canada

Source: From the list of lobbyist registrations at the website for the Office of the Commissioner of Lobbying of Canada; available at www.ocl-cal.gc.ca/epic/site/lobbyist-lobbyiste1.nsf/Intro.

as possible. However, lobbying becomes worrisome when special interests use money, cash, gifts, or donations to campaign funds, and so on to seek favours and thereby cross the line between persuading politicians or bureaucrats and bribing them.

To make lobbying open and fair, Parliament has established rules to regulate it. The *Lobbyists Registration Act* of 1989 set basic requirements for the registration of paid lobbyists, including that lobbyists were to provide information about themselves and the subject matter of their lobbying. This confirmed the legitimacy of lobbying and set up a registry for lobbying consultants.

Although the term *lobbying* covers any effort to interact with government on matters of policy or procurement, federal restrictions apply only when such activities are undertaken for compensation. Only paid lobbyists have to register. This rule is not stringent enough for many observers. One lobbyist even declared that the registration rules were a farce, estimating that, at the federal level alone, roughly 100 000 people "devote a significant portion of their time trying to convince government of the rightness of their position."[14]

In 1993, the Liberal Party campaigned on reforming the lobbying business. In June 1995, the government passed Bill C-43, which made some relatively minor amendments to the *Lobbyists Registration Act*, including strengthening the disclosure requirements. This was followed by several more relatively minor amendments clarifying definitions in the Act, changing the reporting structure for lobbyists, and so on. In 2008, however, the Conservative government of Stephen Harper brought in a new *Lobbying Act*. It identified three types of lobbyists:

1. Consultant lobbyists: Lobbyists hired to communicate on behalf of a client. They could be professional lobbyists or any other individuals.

2. In-house lobbyist (corporations): Someone who is paid to work for an entity that operates for profit.

3. In-house lobbyist (organizations): Someone who works for compensation in a non-profit entity.

The 2008 *Lobbying Act* brought in some tough new measures.[15]

- It established a new **commissioner of lobbying** as an independent agent of Parliament, giving the commissioner enhanced investigative powers and a mandate to enforce compliance with the *Lobbying Act* and the Lobbyists' Code of Conduct.

- It placed a five-year ban on lobbying for ministers, ministerial staffers, and senior public servants after leaving office.

- It banned the payment of contingency fees based on the outcome of a consultant lobbyist's activity and required that all government contracts and agreements state that contingency fees will not be paid.

- It required that all contacts with designated public office holders be recorded.

commissioner of lobbying: An independent agent of Parliament with investigative powers and a mandate to enforce compliance with the *Lobbying Act* and the Lobbyists' Code of Conduct.

The regulations were intended to make the lobbying registration procedure more *transparent*; provide equitable, not selective or privileged, public access to government officials; and allow the public the opportunity to be aware of who is attempting to influence the government and in what regard.

Targets of Interest Group Activity

In seeking access to the political system to further their particular cause, interest groups and lobbyists in democracies focus on one or more of three main target areas: *politicians*, *bureaucracy*, and *political parties*. It is important for interest groups to use the access points provided within the political system and establish a framework for mutual consultation (see Close-Up 10.1). Once a pattern is established, it indicates that the group has obtained recognition as the representative for its particular interests. The Canadian Council of Chief Executives has achieved recognition as the lobby for business interests and, for example, was extraordinarily successful in campaigning for the Canada–U.S. Free Trade Agreement (FTA) and North American Free Trade Agreement (NAFTA).

Close-Up 10.1

Who Lobbies Federal Government Officials the Most?

Lobby groups that had the most contact with federal officials in the year before the 2015 election (June 2014 to June 2015) were:

1. Alliance of Manufacturers and Exporters Canada (239 contacts monthly)
2. Heart and Stroke Foundation of Canada (200 contacts monthly)
3. The Canadian National Railway Co. (144 contacts)
4. The Mining Association of Canada (138 contacts)
5. Federation of Canadian Municipalities (127 contacts)
6. Canadian Federation of Students (117 contacts)

The Canadian Federation of Students was lobbying a wide range of government institutions, including Aboriginal Affairs and Northern Development Canada, Elections Canada, and Industry Canada, on topics that included Canadian summer jobs programs (seeking to increase their annual budget) and Canada Graduate Scholarships (seeking to increase reward levels and expansion of recipients). They also held discussions with MPs and senators about national framework legislation for post-secondary education funding.

For a complete list of who lobbies and whom and what issues are being lobbied, see the 12-month lobbying summary at www.ocl-cal.gc.ca.

Groups target different access points depending on the type of group, its resources, the type of issues involved, and the circumstances of the government—whether majority or minority. Most lobbyists establish friendly relationships with legislators, bureaucrats, and media, or other group contacts, in order to present their cases in informal, persuasive ways.

In Parliament, access to the policy process is available through individual MPs, via the committee system or caucus, and of course through the Cabinet. Successful access requires knowledge of the institutional and procedural structures of government and the legislative system. Legislation and expenditures are generally approved by the executive as a package. By the time a particular package reaches Parliament, the government has publicly committed itself to the policies therein, and little can be done to change the details. The early stages are particularly important for interest groups because although Parliament passes laws it rarely originates them. Some lobbies, however, have been powerful enough to delay legislation or cause it to be altered at later stages (see Close-Up 10.2).

Since it is responsible for initiating legislation, *Cabinet* is a natural target for interest group activity. In the pre-parliamentary stages of a bill, the minister preparing a new policy is responsible for gathering information from interest groups. At the same time, government secrecy requires that the groups cannot be informed about the government's intentions regarding decisions or policy details.

The *bureaucracy* is a significant access point in the pre-parliamentary stages of a bill because it is concerned with policy in its earliest formation. Civil servants are required by their ministers to research and evaluate policy proposals for Cabinet, give advice on the public acceptability of these policies, and even help to educate and inform the public about them. Another opportunity for pressure exists during the drafting and amendment of a bill, but this is more difficult to achieve.

Interest groups seek access to *individual MPs* more for their long-term political influence than for immediate assistance. Without special information or interest, an MP can be of little direct help. Sometimes, however, an MP may take up the cause of an interest group—perhaps because it is politically expedient to do so, or because the group provides information for a well-informed question or speech in the House that might earn the MP credit and recognition within party caucus or in his constituency.

The *committee system* is an attractive access point for interest groups because the purpose of committees is to gather information. When legislation is before a House committee, all interests are invited to present briefs. It is not uncommon for interest groups to have representatives on legislative committees. Some interest groups prefer to lobby Senate committees rather than House committees. Senate committees tend to handle testimony from corporations less politically than do House committees.

Interest groups also attempt to influence *parties*. Political parties provide government leaders, and therefore party decisions may become government policy decisions. Some interest groups, particularly labour associations, openly collaborate with specific political parties, and even affiliate with them, providing both financial and political support for the party (as the Canadian Labour Congress has been affiliated with the NDP). Sometimes, however, groups do not want to be identified with one particular party in case it might harm their cause. Parties also are often wary of affiliation with specific interest groups, particularly if such a connection might alienate voters. They often prefer discreet collaboration and support.

The Government vs. Lobbyists in the "Smoking Wars"

The "war" began in earnest in 1987–1988 over the government's Bill C-51 to ban tobacco advertising and promotion. Regulating the industry was not an easy decision for the government. On one side were the tobacco companies; on the other were various health groups, such as the Canadian Medical Association (CMA) and the Non-Smokers' Rights Association. The tobacco industry has many influential allies; some are directors of tobacco companies or on their boards, and other allies are in Parliament itself. Tobacco companies have been generous contributors to the coffers of political parties, and governments make huge sums of money from cigarette taxes.

However, the Liberal government was determined to ban tobacco advertisements. Health groups banded together to support the bill, while the tobacco manufacturers engaged lobbyist William Neville to prevent regulation of their industry. The campaign quickly went public with newspaper advertisements and a sophisticated direct-mail campaign by both sides.

The tobacco lobby appealed to the Supreme Court of Canada and in 1995 received a ruling in its favour. The Supreme Court found the 1988 *Tobacco Products Control Act* unconstitutional because Ottawa's nearly total advertising ban violated the industry's right to free speech. Companies were allowed to put their logos and trademarks back on their promotional items and to resume all forms of advertising.

The Supreme Court did preserve Parliament's right to legislate in the matter, however. It said that the federal government could pass a new law if it wanted to restrict tobacco advertising. In late 1996, the government tabled another bill on smoking. Bill C-71 was designed to give the feds sweeping powers to regulate the content of tobacco products and to severely limit advertising—including where and in what form tobacco company logos could appear on advertisements for arts and sporting events.

The tobacco CEOs and their allies made the survival of the industry a national unity issue by arguing that since most of Canada's cigarettes were made in Québec, impeding the tobacco industry would badly hurt the depressed Montréal economy. The industry also appealed to Canadian nationalism. Tobacco companies for some time had sponsored sports teams and events such as car races, and arts events such as the Vancouver International Film Festival. Many of these groups depended on tobacco sponsorship and several threatened to leave Canada if the government went ahead with its policy.

After more than a decade, the *Tobacco Act* finally was passed in 1997, with regulations that included restrictions on how tobacco was to be manufactured, packaged, displayed, and sold. Packages had to display information about the product, its emissions, and the health hazards associated with it. The Act banned tobacco ads in public places and inside stores but permitted them in print publications with a "primarily adult readership." Display of brand names at cultural or sporting events were limited to 10 percent of available signage. It became more difficult for young people to buy cigarettes. An amendment to the Act allowed a five-year transitional period leading to a full ban on sponsorship promotions on October 1, 2003.

While the controls achieved have been significant, as of 2014 roughly 16 percent of Canadians 15 years of age and older still smoked, with prevalence highest among young adults 25 to 34 years of age (22 percent).* Meanwhile, more than 85 percent of lung cancer cases are still related to smoking.

The anti-smoking lobby is winning. Apart from pressing for federal legislation, it continues to be active at provincial and municipal levels of government and has achieved legislation in several provinces restricting smoking in public places. However, the smoking lobby has kept its products on the market. The tobacco wars have already lasted more than 20 years and are certain to continue as new "spitless, smokeless, and flavoured" forms of tobacco use are being researched by tobacco firms, and electronic cigarettes are on the market.

Does the fact that smoking-related diseases kill nearly 45 000 Canadians a year justify even tougher government restrictions on the industry?

*Health Canada, "Tobacco Use in Canada: Patterns and Trends, Canadian Tobacco Use Monitoring Survey," www.hc-sc.gc.ca. Accessed August 2015.

Lobbying MPs is probably least effective when a policy is already before Parliament in the form of legislation. Once it has reached this stage, legislation is more apt to be blocked or delayed than changed. The most effective form of lobbying, therefore, is generally to target key bureaucrats and ministers while policy is in the gestation stage and before it is introduced in Parliament.

To be successful, groups must be flexible enough to approach and adapt to all available access points. Often, the key to lobbying success is in the timing. If lobbyists have failed at the pre-parliamentary phase, they can try again when legislation is before the House of Commons. To be successful, lobbyists must "throw out their line everywhere," especially during general elections. In a notable case during the 2015 election, such a "line" was thrown not by lobbyists but by the Liberal campaign co-chair, who sent a detailed email to people behind the Energy East pipeline with advice on how and when to lobby a new government.[16] (The individual in question was asked to resign for his behaviour.)

During minority governments, the channels of access for interest groups shift somewhat. The diffuse structure of minority governments makes it difficult for those in power to develop coherent programs. They must continually bargain for support. Therefore, individual MPs and opposition parties become more significant access points for interest groups because their votes are vital to the government.

Discussion Questions

1. How would you depict and classify the Canadian party system?

2. Would Canada function better if it had only two national political parties? If so, which would you choose?

3. Have party leadership contests changed for the better or worse over recent years?

4. Are lobbyists sufficiently well regulated?

5. If you were advising a group that wanted the government to lower the voting age, what access points would you advise them to target?

Chapter 11

Elections and Political Behaviour

The Contests and the Messengers

Learning Objectives

After reading this chapter, you should be able to

1   Explain how and why the electoral map was drawn and revised for the 2015 general election.

2   Outline the basic rules concerning how elections are called, who can run, who can vote, and how elections are financed.

3   Explain the strengths and weaknesses of the single-member constituency plurality voting system and compare it to the benefits and drawbacks of proportional representation systems.

4   Explain the advantages and drawbacks of referendums.

5   Describe the 2015 general election results in terms of regions, parties, issues, and platforms.

6   Describe the changing role of the media and polls in elections.

Elections are indispensable to democratic government. They link political authorities with the public and bring together political and state institutions. They are "championship" contests that bestow power and prestige on the winners. As well, they provide voters with the opportunity to make individual political decisions, which, taken together, determine the composition of the government. But all elections are not equal; they range from highly democratic elections to "show" elections that are rigged to produce a specific result. Understanding the democratic rules is vital to evaluating elections.

Elections enable voters to choose fellow citizens to serve for a limited time in positions of political power. They also enable a peaceful way of resolving disputes. Above all, they provide for the orderly succession of government by the transfer of authority to new leaders. Competitive elections are a crucial difference between democratic and non-democratic states. Without elections, leaders emerge through heredity (as in a monarchy) or by force (as in a military government).

In democracies, public opinion and the media also provide a link between politicians and the people. Politicians depend on the media to communicate with the public. They do their best to control what the public will hear and see, but they cannot do this entirely because the media, to a large extent, are independent of the political process.

Both politicians and journalists rely heavily on being able to gauge public opinion through opinion polls.

In this chapter, we survey Canada's electoral history up to the 2015 election and the rules governing these tumultuous events that determine political winners and losers. We examine aspects of the electoral system and assess the 2015 election and its results. In the last section of the chapter, we review the role of the media and polls in elections.

FEDERAL ELECTIONS IN CANADA

Voting is the main political activity of most Canadians. When they participate in elections, Canadians authorize that a new government be formed. When they express confidence in the system through their participation, they also provide governments with the legitimacy they need to generate support and acceptance for their policy decisions. In short, by participating they help to govern the country.

In 2015, Canada held its forty-second general election. If founding father and the country's first prime minister, Sir John A. Macdonald, had been alive, he would have been amazed to see how elections have changed since Confederation. Over time, electoral law has become much more democratic. The basic structure of the Canadian system was imported from Britain, where competitive elections were established during the eighteenth and nineteenth centuries. As British society changed over time, the **franchise**—the right to vote—was gradually extended.

franchise: The right to vote.

At Confederation, Canada accepted the British concept of representative government. As in Britain, voting was restricted to a chosen few—only males were enfranchised, and they had to own property. In the first two elections after Confederation, people voted orally, which meant that they were open to intimidation and bribery. Different constituencies voted on different days, which allowed the government to manipulate public opinion by calling the election in safe areas first, hoping that they could create a bandwagon effect in their favour.

As we shall see, a great many reforms have been made since those early days, among them who is qualified to vote. The property requirement was gradually eliminated. In 1917, the vote was extended to women who served in World War I or who were related to men fighting overseas. At the same time, however, the vote was denied to Canadian citizens who had come from "enemy alien" countries. At the end of the war in 1918, the right to vote was extended to all women, and two years later, in 1920, a uniform federal franchise was established. Restrictions on Canadians of Asian ancestry were removed by 1948, but religious conscientious objectors, mainly Mennonites, who had been disenfranchised as early as 1920, did not have their voting rights restored until 1955. Inuit people first received the vote in 1950 and Aboriginal people living on reserves were enfranchised in 1960. In 1970, voting age was lowered from 21 to 18, and in 1975, British subjects who were not Canadian citizens lost their right to vote here.

By 2002, a few more electoral disqualifications for specific groups had been eliminated—including judges, and persons who are inmates in a correctional institution or a federal penitentiary regardless of the length of the term they are serving. New mechanisms were also established to allow Canadian citizens to vote if they are absent from Canada at election time.

The electoral system itself and other electoral rules have also seen many changes. In light of the *Canadian Charter of Rights and Freedoms*, which states that every citizen of Canada has democratic rights "subject only to such reasonable limits prescribed by law as can be demonstrably justified in a free and democratic society," governments have amended the *Canada Elections Act* law to prohibit corrupt or illegal practices and make elections more fair. The most recent changes were made through the *Fair Elections Act* of 2014.

THE ELECTORAL SYSTEM AND ITS RULES

The term **electoral system** refers to the means by which votes cast for candidates are translated into legislative seats. No electoral system is neutral. Each has advantages and inherent biases. The basic rule of the Canadian system is that governments are formed on the basis of the number of members of Parliament (MPs) elected to the House of Commons, regardless of the overall percentage of votes their parties achieve.

A **constituency** (also called a riding or an electoral district) is the geographical area that is represented in the House of Commons by an MP. Canada has a **single-member plurality electoral system** (commonly referred to as first-past-the-post) in which one member or representative is elected from each constituency. This member does not need to gain an absolute majority of votes—just more votes than any other candidate (called a plurality).

The rules concerning the conduct of elections are set down in the *Canada Elections Act*, which was passed in 1974 and has been amended many times since. **Elections Canada** is the government agency that administers elections and is responsible solely to Parliament, not to the government.

When Are Elections Called?

The prime minister advises the governor general on the dissolution of Parliament and when an election should be called. **Dissolution** is the formal ending of the life of a particular Parliament. In minority governments, the government may be defeated in a vote of non-confidence in the House of Commons, causing dissolution to occur earlier than the set date on which it might otherwise have happened. Once Parliament is dissolved, the MPs are regular citizens once again and an election is held.

In 2007, legislation was passed to set fixed elections dates for the House of Commons every four years, on the third Monday in October. The fixed election date was a significant change in electoral law. Previously, prime ministers were required to ask the governor general to dissolve Parliament and call an election at least once every five years, at the prime minister's discretion. This allowed the prime minister leeway to set the date at the most favourable opportunity for the governing party. As we saw in Chapter 7, the new fixed-date legislation limited, but did not eliminate, the possibility of an earlier dissolution. Following the new rules, the 2015 election was the first to be held on the fixed date of October 19, after considerable speculation about whether Prime Minister Stephen Harper would call it earlier.

electoral system: Refers to the means by which votes cast for candidates are translated into legislative seats.

constituency: A geographical area that elects one MP and is the locus of the local organization of political parties; also known as a *riding*.

single-member plurality electoral system: Commonly referred to as first-past-the-post, a system by which the candidate who receives the most votes, a plurality in each constituency, wins that constituency.

Elections Canada: A government agency that administers elections and is responsible solely to the House of Commons.

dissolution: The end of a particular Parliament, which occurs at the request of a prime minister who seeks a new mandate, or whose government has been defeated in the House of Commons.

How Are the Number of Seats and Constituency Boundaries Determined?

Provinces vary widely in population size, and cities are highly populated while rural areas are sparsely occupied, so it is difficult to draw constituency boundaries to make votes equal across the country and within provinces. The *Representation Act, 1985* was passed to achieve representation by population as closely as possible, while at the same time guaranteeing the smaller provinces a minimum number of MPs.

To achieve this dual objective of "rep by pop" and fairness among provinces, four steps are followed in deciding how many constituencies, or seats, each province will have, and how the boundaries are drawn to achieve as similar population size as possible:

1. An electoral quotient is established based on the population of the provinces. It was set at 111 166 for the 2015 election. In future elections, the electoral quotient will be adjusted to reflect average provincial growth since the last redistribution.

2. The population of each province is divided by this electoral quotient to obtain the number of seats to which each is entitled.

3. Adjustments are made to account for the "senatorial clause" and the "grandfather clause." The senatorial clause in the Constitution guarantees that no province can have fewer members in the House of Commons than it has in the Senate; the "grandfather clause" guarantees that no province shall have fewer seats than it had in 1976, during the thirty-third Parliament.

4. A "representation rule" is applied for provinces whose population was over-represented at the end of the last redistribution process. If a province's population is under-represented at this point in the process, the province is given extra seats so that its number of seats is proportional to its share of the population.

These four steps establish the number of seats each province will have. Then, three more seats, one for each territory (Northwest Territories, Yukon, and Nunavut), are added to this seat allocation total to determine the number of seats in the House of Commons. This process provides for a gradual increase in the size of the House based on overall population increases (see Figure 11.1). The number of MPs from each province and the overall total in the House of Commons therefore changes based on population as determined by the decennial census, the last of which was held in 2011.

Following these rules, and based on the 2011 census results, the House of Commons membership increased to 338 seats from 308 for the 2015 election. Ontario got 15 additional MPs, Alberta and British Columbia each got 6, and Québec got 3. The redistribution reflected that three provinces—Ontario, B.C., and Alberta—have been growing more quickly than the others.

When the number of voters in a constituency increases, boundaries may also have to change to make room for new districts. After each full census, 10 federal boundary commissions are established, each with three members: a judge (designated by the chief justice of the province) and two other residents of the

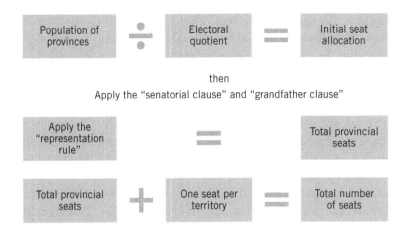

Figure 11.1 Formula for Calculating Representation in the House of Commons

province (appointed by the speaker of the House of Commons). These officials note the total changes in population that have taken place in the provinces and also the details about which cities, towns, and rural areas have grown or become less dense. Where necessary, they adjust boundaries to make constituencies more equal, and add more constituencies in provinces that have grown. The redistribution following the 2011 census altered many boundaries within all provinces, reflecting the shift of population away from the Atlantic provinces and from rural areas into big cities. Nunavut is Canada's largest electoral district by area, but it had the smallest number of voters listed in 2015—19 223. The median size for ridings is about 78 600 voters.

Historically, adjustments were not always this fair. The procedure used to be controlled by the House of Commons, and the majority party often engaged in **gerrymandering**—wherein a party sought to take advantage of its position in government by redrawing electoral boundaries in such a way as to enable it to win more seats in the future. Gerrymandering is no longer an accepted part of the political culture and is prohibited by law. Since the *Electoral Boundaries Readjustment Act* brought responsibility for constituency boundaries under the control of independent electoral boundaries commissions, the unfair practice has ended.

gerrymandering: When a party seeks to take advantage of its position in government to redraw electoral boundaries in such a way as to enable it to win more seats in the future.

Who Can Run and Who Can Vote?

Virtually any Canadian citizen who is 18 years of age or older can become a candidate (except persons convicted of certain crimes, mental patients, and those holding certain public offices or appointments). All that is necessary is to file nomination papers, including the signatures of 100 other electors, and deposit $1000 with a returning officer. However, since very few independent candidates win, most candidates seek official party endorsement.

Thanks to electoral reforms over the years, nearly every Canadian 18 years of age or older can vote. The only persons still specifically prohibited from voting include the chief electoral officer, the assistant electoral officer, returning officers in each riding, and Canadians who have lived abroad for more than five years.

To vote, citizens must be registered. Enumerators used to fan out across the country to register voters, but since 1999 the National Register of Electors provides the basis for federal elections. The list is compiled from a variety of databases, including tax returns. Registration notices are mailed to Canadian citizens 18 years of age and older who are not registered to vote but may be qualified. To register, the citizen fills in the form or registers online. Voting takes place at a designated poll location on election day, on advance voting days, or at any Elections Canada office across the country before a given deadline.

The *Fair Elections Act* (passed in 2014) eliminated a controversial procedure called vouching. If someone wants to vote but does not have a proper ID, a voter in the polling area who knows that person can no longer vouch for him or her, thereby allowing the person to vote. Instead, a voter who has an ID but cannot prove a current address can sign an oath confirming where he or she lives. This must be confirmed by another valid voter signing an oath.

Key Electoral Participants: Coaches, Players, and Referees

Many individuals and groups play a role in general elections. Some, like candidates for election, are easily distinguishable as players. Others, like the media, seem to seek a dual role as both players and referees.

> *If you have good players on the ice, it's because you have a coach who knows the game.*
>
> Jean Chrétien, *former prime minister*

The Prime Minister and Cabinet The prime minister advises the governor general on the dissolution of Parliament when an election is to be called. Following dissolution, the government, through the governor general, formally instructs the chief electoral officer to issue writs of election to each constituency. A **writ** is a document commanding that an election be held, giving the date of the election, the date by which nominations must be received, and the date by which results must be finalized. The Cabinet continues to govern with certain restrictions until the new House of Commons is elected. Party leaders have the paramount role in the national campaign. They are the focus of intensive media attention, and their image may impact greatly on the election results.

The Chief Electoral Officer and the Electoral Commissioner The **chief electoral officer (CEO)** is a public employee appointed by the Cabinet, for a 10-year term, to head Elections Canada.[1] The current CEO is Marc Mayrand. In preparation for an election call, the CEO informs the electoral commissions how many seats will be allotted to each province and provides electoral boundary maps. Elections Canada provides information explaining how and where to vote, but the *Fair Elections Act* stopped it from overtly encouraging people to vote.

The **Commissioner of Elections Canada**, currently Yves Côté, is an independent officer responsible for ensuring that political entities fulfill their obligations

writ: A document commanding that an election be held, giving the date of the election, the date by which nominations must be received, and the date by which results must be finalized.

chief electoral officer (CEO): A permanent public employee appointed by the Cabinet under the authority of the *Canada Elections Act* to head Elections Canada.

Commissioner of Elections Canada: An independent officer responsible for ensuring that political entities fulfill their obligations under the *Canada Elections Act*.

The robocall scandal in 2011 created friction between the Conservative party and Elections Canada, which was responsible for following up on voter complaints.

under the *Canada Elections Act*. He investigates possible election wrongdoing and addresses complaints. His office clarifies new offences such as impersonating candidates or election officials, along with fines for those found guilty. Automated calls (robocalls) made by, or on behalf of, candidates or political parties are permitted, but they are not allowed to mislead or prevent electors from voting, as happened in the 2011 campaign. Following that election, a Conservative campaign worker was sentenced to nine months in prison for his role in a robocall stunt that sent voters to the wrong polling station in Guelph, Ontario.

Returning Officers, Candidates, Leaders, Parties, and Voters Returning officers have a significant role in activating the formal election machinery. They are officially appointed for each constituency by the CEO for a 10-year period following a merit-based selection process. Since 2014, local party associations or national parties are able to nominate deputy returning officers and poll clerks (previously done by the parties' local candidates).

Prospective candidates for the House of Commons do not need the backing of a political party or even have to reside in the constituency they would like to represent. However, it is extremely difficult to be elected without party endorsement, and candidates normally run in their home constituency. Local party organizations generally take the initiative in recruiting and choosing candidates at delegate conventions. The *Canada Elections Act* gives national party leaders a veto over their party's candidates, but they normally do not interfere with local nominations. On the other hand, a statement signed by the party leader or a designated representative confirming the party's endorsement must be filed with a candidate's nomination papers. The ability to withhold endorsement is a significant sanction. During the thirty-fifth Parliament, Prime Minister Jean Chrétien threatened not to endorse dissident backbenchers for the next election. Stephen Harper and his Conservative Party election campaign boss, Doug Finley, exercised considerable influence in candidate selection and rejection after losing the 2004 federal election.

Once a candidate is selected in a given constituency, the party helps to prepare for the campaign. A campaign committee is established, with subcommittees responsible for jobs such as fundraising, advertising, canvassing, etc. The candidate hires a campaign manager. Party headquarters supplies literature, guidance, and most of all a recognizable label, which gives the candidate immediate recognition as well as association with a (hopefully popular) party leader. Party volunteers phone constituents, distribute literature, and assist voters to and from the polling booths.

All parties must be registered by the CEO. Recognized parties and their candidates receive partial compensation for electoral expenses. In turn, the parties assume certain legal responsibilities. Official agents of the parties and candidates keep track of and report all revenues and expenses incurred following the issuance of writs for an election.

Parties provide much of the organization for elections. When an election is called, the national headquarters of the largest parties become nerve centres of nationwide campaigns. Party advisers plan strategy, collect public opinion data, coordinate meetings and tours of party leaders, issue literature, arrange broadcasts, employ public relations firms, issue news releases, and so on. Party advisers include media specialists, policy experts, public relations experts, and public opinion pollsters who focus on the national campaign, where the aim is to elect the party, and 338 separate constituency campaigns, where the aim is to elect individual candidates.

ELECTORAL STAGES: FROM DISSOLUTION TO A NEW GOVERNMENT

Electoral Preparations and the Campaign

An election call initiates a frenetic scramble at the upper levels of each party, as each endeavours to ensure that candidates are in place, sufficient funds are at hand, platforms and literature are ready, and campaign organizers and strategists are appointed and prepared to begin directing the campaign. At the constituency level, the returning officers appoint assistants at each poll from lists supplied by the incumbent party, and the returning officer assigns voting venues for each poll, generally a public building such as a school.

Once candidates are nominated, the returning officer has ballots printed, listing the candidates in alphabetical order and showing party affiliation. Candidates not representing a registered party are listed as independents unless they request to show no designation.

Campaigns are the visible part of elections. From the issuing of the writ to the closing of the polls, Canadian elections last a legal minimum of 36 days. Compared to the United States, where elections take well over a year, campaigns are very short; even the 2015 campaign, which was one of the longest, was only 78 days. During that time, voters are bombarded with party and candidate literature, advertising, debates, and daily news reports about leaders. Campaigns matter. In the 1988 election, the major issue was free trade, and objective studies have confirmed that opinion on this issue, as well as voting intentions, changed considerably during the campaign.[2]

At the national level, experts constantly monitor and revise their overall campaign strategies. In what regions does a party have a good chance to win seats? Where is there little chance? What issues would it be most advantageous to stress or avoid? How should financial and other resources be allocated? Party campaign strategists do their best to answer these and many other such questions.

At the constituency level, candidates make speeches, do door-to-door canvassing, attend coffee parties, and make media appearances as they attempt to retain traditional party supporters and attract as many undecided and opponent votes as possible. Analysis and targeting of the various voting groups in the constituency is essential.

The Vote

On election day, balloting is overseen by deputy returning officers and their clerks. The voter identifies himself or herself to the polling clerk, who has a list of eligible voters for that polling station and gives the voter an official, bilingual ballot. Voters mark their ballot in a private booth and place it in the box. When the polling booth closes, the deputy returning officer, with the polling clerk and scrutineers, counts the ballots, seals them in the box, and delivers them to the returning officer. An unofficial result is made public shortly after balloting is closed. The official count by the returning officer is not made until later, in some cases not for several days until the overseas vote is in. A recount is automatically requested by the returning officer if the difference between the first and second candidates is less than one one-thousandth of the ballots cast. In the very rare event of a tie vote, the returning officer casts the deciding ballot.

Who Pays for Elections?

Elections are funded both privately and publicly according to election laws that have been changed many times over recent decades. Before 1974, the financing of parties and elections was largely unregulated. Questions were constantly raised about the degree and fairness of political competitiveness. Did the expense of the process hinder or exclude individuals, groups, and parties from active involvement? Were wealthy individuals or groups able to "buy" elections?

The *Election Expenses Act* of 1974 represented the first major attempt to address such issues. Political parties received state funding in return for greater regulation of their finances. The Act established a tax credit system for donations and a system of reimbursement for election expenses. It also required federal candidates, for the first time, to give a detailed accounting of money received and spent, and compelled them to observe spending limits. The *Election Expenses Act* also brought party financing into the open. No longer were parties able to hide the extent of their financial dependence on specific sources. Suspicion that corporations, unions, and wealthy individuals might have undue influence on the selection of leaders or the determination of party policies was alleviated, but not eliminated.

The *Election Expenses Act* was amended in a major way in 2004 by the departing Chrétien government in order to make the process even more transparent and shift the main financing of political parties from private to public funding—that is, from corporate and union donations to the taxpayers. Each qualifying party in Parliament was allotted a quarterly allowance based on the number of votes it had received in the last election. To receive these public funds, parties were required to produce detailed financial reports, including a statement on revenue and trust funds. Similarly, they were required to file detailed returns after each election. This was a major move toward preventing large donors from influencing elections, yet ensured that parties would receive fair funding on the basis of past performance. Individual donations to candidates were limited to $5000 and, to keep public funds the main source of party finances, donations from corporations and unions were severely capped, upending traditional relationships between money and power.[3] Party bagmen whose job was to search out large donations became almost obsolete.

These 2004 changes affected the competitive balance between the political parties. The Conservative Party prospered because it had a good base of individual donors. The Liberals, who had previously relied on corporate donations, were hurt most by the new rules. The New Democratic Party (NDP) did reasonably well, even though donations from trade unions were restricted. The Bloc Québécois (BQ) did very well because it now had a quarterly allowance with which to promote separatist interests.

In 2006, the rules were made even tougher by reforms included in the massive *Federal Accountability Act* (Bill C-2) passed by the Harper government. The Act eliminated corporate and union donations entirely and lowered the maximum individual donation to $1000.

Two years later, the Conservative government introduced legislation to remove the quarterly allowance entirely. The opposition parties united against the move and tried to form a Liberal–NDP coalition supported by the Bloc Québécois to replace the minority Conservative government. Their plan was foiled when the prime minister called a new election and won a majority. In 2011, the new Harper government proceeded to phase out the quarterly allowance and replace it with solicited individual donations from the parties.

In 2014, the Conservative government passed the highly political and controversial *Fair Elections Act* (Bill C-23), which made even more amendments to Canada's electoral finance laws. This was unilateral reform by the Conservative Party. Critics found the rules limiting voter franchise offensive, and criticized the measures to limit the role of the chief electoral officer.[4] Among many other changes, the Act increased the amount that individuals could donate to political parties and candidates and also increased spending limits.[5]

Financial Rules for the 2015 General Election

Private Funding Sources Party candidates could donate $5000 to their own campaigns. Individual contributions from the general public of $1500 annually (increasing yearly by $25) were allowed to each of the following:

- a registered political party[6]
- the various entities of each registered political party (registered riding associations, nomination contestants, or candidates)
- each independent candidate for an election

Public Reimbursement for Parties and Candidates If *registered parties* comply with technical requirements, and if they spend at least 10 percent of an expense ceiling as determined by Elections Canada, they are reimbursed for 50 percent of their expenditures. They also receive half of the costs they incur in the purchase of permitted radio and television advertising time. Similarly, *candidates*, too, receive refunds from Elections Canada. Those who garner at least 10 percent of the valid votes cast in their electoral district are refunded their deposit and, if conditions are met, are reimbursed by the receiver general for Canada for up to 60 percent of their paid election expenses and personal expenses during the campaign.

Tax Credits Generous tax credits (up to 75 percent for donations of up to $400) are allowed for individual donations to parties and candidates. However, individual tax credits cannot exceed $650 a year, because the donations are limited.

Spending Limits Registered parties are limited in the amount they can spend during an election. The formula for deciding how much a party can spend is 70 cents multiplied by the number of names on the list of electors for each electoral district in which the registered party has endorsed a candidate (nearly $55 million for parties with a full slate of candidates in 2015). A new allowable electoral expense for a registered party is the cost of election surveys and research during an election period. Spending limits also apply to individual candidates in an election campaign. The limits vary according to the number of electors in a constituency.[7] Political parties have no limits on what they can spend on advertising before an election period formally begins.

Third-Party Spending In 2000, concerned with unrestricted spending by persons or groups other than candidates and political parties, Parliament passed new spending limits for third parties that are still in effect. Groups and individuals had to register with the CEO if they spent $500 or more on promoting or opposing a party or candidate, and groups could not collude to avoid spending limits. In 2015, 110 third parties were registered. They had no obligation to report spending prior to the dropping of the writ. However, in 2015, a new vehicle of organized interests—political action committees (PACs)—became active in the months before the election. Broad coalitions formed that collected and polled contributions from members to endorse or oppose political candidates on specific issues. PACs such as GreenPAC and HarperPac spent money early before the campaign officially began, testing third-party boundaries.

Evaluating Electoral Financing

There is an ongoing controversy about the proper balance between public and private financing. Have all of the changes to election financing since 1974 achieved their goals of fairness and transparency? Those who support the quarterly publicly financed allowances to parties that were initiated in 2004 by the Liberal Party say that it promoted transparency and reduced opportunities for corruption and influence. Those who support the removal of public funding allowances in favour of individual donations by the Conservative government in 2011 argue that parties will receive adequate donations if the public supports them. They add that Canadian taxpayers outside of Québec did not appreciate that taxpayer money in the form of quarterly payments helped to fund the separatist BQ. Individual donations that generate tax credits are not transparent, but they do encourage parties and candidates to interact.

Fixed election dates are also a controversial feature of election financing because election spending limits come into effect only when an election is called, and apply only to the actual days of the campaign. This encourages parties, candidates, and third parties to advertise heavily before the election is called, making spending limits less effective.

THE NET WORTH OF A VOTE: DOES CANADA NEED A NEW ELECTORAL SYSTEM?

Some people believe that elections in Canada could be made more just and democratic.[8] Little remains of fraudulent election irregularities from earlier times such as multiple voting (ballot stuffing), impersonating, bribing, intimidating, and either excluding real names (false enumeration) or adding fictitious names (padding) to voters' lists. However, some question the very framework of the electoral system from a point of view of fairness.

Canada's "first-past-the-post" electoral system makes it theoretically possible for a political party that has won a high percentage of the total vote across the entire country to receive absolutely no seats in the House of Commons. At the same time, a party that has won only a small percentage of the popular vote, but has benefited from votes clustered in a particular area, may be overrepresented in the House. In addition, although Canadians commonly talk about the government as reflecting the will of the majority, this is rarely the case when multiple parties are involved.

When there are more than two parties, it is usual for the government to have the electoral backing of much fewer than 50 percent of all voters. When fewer than 50 percent of voters cast their ballot for one party, that party may still receive much more than 50 percent of the seats in the House. There is considerable discussion about changing Canada's electoral system to make it represent voters more accurately. In the 2015 general election, the Conservatives were the only party that supported the status quo—not surprisingly, since all parties generally favour what benefits them most. They wanted to keep the existing electoral system and make it more difficult to change. Both the NDP and the Liberals said that they favoured some form of proportional representation, with Trudeau declaring that he personally preferred a preferential voting system. Now that the Liberals form a large majority government with only 39.5 percent of the popular vote, they may not be so keen to change the system. They benefited directly from the first-past-the-post system!

We have seen that, to preserve electoral equality, the electoral boundaries commission in each province tries to ensure that constituency boundaries follow the established boundaries of cities, towns, and counties. Rural and northern constituencies are thinly populated, however, and to allocate them the same number of voters as in cities or towns would make them geographically huge and unmanageable. As a result, these constituencies are generally larger with smaller populations than their urban counterparts, so that individual votes there count more than in a more densely populated area.

Similarly, the electoral weight of sparsely populated provinces is protected by rules that distort the general rule of representation by population. An individual's vote in Prince Edward Island has more weight than it would in Ontario, for example. The rule that boundaries must be redrawn after every major census (every 10 years) is meant to keep the value of votes relatively similar by adjusting for major population shifts. However, legislation is not always passed in time for the next general election after a major census.

Another distortion in the value of an individual vote can be caused by low voter turnout. In 2000, because voter turnout was so low, with only 41 percent of the votes cast (or about 25 percent of registered voters) the Liberal Party was given a large majority. The 2008 turnout was the lowest ever in Canada, at 59 percent (it was 65 percent in 2006, 61 percent in 2011, and 69 percent in 2015). In 2011, the Conservatives won a majority government with only 39.6 percent of the popular vote.

In some countries, such as Australia, this problem convinced leaders to implement compulsory voting. If everyone turned out to vote, it was argued, then whatever the result, the government's laws and decisions would carry more legitimacy and be considered binding on the whole community. The argument against compulsory voting, of course, is that citizens should have the right *not* to vote. As well, should election results be determined by the votes of those with no knowledge or interest in the political issues at stake? In Australia, many electors, who are forced to vote, cast a protest ballot by voting for the first name on the list—a so-called "donkey" vote.

Single Member Plurality vs PR Systems The major distortions in the value of an individual vote, and those most subject to debate in Canada, are caused by the type of electoral system itself. One of the big advantages of a *single-member plurality system*—sometimes known as first past the post (FPTP)—is that it is simple to comprehend and to administer. The individual who gets the most votes in a given constituency wins that seat; he or she does not have to win a majority. More important, however, is that on the whole, but not always, this type of electoral system tends to produce more stable, majoritarian governments than do other types.

There are disadvantages associated with the single-member plurality system, however. The most significant drawback is that party seat allocation in the House of Commons is not determined by the national percentage share of the popular vote for each party. If the electorate were to vote in a similar fashion across the country, there would be an arithmetic tendency to favour the two largest parties, with an additional "bonus" of seats for the larger one, and, conversely, a tendency to underrepresent third or minor parties in the House of Commons, especially those whose support was spread fairly evenly but thinly across the country. As a consequence,

Canada's electoral system is often said to favour the development or maintenance of one dominant party. Of course, when there is a maldistribution of the votes across the regions, this still may result in a multi-party system, as has been the case many times since World War I.

According to political scientists, there are two reasons why a single-member plurality system tends to reward the party that comes first with more seats than it deserves and leaves the second and following parties with fewer seats.[9] First, an arithmetic consequence rewards the party that gets the largest share of the vote with more seats. An exception to this general rule occurs only when a minor party has its support concentrated in a particular region. Second, voters who might otherwise support a minor party tend to refrain from voting for it for fear of "wasting" their votes—casting votes that have no effect on the election of individual representatives or on the formation of a government. Thus, for some observers the association between the single-member plurality electoral formula and the two-party system is close to being a "true sociological law."[10]

Examples make this clear. In 1993, the Liberals won 177 seats (60 percent) with only 41 percent of the vote. The Progressive Conservatives (PCs) were reduced to 2 seats (less than 1 percent) even though they had won 16 percent of the vote. It took roughly 31 320 votes to elect a Liberal but more than 1 million to elect a Conservative! In 1997, the PC and Reform parties each won 19 percent of the vote, but Reform got 60 seats and the Tories only 20. The BQ got 44 seats with only 11 percent of the national vote. In 2000, the BQ took 38 seats with just 11 percent of the vote, while the PCs got only 12 seats with 12 percent of the vote. The Liberals formed a majority government, collecting 54.4 percent of seats with a vote of only 39.5 percent of the electorate. A party with a wide but scattered following is severely disadvantaged by the electoral system compared to a party with support that is concentrated geographically.

The type of electoral system has an impact on the formation of governments. The plurality formula often favours the development of a two-party or single-party dominant system, resulting in relatively stable governments. This means that Cabinets are based on one party, and that fact promotes stable, responsible government. Voters know which party to hold responsible for laws and policies and they can either vote for it or vote to "throw the rascals out" at the next opportunity.

Many countries have chosen to forgo such a simple electoral process in order to achieve more voter equality. They place a high premium on the concept of equal "representation," in that their electoral systems are designed to ensure that all significant shades of public opinion are represented in the House of Commons. The simplest such system is known as **proportional representation (PR)**—an electoral system that attempts to ensure that parties receive representation in the House of Commons in proportion to their respective shares of the popular vote.[11] There are many varieties of PR. In the simplest type, for example, a voter casts a ballot for a party as opposed to a candidate. When the votes are counted, parties are awarded their number of seats in proportion to the percentage of votes that each received. In 2015, 25 parties ran candidates. Table 11.1 shows how extremely fractured Canada's House of Commons would have been if PR had been used in the 2015 election.

The general problem with PR systems is that they tend to promote multiple parties, and multi-party systems in turn may give rise to extremist or narrow-interest

proportional representation (PR): An electoral system that attempts to ensure that parties receive representation in the House of Commons in proportion to their respective shares of the overall popular vote.

Table 11.1 How Votes Translated into Seats in the 2015 Election, and How They Would Have Translated in a Pure PR System

Party	Popular Vote (%)	% Seats Won under Current Single-Member Plurality System	Actual Seats Won under Single-Member Plurality System	Theoretical Seats That Would Have Been Won under Pure PR*
Liberal	39.5	54.4	184	134
Conservative	31.9	29.3	99	108
NDP	19.7	13.0	44	67
BQ	4.7	2.3	10	16
Green	3.5	0.3	1	12
Other	0.5	0	0	2

*Numbers do not total 338 due to rounding.

Source: Based on provisional data from Elections Canada.

parties because they can easily win enough votes across a whole country to gain some seats. Generally in PR systems, no party wins a majority of seats, so Cabinets are based on fragile coalitions. This may promote Cabinet instability and increase the possibility of governmental problems and constant elections. Most important, and often overlooked, the public has no opportunity to vote for or against specific would-be coalitions, and voters do not know which party to hold responsible at the next election.

To a large extent, *representation* and *governing* are competing and contradictory principles. Democracy requires an acceptance of *both* of these principles. Obviously, in a democracy the people need to be represented in some form or other. Equally, democracy requires a government that can produce policies to be judged by the electorate. It may be impossible to have perfection in both areas at once. Even "perfect" representation of every group in society would be of little benefit if it produced fractious, unstable governments based on ever-changing coalitions.

In the past several federal elections, the second and third parties have received considerably fewer seats than warranted by their popular support. Proponents of change in the provinces and at the federal level point to chronic misrepresentation of voter support in legislatures throughout the country. Could Canada's electoral system be made fairer in this regard? As Table 11.1 shows, if pure PR had been adopted for the 2015 election, a minority government would automatically have been put in place, as the Liberals would have received only 134 seats, while the Conservatives, NDP, BQ, Greens, and Others would have had 204 seats. If the Conservatives and NDP could have come to an agreement, these two parties would have been able to form a coalition government. In other words, PR would have given Canada a highly fractured party system and a totally different government.

Stable governments elected by versions of PR do exist, but they require conditions such as a relatively small geographical area to administer and a form of coalition spirit found in what are called *consociational democracies*.[12] The cultural and procedural consensus required to make governments effective in countries with PR has been well documented. The few European countries with PR and stable governments *are exceptions*. New Zealand is often held up as a positive example of PR, but its recent history is mixed, with its relatively complex PR system having produced both stable and unstable governments. Therefore, advocates who wish to reform the electoral system often present blended electoral systems that combine the advantages and disadvantages of PR and the single-member constituency system.[13]

In 2004, the Law Commission of Canada produced a report that called for a mixed-member proportional electoral system. Such a system would provide dual forms of representation—some members would be elected in single-member constituencies and others by a PR system. Such mixed-member systems are used in New Zealand and Germany, and in regional elections in Scotland and Wales. Citizens can vote for the same party or split their tickets—that is, vote for a candidate of one party in the riding and choose a candidate from another party in the PR system. The Law Commission recommended that two-thirds of the members of the House of Commons should be elected in constituencies using the first-past-the-post method, and the remaining one-third should be elected from provincial or territorial party lists. In addition, it said that one list seat should be allotted to each of the three territories.[14]

Such a system would allow approximate congruence between votes and seat allocations, making it easier for minor parties to gain representation. However, it would also reduce the chances of majority governments being elected and threaten the integrity of the responsible Cabinet system. Canada does not possess all of the components of the few countries that have adopted PR successfully, so the trade-off of stable government for better representation could have repercussions that have not yet been adequately considered.

preferential system: An electoral system in which voters rank their candidates in order of preference.

Another system under consideration is a **preferential system** or single-member majoritarian system. In this type of system voters rank their preferred candidates first, second, third, and so on. The means of counting ballots in preferential systems varies, but in the "alternative vote" method, the winning candidate must achieve at least 51 percent of the vote. If no candidate reaches that threshold, the candidate with the lowest number of votes is dropped and those ballots are reallocated to the candidate listed as second choice, and this continues until one candidate obtains a majority, i.e., wins.[15]

In electoral system reform it is best to remember that there is no such thing as a system without consequences!

BY-ELECTIONS

by-election: An election held in a constituency to fill a legislative seat that has fallen vacant between general elections.

A **by-election** is an election held in a constituency to fill a legislative seat that has fallen vacant between general elections. Within six months of the date at which the speaker of the House must issue a notification warrant acknowledging the vacancy, the prime minister may choose any date for the by-election. By-elections may be held soon after a vacancy appears, a year or more later, or not at all if the writs for a general election are issued before the by-election takes place. The prime minister and his or her advisers are not keen to call a by-election if they believe that the result will be perceived as unfavourable, a hesitancy that is reinforced by the tendency of governments to be defeated in many by-elections. Usually, a by-election is called because an

MP dies or resigns, but occasionally an MP will be asked to resign in order to allow another individual to win a seat.

REFERENDUMS

A **referendum** is a means by which a policy question is submitted directly to the electorate for a decision rather than being decided exclusively by elected representatives. Around the world, some referendums are merely consultative, providing a kind of official public opinion poll on an issue in order to guide politicians. Others are binding in that the government must follow the majority decision that the referendum provides. Still others are essentially instruments of ratification, the final seal of approval on a course of action adopted by a law-making institution; for example, where proposed constitutional amendments must be ratified by the electorate, as is required in Australia.

referendum: A means by which a policy question is submitted directly to the electorate for a decision rather than being decided exclusively by elected representatives.

Most countries use referendums with extreme caution and only in specific circumstances because there are many problems associated with them. Arguments for and against can be summarized as follows.

Arguments for referendums:

- They represent a form of direct democracy.
- Widespread consultation increases the legitimacy of political decisions.

Arguments against referendums:

- They detract from the sovereignty of Parliament, downgrading its importance as a sovereign law-making body.
- They can be extremely divisive, because they divide the electorate into winners and losers, and such division can have severe negative impacts when it is along regional or ethnic lines.
- They require a Yes or No answer to sophisticated and complex questions, and do not allow for any compromise solution.
- Citizens may be relatively uninformed to make decisions, especially on technical or legal matters.
- It is not feasible to consult citizens on every issue that might be regarded as fundamental.
- Often they do not offer a meaningful choice but are merely symbolic.

Although there have been several referendums at the provincial level in Canada, only three have been held at the national level, all of which were of the consultative type. The first was held in 1898 when the federal government was contemplating the prohibition of alcohol. Although a small majority voted in favour of prohibition (51 percent), there was a very low turnout (44 percent) so Prime Minister Wilfrid Laurier did not believe that the level of support was strong enough to go ahead with the plan (see Chapter 6).

The second national referendum was called during the Conscription Crisis of 1942. Prime Minister William Lyon Mackenzie King proceeded with conscription only after a referendum that asked the people whether the federal government could overturn its previous electoral pledge not to institute a draft. The referendum received the support of 65 percent of the voters. Québec, however, voted heavily against conscription (71 percent), thus exacerbating relations between English and French Canadians. King delayed conscription to reduce the potential impact of the issue (see Chapter 5).

The third and most recent referendum was on the Charlottetown Accord in 1992. After considerable bickering, 54.4 percent voted against the agreement and 44.6 percent for it, a result that represented a humiliating defeat for Prime Minister Brian Mulroney. It set the stage for his retirement and the massive defeat of the Progressive Conservative Party in 1993 (see Chapters 3 and 5).

ELECTORAL BEHAVIOUR: VOTING PATTERNS IN CANADA

Political scientists study Canadian elections in order to analyze what motivates people to participate in them and why elections turn out as they do. Two decades ago, when Jerome Black examined Canadian voter turnout from a comparative perspective, analyzing voting in 18 countries, he concluded that participation in Canada consistently ranked in the lower quartile of democratic nations.[16] Later data, particularly in the 2015 election with a turnout of 69.1 percent, indicated that Black's analysis was limited to a particular period of Canadian history (see Figure 11.2).

Low voter turnout is worrying to some commentators, especially those who blame it on increased cynicism about elections, governments, politicians, and elected officials. Many are particularly concerned with the lack of interest and participation among Canadian youth. To this end, proposals abound about how to reduce the so-called "democratic deficit" and provide more incentive to participate.

Meaningful, objective generalizations about political participation—why people vote or not—are difficult to make with precision and over time. However, some studies have given some clues as to what motivates people to cast a ballot. One aggregate-level study of turnout levels concluded that the most important determinants of voter turnout are regional and socio-economic. The strongest predictive variables in the study were residential stability and economic affluence.[17] There is little doubt that socio-economic factors are significant in motivating political participation. The poor and uneducated are much less apt to vote than are individuals with higher income levels and university educations. The wealthy may feel that they have more at stake in an election outcome, and more highly educated people are generally better informed and more interested in political issues. Workers at the lower end of the socio-economic spectrum tend to be preoccupied with factors of survival and have a low feeling of efficacy. Those at the other end of the spectrum are more apt to believe that they can further their own and society's interests by electing the right candidate.

Other factors undoubtedly are involved in voter participation. Voter turnout in Canada is highest in the middle-age range; the youngest and the oldest voters tend to abstain most. Over time, studies have found little significant difference between ethnic groups in terms of whether or not they vote, and levels of participation have also been found to be roughly similar in the various regions across the country.

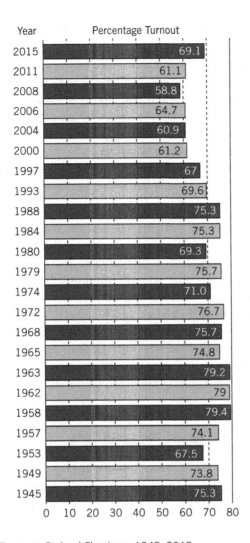

Figure 11.2 Voter Turnout, Federal Elections, 1945–2015

Source: Elections Canada. Official voting results.

Short-Term and Long-Term Factors in Voting Behaviour

Factors that could influence *how* Canadians vote can be grouped loosely into long-term and short-term factors. Long-term factors contribute to an individual's basic *party identification* with a political party. They include socio-economic indicators such as class, religion, gender, ethnicity, urban–rural distinctions, and so on. Short-term factors arise from the specifics of election campaigns, including issues, leaders, candidates, debates, polls, and media coverage.

Long-term factors begin early in life, as attitudes toward politics and political parties are acquired through socialization and social group factors. These factors influence one's political ideas, party identification, and voting intentions to varying degrees.

Long before an election campaign starts, some individuals may have acquired a degree of party identification.

Short-term factors take effect during an election campaign, making impacts on voters that confirm or change the effect of long-term factors. Two short-term factors in particular have been significant in recent elections: leadership and issues. These, of course, change from one election to the next. Changing technology, campaign strategies, and the media, especially television and social media, have increased the impact of short-term factors on voting in recent years.

Of the long-term factors, region and urban–rural divides have often proven to be the most significant. Class has rarely been very significant.

Region While early Canadian elections often showed region to be a dependable voting factor, it has become less predictable over the years. Regional voting patterns have not been consistent over the long term even in the Maritimes. Newfoundland voted strongly Liberal from 1949 to 1968 (while Joey Smallwood led the Liberal Party in the province), but that support diminished (particularly while Robert Stanfield was leader of the Conservatives) until 1993, when Newfoundlanders once more gave the Liberals all of their seats. In 1993, the Liberals won 31 of the 32 seats in the Atlantic region. This was reduced to 11 in 1997, restored to 19 in 2000, and remained in that range until 2011 when the Liberals had their worst showing ever across the country (the Conservatives took 14 seats in the Atlantic region). In 2015, the Atlantic provinces went solidly Liberal in taking all 32 seats (see Table 11.2).

Table 11.2 Regional Votes, 2011 and 2015

Party							
	BC	**Prairies**	**Ontario**	**Québec**	**Atlantic**	**North**	**Total**
			Seats, 2011				
Cons	21	51	73	5	14	2	166
Liberal	2	2	11	7	12	–	34
NDP	12	3	22	59	6	1	103
Green	1	–	–	–	–	–	1
BQ	–	–	–	4	–	–	4
Total seats	36	56	106	75	32	3	308
			Seats, 2015				
Cons	10	44	33	12	–	–	99
Liberal	17	12	80	40	32	3	184
NDP	14	6	8	16	0	–	44
Green	1	–	–	–	–	–	1
BQ	–	–	–	10	–	–	10
Total seats	42	62	121	78	32	3	338

Source: Elections Canada. 2015 data are provisional.

People in specific areas of the country have traditionally supported one party over others and shifted their allegiance only periodically, and in unusual circumstances. However, in recent decades, realignment has often taken place throughout the country. Regions have shown wide variations in voter support. Québec, for example, voted massively Liberal through most of the twentieth century from the days of Laurier until 1984. Aberrations in this pattern occurred, first with the severe defeat of the Liberals by the PCs under John Diefenbaker in 1958 and then again by Brian Mulroney's Tories in 1984 and 1988. From 1993 to 2004, the BQ dominated Québec federally. In 2011, the NDP, led by Jack Layton, controlled the province. In 2015, it was once again the Liberals who unexpectedly surged to take 40 of the province's 78 seats; the BQ won only 10 seats, not even enough for official party status.

Populous Ontario has by far the most ridings—121 in 2015. It is hard to form a government without adequate support in this province. The two major parties have alternated as the favoured party throughout Canada's history. In 2011, the Conservatives did well with 73 seats. In 2015, the Liberals won 80 seats, reverting to an electoral map much like that in 2004, when the last Liberal majority was elected.

The Prairie provinces and British Columbia voted heavily PC in federal elections from about 1957 to 1993. The Prairie provinces have a tradition of supporting protest parties—they gave rise to the Progressives, the CCF/NDP, and more recently Reform/Alliance. From 1993 to 2004, they supported the new, populist Reform Party, which became the Canadian Alliance, and then transferred their allegiance to the new Conservative Party of Canada. In 2015, the Conservatives still dominated in the Prairie provinces, but the Liberals and NDP both made breakthroughs with urban voters in Calgary, and the Liberals also gained seats in Saskatoon and Winnipeg. British Columbia, Saskatchewan, and Manitoba also have a history of periodic support for the NDP. British Columbia's 36 ridings were strongly Conservative in 2011, with the NDP in second place. In 2015, the province split three ways, but in keeping with their momentum elsewhere, the Liberals took the lead with a record 17 seats of 42.

While Liberals tend to attract a disproportionate number of urban voters, the Conservatives and Western protest parties traditionally received a higher degree of rural support. However, these associations may not be statistically meaningful. In Canada, the impact of community size on voting is likely to be associated with several other cleavages and voting influences, and so it is impossible to separate its impact from other variables. In any case, the Liberals have been the party most able to attract a variety of voters by cutting across urban–rural lines. Their 2015 majority victory gave them representation in every region.

ANALYSIS OF ELECTORAL OUTCOMES

Since Confederation, Canada has held 42 general elections, which either the Liberals or the Conservatives have won. The Liberal Party held power for most of the twentieth century (see Table 11.3). The longest continuous time it has been in opposition was when the Progressive Conservatives under Brian Mulroney governed from 1984 to 1993. The dramatic collapse of the PCs in the 1993 election left the Liberals with no strong, united challenger until 2004, when the Conservative Party of Canada was formed.

Table 11.3 General Election Results, 1945–2015

Election Year	Gov't Formed	Total Seats	PC Seats	PC % Votes	Lib Seats	Lib % Votes	Con Seats	Con % Votes	CCF/ NDP Seats	NDP % Votes	Ref** Seats	Ref** % Votes	BQ Seats	BQ % Votes	Oth**** Seats	Oth % Votes
1945	Lib	245	67	27	125	41	–	–	28	16	–	–	–	–	24	16
1949	Lib	262	41	30	190	49	–	–	13	13	–	–	–	–	18	8
1953	Lib	265	51	31	170	49	–	–	23	11	–	–	–	–	21	9
1957	PC	265	112	39	105	41	–	–	25	11	–	–	–	–	23	9
1958	PC	265	208	54	48	34	–	–	8	9	–	–	–	–	1	3
1962	PC	265	116	37	100	37	–	–	19	14	–	–	–	–	31	12
1963	Lib	265	95	33	129	42	–	–	17	13	–	–	–	–	24	12
1965	Lib	265	97	32	131	40	–	–	21	18	–	–	–	–	16	10
1968	Lib	264	72	31	155	45	–	–	22	17	–	–	–	–	15	7
1972	Lib	264	107	35	109	38	–	–	31	18	–	–	–	–	16	9
1974	Lib	264	95	35	141	43	–	–	16	15	–	–	–	–	12	6
1979	PC	282	136	36	114	40	–	–	26	18	–	–	–	–	6	7
1980	Lib	282	103	33	147	44	–	–	32	20	–	–	–	–	0	3
1984	Con	282	211	50	40	28	–	–	30	19	–	–	–	–	1	–
1988	PC	295	169*	43	83	32	–	–	43	20	–	–	–	–	–	4
1993	Lib	295	2	16	177	41	–	–	9	7	52	19	54	13	1	4
1997	Lib	301	20	19	155	38	–	–	21	11	60	19	44	11	1	2
2000	Lib	301	12	12	172	40	–	–	13	9	66	26	38	11	–	2
2004	Lib	308	–	–	135	37	99	30	19	16	–	–	54	12	1	6
2006	Con	308	–	–	103	30	124	36	29	18	–	–	51	11	1	5
2008	Con	308	–	–	77	26	143	38	37	18	–	–	49	10	2	8
2011	Con	308	–	–	34	19	166	40	103	31	–	–	4	6	1	4
2015***	Lib	338	–	–	184	40	99	32	44	20	–	–	10	5	1	4

*169 Conservatives were elected on November 21, 1988, but one died before being officially sworn in, leaving the seat technically vacant.

**Includes Alliance.

***Provisional data from Elections Canada.

****Other includes the Green Party, which won 1 seat with 3.9 percent of the vote in 2011 and 1 seat with 3.5 percent of the vote in 2015.

Source: Data available at www.elections.ca.

The 1993 federal election created a fundamental realignment of parties, from which the Liberals profited. Capturing 41 percent of the vote, the Liberals obtained 177 seats in the House of Commons, regained power, and formed a strong majority government. After the election, it was the only party that could claim national status. The BQ ran candidates only in Québec, and Reform avoided Québec altogether. The Tories were reduced to a historic low of 2 seats, even though they won 16 percent of the popular vote nationwide. The most important element in the Liberals' success in earlier years had been the capture and maintenance of Québec.

In 1997, the Liberals won a razor-thin majority with 155 seats, but like the four opposition parties, their representation was basically regional. Roughly two-thirds of the Liberal caucus was from Ontario. Reform replaced the BQ in second place and therefore won recognition as the Official Opposition. In 2000, the Liberals regained a strong majority government. In 2004, they were restricted to a weak minority government, which fell in early 2006. They lost to the Conservatives in the ensuing election, and again in 2008 and 2011.

THE 2015 FEDERAL ELECTION

Background

The 2011 general election produced a Conservative majority of 166 seats and a dramatic reversal of fortune for all opposition parties. The NDP rode a wave of support in Québec when the electorate abandoned the BQ in droves. The NDP took 59 seats in Québec, and that, combined with modest gains particularly in Ontario and British Columbia, brought them to 103 seats and enabled the traditional third party to become the Official Opposition for the first time. The Liberals, with relatively poor leadership and still suffering negative public opinion from the sponsorship scandal that had helped to bring them down in 2006, received their worst-ever results, dropping to 34 seats and risking oblivion. The BQ was reduced to 4 seats, losing its official party status, while the Green Party elected its first MP.

This was a dramatic win for Stephen Harper after uniting the fractious right-wing parties into the Conservative Party of Canada in 2003 and then leading two minority governments. He moved quickly to enact legislation to consolidate his party's position. Initially, the economy was buoyant, resource prices were high, and the country maintained a competitive dollar. As the fifth largest oil producer in the world, the Conservative government's emphasis on developing oil and pipelines was popular, even as manufacturing declined in Ontario. Harper avoided fractious behaviour by his MPs, which he had endured in his first minority government, by imposing strict discipline on his members and centralizing power in his office.

The NDP, meanwhile, lost its very popular leader, Jack Layton (who died shortly after the election), and elected Tom Mulcair in his stead. The Liberals also elected a new leader, Justin Trudeau, the eldest son of former prime minister Pierre Trudeau. The party he took over was dispirited and disorganized, with relatively few resources, and on the brink of extinction.

As the October 2015 deadline for the next election approached, the country's economy was moving close to a recession and the Canadian dollar plummeted to 75 cents against the U.S. dollar. There were other ominous signs for the Conservatives and for Harper in particular, including the trial of Senator Mike Duffy on charges that included conflict of interest and fraud.

The 2015 Federal Election Campaign

The governing Conservatives prepared well in advance for the election, producing a balanced budget, limiting the influence of special interests in elections, and amassing more money than their opponents. As a prelude to the election call, they spent billions of dollars of government funds, all publicized through government advertising. The spending included a one-time $3 billion boost to the Universal Child Care Benefit program that the government had introduced earlier in the year. Cheques

Table 11.4 MPs Elected in 2011 and at Dissolution in 2015

Party	Elected 2011	Party Standing at Dissolution
Conservative	166	159
NDP	103	95
Liberal	34	35
BQ	4	2
Green	1	2
Strength in Democracy	–	2

retroactive to January 1, 2015, were sent to families with children just before the election call.

On August 2, 2015, Prime Minister Harper asked the governor general to drop the writs of election, and official proclamations were issued on August 4, triggering a long 78-day campaign, the longest in modern Canadian history. Beginning the campaign early silenced prospective hostile advertisements from unions and other anti-government groups because strict spending limits prevented them from producing ads during the campaign period. It also allowed the Conservatives to benefit from their larger financial reserves. At dissolution there were six parties in Parliament, reflecting changes since the 2011 election (see Table 11.4).[18]

The Conservatives began with the theme of sound leadership, but ran a largely negative campaign, focusing at first on undermining Trudeau through ads claiming that he was "just not ready." (Before the first debate, a Conservative staffer even commented that expectations for Trudeau were so low that to be successful he simply needed to arrive at the debate with his pants on.) For the first two weeks of the campaign, the trial of Senator Mike Duffy was in the headlines and the scandals associated with it reflected badly on both the Conservative Party and Stephen Harper (see Chapter 7 and 13). The trial took the Conservatives off their economic and security messages.

From the beginning, the Liberals ran a well-organized, positive campaign on the theme of "Real Change." Their biggest imperative when they began in third place was to beat the NDP and avoid the risk of disintegrating as a party. The campaign was a test of Trudeau's maturity and competence and of the new organization of his party.

In May, before the campaign even began, Harper declared that he would not participate in the traditional leaders' debates (held by the consortium of the major TV networks), but instead would participate in up to five independently staged debates. In the end, there were five leadership debates, each on a specialized theme, with one in French sponsored by the French-language TVA (Québec media).

As the debates took place and Trudeau clearly held his own, the Conservative slogan of "just not ready" began to lose traction. Voters seemed to warm to the young Liberal leader and, by the second-last week of the very long campaign, polls indicated that the Liberals had reached their goal of surpassing the NDP. By the last week of the campaign, Trudeau was asking for a majority and switched to the slogan "Ready."

Important Issues in the Election Several issues were discussed during the long campaign, but having announced their plans well in advance the Conservatives had little new to say. The Liberals, meanwhile, were able to craft competitive counteroffers like larger benefits and tax cuts. The *economy* was entering a recession, but the Conservatives defended the economic policies they already had in place. Harper stressed his stewardship of the economy. This included budgetary prudence through low taxes, targeted tax breaks, and eliminating the deficit for 2015. The NDP also ran on a platform that promised fiscal responsibility with no deficits.

The Liberals broke rank with the other two parties and proposed modest deficits of up to $10 billion a year for three years, to provide money for infrastructure projects that would stimulate growth. They proposed raising the federal tax rate on income over $200 000 a year, claiming that they would have the wealthiest citizens pay a combined federal–provincial rate of more than 50 percent while giving middle-class Canadians a tax cut. They said they would target family benefits to all but the rich, and assist with pension reform. This approach and combination of proposals allowed the Liberals to present a more ambitious agenda than the other parties and claim that they were prepared to help the middle class most. Their policies targeted many groups, including Aboriginals, visible minorities, immigrants, women, students, and environmentalists, as well as the middle class.

During the campaign, the Conservatives announced the completion of a new trade agreement, the Trans-Pacific Partnership (TPP), proclaiming it a winner for the Canadian economy. The NDP criticized the TPP for making concessions on auto parts and the dairy industry and argued that it would cost tens of thousands of Canadian jobs. The Liberals did not take issue with the agreement, saying that the details were not yet known. Both parties refused the opportunity to have Privy Council Office briefings on the details of the pact.

Immigration became a controversial issue because of a shocking photo of the dead body of a small Syrian boy who had washed up on a Turkish beach. His family's asylum request had been turned down by Harper's government. In spite of the widespread emotional response to the plight of Syrian refugees, the Conservatives chose to retain a relatively restrictive refugee policy. The Liberals, by contrast, stressed the need to be open and inclusive and claimed they would let in 25 000 Syrian refugees by 2016, omitting to say how administratively difficult this policy would be to implement.

The *environment* was another controversial issue. The Conservative government had withdrawn Canada from the Kyoto Treaty in 2011, a move that was widely regarded as a symbol of Harper's lack of concern for environmental targets. The Liberals, on the other hand, stressed the need to move toward higher environmental standards, invest more in clean technologies, subsidize renewable energy sources, increase environmental requirements on business, and impose taxes on carbon emissions. They proposed to develop a new "pan-Canadian framework" for setting climate change targets and negotiating with the United States and Mexico. They also came out against the Northern Gateway pipeline project that was strongly supported by the Conservatives.

The Liberals also appealed to *Aboriginals* on many levels. When the Conservatives did not address rising Aboriginal incarceration rates, the lack of clean water and decent housing on reserves, or the 1200 murdered or missing Indigenous women and girls over the last 30 years, the Liberals did. They promised to launch an immediate inquiry into the missing or murdered Aboriginal women. As well, Trudeau promised a nation-to-nation process to improve Aboriginal education, accommodating to the terms of First Nations negotiators that the Harper government had refused. He also promised increased funding for reserve schools and employment training.

The *electoral system* itself was a source of contention. The Conservatives proposed to keep the current first-past-the-post system and make it more difficult to change. The NDP said that it would change the system to some form of proportional representation. The Liberals said that if they won this time, it would be the last election using the current system. Trudeau said that he would set up a special all-parliamentary committee to study the alternatives, but stated that he personally favoured some form of preferential ballot.[19]

Security was an issue in that criticisms of Bill C-51 continued to play out, with the opposition parties branding the Conservatives as trying to frighten and divide Canadians through their stress on public safety and generally acting as harbingers of doom. The Liberals said they would amend the sweeping anti-terrorism laws that had been brought in by Harper after a gunman killed a soldier and fired on more people in Parliament in 2014 (see Chapter 12).

Marijuana was a controversial issue. Against Conservative objections, the Liberals proposed to legalize recreational marijuana, but in an evidence-based way. Trudeau noted that there were already more than 100 illegal marijuana dispensaries in Vancouver and that approximately 450 000 Canadians already use marijuana medicinally. The Liberals maintained that legalization of marijuana would bring in $1 billion to $6 billion in government revenue. The marijuana policy appealed to young people, as did the Liberal promise to cap university tuition. Women, meanwhile, were promised new strength in politics, as Trudeau pledged that his Cabinet would be divided equally between both genders.

The Conservatives raised three targeted issues of *identity politics* during the campaign. One was the suggestion of launching a "barbaric cultural practices" hotline for Canadians to inform officials about un-Canadian activities. The second took the form of a drafted law—Bill C-24, "Strengthening the Canadian Citizenship Act"—that would strip citizenship from dual nationals if they were convicted of serious offences such as terrorism or treason. This bill was widely misunderstood among immigrant communities, where many feared being deported. The third issue, the niqab, was perhaps the most damaging politically. This issue (discussed in Chapter 2) ignited controversy when the Conservative government refused to accept a court ruling that allowed Muslim women to wear their niqab veil during citizenship ceremonies, and vowed to appeal it to a higher level. (Polls showed that Quebeckers highly disapproved of the niqab, so it should have been a good issue for the Conservatives.) The Liberals and NDP took the stand that the government had no business interfering in this matter.

In foreign policy, the Liberals said that they would withdraw Canadian planes from the combat mission in Syria and focus instead on training and humanitarian support. They proposed less emphasis on military solutions (they were against purchasing F-35 fighter planes, for example) and more on active participation in the United Nations, breathing new life into peacekeeping missions that Canada had abandoned in recent years.

All of the major parties conducted highly regional campaigns, distributing promises and catering to regional sensibilities—unemployment insurance in the Atlantic region, the aerospace industry in Québec, and so on. They tailored their ads to the regions. In the end, the election results exhibited wide regional differences in support for the parties.

Results and Analysis

By election day the polls indicated that the Liberals would win, but few predicted that it would be by such a substantial majority. A relatively large turnout of 69 percent (the highest since 1993) helped the party to defy the odds and win 184 seats with 39.5 percent of the popular vote, an astonishing increase of 150 seats and 20.6 percent of the vote from the last election—more than 4 million new votes. It was the biggest seat gain in Canadian history, and it allowed the Liberals to renew their dreams of being a truly national party. Liberals won 86 seats from the Conservatives, 56 from the NDP, and 2 from the BQ.

The Conservatives won only 31.9 percent of the vote (a decrease of 7.7 percent) and 99 seats. According to the polls, their support did not vary much throughout the campaign, even when they changed their focus to social identity issues. They lost only 50 000 votes from 2011. Stephen Harper's core vote held well even though the election campaign turned into a "Harperendum," a referendum on Harper and his personality as prime minister. Voters in Québec did not rally behind the Conservatives; instead, soft NDP votes moved to the Liberals. In the end, the Conservatives finished second and formed the Official Opposition in the House of Commons.

Newly elected Prime Minister Justin Trudeau and his wife, Sophie Grégoire-Trudeau, on election night in 2015.

Table 11.5 Seats Won in the 2015 General Election by Province*

Province	Con	Lib	BQ	NDP	Green	Other	Total
Alberta	29	4	0	1	0	0	34
BC	10	17	0	14	1	0	42
Manitoba	5	7	0	2	0	0	14
Saskatchewan	10	1	0	3	0	0	14
New Brunswick	0	10	0	0	0	0	10
Newfoundland and Labrador	0	7	0	0	0	0	7
Nova Scotia	0	11	0	0	0	0	11
PEI	0	4	0	0	0	0	4
Ontario	33	80	0	8	0	0	121
Québec	12	40	10	16	0	0	78
Nunavut	0	1	0	0	0	0	1
NWT	0	1	0	0	0	0	1
Yukon	0	1	0	0	0	0	1
National Total	99	184	10	44	1	0	338

*Based on provisional data from Elections Canada.

The NDP led a "no risk" front-runner campaign, but its orange wave of 2011 folded, and in the last week of the campaign the party returned to its third-party pre-wave condition. The NDP won 44 seats and 19.7 percent of the popular vote, a loss of 51 seats and a decrease in popular vote of 10.9 percent. It was the only party to lose a large number of votes—almost a million—and more than half of its seats. It was pushed back to rely on its core support in the West and a few seats in rural Ontario and Québec (see Table 11.5), roughly where it was after the 2004 election.

The new alignment looked a lot like it had 35 years earlier when Pierre Trudeau was prime minister, well before either Stephen Harper or Justin Trudeau appeared on the political scene. It also suggested a somewhat regionally fragmented polity.

In the Atlantic provinces, where the Liberals had the advantage of strong provincial parties and popular premiers (three of the four provinces had Liberal governments), the entire region went Liberal. Peter MacKay had been the regional standard bearer of the Conservatives in the Atlantic region, but he retired shortly before the election call. High-profile New Democrats lost their seats in the Liberal sweep.

In Québec, some had believed that a Trudeau would never get elected again. However, this time the province divided its vote among four parties. Quebeckers gave 40 seats to the Liberals, giving their province a strong voice in federal government and politics for the first time since 2000 with Jean Chrétien. The result was a major breakthrough for the Liberals, who had been excluded from Québec after the sponsorship scandal, replaced first by the BQ in 1993 and then by the NDP in 2011. The NDP kept 16 seats, with Québec still its biggest base, and the Conservatives retained 12 seats. This was the only province in which the Conservative share of the vote increased from 2011, and then it was by considerably less than 1 percent. The BQ came back from 4 seats to 10, but was still short of party status and its leader lost his seat.[20]

In Ontario, the Liberals reclaimed 80 seats, the Conservatives took 33, and the NDP won 8. The Liberals had countered the Conservative immigration policies to attract concentrations of new immigrant voters in places like the 905 area code outside of Toronto. This was a hotly contested area because from 2004 to 2011 it indicated which party would win the election and whether it would form a majority or minority government. They also said that they would support provincial premier Kathleen Wynne in reforming the province's pension policies. Several Conservative Cabinet ministers were defeated in Ontario, and the NDP lost badly in Toronto.

In the Prairie provinces, the Conservatives kept most of their support, but the Liberals made a breakthrough, winning 12 seats (mostly in large cities), and the NDP won 6. For the Liberals to win that many seats in the Prairie provinces, where they had been inconsequential for decades, was a big step forward. The party drew votes from young professionals in Calgary, Edmonton, Saskatoon, and Winnipeg. In Alberta, the Conservatives saw a total rise in their votes, but due to high voter turnout their share of the vote fell by seven points. British Columbia split its votes three ways, with the Liberals taking 17 seats, the Conservatives 10, and the NDP 14 (its second largest provincial vote after Québec). Many high-profile local issues were debated there, as well as the economy and other national issues. In the North, the three territories all returned Liberal MPs.

The Liberals won seats in every province, but the Conservatives held the bulk of their support in their base regions, the West and rural Ontario.[21] Conservative support came largely from white, rural, well-off voters and suburbia. Liberals polled well in major cities. The Liberals did well in ridings with visible minority populations (those where 26.8 percent or more were visible minorities, according to the National Household Survey). This trend applied across the country, but was especially true in Ontario and Québec. In Ontario, the Liberals won 91 percent of high visible minority ridings. The Conservatives won only 7 percent, losing seats in Toronto, Brampton, and Mississauga that they had won in 2011.[22]

The fact that the Conservatives had no persuasive message that appealed to voters meant that their tone was negative, and they were easily thrown off course as they grasped at issues involving refugees and social identity, particularly the niqab issue, that in the end did not help them. The negative ads that the party used to label Trudeau as young and "not ready" seemed to be effective initially, but the 43-year-old Liberal leader did well in the first debate and ran a consistently good campaign, making it clear that he was no bogeyman. Rather, he inspired the same excitement and loyalty as his father had in his political debut almost five decades earlier. The Liberal slogan of "Real Change" was reminiscent of the slogan that had brought Democratic leader Barack Obama to power in the United States. It fit the mood of the electorate as they turned on Stephen Harper. After nearly 10 years of Conservative rule, many voters simply wanted something new. The question was which party and leader would provide the desired change.

The long campaign ended up being a bad decision for the Conservatives, a tactical error. The campaign had intended to show Stephen Harper as the safe, known, and knowledgeable leader, but by the end of the campaign voters were reminded of the many traits they disliked in his leadership. The litany of complaints included how he drove wedges among groups by using social, emotional issues; showed disregard of facts from scientists and civil servants; created spin around everything his government did; evinced a bunker mentality; instructed Conservative MPs on how to manipulate and control parliamentary committees; bulldozed legislation through Parliament in omnibus bills, minimizing parliamentary scrutiny; and saw enemies everywhere, especially among elites. In addition to this litany, Harper had marginalized moderate conservatives and concentrated power in his own hands, giving the impression of paranoia and alienating many in his caucus.

These negative perceptions (whether fair or not) obscured Harper's strengths. Among them, he had shown economic leadership through difficult times, put in place policies that created jobs, and increased trade links. He had helped families and the middle class. He had shrunk the size of the federal state by sharing money, authority, and taxing powers with the provinces. He was tough on national security and immigration policy. Perhaps most of all, he had brought the West back into the federal government and politics.

In contrast, the long campaign gave Justin Trudeau time to overcome the doubts and low expectations that had been set for him. He showed that he was well informed, hard-working, energetic, competent, and likeable, with a sunny disposition that contrasted with Harper's dour personality. He epitomized freshness and hope. As well, he had roots in three provinces—British Columbia, Ontario, and Québec—all of which ended up giving him considerable support.

The long campaign also provided time for NDP leader Tom Mulcair to impress the electorate, but he failed to do so. He moved his party to the centre and the Liberals profited from the progressive vacuum he left behind. He did not stress income inequality as a defining issue, and would not admit that he might need to raise taxes on the wealthy. Nor would he support small deficits to provide income for his programs. Having run as a safe, comfortable prime minister–in-waiting, Tom Mulcair and his party emerged as worthy but not a ruling party. In the end, voters did not see Mulcair as the leader best positioned to unseat Harper. The NDP share of the vote increased from 2011 only in Prince Edward Island, Nunavut, and Yukon.

When they called the election earlier than necessary, the Conservatives had considerably more money than the other parties. During previous elections, they had developed sophisticated software to develop and promote political issues that would help them target and attract large numbers of small donations and identify supports to get out the vote. It was effective data mining based on scientific marketing that helped the party formulate policies and messages tailored to the needs and wants of swing voters. It was a strategy that provided win-ability. The Liberal Party, by contrast, was in shambles when Justin Trudeau took over, and badly needed to revamp its fundraising and organization. By 2015, although the Liberals were still behind financially, they had caught up to the Conservatives in their use of new technology.

The Liberals ran an aggressive campaign. They conducted extensive training sessions for volunteers before the election, claiming to have more than 80 000 ready to knock on over 10 million doors. They were better prepared to mount local campaigns. Instead of relying on telephones, their volunteers accessed a mobile app that allowed them to input information collected from their canvasing. Experts at party headquarters took it from there, developing predictive modelling that they claimed enhanced their knowledge of which types of voters to target and how. The NDP said that they had more than 40 000 trained volunteers, and were particularly active in Québec. They also had a tracking system, but it proved less sophisticated than the Liberals' system.

By the morning after the election, the country had changed. Canadians had voted to return to moderate, big tent government. Harper resigned after speaking to his supporters on the night of the election. He left no obvious successor. The NDP was back to its traditional third-party status, although it kept a substantial number of seats in Québec, British Columbia, and Ontario. Both the NDP and the Conservatives immediately began post-mortems to see where they had gone wrong. For the Conservatives, the explanation involved a long series of "ifs"—*if* the price of oil had not highlighted the weakness of the Conservative economic strategy, *if* the Mike Duffy trial had not coincided with the campaign, *if* the Syrian refugee crisis had not happened, *if* the niqab issue had not been raised, and *if* the campaign had been shorter, things might have gone differently for them.

The Liberals inherited a weak economy with which to finance their domestic ambitions. Low prices for oil and other commodities weighed heavily on the economy as they began their new government. Research indicates that the electorate has high expectations of the new government in terms of tone; ethical conduct; and the values of civility, inclusion, and collaboration.[23] Justin Trudeau showed that he has mastered the skill of campaigning. Now he needs to master governing if Canada is to avoid plunging back into social depression and chronic deficits. The Liberal Party platform proposes a more interventionist federal government on economic matters such as infrastructure, pensions, and the environment.

MEDIA, POLLS, AND ELECTIONS

Media have become vitally important links between political institutions and private citizens, especially during elections. By media, we mean the traditional communication technologies—radio, television, newspapers (both broadsheet and Internet varieties), and magazines—as well as the newest systems of communications that are rewriting the political landscape—including social networking, citizen journalism, and blogs. As intermediaries between government and the population, they play a significant role in legitimizing government, making it more effective, and preventing abuses of power.

Communications guru Marshall McLuhan noted decades ago, in his book *Understanding Media*, that the "medium is the message," by which he meant that we should look beyond the content of the media to understand the effects that various forms of media have on our lives and on our thinking. Mass media are crucial sources of political information, suggesting topics that citizens ought to know about and what to think about those topics. They play an important role in helping citizens make informed decisions at election time. During elections, most newspapers endorse a party. In 2015, *The Globe and Mail* endorsed the Conservative Party, but said that Stephen Harper should resign.

Changes in communications technologies are affecting the way in which elections are portrayed. About 68 percent of Canadians use smartphones. Newspapers have devised applications (apps) to help users stay informed. Social networking (such as Facebook, YouTube, and Twitter), citizen journalism, and blogs are playing a much greater role than ever before, allowing interaction with parties and leaders and opportunities to express opinions. New digital broadcasters made significant contributions during the 2015 campaign. When the Conservatives refused to participate in the traditional consortium debates, YouTube/Google Canada transmitted debates organized by *Maclean's* and *The Globe and Mail*. However, while there is little doubt that these formats are influential in politics, there is little empirical evidence about exactly *how* they affect election campaigns. They are heavily used by Canadians but it is uncertain how, or how much, they affect election outcomes.

Polling is a staple of election campaigns, to track changes in voter support. There was an abundance of public opinion polling before and during the 2015 election campaign. However, while the variation in their predictions, contradictions, and even silly trending made them entertaining, they were basically inconclusive and unreliable—a result that has also been true in most modern-day elections in other countries. As the campaign reached day 78, most polls became more accurate in predicting the relative support for the parties. However, as usual, they were not able to accurately predict the number of seats for each party or even the possibility of a majority government. The reason is obvious: Canadian elections do not produce a uniform swing of votes across the entire country, and therefore without much larger targeted samples polls cannot predict results in particular geographical territories, and certainly not in single ridings. Moreover, the effort to extrapolate from national surveys to provincial or local results provides such wide margins of error that almost any prediction is possible (and usually attempted!). On the whole, the media receive free survey data from pollsters, who then use the resultant publicity to sell their wares to others consumers such as businesses. The media use the free information to provide dramatic "horse race" and sales-promoting strategies. Media, too, are businesses, after all.

Discussion Questions

1. In what respects could Canadian elections be made more democratic? Be sure to consider the method of determining who wins, the technique for counting votes, who runs for office, who is allowed to vote, who finances political parties, and how electoral boundaries are drawn.

2. Should Canada adopt compulsory voting? Should Canada get rid of the single-member plurality electoral system? Why or why not?

3. Do you think that Canada should hold more referendums to allow more direct citizen input into decision making? Why or why not?

4. Was Justin Trudeau elected because of his policies or his personality? Did the personality and/or the role of outgoing prime minister Stephen Harper affect the results?

5. The media are not elected, yet they influence what voters see, hear, and think about during an election. Do politicians use the media, or do the media use politicians?

Chapter 12
Canadian Foreign Policy
Constraints, Opportunities, and Sacrifice

Learning Objectives

After reading this chapter, you should be able to

1   Define foreign policy and distinguish it from domestic policy.

2   Define globalization and assess its importance for Canadian economic policy.

3   Trace the history of Canada's trade policy from the National Policy to the free trade agreement with the United States and NAFTA.

4   Outline Canada's policies towards a) terrorism, b) Arctic sovereignty, and c) pipeline issues.

5   Describe Canada's foreign military expeditions in the nineteenth and twentieth centuries, and assess Canada's recent military involvement in Afghanistan, Libya, Iraq, and Syria.

Canada is far from self-sufficient in either economic prosperity or national security. Increasingly, the safety and well-being of Canadians depend on how the government responds to the dangers, constraints, opportunities, and obligations that flow from the international environment. The world has entered an era of violence and increasing interdependence. In Chapter 9, we discussed terrorism and Canada's security policies and laws. Here, we examine more generally how understanding Canadian government and politics requires a broad grasp of global affairs.

Students of international relations have difficulty depicting Canada's place in the international power hierarchy. Some scholars accept the description of Canada as an influential *middle power*. The Canadian government endorsed this notion after the end of World War II, when it rallied with like-minded states to contest the domination of the United Nations by the "great powers." After that period, officials and scholars alike began to use the phrase somewhat indiscriminately. Andrew Cooper boldly states that the middle power framework became "the consensual champion among the competing conceptual frameworks."[1]

Those on the intellectual left have never accepted the term *middle power*. They argue that the country depends overwhelmingly on its southern neighbour for security as well as prosperity. For them, Canada went from being a colony of Britain to one of the United States. While this argument has some merit, it is nevertheless true that Canada has frequently opposed U.S. policies and acted independently; Canada's opposition to the U.S. war in Vietnam and the second war in Iraq are major cases in point. On October 20, 2015, the day after he assumed office, prime minister–elect

Justin Trudeau announced that he would not follow the U.S. lead and would instead halt Canadian aircraft bombing of ISIS in Syria.

A third group asserts that Canada is a more significant country than the terms *middle power* or *satellite of the United States* would imply. They claim grandly that Canada is a "foremost" or "major" power. Justifications for this high ranking include public opinion surveys that show this is how many Canadians regard their country, membership in the prestigious economic G7 club, and—at least in theory—the somewhat reduced bipolarity of the world after the Cold War that has allowed countries such as Canada to ascend to new power positions.

In the final analysis, whether Canadians consider their country to be a major, middle, or dependent power may be irrelevant. What matters more is what *other countries* think about Canada's significance in the global competition. But here, too, the record is mixed. Determining Canada's relative economic performance in terms of its gross domestic product (GDP) is much easier than measuring overall international power. By this measure, Canada certainly hovers in the top group. In 2014, for example, Canada had one of the largest economies in the world, and its per capita income was measured at US$41 887. This means that, in a global perspective, Canadians are economically very well off. In 2015, the UN Human Development Index placed Canada ninth in its ranking of all countries in the world.

In this chapter, we provide information necessary to assess these viewpoints. First, we examine the concept of foreign policy itself. Then, we turn to a discussion of its main components: trade policy, security, and defence policy. In examining trade policy, we consider Canada's role in the world and in particular its relationship with the United States, as well as more specific issues such as Arctic sovereignty. In examining defence policy, we focus on Canada's role in defence organizations, war, and peacekeeping.

WHAT IS FOREIGN POLICY?

international relations: The broad network of relations among states, including the activities of citizens and non-state institutions.

global system: The sets of relationships among states and other significant actors in the world.

foreign policy: State or government behaviour that has external ramifications.

The study of **international relations** focuses on the broad network of relations among states, including the activities of citizens and non-state institutions. The **global system** consists of sets of relationships among states and other significant actors in the world. The **foreign policy** of countries, on the other hand, is much narrower than either of these concepts. It concerns state or government behaviour that has external ramifications. It includes diplomatic and military relations among states, as well as their cultural, economic, technological, and, increasingly, ecological and security interests.

There are basic similarities and dissimilarities between domestic and international affairs. Both consist of the struggle for advantage among organized groups with different interests and values. In neither case can all of the interests and values at stake be satisfied; therefore, disputes and conflicts often erupt. In domestic politics, such conflict may lead to criminal acts or revolution. In international and global politics, the result may be economic catastrophe, international terrorism, or even warfare.

The main distinction between domestic and foreign politics is that the international system has no world government to mitigate disputes and determine "who gets what, when and how." The world's states exist in a kind of anarchy without a higher form of government to guide them. They compete in a world of insecurity and danger. Of course, states sometimes cooperate to further their own interests, and in that sense they develop "law-like" customs and practices that shape their behaviour. On the whole, therefore, the external behaviour of states is characterized by legal and political anarchy as well as by customs and norms about proper behaviour.

Politics among states takes many forms, ranging from diplomacy to war. Routine relations include negotiations between diplomats and other officials who assert the claims of their states in "bilateral" (between two of them) and "multilateral" (among several of them) frameworks. Diplomacy may result in agreement or conflict. Treaties and protocols may be negotiated and signed, but if agreement cannot be reached among states, other approaches may be sought, ranging from public complaints to propaganda, subversion, and even outright war.

Making foreign policy is considerably different from making domestic policy. The state has authority over its internal environment, but a government has no legal authority outside its borders. As a result, foreign policy decisions must be set within the context of the opportunities and constraints of the international system. In concrete terms, foreign policy-making differs from domestic policy-making because the former may be little more than striking an image. Only rarely is legislation necessary; normally Parliament and even the bureaucratic elite have little more than spectator status, as the prime minister and the ministers of defense, foreign affairs, and international trade dominate.

Unlike domestic politics, which takes place within a set of more or less developed laws and which ultimately is related to the authority of government and sovereignty of the territory, international politics has no international government that can impose its laws on people everywhere. States may join international organizations for mutual benefit, but few accept the authority of decision makers or laws other than their own domestic authorities. At the same time, to be realistic, powerful countries often dominate their weaker neighbours and even on occasion colonize them.

While Canadian provinces have some power in international affairs, advocates of *exclusive* federal competence in all international matters argue that the prerogative of treaty-making power was vested exclusively in the Queen in 1867, as stated in Section 9 of the *British North America Act*. Through a process of evolution from 1871 to 1939, direct power over foreign affairs devolved to Ottawa. However, while the federal government might like to prevent provincial government initiatives, jurisdictional realities necessitate accommodating them.

The province of Québec shares many of the same international interests and objectives as the other nine provinces. However, because of the sovereigntist aspirations of some of its governments, it also has sometimes followed its own unique agenda. Québec nationalism is discussed in Chapter 5, but it is important to note here the impact of the nationalist agenda on Québec's relations with foreign countries, and the consequent strain this has often placed on Ottawa–Québec relations. As Kim Nossal notes, once the Parti Québécois came to power in Québec in 1976, what had begun as "an external expression of functional provincial interests" became "an issue of symbolic national interest for the Québec government."[2] As the nationalist goal began to shift toward the separation of Québec from Canada by gaining international recognition of Québec's sovereign status,[3] Québec began to challenge the federal government's monopoly over the conduct of Canada's foreign relations.

During the 1995 Québec referendum, French president Jacques Chirac promised that France would recognize Québec after a Yes vote. This was a break from the more qualified approach of "non-interference but non-indifference" that had held since the failure of the 1980 referendum. On the other hand, the United States followed its standard line—that the United States prefers a united Canada, but it is up to Canadians to make their own decisions.

ECONOMIC AND TRADE POLICY

Canada's prosperity relies on the export of goods and services as well as foreign investment in its currency, stocks, and bonds. The country has a low ratio of population to land and resources and is by necessity one of the largest trading states in the world. The domestic population of more than 35 million is too small to sustain all of the country's flourishing industries, so around one-third of the GDP depends on exports. Most of these exports are from primary industries based on natural resources.

Canada has three main kinds of natural resources. The first is agricultural land, which climatic and soil conditions make amenable to cultivating crops and raising livestock. It is limited to the southernmost part of the country and is steadily encroached on by industrial development and urban sprawl. Canada is one of the largest exporters of agri-food products. The second category is non-renewable resources, such as mineral deposits. Canada is a leading exporter of minerals—crude petroleum, natural gas, iron ore, nickel, and copper. The third type of natural resource consists of renewable resources, of which wood, fish, fur, and grains have been particularly important to Canada's economic growth.

This present-day pattern of the Canadian economy was laid out in the colonial period. Basically, Canada exports primary resources and imports secondary or manufactured products. Most Canadians live and work in urban, industrialized areas, but agricultural products, lumber, and mineral resources provide the bulk of exports and pay for imported manufactured goods. In 2014, Canada's exports amounted to $529 billion compared to $524 billion in imports.

Manufactured goods such as motor vehicles and parts, metals, minerals, pulp and paper, lumber and sawmill products, natural gas, and wheat sell extremely well. However, Canada consumes more *services* (such as tourism, freight, and government procurement) from other countries than it sells, and pays more interest to investors abroad than it earns on foreign investments.

Trade between Canada and its main trading partners requires careful day-to-day management. However, the fact that the contractual framework for most of Canada's bilateral trade is provided by international treaties illustrates the important multilateral dimension of economic relations. As an export-oriented economy, Canada's prosperity is vitally linked to maintaining a multilateral, transparent, and rules-based world trading system.

CANADA AND GLOBAL ECONOMICS

At the end of World War II, the leading economic countries met at Bretton Woods in the United States to reorganize the war-torn economies of the trading world. They decided to fix (peg) the exchange rate of the U.S. dollar to the gold standard, and other currencies to the U.S. dollar. The currencies could be "unpegged" only within stipulated regulations. Eventually, however, the rules unravelled due to pressures on the U.S. dollar and the entire exchange system became unregulated. Since then, currencies have floated freely, as Canadians who experienced the 69-cent dollar in 2016 will understand.

As for international trade, the United States, Britain, and Canada were the principal proponents of a new order that resulted in the 1947 **General Agreement on Tariffs and Trade (GATT)**, an agreement that sought to establish a trading order based on reciprocity, non-discrimination, and multilateralism. It covered most of world trade and included most major industrialized countries. The GATT established a code of rules for the conduct of trade; as an institution, it oversaw the application of the trade rules and provided a forum in which countries could discuss trade problems and negotiate reductions in trade barriers.

General Agreement on Tariffs and Trade (GATT): A 1947 agreement that established a trading order based on reciprocity, non-discrimination, and multilateralism among most major industrialized countries.

As a signator of the GATT, Canada could negotiate basic resource needs with its powerful southern neighbour more easily. In 1994, participants agreed to transform the GATT secretariat into a somewhat more powerful *World Trade Organization* (WTO) and to reduce tariffs on a long list of goods. As of 2014, there are 161 members in the WTO, including China, which joined in 2001.

As the global economy grows, the significance of other international economic multilateral organizations such as the *International Monetary Fund* (IMF) and the *World Bank* increases. Both organizations were established at the end of World War II. The purposes of the IMF are to foster stability in money markets, encourage cooperation among states on monetary matters, aid in the establishment of a payment system, and promote international trade. Currently, 188 states are members of the IMF, which lends funds to member states and provides technical assistance to their economies. The World Bank also lends money. It focuses on countries or states that commercial banks or other lenders will not support, and generally tries to reduce poverty among its members. A total of 188 countries belong to the World Bank. The importance of each state within these organizations is based on its voting strength as determined by its financial contributions to the funds.

Canada belongs to many other multilateral organizations that concern the global economy and development. The best known is the **G7**, which includes the world's seven largest industrialized democracies—United States, Japan, Germany, Britain, France, Italy, and Canada—and the Commission of the European Union. (The organization is called G8 when Russia is included.) This prestigious group holds annual economic summits, maintaining a tradition that began in 1975 at Rambouillet in France. The summits have taken on a semi-permanent character, although there is no permanent secretariat. They have become huge media events at which leaders discuss economic issues and other international topics.

G7: A multilateral organization of the world's seven largest industrialized democracies. It deals with issues concerning the global economy and issues of the day.

The G7 is important to Canada for several reasons. First, it provides recognition of status; political leaders want to be part of this elite group. But more important is Canada's major stake in the economic relationships among the "Big Seven." Of the seven, Canada is affected most by the economic policies of the United States. Prime ministers therefore usually express strong satisfaction with how the G7 serves Canadian interests and foreign policy. On the other hand, many observers believe that the summits are meaningless exercises. A balanced view is that they are significant, but that their importance is easy to exaggerate.

Canada has also been affected by world economic trends. Strong multinational corporations, combined with more open trade rules, have given rise to what many

Globalization

Globalization is defined as the integration of states through trade, communications, and contact. It is widely used to explain various major international events, from world economic relations to world terrorism.

Globalization is a reorientation of cultural, economic, political, and technological activities and processes in such a way that they transcend state or country borders. It is a cluster of interconnected factors that make states more economically interdependent and transform world politics, including the integration of goods, services, capital, and markets. But that

is not all. The speed of the flow of capital around the world—calculated at more than $2 trillion per day—and the growing importance of non-state actors have also undermined states' abilities to regulate their own economies.

While the state retains its primary responsibilities in the military and security fields, it increasingly shares power with broader forces in other aspects of international life. To some extent, the forces of globalization are determining which countries and individuals win or lose in the world market of commerce and ideas.

globalization: The integration of states through trade, communications, and contact.

observers call *globalization* (see Close-Up 12.1). Its impact on the Canadian economy has been dramatic. A *global* economy has emerged in terms of not just trade but also all of the elements of wealth creation—finance, investment, production, distribution, and marketing. The changing structure of the world economy has seriously affected the Canadian economy and trade patterns in many ways. Rapidly developing technologies have forced industries in developed countries such as Canada to become more competitive or be left behind as standard technologies are taken over by developing countries with lower labour costs.

For historical and political reasons, Canadian foreign policy has always been directed predominantly toward Europe (especially Britain) and the United States. Political relations, defence, and economic policies have developed certain basic continuities. Long-standing defence ties exist with the United States and Western Europe through the North Atlantic Treaty Organization (NATO) and North American Aerospace Defense Command (NORAD). Multilateral relations are primarily conducted through the United Nations and its related agencies. Bilateral political and economic relations are strongest with the United States, the Commonwealth, Western Europe, and the French-language community. However, Asia, especially China and Japan, have recently become even more important to Canada than Europe is in purely economic relations.

The Commonwealth

At Confederation, Canada was part of the British Empire, exercising autonomy in domestic policy but dependent on Britain in foreign affairs. World War I was the catalyst for Canada to attain complete autonomy, and for the transformation of the British Empire into the Commonwealth. The transition was achieved at a succession of imperial conferences, culminating in 1926 with the Balfour Declaration, which concluded that the dominions were equal, autonomous communities united by a common allegiance to the Crown and freely associated as members of the

Commonwealth of Nations. This sentiment was enshrined in the 1931 *Statute of Westminster*, which formally laid the old Empire to rest.

The Commonwealth at that time consisted of Britain, Australia, Canada, Newfoundland, the Irish Free State, the Union of South Africa, and New Zealand. Now, almost a century later, it numbers 53 member states and embraces about a third of the world's population (about 1 billion people) and about a quarter of the Earth's surface. Prime ministers Louis St. Laurent and Lester Pearson played important roles in the evolution of the new Commonwealth. Pearson, in particular, was key in negotiating an acceptable formula for new admissions—a development that changed the essentially Anglocentric focus of the Commonwealth association. Today, the organization has no binding rules of membership, and decisions are made by consensus rather than by vote.

Commonwealth of Nations: An association of 53 states united by a common historical tie. Some owe allegiance to Queen Elizabeth II, some have their own monarchy, and some are republics.

Canada and the United Nations

Canada played a central role in creating the United Nations (UN) and in directing its evolution as an international organization. Canada's sponsorship of the UN demonstrated a radical change from the pre-war policy of isolationism to postwar internationalism as a means of avoiding war. Both Louis St. Laurent, Secretary of State for External Affairs in 1946, and Lester Pearson, who followed in that position, were avowed internationalists. Pearson wrote in his memoirs, "Everything I learned during the war confirmed and strengthened my view as a Canadian that our foreign policy must not be timid or fearful of commitments but activist in accepting international responsibility."[4]

Initially, the UN had 57 charter members, and in the 1950s Canada was a major participant. The club was very restrictive. In 1955, Paul Martin, Sr., chair of the Canadian UN delegation, persuaded the UN Security Council to agree to a package deal for accepting new members. They flooded in, and today Canada is no longer a principal player, but merely one of 194 countries that belong to the UN.

No organization has arisen to replace the UN as a forum for the discussion of world problems. Canada has played a role in several significant issues, including the law of the sea, the north–south dialogue between rich and poor nations, human rights, chemical warfare, abolition of land mines, halting traffic in small arms, and ending the conscription of children. Canada is also a strong supporter of the UN's many specialized multilateral agencies, such as the World Health Organization and the International Labour Organization. As president of the UN General Assembly, Lester Pearson was responsible for introducing one of its most important innovations: the concept of a peacekeeping force. The UN Charter provided for a standing army but none was ever created.

The rather tarnished contemporary image of the UN may be a result of exaggerated expectations of what it can accomplish. John Holmes summarized the situation this way: "When people worry whether the UN has lived up to the ideals of the Charter, in some ways it's the wrong question. Rather than see whether it has been able to carry out a mandate carved in stone it may be better to ask whether it has been able to grow and fit in with changing circumstances. . . . To a great extent it has."[5] Holmes was correct. Unfortunately, not all agree. In 2010, Canada was denied a position on the Security Council despite campaigning strongly to secure a seat.

Canada's Relations with the United States

U.S. President John F. Kennedy once said of Canada that "geography made us neighbours, history made us friends and economics made us partners." He was correct. There is no more important external relationship for Canada than that with the United States. But the long history of cooperation in NATO and NORAD belies the fact that much of Canada's history, including Confederation itself, was inspired by efforts to be independent of the United States and protected from American domination.[6]

The United States is Canada's largest trading partner. Approximately $850 billion in trade crossed the border in 2014, the world's leading two-way trade relationship by a large margin. The United States accounts for about four-fifths of Canadian exports and two-thirds of its imports. On the other hand, Canada takes only a small percentage of total American exports and provides even less of its total imports. Even at these significantly lower percentages of total trade, however, Canada is the most important trading partner of the United States.

The high degree of dependence is not mutual. Although geography and history provided the backdrop for the early special relationship, that tie has inevitably been one-sided. This is perhaps best illustrated in symbolic terms by the relative urgency assigned to initial political visits at the highest level. The first Canadian prime ministerial trip to Washington was in 1871; the first official U.S. presidential visit to Ottawa did not occur until more than seven decades later, in 1943. The relationship between these unequal neighbours over the years has been friendly, but, on the part of Canadians, necessarily guarded, as the attitudes of U.S. leaders have fluctuated from extremes of annexation to complete indifference. Ulysses S. Grant, for example, aspired to absorb Canada into the United States in time for his 1872 election bid—in fact, he wanted the British to cede Canada in exchange for damage caused by a British ship![7]

The two governments have different approaches to the role of government in the economy. In Canada, both federal and provincial governments are active in the marketplace to a degree unacceptable in the United States. Perhaps the most obvious difference, however, is that Canada's population is only approximately one-tenth that of the United States, making Canada vulnerable to pressures from the United States in the fields of economy, defence, and culture.

Most foreign capital enters Canada in the form of direct investment, not interest or portfolio investment. This means that rather than involving bank loans or bonds, which can be paid off, investment in the Canadian economy often brings a high degree of control and ownership, especially in the manufacturing and resource sectors. Branch plants allow the importation of U.S. technology and market access as well as American values. They are subject not only to market forces and Canadian government regulation, but also to U.S. national interests.

There can be little doubt that foreign investment improves Canada's standard of living and has helped to transform Canada into an industrialized country. However, there is equally little doubt that it has increased the dependence of Canada's economy and culture on the United States.

Free Trade: FTA and NAFTA One of the most controversial ongoing trade issues concerns free trade, a recurring theme in Canada's relationship with the United States. The issue originated—and caused heated debate—as far back as the 1870s.

In the early years of statehood, Conservative Prime Minister Sir John A. Macdonald won the hearts of Canadians with his National Policy of high tariffs to protect fledgling Canadian industries. In 1911, Sir Wilfrid Laurier failed to win re-election partly because he wanted to eliminate tariffs on one-quarter of cross-border trade. He could not compete with the Conservative opposition slogan: "No truck or trade with the Yankees."

Much later, in the early 1980s, controversy developed over whether to move toward full free trade across the border or, as the Liberal government recommended, to build *sectoral free trade* in selected items, among them steel and agricultural equipment. This type of policy had been implemented in the 1965 Auto Pact and had proven successful in increasing the flow of Canadian automobiles and parts across the Canada–U.S. border. However, the idea of sectoral free trade was abandoned when the Conservatives came to office in 1984. Prime Minister Brian Mulroney reversed the Conservative Party's traditional position against free trade and entered into negotiations for a comprehensive, general free trade agreement with the United States. The new government's position was buttressed by the 1985 report of the Royal Commission on the Economic Union and Development Prospects for Canada, which argued strongly in favour of *general free trade*.[8]

Opponents argued that general free trade would destroy many Canadian companies and inevitably lead to the formation of common institutions dominated by the United States, thereby eroding Canada's political sovereignty. At the time, many Canadian business people were worried about a growing demand for protectionism in Washington due to a massive U.S. trade deficit. Two major trade disputes came to the fore while the free trade negotiations were taking place. In 1986, the United States introduced a countervailing duty against softwood lumber imported from Canada. Canada negotiated with the United States to apply its own 15 percent export tax rather than submit to the countervailing duty. Later the same year, the United States imposed a five-year tariff on Canadian red cedar shakes and shingles, and Canada was forced to retaliate.

Negotiations for a comprehensive free trade agreement began, and two years later the legal text was released and signed on January 2, 1988. Meanwhile, federal Liberal leader John Turner called on the Liberal-controlled Senate to block the agreement. The 1988 election ensued, with the free trade deal as the primary election issue. The Tories won the election, and the controversial agreement came into force on January 1, 1989.

The *Canada–United States Free Trade Agreement* (FTA) was intended to enhance market access and reduce trade conflicts between the two countries. It provided a set of *dispute resolution mechanisms* and the goal of gradual elimination of all tariffs between the two countries. Special and technical agreements were made in many fields; however, free trade as such was never completed. Each country reserved the right to continue to impose trade retaliation in the form of countervailing duties, anti-dumping, or other trade remedies. Each country also reserved the right to change its trade legislation after the FTA came into force.

Opposition to the FTA was widespread in Canada and centred on three issues. First, it was argued that the deal did not obtain *secure* access to the U.S. market for Canadian products since American trade remedies continued to apply. Second, the agreement was attacked as giving away too much in investment, financial services, agriculture, energy, and service sectors, and getting too little in return. A third issue involved what constituted a trade "subsidy"; opponents of the deal argued that Canadian social programs, such as unemployment insurance and provincial health insurance, could fall into this category and therefore be subject to retaliation.

Questions about the impact of the FTA on Canadian interests and Canadian sovereignty lingered. The Canadian government immediately began negotiations with Mexico and the United States for a *North American Free Trade Agreement* (NAFTA). This agreement called for a three-country deal that incorporated the FTA and expanded it to include clauses on intellectual property, medical services, and more explicit rules about national treatment. In the November 1993 general election, the Liberals under Jean Chrétien promised to reopen some of the most controversial parts of NAFTA. However, despite the Liberal victory, NAFTA was made law on January 1, 1994, without the resolution of any of those issues (see Table 12.1).[9]

The free trade debate continues, but today all three major Canadian parties seem to agree that, as neighbours on this continent, the only reasonable policy to adopt is one that fosters a mutually satisfactory free trade relationship. In 1994, at the Summit of the Americas, negotiations were announced to extend NAFTA into a hemispheric free trade zone, but discussions continually broke down and eventually progress became non-existent.

At the bilateral level, two relatively new issues have dominated U.S.–Canada relations in recent years: pipelines and Arctic sovereignty.

Canada–U.S. Pipeline Issues Canada has had many specific issues with the United States over pipelines in the past, but none as direct and controversial as the proposed 1711-kilometre Keystone Pipeline XL. If approved by the U.S. government, this pipeline would have transported diluted bitumen from the Athabaskan oil sands in northeastern Alberta to refineries in the Midwest United States and the Gulf Coast of Texas.

Table 12.1 The NAFTA Equation, 2014

	United States	Canada	Mexico
Population (millions)	319	33	120
Life expectancy at birth (years)	79	82	78
Mean years of schooling	12.9	12.3	8.5
Per capita GDP (PPP US$)*	52 308	41 887	15 854
Exports (as % of GDP)	13.5	31.6	32.7
Adult literacy (%)	100	100	95
Human Development Index 2014 (rank)	5th	8th	71st

*Purchasing power parity (PPP) is a technique used to determine the relative value of different currencies.

Source: Adapted from the *Human Development Report, 2014. Sustaining Human Progress: Reducing Vulnerabilities and Building Resilience*. (New York: United Nations, 2014).

The pipeline proposal was advocated by Canadian industry and the Canadian government but opposed by U.S. environmental groups. President Barack Obama delayed the decision until several environmental studies were completed, and then vetoed the legislation when it became clear that the United States had become less dependent on oil imports than earlier believed because of the development of "fracking." The clincher came when the U.S. Energy Information Agency declared that the United States had become the largest producer of oil and gas in the world and might have as much as 60 billion barrels of recoverable shale oil. The dispute is ongoing and is likely to go to court.

In view of President Obama's veto, Prime Minister Stephen Harper's declaration that Canada was about to become an "energy superpower" was replaced with a defensive stance that Canada would build other pipelines from Alberta to the Pacific and seek new Asian markets for its oil. This policy met with significant resistance from Aboriginal groups and environmentalists (see Chapter 5).

Arctic Sovereignty

Few topics in Canada–U.S. relations have been plagued with more hysteria, histrionics, and hypocrisy than the Arctic. Since the North emerged as a romantic notion in Prime Minister John Diefenbaker's vision for Canada, the people of the North have been a centrepiece of political posturing, debates, policy, and expenditure by the federal government. Saber-rattling and serious negotiations have gone hand in hand.

The North comprises three political and administrative regions: Yukon, Nunavut, and the Northwest Territories (see Figure 12.1). Its total area is huge, comprising about two-fifths of the total mass of Canada and a coastline more than 162 000 kilometres in length (more than half of Canada's total coastline). After being isolated from the world for hundreds of years, inhabitants of the North are now being touted as the future source of development and prosperity. This abrupt reversal resulted from the discovery of oil and other resources in the region that were suddenly made more accessible because of climate change. As the ice fields melt, the fabled Northwest Passage is also expected to be open during summer months, allowing ships to pass directly between the Pacific and Atlantic Oceans. Various surveys have concluded that the Arctic region possesses about a quarter of the world's undiscovered oil and gas.

The wealth of resources in the North has given rise to mounting claims and even military activity in the Arctic. In 1996, Canada, Denmark, Finland, Iceland, Norway, Russia, Sweden, and the United States created an Arctic Council to manage the Arctic region as the polar ice melts, revealing new resources.

Canada has many interests in the region. It claims ownership of the Northwest Passage and therefore the right to control movement through it. Other countries, including the United States, dispute that assertion and claim that the Northwest Passage is an international strait that countries should be able to navigate freely. Canada also has rights over extensive seabeds in the Arctic that involve minor disputes. Denmark and Canada contest ownership of Hans Island, a 1.3-kilometre island between Greenland and Ellesmere Island, and there are issues with the United States over a segment of the Beaufort Sea north of Yukon. There are also unresolved

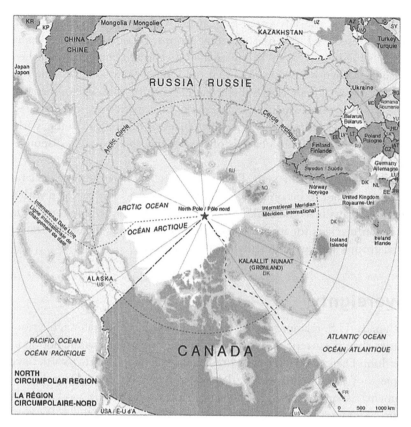

Figure 12.1 The Arctic

Source: North Circumpolar Region - The political map of the North Circumpolar Region. Natural Resources Canada.

issues with Russia over the Lomonosov Ridge (an undersea ridge that runs under the North Pole from Greenland to Russia) and periodic signs of Russian aggressiveness in the North.

Given the nationalist symbolism of the North, and the possibility of significant economic returns, Canada took several steps to protect its sovereignty in the region as part of Prime Minister Harper's "Northern strategy." Examples include:

- The Canadian High Arctic Research Centre, which is being built in Cambridge Bay, Nunavut.

- Construction to complete the Dempster Highway from Inuvik to Tuktoyaktuk.

- A promise of more than $3 billion to build five and perhaps six new Arctic patrol boats, the first of which will be delivered in 2018. Their purpose will be to patrol the length of the Northwest Passage. Presently, the Canadian Coast Guard employs two medium-sized icebreakers and four small icebreakers, but the ships are aging. (One, the *Louis St. Laurent*, is more than 44 years old.)

There are several domestic issues concerning Canadian policy in the North. First, the North exhibits the same types of problems among Canada's Aboriginal peoples that plague them elsewhere—alcoholism, low life expectancy, high suicide rates, and inadequate housing. Second, Canada needs to be able to respond to disasters, rescue people, regulate economic development, and defend the territory if it is to assert its sovereignty in the North. Unfortunately, Canada has only four second-hand submarines (bought from the UK), and these are able to operate under the ice caps for only short periods of time. Also, while Canada carries out periodic military exercises, it has only one 5000-member Ranger unit, a mainly indigenous army reserve force. It is not a fighting force but rather a symbolic Canadian footprint in the region.

Canada and Europe

Canada's historical and cultural ties with Western Europe have always been close, and Canadian governments have counted on this region to counterbalance U.S. influence. In the 1970s, in particular, fears were rife that Canada was too dependent on U.S. markets. At that time, Prime Minister Pierre Trudeau initiated his so-called "Third Option," to increase trade with Western Europe and Japan in order to diminish reliance on the United States. As an extension of that philosophy, Trudeau achieved a weak contractual link with the European Community, known as the Framework Agreement. However, little but platitudes came from this document, and trade with the United States continued to increase while it stagnated with Europe.

The countries that make up the European Union (EU) constitute the world's largest single economic entity. It is one of Canada's largest markets for agricultural products and several others that are resource-based, including forest products and fish. Since trade with Canada represents only a small percentage of total EU imports, the relationship is more important to Canada than to the EU.

Access to EU markets is difficult for Canadians to achieve, and despite traditional political ties, the trade relationship is unlikely to improve much. EU members have generally wanted access to Canada's pulp, oil, uranium, and other mineral resources in return for selling Canadians manufactured goods. The Canadian government is justifiably reluctant to accept these nineteenth-century conditions of trade.

In 1990, Canada and the EU signed the Transatlantic Declaration, which brought the two together but did very little for economic interests. In 1996, the two signed a Joint Action Plan (JAP), which is very broad in scope but does not include a free trade agreement.

In 2015, Canada negotiated a Comprehensive Economic and Trade Agreement (CETA) with the 28 members of the EU, but so far it is neither signed nor ratified. In Canada, the agreement is receiving the same criticism as NAFTA.

Canada and the Pacific

While Canadian trade with Western Europe stagnated in recent years, it increased rapidly with the Pacific Rim. In 1983, for the first time, Canada traded more with Asia than with Western Europe, and China is now Canada's second largest trading partner. It is increasingly evident that trans-Pacific trade is another opportunity to counterbalance the U.S. domination of the Canadian economy; it may eventually become another "third option."

Countries of the Pacific Rim—Japan, Korea, Taiwan, and Singapore, in particular—are challenging world markets with outstanding management, technology, and production techniques. While Japan's economy has slowed, those of the "Asian tigers" continue to grow. Despite their recent sluggish economies, Japan and China remain Canada's fastest-growing export markets. However, trade relations with these two countries are those of a resource-rich supplier with resource-poor industrial nations: Almost all of China and Japan's exports to Canada are fully manufactured, while most of Canada's exports are either raw materials or semi-processed products. China has one of the largest economies in the world and is likely to become an even more significant international player. However, when China suffers economic problems, Canada's resource market also suffers.

In October, just before the 2015 federal election, Canada signed a free trade agreement—the Trans-Pacific Partnership (TPP)—with 11 countries of the Pacific Rim. If ratified, this would create a massive free trade zone of 800 million people. Canada faced severe pressures from countries such as Australia, New Zealand, and the United States to open up its market for products such as milk and poultry. Canada has high tariff walls on these products and found it politically difficult to change the rules that protect them. The agreement may prove as contentious as the 1988 Free Trade Agreement with the United States. The new Liberal government has been slow to clarify its intentions regarding ratification of the TPP.

CANADIAN DEFENCE POLICY

Defence and security policy are intertwined with foreign policy objectives and, more specifically, with deterring aggression.[10] Canadian objectives in this field have varied over time according to changes in the international strategic environment and the political configuration of the country, but at all times there has been a commitment to preserving the country's independence, borders, institutions, and values, and the pursuit of peaceful settlements to prevent hostilities and warfare.

Almost all Canadians accept these high aspirations. However, the policies and programs required to fulfill them are constantly in dispute. Should Canada continue to be a member of a collective security arrangement such as NATO or, like Sweden, be completely independent? Should Canada be part of the nuclear bomb club or continue to keep nuclear devices off of native soil? Even if there were agreement on such general policies, an analyst would still need to know what costs would be required to execute them. These are difficult questions that touch on the basic values of the country. Indeed, what policies could protect Canadian citizens and defend the second largest land mass and longest coastline in the world?

History and Context of Canadian Military Policy

Canada's earliest military engagements were as British colonies. As members of the British Empire, Canada took part in two British overseas expeditions in Africa. Sixteen Canadians died in the 1884 Nile Expedition and 8300 died in the 1899–1902

Boer War in South Africa. The country also joined the 1918–1919 British expedition to Siberia to support the White Russian government during the civil war. Almost all of the 4192 soldiers sent to Vladivostok returned home safely.

In World War I (1914 to 1918), Canada as a colony was again automatically at war with Germany and others when Britain declared war. More than 600 000 troops were sent overseas to help defend the motherland. Québeckers vehemently opposed conscription, but many of them served. In total, almost 60 000 Canadians gave their lives in the name of the Crown. As the war drew to a victorious conclusion, Canada was increasingly recognized for its contributions to the war. The 1926 *Balfour Declaration*, a resolution of the Imperial Conference, declared that Britain and her dominions were autonomous and equal communities that pledged allegiance to the Crown and were free to join the British Commonwealth of Nations. As we saw in Chapter 3, Canada's independence was established by the British *Statute of Westminster* in 1931 and confirmed by the patriation of the Constitution in 1982.

Canada entered World War II (1939–1945) to fight Germany and its Nazi allies a week after Britain did, perhaps illustrating its newly achieved autonomy and sovereignty. Just over a million Canadian soldiers served in the forces and some 42 042 died as a result of the war. Relations with the United States grew closer during this time. In Korea (1950–1953), there were 1557 Canadian casualties and 1312 deaths. In total, Canada has contributed and sacrificed in 12 major violent conflicts (see Table 12.2).

The focus of Canadian defence policy has changed dramatically over the years. At the end of World War II, Canada punched far above its weight in international affairs. When the Cold War began, in about 1949, Canada entered perhaps its most dangerous period internationally. Fear of Russian aggression pushed the number of "peacetime" Canadian troops to more than 120 000. Fourteen thousand Canadian troops were kept in Europe, and Canada spent roughly 7 percent of its GDP on defence. For some time it ranked fourth among NATO partners on defence spending per capita, and for a while it even allowed foreign nuclear weapons on Canadian territory.

Table 12.2 Canada's Overseas Combat Missions

Sudan (Nile Expedition)	1884
South Africa (Boer War)	1899–1902
World War I	1914–1918
Siberia (Expeditionary Force)	1918–1919
World War II	1939–1945
Korean War	1950–1953
Gulf War I (Iraq)	1990–1991
Yugoslavia	1999
Afghanistan	2002–2013
Libya	2013
Iraq, Syria	Ongoing effort to destroy ISIS

However, the Cold War, which had defined world politics after 1949, ended suddenly when the Berlin Wall fell in 1989. The two superpowers no longer threatened to collide in warfare. Canada did not withdraw from NATO, but it removed all of its bases from Europe and government budgets earmarked for NATO were reduced. The number of men and women in the armed services and the amount spent on defence have continually fallen since then, and Canada's strategic importance has declined accordingly.

Canada's geographical location between Russia and the United States is not as important as it used to be. For example, while NORAD remains operative, the North Warning System was downsized and NORAD's tasks were shifted to emerging issues such as counternarcotics monitoring and surveillance. Since 2001, initiatives against terrorism dramatically increased.

When the September 11, 2001, terrorist attacks took place in Pennsylvania, Washington, and New York, they shook Canadians' faith that North America is immune to overseas attack. After that, Canada has participated in the hunt for terrorists and joined other NATO countries in supplying troops and advisers in Afghanistan. Anti-terrorism activities have increased the budgets in the Department of National Defence (DND), the Canadian Security Intelligence Service (CSIS), and other agencies and focused attention on a new series of responsibilities and priorities.

Canada and the United States also announced an expanded role for NORAD as an alternative to Canada's participation in the U.S. ballistic missile defence (BMD) program. NORAD added radar and satellite monitoring responsibilities to the U.S. command. As Canada holds the deputy commander position in NORAD, any enhancement of the role of this institution draws Canada further into BMD policy development.[11] Domestic controversy over this topic ranges from the view that if Canada joins the BMD program, it will have "lost its soul," to the belief that it will eventually be "irresponsible" not to join Americans in this new defence system. Unlike the Liberals, New Democratic Party, and Bloc Québécois, Stephen Harper implied on occasion that he favoured some positive moves in this direction. It is not yet clear how the new Liberal government will proceed, but caution is likely.

Since the end of World War II, Canada has sought security in collective agreements; it has not been neutral. The mission of the DND is to defend Canada and its interests while contributing to international peace and security. The basic pattern of the international environment today is one of decreased East–West differences and a large increase in local, religious, and regional conflicts, particularly in the Middle East and South Asia. Explanations for hostile and terrorist acts throughout the globe are beyond the scope of this book, but they include economic, cultural, religious, and ideological frustrations and aggression.[12]

Given issues such as international terrorism and internal war in Afghanistan, Iraq, Libya, and Syria, it could be said that Canada's expenditure on defence is insignificant. However, the size of Canada's population and the few "direct" conflicts in which Canada is engaged render its military commitment reasonable even though NATO partners, including the United States, disagree. The government faces many critics on this topic both inside and outside the country.

In 2015, after many years of reductions, the government approved a rise in defence spending. Approximately $20 billion was included in the budget for the defence envelope, with a promised 3 percent annual increase over the next decade. This budget sustains 68 000 regular force members, 27 000 reservists, and 24 000 civilians. The new figure placed Canada very high among NATO contributors in terms of its total budget, but still near the bottom of NATO contributors in terms of military spending as a percentage of GDP. Canada spent considerably less than 2 percent of GDP, the recommended minimum target for NATO countries.

The Canadian Armed Forces

Since 1968, the Canadian Armed Forces have had a unified command structure of air force, army, and navy. They perform a number of roles, including surveillance of Canadian territory and coastlines to protect sovereignty, the defence of North America in cooperation with U.S. forces, the fulfillment of NATO commitments, and international peacekeeping roles. It also provides assistance to other federal government departments, civil authorities, and civilian organizations.

Where are military expenditures allocated? About three-quarters of the funds go toward the combined maritime, land, and air forces. They cover costs related to the defence of Canada's territory, including the special partnership with the United States in NORAD and membership in NATO. Although Canada is involved in strategic nuclear planning, it has no nuclear weapons of its own. The country's role in NATO initially involved stationing Canadian land and air forces in Europe as part of the forward defence strategy. In 1994, Canada closed these bases and brought all troops home from Europe.

In keeping with the fundamental nature of Canadian security policy, the government's most visible activity has until recently been in the field of international peacekeeping and peace enforcement. Since 1947, Canada has sent troops to almost all UN and NATO peacekeeping missions. More than 100 000 members of the Canadian Armed Forces have served in hostile areas all over the world.

In recent years, especially during the war in Afghanistan, it became evident that Canada's commitment to peacekeeping had severely declined. Until 1989, Canada had served in every UN peacekeeping mission—it was the world's leading peacekeeper. Then it became more selective and refused to help in many missions. As the nature of peacekeeping changed, with many missions shifting from supervising ceasefires and separating combatants to actually *enforcing* the peace, Canada lost its will to participate. Its significance as a peacekeeping country declined accordingly. Today, there are only 85 Canadian police officers, 9 military experts, and 18 military officers serving among the 123 945 personnel at 16 UN missions.

Canada in Afghanistan

The invasion and occupation of Afghanistan (unlike the second attack on Iraq) was sanctioned by the United Nations. The defeat of the forces of Mullah Omar and Osama bin Laden in 2001 was swift and decisive. The United States continued to fight the terrorists along the Pakistan border, but quickly pulled out its troops to prepare for war with Iraq. In the early stages, insufficient new troops replaced them. Then, a NATO-led coalition of 37 countries, including Canada, took over much of the fighting in south and southeast Afghanistan. As of 2015, UN activities in Afghanistan have concluded, but the job remains largely unfinished and the threat of resurgent global terrorism from Taliban bases is growing. The West has largely failed to prevent the Taliban from providing a home for al Qaeda and other terrorist groups.

The Canadian military played a vital role in Afghanistan. It was not a peacekeeping mission. Canadian efforts were governed by the Afghanistan Compact, NATO, and agreement with the Afghan and foreign governments to stabilize the country in the face of continued violent threats from the Taliban and al Qaeda. Canada's contribution consisted of about 2500 personnel, divided into three missions. *Operation Athena* was Canada's commitment to the NATO-led International Security Assistance Force (ISAF) sanctioned by the UN in December 2001. Canadian General R.J. Hillier, chief of the defence staff, was the first commander of ISAF. The operation consisted of five regional military commands and, after 2005, a Provincial Reconstruction Team (PRT) with both military and civilians carrying out various types of reconstruction in the Kandahar region. Canadian military personnel also contributed through *Operation Archer* to the U.S.-led Operation Enduring Freedom, working in Kabul, Bagram Air Base, and Afghan military and training operations. Finally, *Operation Argus* involved the Strategic Advisory Team working directly for the Afghan government.

Canadians fought as part of the 37 000 soldiers under ISAF and among the separate 11 000 American-led Operation Enduring Freedom troops. In the final analysis, 152 Canadian soldiers were killed before Canada withdrew from Afghanistan in 2014—the first Canadians to die in military action since Korea.

Recent Military Engagements

After the American tragedies of September 11, 2001, the Canadian government committed to supporting efforts to end "global terrorism." However, there was considerable controversy and anguish about whether Canada should join the United States and the so-called "coalition of the willing" to depose Iraq's leader Saddam Hussein (who allegedly, but incorrectly, possessed weapons of mass destruction). The Liberal government declined the offer.

When the Conservatives came to power, Stephen Harper began to reverse Liberal policies, saying that he didn't want to make commitments and then run away at the first sign of trouble. In July 2011, Harper was quoted as saying that international politics is a perpetual struggle between Good and Evil, and that Canada's foreign policy should be on the side of the "Good." After that, Harper took a bellicose position on international relations in Libya, Iraq, Syria, and Iran and promoted strong and aggressive relations with Russia over Ukraine.

In March 2013, under the auspices of the UN and the "Responsibility to Protect" concept, Canada took a leading part in airstrikes against Colonel Gaddafi's forces in Libya and helped to force him out of office. The action helped to defeat

Canada sends aircraft to bomb ISIS in Syria in 2015.

Gary Clement/National Post

Gaddafi but left Libya in a state of disarray and economic ruin, with multiple militia groups continuing to rule various sectors of the country even today.

After the war in Iraq, Canada concurred with the U.S. decision to vacate the country, but soon found itself supporting U.S. actions against the Islamic Front (ISIS), which had captured much of central Iraq. When ISIS began controlling large portions of Syria as well, Canada expanded its mission to include bombing inside Syria. The mission was not approved by the UN or NATO. Syria was not at war with Canada, yet Canada continued to drop ordnance inside the country on the basis that it was helping to defend Iraq. Canada had six CF-18s bombing the so-called Islamic State in Iraq and Syria, plus two surveillance planes and one refuelling plane as well as about 600 personnel supporting this mission from Kuwait.

The missions inside Iraq and Syria were extended until March 30, 2016 by the Conservative government. This was the first time Canada had provided armed intervention without a request from a state under attack, the UN Security Council, or NATO. The Conservative government defended the policy by arguing that the Iraqi government had asked for Canada's help because ISIS has created safe havens inside Syria from which to attack Iraq. In defence of their position, Prime Minister Harper and Defence Minister Jason Kenney relied on UN Article 51, which provides for the right to collective defence. However, this action still constituted a violation of Syria's sovereignty and the two main Canadian opposition parties both opposed the action, saying that Canada did not have legal grounds for the aggression. Immediately upon being elected in 2015, prime minister–elect Justin Trudeau suspended the policy.

The use of pre-emptive strikes against possible future aggressors is always questionable in international law, and yet the United States has used "the war on terrorism" to defend its right to go to war in Yemen, Nigeria, Somalia, Libya, Pakistan, and Afghanistan—and now in Syria. Canada joined only in Syria. A case for international action based on humanitarian need might have been a better political strategy, as Syria has turned into one of the worst humanitarian crises in decades.

Canada also took a firm stand on nuclear weapons in Iran. Harper strongly supported Israel and took a very aggressive hard line against Tehran. He closed Canada's embassy in Tehran, kicked Iranian diplomats out of Canada, imposed economic sanctions, and was skeptical of the U.S.-led P5 nuclear agreement with the Iranian government, aligning Canada close to Israel.

Canada's policies toward Russia have hardened since the Russian occupation of Crimea in March 2014. Since that illegal occupation, Canada has imposed economic sanctions on Russian personnel and products and taken an aggressive stance in favour of the continued independence of Ukraine. It has loaned Ukraine more than half a billion dollars, gave the government non-lethal military equipment, and sent troops to train Ukrainian forces in their fight against Russian-backed rebels.

Canada has also been aggressive in supporting increased NATO activity in Eastern Europe and in confronting Russian actions in the area. It has supported an enhanced NATO, joined manoeuvres in Eastern Europe, and agreed to repositioning munitions and supplies in Poland and three Baltic states. It supported Poland with a new armed forces command centre and is helping to form a kind of tripwire for the West by offering to join a rapid reaction force against possible Russian aggression.

Policy and Strategy Canada has few military resources with which to police the world. Its politicians should be mindful that sermons are not strategies. Hurling moral slogans and metaphors is not an excuse for well-thought-out policy. Politicians have to respond to shifts in public opinion, but they fail if they slavishly follow public opinion rather than leading it. High moral standards without practical backup collapse when reality sets in.

The issue is for Canadians to decide—have Canada's recent aggressive actions in the Middle East and South Asia increased or decreased international stability? Did the Harper government choose the right Canadian foreign policies from the marketplace of ideas to protect Canada's national interests? What path should the Trudeau government follow?

Discussion Questions

1. What are the components of "foreign policy"?
2. Should trade rules be considered domestic policy?
3. Should Canadian foreign policy be a projection of the country's national interests?
4. Was the government's policy in Afghanistan in Canada's national interest? What about its policy in Iraq? In Libya? In Syria? In Ukraine?
5. Does Canada's military policy reduce the chance of terrorism in Canada and the world? Does it reduce civil liberties at home?

Chapter 13
Ethics in Canadian Government and Politics
Honesty and Corruption

Learning Objectives

After reading this chapter, you should be able to

1 Distinguish between patronage and conflict of interest.

2 Identify the rules in place to prevent misconduct by members of Parliament, senators, and Cabinet ministers.

3 Critique the ethical rules introduced by the Chrétien, Martin, and Harper governments.

The *Criminal Code, the Parliament of Canada Act*, Standing Orders of the House of Commons, and Rules of the Senate have always applied to any minister or ordinary member or senator involved in fraud, influence peddling, or breach of trust. The *Criminal Code* makes certain practices such as bribery illegal; the *Parliament of Canada Act* forbids members of Parliament (MPs) from having government contracts; and the Standing Orders of the House of Commons and Rules of the Senate ban certain behaviour and require activities, such as disclosing a financial interest when speaking or voting in Parliament. However, much of the so-called unethical conduct that has taken place in Parliament has not been illegal or even against precise parliamentary rules. Most of it has been about broad so-called unethical behaviour not covered by legal rules, and much of it has been sensationalized by political gossip and manoeuvring.

Almost every government in recent years has been plagued by scandals. Pierre Trudeau's outgoing patronage appointments in 1984 created a furor that largely cost John Turner a renewed mandate as prime minister. Scandalous behaviour eventually brought down the Mulroney government and damaged Kim Campbell's chances of forming a durable government. Scandals in Jean Chrétien's government undermined the government of his successor, Paul Martin. The political chicanery uncovered by the auditor general (in a scandal known as AdScam) and exposed in the Gomery Inquiry in 2005 helped to bring down the Martin government and led the Conservative government of Stephen Harper to make major changes to ethics rules in Canada. In spite of his changes, however, Harper's government in turn was plagued by issues of questionable conduct in the Senate that was linked to the prime minister.

When politicians engage in conflicts of interest, patronage, pork-barrelling, or other forms of unethical conduct, they create situations in which they may be beholden to private interests. Cabinet ministers, MPs, and senators are in positions of public trust. Canadians expect a high degree of integrity from them but, on the whole, rules governing their ethics have emerged haphazardly and as the result of scandals.

CONFLICT OF INTEREST

Public attitudes have changed considerably over the years. Questions of ethics in Parliament that were considered acceptable a few decades ago now engender public condemnation. Until relatively recently, MPs routinely ran their private businesses even after becoming ministers. Conflict-of-interest queries were not raised unless ministerial decisions clearly and publicly produced private advantage for someone. In those years, politics was still a part-time, rather poorly paid occupation, and ministers and prime ministers frequently engaged openly in activities that were potentially conflicting. They sat on boards of directors, carried on legal practices, and possessed private trust funds. It is even said that C.D. Howe, a respected Liberal minister, routinely checked his stock listings before attending Cabinet to make important economic decisions for the country.

A **conflict of interest** is regarded as a situation in which a prime minister, Cabinet minister, MP, senator, or public servant has a private, personal economic interest sufficient to influence how he or she exercises public duties and responsibilities. Such conflict may or may not be illegal. Even if it is legal, it may create public doubts or suspicions that the decisions or actions taken are not impartial.

MPs and senators have always been subject to specific rules from the *Criminal Code*, the *Parliament of Canada Act*, and the rules of the House and Senate that prohibit certain forms of behaviour. Reformers have tried to make the rules more specific, but until recently this was to little avail. There was a general abhorrence of being regulated. In 1973, Allan MacEachen tabled a Green Paper titled *Members of Parliament and Conflict of Interest*, which called for legislation that would apply to *all* politicians. The Green Paper defined conflict of interest as a "situation in which a Member of Parliament has a personal or private pecuniary interest sufficient to influence, or appear to influence, the exercise of his public duties and responsibilities."[1] Opposition to such legislation was great in both Houses. On the first attempt, the Senate blocked the proposal; on the second attempt in 1979, Parliament was dissolved before the bill reached second reading.

During this period, Cabinet members did receive letters from the prime minister admonishing them to be ethical. Blind trusts became mandatory for all ministers, and for two years after leaving Cabinet, ex-ministers could not serve on boards of directors of corporations with which they had dealt as ministers; they also could not act on behalf of such people or corporations, or act as lobbyists. For one year, ministers could not accept jobs from companies with which they had dealt, nor could they act as consultants for them.

In 1984, the government set up a Task Force on Conflict of Interest (culminating in the Starr–Sharp Report), which concluded that there was a need to improve

conflict of interest: A situation in which a prime minister, Cabinet minister, member of Parliament, or public servant has a private, personal economic interest sufficient to influence how he or she exercises public duties and responsibilities.

regulations, and proposed appointing two ethics officers: a counsellor and a commissioner. The commissioner would function as a police officer seeking out and investigating potential conflicts of interest, while the ethics counsellor would inform ministers what the law and ethics code demanded of them so that they could obey it. No action was taken on the report.

In 1985, Prime Minister Brian Mulroney introduced new conflict-of-interest guidelines for Cabinet ministers and civil servants. It stopped short of full, mandatory disclosure in order to strike a balance between protecting the public interest and the private affairs of ministers. Regulations made it clear that ministers could not hire their own immediate relatives (or other ministers' relatives) for government jobs.

Ambiguity and lack of enforcement provisions in Mulroney's code led to a major conflict-of-interest case. In 1987, Cabinet minister Sinclair Stevens was faced with a series of conflict allegations. Stevens had placed his assets in a blind trust—that is, he did not sell them but had to put them in the hands of someone else. However, the trust was less than blind. The Parker Commission, which investigated the case, concluded that Stevens had violated the conflict code 14 times because his wife and special assistant participated with him in the management of the assets.[2] However, 17 years later, in 2004, a federal court judge exonerated Stevens by overturning the report of the public inquiry.

Meanwhile, Prime Minister Mulroney introduced conflict-of-interest legislation to force enough disclosure to keep government leaders honest, yet not infringe unduly on their private lives. However, Bill C-114 died on the Order Paper in 1988 when the general election was called. Various other attempts to legislate on conflict of interest also failed. In the last days of the next Mulroney Conservative government in 1993, another more stringent bill (Bill C-43) was introduced but it, too, died on the Order Paper when the 34th Parliament was dissolved. Legislative success was not achieved until 2006 with the Conservative government of Stephen Harper, as we see below.

POLITICAL PATRONAGE

patronage: In the broad sense, concerns the awarding of contracts, employment, and other material benefits to individuals or groups on the basis of partisan support rather than merit.

Political **patronage** in the broad sense refers to awarding contracts, employment, and other material benefits to individuals or groups on the basis of partisan support rather than merit. Patronage is usually distributed carefully in order to avoid charges under the *Criminal Code*. It is generally claimed to be part of the normal democratic practice of rewarding followers, constituents, regional representatives, and political friends for their support. However, patronage can include illegal practices such as vote-buying, "treating" (paying for votes with liquor), and other forms of bribery that are against the law. **Pork-barrelling**, on the other hand, extends favours to whole regions or communities as an inducement for support. Like patronage, pork-barrelling usually breaks no laws but often raises questions about ethical conduct.

pork-barrelling: An abuse of power whereby politicians extend political favours to whole regions or communities as an inducement for support.

Several aspects of patronage raise problems. It plays to human weaknesses, encouraging unethical behaviour by individuals, institutions, and groups in society. It also has an inflationary aspect: one reward creates a demand for more, and the demand may exceed supply. Clearly, many prime ministers have been unable to resolve the problem of dispensing patronage without compromising their public position. In fact, public cynicism and media investigations make all major forms of government expenditure and preferment suspect.

Some commentators regard patronage and pork-barrelling as essential to politics, providing the "oil" that makes the system run smoothly and the "glue" that keeps parties together and the political system stable. For others, patronage and pork-barrelling are corrupt, immoral activities that impede honest, efficient government services. All would agree, however, that patronage has been an enduring feature of the Canadian political system. It persists in the shadowy world where interest group behaviour, conflict of interest, and pork-barrelling meet, and where influence and favours may result in corruption.

Government contracts are perhaps the most noticeable form of patronage. Most large contracts come under strict rules of tendering, but a few contracts—especially smaller, personal ones—are let without tender, and sometimes there are preferred suppliers with political connections. The auditor general, who reports to Parliament on government expenditures, has significantly reduced patronage and inefficiencies in the field of contracts. However, as the Gomery Inquiry showed, questionable practices continue, though for the most part in a more nuanced fashion.

Patronage extends well beyond the scope of public relations for the government. Even inside the public service, the government has considerable patronage to hand out in the form of senior appointments. In all, there are more than 3000 political appointments in the federal government to be made by the prime minister and Cabinet.

The history of patronage crosses party lines. In 1979, Prime Minister Joe Clark incurred the wrath of his party's rank-and-file after he delayed too long and lost his chance to dispense rewards before his minority government was defeated. John Turner lost the 1984 election when he declared that he had "no option" but to honour the plethora of appointments demanded by the departing prime minister, Pierre Trudeau. Brian Mulroney made a major issue out of patronage in his 1984 election campaign, but then proceeded to fill patronage positions and award government business to party and personal friends. The new Chrétien, Martin, and Harper governments promised to decrease patronage appointments, but the country waited in vain for it to happen.

RULES FOR MINISTERS, PARLIAMENTARY SECRETARIES, AND SENIOR OFFICIALS

When he came to office in 1993, Jean Chrétien took a novel approach to conflict of interest. He said that rather than pass laws or even regulations concerning ethics in his government, he wanted to set up an "integrity regime," in which he would be responsible for his ministers' actions. He hired former minister Mitchell Sharp as ethics adviser on integrity in government for $1 a year, stating that integrity in government is not just about rules and regulations, but also a matter of personal standards and conduct. He asked Mitchell Sharp to interview prospective Cabinet ministers in order to identify anything in their records that might embarrass the new government. Sharp interviewed all candidates for Cabinet, asking them whether they and their spouses could live with conflict-of-interest guidelines, and whether they had any skeletons in their closet, tax arrears, or personal problems. This procedure blocked some individuals from Cabinet and caused a few others to request a change of portfolio to avoid potential conflicts. Then, in June 1994, Chrétien unveiled yet another "ethics package," which included a conflict-of-interest code for senior officials and rules for lobbyists.

Jean Chrétien's 1994 code covered all members of Cabinet, parliamentary secretaries, members of the ministers' staffs, and more than 1200 senior officials in the federal public service. Section 3(1) of the code declared that "public office holders shall act with honesty and uphold the highest ethical standards so that public confidence and trust in the integrity, objectivity and impartiality of government are conserved and enhanced." It listed the principles and compliance measures that were intended to prevent "real, potential or apparent conflicts of interest." All public employees were required to report to an ethics counsellor about their assets, liabilities, and outside activities. The counsellor then would advise the public official appointees what to do to be in accordance with the code.

Appointees' assets were listed and monitored. Exempt assets, such as homes, vacation properties, bank accounts, fixed income investments, and mutual funds, were not controlled. "Declarable" assets had to be made public, but the officeholder could continue to handle them. These included ownership of family or local businesses, farms under commercial operation, and rental properties. "Controllable" assets were those such as publicly traded securities, including shares in a stock market, that could be affected directly or indirectly by government action. Officeholders were required to divest themselves of all of these types of controlled instruments.

Officeholders could (1) sell the assets; (2) put them in a "blind trust" (i.e., they would not be allowed to obtain information on the composition of their assets, as they would be managed at arm's length); or (3) in certain cases, create a "blind management" agreement (e.g., if one owned a private company that might do business with the government). In the latter case, the officeholder was prevented from making any decision on the management of his or her assets.

Only one position, that of ethics counsellor, was formally created, not two, as envisioned in 1984. On June 16, 1994, Howard Wilson was appointed as Prime Minister Chrétien's ethics counsellor and reported directly to him. It was Wilson's duty to uphold the code of conduct for public officeholders and enforce a law—the *Lobbyists Registration Act*. Although the code was *unlegislated*, the ethics counsellor's most important responsibility was to probe the conduct of Cabinet ministers whenever requested to do so by the prime minister.

Prime Minister Chrétien also declared that ministers should not communicate with government tribunals except under very specific circumstances. The ethics counsellor summarized this rule as "Ministers shall not intervene, or appear to intervene, on behalf of any person or entity, with federal quasi-judicial tribunals on any matter before them that requires a decision in their quasi-judicial capacity, unless otherwise authorized by law."[3] The rule did not restrict ordinary MPs in their dealings with administrative tribunals, but it did hold ministers to a high standard of accountability. At issue was finding the right balance between ensuring that ministers could not use their positions to unduly influence tribunals, yet giving them enough freedom to help their constituents and pursue their policy objectives.

General Conflict-of-Interest Rules for MPs and Senators

- Under the *Criminal Code*, it is illegal for any Cabinet minister, MP, or senator to accept or solicit bribes or to accept a benefit for helping someone in a transaction with government (influence peddling).
- The *Parliament of Canada Act* declares that senators and MPs cannot be a party to any contract paid for with federal funds. Nor can they sell their services.

- Standing Orders of the House of Commons prevent MPs from voting on any question in which they have a direct financial interest.
- Senate rules declare that senators cannot vote on any question or sit on a committee dealing with a matter in which they have a financial interest not generally held by members of the public.

MEMBERS OF PARLIAMENT AND SENATE

There still was no specific legislation or even a code of conduct for regular MPs regarding conflict of interest. Several bills on the topic had been introduced, but none was passed. A Joint Committee of the two Houses in the 36th Parliament concluded that there should be a code for both senators and MPs, but a bill was never produced, as senators and MPs behind the scenes said that they would not approve the legislation.

The *Criminal Code* and House and Senate Rules continued to apply, but alas, without an ethics code. The rules that did apply were not codified or coherent, and were often contradictory. Loopholes existed in many fields. Free foreign travel was unregulated, although MPs (but not senators) had to declare trips. Fees for speaking and consulting did not have to be declared, and relations with lobbyists were uncontrolled. In other words, there was no systematic transparency. Under the Standing Orders, MPs had to declare any private interests in any matter before the House, but there was no annual registry as in the UK or Australia to publicize this material (see Close-Up 13.1).

COMPLICATIONS AND PROBLEMS WITH ETHICS REGULATION

The Chrétien reforms moved conflict of interest codes significantly forward, but there remained problem areas in the rules concerning ministers:

1. *Ad hoc nature of rules:* The rules were unique to each prime minister so that the next prime minister could change them at will. The rules were not regularized in the form of regulations or laws approved by Parliament.

2. *Lack of independent investigative powers:* The ethics counsellor, Wilson, was responsible for investigating conflict-of-interest allegations against anyone the prime minister asked him to investigate. He then reported his findings directly to the prime minister. There was nothing to compel Wilson to investigate conflict-of-interest allegations raised in the media or by the House of Commons. He merely advised

those who asked him what the law was, so that they could obey it. There was no way he could legitimately investigate the prime minister.

3. *Lack of accountability and openness:* The Liberals promised that the "ethics counselor . . . would report directly to Parliament." However, Wilson was not accountable to Parliament—he reported, personally and privately, to the prime minister.

Just how effective the new institutions were in regulating levels of honesty in public life is difficult to assess, as the officials carried out their activities in secret. Mitchell Sharp's interviews produced some notable successes. Two potential ministers withdrew their names for Cabinet appointments in 1994 when they were told of the conditions in the prime minister's code. However, both MPs joined the Cabinet at a later date. No potential ministers were prevented from joining the Cabinet in later Chrétien administrations.

On taking office, Paul Martin updated the conflict-of-interest and post-employment Code for Public Officeholders and named a new ethics commissioner. The code covered ministers, ministers of state, parliamentary secretaries, members of ministerial staff, and all order-in-council appointees. Martin did not delete the old code but added new rules to reduce the possibility of improper use of government aircraft; require that all gifts worth more than $1000 be put into a government inventory; require approval of the commissioner before accepting any gifts, hospitality, or benefits; and require public disclosure of liabilities. The prime minister was also required to make a public statement to the commissioner about his own compliance with the rules.

In 2004, Parliament formally created the position of ethics commissioner and also a Senate ethics officer. As well, just before the 2004 election was called, new conflict-of-interest rules were added to the Standing Orders. Essentially, the 25th Report of the Standing Committee on Procedure and House Affairs was added to the Orders and made applicable to MPs at the beginning of the next Parliament. These rules required MPs to disclose all major assets, liabilities, and outside income of themselves, their spouses, and their dependent children within 60 days of the resumption of Parliament.[4]

THE GOMERY COMMISSION

At the end of the Chrétien era, new scandals erupted. After the separatists' near-success in the 1995 Québec referendum, the federal Liberal government had acted to strengthen support for Canada in Québec. It spread money throughout the province to demonstrate Ottawa's largesse and help hold the country together. In what became known in the press as the AdScam scandal, questionable decisions and sloppy administration led the auditor general to conclude that the program had been administered outside normal Treasury Board and Public Works guidelines. She found that more than $100 000 had been misappropriated and given to a handful of Liberal advertising firms. The Crown corporations Via Rail, Canada Post, Old Port of Montréal, and Business Development Bank (BDB) were all implicated.

Political fallout, a Royal Canadian Mounted Police (RCMP) investigation, Commons committee hearings, and a judicial enquiry followed to determine if there had been any wrongdoing or criminal activity. Among the casualties were former public works minister Alfonso Gagliano; head of the BDB, Michel Vennat; head of Canada Post, André Ouellet; and head of Via Rail, Jean Pelletier.

The **Gomery Commission**, formally the Commission of Inquiry into the Sponsorship Program and Advertising Activities, headed by retired Justice John Gomery, was set up in 2005 to follow up on the auditor general's report on allegations of corruption related to the Québec sponsorship program. The final report of February 1, 2006, basically cleared Prime Minister Paul Martin of wrongdoing, but named several businessmen as being involved in scandals and implicated Jean Chrétien and his senior staff in the affair. The report also made suggestions about the need to reform central government institutions with regard to conflict of interest.

Two years later, in mid-2008, a federal court judge ruled that Justice John Gomery had been biased when he held Jean Chrétien and his senior staff accountable for the Liberal advertising scandal in Québec. However, the ruling was too late to prevent serious political fallout for Chrétien's successor, Paul Martin, who had been minister of finance during AdScam. Although Martin declared that he knew nothing about the scandal until it became public in 2001, allegations of corruption helped to turn the public against Martin and the Liberal Party for years.

Gomery Commission: A commission headed by retired Justice John Gomery, created to follow up on the auditor general's report on allegations of corruption related to the Québec sponsorship program (a.k.a. AdScam).

THE FEDERAL ACCOUNTABILITY ACT, DECEMBER 2006

During the federal election of 2006, Stephen Harper exploited the ethical difficulties in the Chrétien and Martin ethics regimes, unveiling a 52-point ethics package. When the Conservatives won a minority government, their first initiative was to change the rules for ethics in government. A comprehensive *Federal Accountability Act* (Bill C-2) was passed and granted royal assent in December 2006. This large omnibus bill outlined new rules for donations to political parties (see Chapters 10 and 11); included a five-year lobbying ban on former ministers, their aides, and senior public servants; amended the *Lobbyists Registration Act* (now with a commissioner of lobbying); and enhanced the power of the auditor general. It also created a new **parliamentary budget officer**, whose mandate is to provide objective economic and financial analysis to Parliament. A new **public sector integrity commissioner** was appointed to promote and protect whistleblowers.

parliamentary budget officer: An officer of Parliament whose mandate is to provide objective economic and financial analysis to Parliament.

public sector integrity commissioner: An officer of Parliament appointed to promote and protect whistleblowers.

The *Federal Accountability Act* also created for the first time a conflict-of-interest law, which came into effect on July 9, 2007. This law created the first legislative regime to govern the ethical conduct of public officeholders and created a new position, **commissioner of conflict of interest and ethics**, to administer the new *Conflict of Interest Act*. The position replaced the ethics commissioner. The legislation covered what had already been included in the Code for Public Office Holders mentioned above. However, the new rules also prevented public officeholders and MPs from holding personal trusts and private interests from which they could derive personal benefit. From now on, public officeholders are required to either sell *all* of their assets in an arm's-length transaction or place them in a *fully blind trust* (see Chapters 7 and 8).

The new commissioner has responsibility to monitor the new Act as well as the Conflict of Interest Code for Members of the House of Commons (which incorporated earlier rules from the Standing Orders). The commissioner has the power to initiate formal investigations, hold politicians responsible for their actions, and even fine violators. The prime minister is prevented from overruling the commissioner on all aspects of government ethics.

commissioner of conflict of interest and ethics: An officer of Parliament who administers the Conflict of Interest Code for Members of the House of Commons and the *Conflict of Interest Act* and advises Canadian MPs and public officeholders on how to prevent conflicts of interest between their public duties and private interests.

It remains to be seen whether these new rules and officials will end conflict-of-interest scandals in Canadian politics or whether new loopholes will be found. The long history of conflict of interest, and especially recent allegations, should make us cautious. The changes may prove valuable, but they did not, for example, prevent Prime Minister Harper from appointing a Mulroney-appointed judge as head of the commission of inquiry into Brian Mulroney's conflict-of-interest case. Moreover, since the Senate objected to its members being included in some of the conflict-of-interest provisions, their conduct continues to be guided by a Senate ethics officer.

SENATE ISSUES AND CORRUPTION

The Senate is responsible for governing itself and how it functions. Senators design and enforce their own rules. In 2014, three Conservative Senators—Patrick Brazeau, Mike Duffy, and Pamela Wallin—and one Liberal, Mac Harb, were accused of various expense illegalities. Harb paid back what he owed, and then resigned. The other two were temporarily suspended pending investigations and then sat as Independents. A trial for Mike Duffy on 31 charges of fraud and breach of trust

Senate oversight mechanisms failed to define and enforce what constituted a second residence that would be eligible for deductions.

is currently in progress. After 61 days of testimony, Judge Charles Vaillancourt is expected to rule on the Duffy case in 2016.

In 2015, during the trial of Senator Duffy, Michael Ferguson, the auditor general, completed a report on Senate expenses from April 2011 to March 2013. In it, he raised serious questions about the Senate's ability to oversee and control its own budgets. He claimed that there was a pervasive lack of evidence for many of the senators' reimbursement claims. Of the 116 senators investigated, Ferguson called for 30 senators (including top Conservatives and Liberals) to repay their misspending, and asked that nine current and former senators be investigated by the RCMP, mostly for claims based on improper residency. The misspending cases have gone to arbitration and the police cases have gone silent.

Most of the auditor's charges are being disputed, and the auditor's claim that the Senate should review the mandate and structure of its Committee on Internal Economy is under savage attack for interfering in the independence of the upper House. The Senate is likely to agree to more transparency in expenditures, but not to more control over its activities. As the new Liberal government was setting up in early 2016, the saga continued.

RESPONSIVENESS AND GOVERNABILITY

Democracy requires a high degree of trust between the government and the governed. Canada is not a direct democracy in which citizens get to vote on all issues. Parliament is a representative institution. For it to function well, it must be responsive to public demands, but the public also needs to be aware of the subtleties and difficulties of governing. The problem is that in an era of 24-hour glib television and irresponsible social media, the time required to reflect on issues is compressed to such a degree that significant issues are often not resolved with a proper foundation of thought or foresight.

Governing and electoral responsiveness are not the same. Sometimes it seems that only the "responsive" part of democracy is given credence in an era in which no one is allowed to say that it is not the politicians but the journalists and the electorate who "have no pants on." To a large extent, politics is interests masquerading as principles, but many sectors of the public and the media are guilty of selfishly looking after their own interests—of using loopholes and questionable tax deductions for personal gain, or engaging in yellow populist journalism. At times, Canadian politics seems to be all about silly signposts and no significant destinations. The country seems to lack a "put it all together" community of concerned citizens *and* leaders who do their best to enhance public trust in our democracy.

Discussion Questions

1. What are some of the major forms of misconduct in government?
2. What are some of the ethical rules that apply to members of Parliament and Cabinet ministers today? Are they satisfactory?
3. How does the Senate differ from the House in terms of ethical rules?
4. What is your view of recent Senate scandals?

Endnotes

Chapter 1

1. Michael B. Poliakoff, *Combat Sports in the Ancient World: Competition, Violence, and Culture* (New Haven, CT: Yale University Press, 1987).
2. Max Weber, *The Theory of Social and Economic Organizations*, A.M. Henderson and Talcott Parsons, eds. and trans. (New York: Oxford University Press, 1947), p. 154.
3. David Easton, *A Framework for Political Analysis* (Englewood Cliffs, NJ: Prentice Hall, 1965), pp. 50–56.
4. Definitions of politics vary widely. See in particular Harold Lasswell, *Politics: Who Gets What, When and How* (New York: McGraw-Hill, 1965).
5. For a comparison of types of governments, see Robert J. Jackson and Doreen Jackson, *Introduction to Political Science: Comparative and World Politics*, 5th ed. (Don Mills, ON: Prentice Hall, 2008).
6. See Robert J. Jackson, "Australian and Canadian Comparative Research," in Malcolm Alexander and Brian Galligan, eds., *Comparative Political Studies* (Sydney, Australia: Pitman, 1992).
7. See Jean Bethke Elshtain, *Democracy on Trial* (New York: Basic Books, 1994); and Robert D. Putnam, *Making Democracy Work: Civic Traditions in Modern Italy* (Princeton, NJ: Princeton University Press, 1993).

Chapter 2

1. The 2011 Census of Canada is the basis for demographic statistics in this chapter unless otherwise indicated. A national census is conducted every five years by Statistics Canada. As of 2011, the census is still mandatory, but respondents may choose to complete a short-form version. This change made the new data unreliable for purposes of comparison with earlier years. The 2015 Liberal government has pledged to return the long-form census.
2. Canada's population growth rate of 1.1 percent was highest among the G7 countries. Statistics Canada, "Canada's Population Estimates: Age and Sex, 2014," *The Daily*, September 26, 2014.
3. Mowat Centre for Policy Innovation, "Canadians' Attitudes toward the Federation," 2010. www.mowatcentre.ca
4. See, for example, Robert J. Jackson and Doreen Jackson, *Introduction to Political Science: Comparative and World Politics*, 5th ed. (Don Mills, ON: Prentice Hall, 2008), Chapter 6.
5. J.T. McHugh, "Toward a Grand Theory of the Study of Canadian Political Thought," *American Review of Canadian Studies*, vol. 43, no. 1 (2013), pp. 123–143.
6. John Locke, *Two Treatises on Government*, Peter Lasleet, ed. (New York: New American Library, 1965).
7. Ibid., "Second Treatise," Chapter 4.
8. Robert J. Jackson, *Global Politics in the 21st Century* (New York: Cambridge University Press, 2013). See Chapter 8, "Politics beyond the State: Identity—Ethnicity, Nationalism, and Religion," pp. 211–243.
9. Statistics Canada, *The Daily*, September 17, 2014. www.statcan.gc.ca/pub/91-520-x/2014001/hi-fg-eng.htm
10. To determine the LICO, Statistics Canada calculates the proportion of its gross income that the average family spends on necessities (shelter, food, and clothing) and then adds 20 percentage points to that figure. It then calculates the level of income at which individual families would spend that percentage on the same necessities.
11. The low income measure (which sets the poverty line at one-half the median income) placed 12.2 percent of Canadians in poverty in 2011. The figures from the first National Household Survey in 2011 cannot be compared to other years except with great caution, because the methodology changed after the federal government cancelled the mandatory long-form census in favour of a voluntary household survey.
12. Ronald Lambert et al., "The Sources of Political Knowledge," *Canadian Journal of Political Science*, vol. 21, no. 2 (June 1988), p. 373.
13. www.oecd.org/edu/Canada-EAG2014-Country-Note.pdf
14. According to the Conference Board of Canada, an Ottawa-based not-for-profit think tank, the United States has the largest gap between rich and poor people in the 17 developed countries examined. Canada's Gini index (a measure of the distribution of money among individuals) was 0.32, compared to 0.38 for the United States. On the Gini scale, 0 represents equality of income and 1 represents maximum inequality. Denmark and Sweden had the lowest Gini scores at 0.23. The gap between the real average income of the top quintile of Canadian earners and the lowest quintile was $117 500 in 2009. "Canadian Income Gap Widened Despite Commodity Boom," *Wall Street Journal*, July 13, 2011.
15. *Children of the Recession: UNICEF Report Card 12*. Released October 28, 2014. www.unicef.ca/en/children-of-the-recession-unicef-report-card-12
16. Riccardo Petrella, "Nationalist and Regionalist Movements in Western Europe," in C. Foster, ed., *Nations without a State* (New York: Praeger, 1980).
17. Ailsa Henderson identified nine distinct regional variant cultures in Canada, each with unique political attitudes and behaviours that cannot be explained by provincial boundaries. See Ailsa Henderson, "Regional Political Cultures in Canada," *Canadian Journal of Political Science*, vol. 37, no. 3 (September 2004), pp. 595–616.
18. Mowat Centre for Policy Innovation, "Canadians' Attitudes toward the Federation," 2010, p. 6. www.mowatcentre.ca
19. Quoted in David Elton and Roger Gibbins, "Western Alienation and Political Culture," in R. Schultz et al., eds., *The Canadian Political Process*, 3rd ed. (Toronto: Holt, Rinehart and Winston, 1979), p. 8.

20. The first important study in this field was David J. Elkins, "The Sense of Place," in David Elkins and Richard Simeon, eds., *Small Worlds: Provinces and Parties in Canadian Political Life* (Toronto: Metheun, 1980), p. 23.

21. According to the Inter-Parliamentary Union, Canada ranked only 47th in its comparative study of women in 188 parliamentary assemblies, October 1, 2013. www.ipu.org/wmn-e/classif.htm

22. Data from the Inter-Parliamentary Union. www.ipu.org/wmn-e/clasif.htm

23. Quoted in *Maclean's*, March 23, 2015, p. 28.

24. www.catalyst.org/knowledge/statistical-overview-women-workplace

25. Leon Dion, *Quebec: The Unfinished Revolution* (Montréal: McGill-Queen's University Press, 1976), p. 180.

26. Immigrants are people who have been granted the right to live in Canada permanently by immigration authorities. Some are recent arrivals; others have lived in Canada for several years.

27. See Neil Bissoondath, *Selling Illusions: The Cult of Multiculturalism in Canada* (Toronto: Penguin Books, 1995). Also see Ted McDonald et al., eds., *Canadian Immigration: Economic Evidence for a Dynamic Policy Environment* (Montréal: McGill-Queen's University Press, 2010).

28. Statistics Canada, "Economic Insights: Twenty Years in the Careers of Immigrant and Native-born Workers." Catalogue no. 15-424-K—No. 032.

29. See Jeffrey Restz and Raymond Breton, *The Illusion of Difference: Realities of Ethnicity in Canada and the United States* (Toronto: C.D. Howe Institute, 1994). Also see Timothy Garten Ash, Edward Mortimer, and Kerem Oktem, "Freedom in Diversity: Ten Lessons for Public Policy from Britain, Canada, France, Germany and the United States," 2015. Available as a pdf file at www.sant.ox.ac.uk/esc/freedomanddiversity.html

30. "Keeping Faith on Immigration," *The Globe and Mail*, July 7, 2015, p. A12.

31. See Jean Leonard Elliot and Augie Fleras, *Unequal Relations: An Introduction to Race and Ethnic Dynamics in Canada* (Scarborough, ON: Prentice Hall, 1992).

32. *The British North America Act*, Section 91(24).

33. *The Globe and Mail*, August 25, 2014, p. 1.

34. See www.conservative.ca/EN/269z/4165

35. The settlement provided at least $1.9 billion for "common experience" payments to former students who lived at one of the more than 130 residential schools.

36. *The Globe and Mail*, June 6, 2015, p. A10.

Chapter 3

1. See Garth Stevenson, *Unfulfilled Union: Canadian Federalism and National Unity*, revised ed. (Toronto: Macmillan, 1982).

2. Letters patent are instruments by which prerogative powers are delegated by the Queen on the advice of her Canadian Cabinet to her representative, the governor general. See also Chapter 6.

3. See Peter J.T. O'Hearn, *Peace, Order and Good Government* (Toronto: Macmillan, 1964).

4. For opposing arguments about Québec's use of the not-withstanding clause in the Charter to defend its language bill, see Reg Whitaker, "The Overriding Right," and P.K. Kuruvilla, "Why Quebec Was Wrong," in *Policy Options*, vol. 10, no. 4 (May 1989), pp. 3–6 and 7–8.

5. *Ontario Film and Video Appreciation Society v. Ontario Board of Censors*, (1984), 45 O.R. 80.

6. *Shaping Canada's Future Together* (Ottawa: Supply and Services, 1991).

7. For more detail, see Robert J. Jackson and Doreen Jackson, *Politics in Canada*, 7th ed. (Scarborough, ON: Prentice Hall, 2009), Chapter 5.

8. See Robert J. Jackson and Doreen Jackson, *Stand Up for Canada* (Scarborough, ON: Prentice Hall, 1992).

9. Ibid.

Chapter 4

1. William H. Riker, "Federalism," in Fred I. Greenstein and Nelson W. Polsby, eds., *Handbook of Political Science Vol. 5: Government Institutions and Processes* (Reading, MA: Addison and Wesley, 1975), p. 101.

2. The Québec City conference on Confederation was decisive. It convened in October 1864 and lasted 17 days. Delegates representing Upper and Lower Canada and Newfoundland worked out the terms of political and economic association. The final agreement was signed in Charlottetown.

3. P.B. Waite, *The Life and Times of Confederation, 1864–1867* (Toronto: University of Toronto Press, 1962).

4. The most recent case occurred in 1961, when the lieutenant-governor of Saskatchewan, Frank Bastedo, without first consulting with the federal government, reserved provincial legislation that he believed was of doubtful validity. The Department of Justice quickly decided that the bill was within provincial jurisdiction and assent was given. R. MacGregor Dawson, *Government of Canada*, 5th ed., revised by Norman Ward (Toronto: University of Toronto Press, 1970), pp. 213–217.

5. Garth Stevenson, "Federalism and Intergovernmental Relations," in M.S. Whittington and G. Williams, eds., *Canadian Politics in the 1980s*, 2nd ed. (Toronto: Methuen, 1984), p. 378.

6. See Alain C. Cairns, "The Judicial Committee and Its Critics," *Canadian Journal of Political Science*, vol. 4, no. 3 (September 1971), pp. 301–345.

7. See Donald Swainson, ed., *Oliver Mowat's Ontario* (Toronto: Macmillan, 1972), especially Bruce W. Hodgins, "Disagreement at the Commencement: Divergent Ontarian Views of Federalism, 1867–1871," pp. 52–68.

8. See D.V. Smiley, ed., *The Rowell-Sirois Report: An Abridgement of Book I of the Royal Commission Report on Dominion-Provincial Relations*, The Carleton Library No. 5 (Toronto: McClelland & Stewart, 1963).

9. D.V. Smiley, "An Outsider's Observations of Federal-Provincial Relations among Consenting Adults," in R. Simeon, ed., *Confrontation and Collaboration: Intergovernmental Relations in Canada Today* (Toronto: The Institute of Public Administration of Canada, 1979), pp. 109–111.

10. J.C. Strick, *Canadian Public Finance*, 2nd ed. (Toronto: Holt, Rinehart and Winston, 1978), pp. 100–101.

11. David B. Perry, "The Federal-Provincial Fiscal Arrangement Introduced in 1977," *Canadian Tax Journal*, vol. XXV, no. 4 (July/August 1977), pp. 429–440.

12. Jennifer Smith, "Informal Constitutional Development: Change by Other Means," in Herman Bakvis and Grace Skogstad, eds., *Canadian Federalism: Performance, Effectiveness, and Legitimacy* (Don Mills, ON: Oxford University Press, 2002), pp. 50.
13. *Maclean's*, February 15, 1999.
14. Ibid.
15. *Ottawa Citizen*, February 28, 1995.
16. *The New York Times*, September 17, 2004.
17. http://pm.ca/grfx/does/QuebecENG.pdf

Chapter 5

1. On the types of nationalism, see Anthony D. Smith, *Nationalism in the Twentieth Century* (Oxford, UK: Martin Robertson, 1979). On the "new" nationalism, see Michael Ignatieff, *Blood and Belonging; Journeys into the New Nationalism* (Toronto: Viking, 1993).
2. Attributed to Albert Einstein in Martin Levin, "Nationalism: Disease or Plague," *The Globe and Mail*, June 15, 1995.
3. There are many interpretations of nationalism. See A.D. Smith, *Theories of Nationalism* (Oxford, UK: Oxford University Press, 1994); and Liah Greenfeld, *Five Roads to Modernity* (Cambridge, MA: Harvard University Press, 1992).
4. Governments cannot use the notwithstanding clause to exempt the application of these Charter guarantees. In early 1993, Parliament and the New Brunswick legislature passed a constitutional amendment guaranteeing equal status for New Brunswick's French- and English-language communities. See Chapters 3 and 4.
5. See Denis Smith, *Bleeding Hearts...Bleeding Country: Canada and the Québec Crisis* (Edmonton: Hurtig, 1971).
6. These include the Parti Patriote in the early nineteenth century under Louis-Joseph Papineau; the Parti Nationale led by Honoré Mercier, elected in 1886; and the Union Nationale led by Maurice Duplessis, elected in 1936.
7. Parti Québécois, *La Souveraineté* (Montréal: Service de communications du Parti Québécois, 1990), a party pamphlet.
8. *The Globe and Mail*, October 31, 1995.
9. In this fourth step, money was seriously misspent, later resulting in damaging scandals for the federal Liberal Party.
10. Quoted in *Maclean's*, December 11, 2006, p. 23.
11. CTV news report, "Québec Nationhood: A Loaded History," November 22, 2006.
12. See Robert J. Jackson, *Global Politics in the 21st Century* (New York: Cambridge University Press, 2013), especially Chapter 13.
13. Stéphane Dion, "Tell the Truth, Bernard," *The Globe and Mail*, March 15, 2001.
14. Quoted in *The Globe and Mail*, April 3, 2014, p. A3.
15. As recorded in documents sent to Québec premier Robert Bourassa, August 20, 1990.
16. *Calder v. Attorney General of B.C.*, [1973] S.C.R. 313.
17. The government has stated that it will cede no more than 5 percent of the total British Columbia land mass to settle all claims, and no privately owned land will be included. Most Crown land will also be protected. This figure was chosen because Aboriginal peoples make up about 5 percent of British Columbia's population.

18. Specific Claims Tribunal Canada. Details available at www.sct-trp.ca.
19. *Tsilhqot'in Nation v. British Columbia*, 2014 S.C.R. 256.
20. The Keewatin case involved the interpretation of Treaty 3, a 141-year-old agreement covering western Ontario and eastern Manitoba.
21. Michael Whittington and Glen Williams, eds., *Canadian Politics in the 21st Century* (Scarborough, ON: Nelson, 2000), p. 109. See also John Hylton, *Aboriginal Self-Government in Canada: Current Trends and Issues* (Saskatoon, SK: Purich Publishing Ltd., 1999).
22. Ibid., p. 115. See also Gurston Dacks, "Implementing First Nations Self-Government in Yukon: Lessons for Canada," *Canadian Journal of Political Science*, vol. 37, no. 3 (September 2004), pp. 671–694.

Chapter 6

1. See R.A.W. Rhodes, John Wanna, and Patrick Weller, *Comparing Westminster* (Oxford, UK: Oxford University Press, 2011); and Robert J. Jackson "Westminster Futures: Australia, Canada, New Zealand and the United Kingdom in Comparative Perspective," in Glyn Davis and R.A.W. Rhodes, eds., *The Craft of Governing* (Crows Nest, Australia: Allen & Unwin, 2014), pp. 227–247.
2. See Chapter 7, "Parliament."
3. The 1968 *Manual of Official Procedure of the Government of Canada* states, "The Governor General does not retain any discretion in the manner of summoning or proroguing Parliament, but acts directly on the advice of the prime minister." The author wishes to make it clear that he was the senior researcher for Henry Davis in developing this manual of government procedure.
4. This is based on area of residence as an adult.
5. For example, all provincial premiers were made privy councillors in 1967 to celebrate Canada's centennial.
6. Malcolm Punnett, *The Prime Minister in Canadian Government and Politics* (Toronto: Macmillan, 1977), p. 56.
7. For a comparison of the Chrétien and Martin governing styles, see "The Chrétien Legacy," *Policy Options* (November 2002), pp. 6–43; and "Paul Martin's Legacy," *Policy Options* (October 2002), pp. 6–18.
8. Denis Smith, "President and Parliament: The Transformation of Parliamentary Government in Canada," in Tom Hockin, ed., *Apex of Power* (Scarborough, ON: Prentice Hall, 1971), pp. 308–325.
9. For discussions of leadership, see Margaret Macmillan, *The Uses and Abuses of History: Dangerous Games* (London: Modern Library, 2009); and James David Barber, *Presidential Character*, 4th ed. (Englewood Cliffs, NJ: Prentice Hall, 1992). For the author's own views, see Robert Jackson, *Global Politics in the 21st Century* (Cambridge, UK: Cambridge University Press, 2013), Chapters 4 and 16.

Chapter 7

1. In theory, the governor general retains some discretionary power in the matter of dissolution (see Chapter 3).
2. The prayer was altered in 1994 to make it non-denominational by eliminating reference to Jesus Christ. Also deleted were archaic references to the British Empire and the royal family.

3. See Robert J. Jackson and Doreen Jackson, *Politics in Canada*, 7th ed. (Don Mills, ON: Prentice Hall, 2009), Chapter 9.

4. See Robert J. Jackson and Paul Conlin, "The Imperative of Party Discipline in the Canadian Political System," in Mark Charlton and Paul Basher, eds., *Contemporary Political Issues*, 2nd ed. (Scarborough, ON: Nelson, 1994).

5. Sydney Sharpe and Don Braid, *Storming Babylon: Preston Manning and the Rise of the Reform Party* (Toronto: Key Porter, 1992).

6. *The Globe and Mail*, March 19, 1994.

7. See House of Commons, *Precis of Procedure*, 4th ed. (Ottawa: Clerk of the House of Commons, 1991) and rule updates from that period forward.

8. This happened, for example, in 1979 under Joe Clark, who had only two Progressive Conservative MPs elected in Québec. Clark addressed the situation by naming three ministers from Québec to the Senate to bolster francophone representation in the federal Cabinet.

9. See J.R. Robertson, "Rejection of Bills by the Canadian Senate: Theory and Practice," unpublished Library of Parliament research paper, 1990.

Chapter 8

1. H.H. Gerth and C. Wright Mills, eds. and trans., *From Max Weber: Essays in Sociology* (New York: Oxford University Press, 1946), pp. 232–235.

2. For elaboration of the theories and models of policy-making, see Robert J. Jackson and Doreen Jackson, *Politics in Canada*, 7th ed. (Scarborough, ON: Prentice Hall, 2009), Chapter 13.

3. Historically, in departments where the minister's official designation was secretary of state (as in secretary of state for foreign affairs), the senior public servant was known as the undersecretary of state rather than the deputy minister.

4. "Government task forces" should not be confused with the "Special Committees" of the House of Commons.

5. See Sharon Sutherland, "Responsible Government and Ministerial Responsibility," *Canadian Journal of Political Science*, vol. 24, no. 1 (March 1991), p. 128.

6. Kenneth Kernaghan, "Power, Parliament and Public Servants in Canada: Ministerial Responsibility Re-examined," in H.D. Clarke et al., eds., *Parliament, Policy and Representation* (Toronto: Methuen, 1980), p. 128.

7. Unless otherwise acknowledged, figures relating to public service employees are drawn from the appropriate Annual Reports of the Public Service Commission and Statistics Canada or the Treasury Board Secretariat.

8. In May 1995, the auditor general issued a report criticizing public servants' ethics. He concluded that too many employees had a limited understanding of public sector ethics. As an example, he claimed that 4 percent would accept a free stay at a ski chalet if offered by a grant recipient, and 11 percent would hire a brother-in-law for an untendered contract. Auditor General, Interim Report (Ottawa: 1995).

9. Donald J. Savoie, "Who Is Auditing the Auditor-General?" *The Globe and Mail*, August 25, 1995.

10. D.C. Rowat, "The Right of Public Access to Official Documents," in O.P. Dwivedi, ed., *The Administrative State in Canada: Essays in Honour of J.E. Hodgetts* (Toronto: University of Toronto Press, 1982), pp. 185–186.

11. Paul Thomas, "Courts Can't Be Saviours," *Policy Options*, vol. 5, no. 3 (May/June 1984).

Chapter 9

1. Governor-in-Council is the formal or legal name under which Cabinet makes decisions. For a full explanation, see Chapter 6 on the executive.

2. Peter H. Russell, "The Jurisdiction of the Supreme Court of Canada: Present Policies and a Programme for Reform," *Osgoode Hall Law Journal* (1969), p. 29.

3. Peter H. Russell, *The Judiciary in Canada: The Third Branch of Government* (Whitby, ON: McGraw-Hill Ryerson, 1987), p. 335.

4. For a summary, see Andrew D. Heard, "The Charter in the Supreme Court of Canada: The Importance of Which Judges Hear an Appeal," *Canadian Journal of Political Science*, vol. 24, no. 2 (June 1991), pp. 289–307.

5. Supreme Court Judge Gérard La Forest, quoted in *The Globe and Mail*, April 14, 1987.

6. Peter H. Russell, *The Judiciary in Canada: The Third Branch of Government* (Whitby, ON: McGraw-Hill Ryerson, 1987), p. 360. For a detailed study of early Charter cases and the Constitution, see Rainner Knopff and F.L. Morton, *Charter Politics* (Scarborough, ON: Nelson, 1992).

7. Mr. Justice Antonio Lamer, quoted in *The Globe and Mail*, April 14, 1987.

8. R.I. Cheffins and P.A. Johnson, *The Revised Canadian Constitution: Politics as Law* (Whitby, ON: McGraw-Hill Ryerson, 1986), p. 152.

9. *The Globe and Mail*, May 26, 1995.

10. Frederick Vaughan, "Judicial Politics in Canada: Patterns and Trends," *Choices: Courts and Legislatures*, vol. 5, no. 1 (June 1999), p. 15.

11. *Maclean's*, March 29, 1999.

12. Mr. Justice Antonio Lamer, quoted in *The Globe and Mail*, April 14, 1987.

13. Frederick Vaughan, "Judicial Politics in Canada: Patterns and Trends," *Choices: Courts and Legislatures*, vol. 5, no. 1 (June 1999), p. 20.

14. R.I. Cheffins and P.A. Johnson, *The Revised Canadian Constitution: Politics as Law* (Whitby, ON: McGraw-Hill Ryerson, 1986), pp. 148–149.

15. Peter H. Russell, "The Political Purposes of the Canadian Charter of Rights and Freedoms," *The Canadian Bar Review*, vol. 61 (1983), p. 51.

16. Quoted in *The Globe and Mail*, April 14, 1987.

17. Statistics are from Statistics Canada, found at www.statcan.ca.

18. The only exception is Newfoundland and Labrador, where the province maintains jurisdiction by a special arrangement with the federal government.

19. Robert J. Jackson, *Global Politics in the 21st Century* (New York: Cambridge University Press, 2013), p. 330.

Chapter 10

1. The collapse of the party system and the reasons for it are discussed in R. Kenneth Carty, William Cross, and Lisa Young, *Rebuilding Canadian Party Politics* (Vancouver: UBC Press, 2000), Chapter 1. For information on the rise of

third parties, see Eric Belanger, "The Rise of Third Parties in the 1993 Canadian Federal Election: Pinard Revisited," *Canadian Journal of Political Science*, vol. 37, no. 3 (September 2004), pp. 561–580.

2. Hugh Thorburn, "Interpretations of the Canadian Party System," in H.G. Thorburn, ed., *Party Politics*, 6th ed. (Scarborough, ON: Prentice Hall, 1991).

3. R. Kenneth Carty, William Cross, and Lisa Young, *Rebuilding Canadian Party Politics* (Vancouver: UBC Press, 2000), p. 158.

4. Ibid., p. 159.

5. Lisa Young and William Cross, "Women's Involvement in Canadian Political Parties," in Manon Tremblay and Linda Trimble, eds., *Women and Electoral Politics in Canada* (Toronto: Oxford University Press, 2003), p. 99.

6. See C. Maille, *Primed for Power: Women in Canadian Politics* (Ottawa: Canadian Advisory Council on the Status of Women, 1990).

7. R.M. Dawson, *The Government of Canada*, 5th ed. (Toronto: University of Toronto Press, 1970), p. 504.

8. See Lisa Young and Joanna Everitt, *Advocacy Groups* (Vancouver: UBC Press, 2004), p. 5. Hillwatch, a leading Canadian Government Relations firm, provides a useful list of hundreds of interest groups and associations as well as think tanks that try to influence public policy in Canada.

9. Robert H. Salisbury, "Interest Groups," in Fred I. Greenstein and Nelson W. Polsby, eds., *Handbook of Political Science*, vol. 4 (Reading, MA: Addison-Wesley, 1975), p. 175.

10. The pluralist perspective is discussed along with other theories and critiques of democracy in Robert J. Jackson and Doreen Jackson, *Comparative Government*, 7th ed. (Scarborough, ON: Prentice Hall, 2009), Chapters 5 and 16. The number of lobbyists is monitored by the Lobbyists Registration Branch.

11. See John Meisel, "The Decline of Party in Canada," in H.G. Thorburn, ed., *Party Politics in Canada*, 5th ed. (Scarborough, ON: Prentice Hall, 1984).

12. This list was set out first by A. Paul Pross, "Pressure Groups: Adaptive Instruments of Political Communication," in A. Paul Pross, ed., *Pressure Group Behaviour in Canadian Politics* (Whitby, ON: McGraw-Hill Ryerson, 1975).

13. *The Globe and Mail*, April 1, 1995.

14. *Ottawa Citizen*, December 2, 1994.

15. The Office of the Commissioner of Lobbying of Canada site is available at www.ocl-cal.gc.ca/epic/site/lobbyist-lobbyiste1.nsf/Intro

16. CBC News, October 14, 2015.

Chapter 11

1. The *Fair Elections Act* placed a limitation on Elections Canada by requiring it to get Treasury Board approval to pay outside experts. It also reduced the term of the CEO from a lifetime appointment to 10 years.

2. Richard Johnston, André Blais, Henry E. Brady, and Jean Crête, *Letting the People Decide* (Montréal: McGill-Queen's University Press, 1992), p. 160.

3. Corporations and unions could no longer donate to political parties, and their donations to individuals were severely restricted.

4. The new Act separated the responsibility for *managing* the election from *regulating electoral practices*. Prosecution of breaches under the *Canada Elections Act* (such as illegal robocalls) are now handled by the Director of Public Prosecutions, under direction of the government.

5. CBC News, "Fair Elections Act: Ex-Watchdog Sheila Fraser Slams Bill as Attack on Democracy," April 3, 2014.

6. Fees paid for a political convention are considered to be contributions to the political party.

7. The limit is calculated at $2.07 for each of the first 15 000 electors, $1.04 for each of the next 10 000 electors, and $0.52 for each elector over 25 000. The formula is subject to certain adjustments and an inflation adjustment factor.

8. In 1989, the Royal Commission on Electoral Reform and Party Financing produced a report (issued in four volumes in late 1991) containing many recommendations for reforms. Many have been enacted by legislation, but others remain as part of the ongoing debate on electoral reform.

9. Maurice Duverger, *Political Parties* (London: Methuen, 1954), vol. II, Chapter 1.

10. Ibid., p. 217.

11. For further information about kinds of electoral systems and the effects they have on electoral outcomes, see Robert J. Jackson and Doreen Jackson, *An Introduction to Political Science: Comparative and World Politics*, 5th ed. (Scarborough, ON: Pearson, 2008), Chapter 17.

12. A. Lijphart, *Democracies: Patterns of Majoritarian and Consensus Government* (New Haven, CT: Yale University Press, 1984).

13. See, for example, Daniel Pellerin and Patrick Thomson, "Proportional Representation Is Likely to Create More Problems Than It Would Solve; The Single Transferable Vote Offers a Better Choice," *Policy Options* (October 2004), p. 104.

14. Law Commission of Canada, *Voting Counts: Electoral Reform for Canada* (Ottawa: Minister of Public Works, 2004), p. 104.

15. British Columbia, Alberta, and Manitoba all tried alternative vote systems for short times in provincial elections, but abandoned them.

16. Jerome Black, "Reforming the Context of the Voting Process in Canada: Lessons from Other Democracies," in Herman Bakvis, ed., *Voter Turnout in Canada, Royal Commission on Electoral Reform and Party Financing* (Toronto: Dundern Press, 1991), pp. 61–82.

17. Munroe Eagles, "Voting and Non-voting in Canadian Federal Elections: An Ecological Analysis," in Herman Bakvis, ed., *Voter Turnout in Canada, Royal Commission on Electoral Reform and Party Financing* (Toronto: Dundern Press, 1991), p. 25.

18. MPs Jean-François Larose of the NDP and Jean-François Fortin of the BQ had abandoned their parties to form a new political party, Strength in Democracy. Both MPs lost their seats in 2015.

19. This proposal was intended as part of the Liberals' 32-point plan "to restore democracy." It included a long list of radical proposals, some of which would be very difficult to implement.

20. The BQ won 80 000 fewer votes in this election, but increased its number of seats from 4 to 10.

21. "How Canadians Voted," *The Globe and Mail*, October 21, 2015, p. A6.
22. Ibid.
23. These were findings of Ensight Canada, a firm that conducted 4 waves of research and 12 focus groups nationally during and immediately after the campaign. See James Wall, "Why the Liberals Struck a Chord with Voters," *The Globe and Mail*, October 23, 2015.

Chapter 12

1. Andrew Cooper, *Canadian Foreign Policy: Old Habits and New Directions* (Scarborough, ON: Prentice Hall, 1997), p. 25.
2. Kim Nossal, *The Politics of Canadian Foreign Policy* (Scarborough, ON: Prentice Hall, 1986), p. 317.
3. Robert J. Jackson and A. Dann, "Quebec Foreign Policy?" in Werner Link and Werner J. Feld, eds., *New Nationalism* (New York: Pergamon Press, 1979). For a U.S. view, see Charles Doran, *Why Canadian Unity Matters and Why American Care* (Toronto: University of Toronto, 2001).
4. Lester B. Pearson, *Mike: The Memoirs of Lester Pearson, Vol. I: 1897–1948* (Toronto: University of Toronto Press, 1972), p. 283.
5. John Holmes, quoted in the *Toronto Star*, November 20, 1982.
6. Geoffrey Hale, *So Near, Yet So Far: The Public and Hidden Worlds of Canada–US Relations* (Vancouver: UBC Press, 2012).
7. See Robert J. Jackson and Doreen Jackson, *Politics in Canada: Culture, Institutions, Behaviour, and Public Policy*, 7th ed. (Toronto: Pearson, 2009), Chapter 15.
8. *Report of the Royal Commission on the Economic Union and Development Prospects for Canada*, vol. 1 (Ottawa: Minister of Supply and Services, 1985).
9. Robert J. Jackson et al., *North American Politics: Canada, USA, and Mexico in Comparative Perspective* (Toronto: Prentice Hall, 2004).
10. See David S. McDonough, ed., *Canada's National Security in the Post 9/11 World: Strategy, Interests, and Threats* (Toronto: University of Toronto Press, 2012).
11. Patrick James, *Canada and Conflict* (Don Mills, ON: Oxford University Press, 2013).
12. See Robert Jackson, *Global Politics in the 21st Century* (Cambridge, UK: Cambridge University Press, 2014); on international conflict and terrorism in the Middle East, see Robert J. Jackson and Philip Towle, *Temptations of Power: The United States in Global Politics Since 9/11* (London: Palgrave, 2006).

Chapter 13

1. Privy Council Office, Canada, *Members of Parliament and Conflict of Interest*, MacEachen Green Paper (Ottawa: Information Canada, 1973).
2. Canada, *Commission of Inquiry into the Facts and Allegations of Conflict of Interest Concerning the Honourable Sinclair M. Stevens* (report) (Ottawa: Supply and Services, 1987).
3. The UK Register of Members' Interests requires the detailing of private interests, holdings, investments, gifts received, trips taken, and other sources of income. See Maureen Mancuso, *The Ethical World of British MPs* (Kingston, ON: McGill-Queen's University Press, 1995).
4. For details, see Report 25, Standing Committee on Procedure, April 27, 2003.

Further Reading

Chapter 1

Cohen, Andrew. *The Unfinished Canadian: The People We Are.* Toronto: McClelland & Stewart, 2007.

Conrad, M., and A. Finkel. *Canada: A National History.* Toronto: Pearson Longman, 2007.

Jackson, Robert J., and Doreen Jackson. *Politics in Canada: Culture, Institutions, Behaviour and Public Policy*, 7th ed. Don Mills, ON: Prentice Hall, 2009.

Chapter 2

Bell, T., R. Dagger, W. Christian, and C. Campbell. *Political Ideologies and the Democratic Ideal*, 2nd ed. Toronto: Pearson Education Canada, 2012.

Byers, Michael. *Intent for a Nation: What Is Canada For?* Vancouver: UBC Press, 2007.

Dickason, Olive Patricia (with D.T. McNaab). *A Concise History of Canada's First Nations*, 4th ed. Don Mills, ON: Oxford University Press, 2006.

Ismael, Shereen. *Child Poverty and the Canadian Welfare State: From Entitlement to Charity.* Calgary: University of Alberta Press, 2006.

Ponting, J. Rick. *First Nations in Canada: Perspectives on Opportunity, Empowerment and Self Determination.* Whitby, ON: McGraw-Hill Ryerson, 1997.

Strong-Boag, V., and A.C. Feldman, eds. *Rethinking Canada: The Promise of Women's History*, 4th ed. Toronto: Oxford University Press, 2002.

Wiseman, Nelson. *In Search of Canadian Political Culture.* Vancouver: UBC Press, 2007.

Chapter 3

(See also further reading for Chapter 9.)

Ajenstat, Janet. *The Canadian Founding: John Locke and Parliament.* Montréal and Kingston: McGill-Queen's University Press, 2007.

Bakan, Joel, and David Schneiderman. *Social Justice and the Constitution.* Don Mills, ON: Oxford University Press, 1992.

Behiels, Michael, ed. *The Meech Lake Primer: Conflicting Views of the 1987 Constitutional Accord.* Ottawa: University of Ottawa Press, 1989.

Cairns, Alan C. *Reconfigurations: Canadian Citizenship and Constitutional Change.* Vancouver: UBC Press, 1995.

Cook, Curtis, ed. *Constitutional Predicament.* Montréal and Kingston: McGill-Queen's University Press, 1994.

Dodek, Adam. *The Canadian Constitution.* Toronto: Dundurn, 2013.

Greene, Ian. *The Courts.* Vancouver: UBC Press, 2005.

Heard, Andrew. *Canadian Constitutional Conventions.* Don Mills, ON: Oxford University Press, 1991.

Hogg, Peter. *Constitutional Law of Canada*, 3rd ed. Toronto: Carswell, 1992; Student Edition, 1999.

Jackson, Robert J., and Doreen Jackson. *Stand Up for Canada: Leadership and the Canadian Crisis.* Scarborough, ON: Prentice Hall, 1992.

Kelly, James B. *Governing with the Charter.* Vancouver: UBC Press, 2005.

Knopff, Rainer, and F.L. Morton. *Charter Politics.* Scarborough, ON: Nelson, 1992.

Lazar, Harvey, ed. *The State of the Federation 1997: Non-Constitutional Renewal.* Kingston, ON: Institute of Intergovernmental Relations, 1997.

Moore, Christopher. *Three Weeks in Quebec City: The Meeting That Made Canada.* Toronto: Allen Lane, Penguin, 2015.

Petter, Andrew. *The Politics of the Charter: The Illusive Promise of Constitutional Rights.* Toronto: University of Toronto Press, 2010.

Chapter 4

Bakvis, Herman, and Grace Skogstad, eds. *Canadian Federalism: Performance, Effectiveness and Legitimacy*, 2nd ed. Don Mills, ON: Oxford University Press, 2008.

Bercuson, David J., and Barry Cooper. *Deconfederation: Canada without Québec.* Toronto: Key Porter, 1991.

Burgess, Michael. *Comparative Federalism: Theory and Practice.* London, UK: Routledge, 2006.

Hueglin, Thomas O., and Alan Fenna. *Comparative Federalism: A Systematic Enquiry.* Peterborough, ON: Broadview Press, 2006.

Kelly, James B., and Christopher P. Manfredi, eds. *Contested Constitutionalism.* Vancouver: UBC Press, 2009.

Peach, Ian, ed. *Constructing Tomorrow's Federalism: New Perspectives on Canadian Governance.* Winnipeg: University of Manitoba Press, 2007.

Stevenson, Garth. *Unfulfilled Union, Canadian Federalism and National Unity*, 4th ed. Montréal and Kingston: McGill-Queen's University Press, 2004.

Westmacott, Martin, and Hugh Mellon, eds. *Challenges to Canadian Federalism.* Scarborough, ON: Prentice Hall, 1998.

Chapter 5

De Pasquale, Paul W., ed. *Natives and Settlers Then and Now: Historical Issues and Current Perspectives in Treaties and Land Claims in Canada.* Edmonton: University of Alberta Press, 2006.

Gibbins, Roger, and Loleen Berdahl. *Western Visions, Western Futures: Perspectives on the West in Canada.* Peterborough, ON: Broadview Press, 2003.

Hébert, Chantal, and Jean Lapierre, *The Morning After the 1995 Quebec Referendum and the Day That Almost Was.* Toronto: Alfred A. Knopf Canada, 2014.

Johnston, Richard, et al. *The Challenge of Direct Democracy: The 1992 Canadian Referendum.* Montréal and Kingston: McGill-Queen's University Press, 1996.

Kernerman, Gerald. *Multicultural Nationalism: Civilizing Difference, Constituting Community.* Vancouver: UBC Press, 2005.

Ponting, J. Rick. *The Nisga'a Treaty: Polling Dynamics and Political Communication in Comparative Context*. Peterborough, ON: Broadview Press, 2006.

Wright, Robert. *The Night Canada Stood Still: How the 1995 Quebec Referendum Nearly Cost Us Our Country*. Toronto: HarperCollins, 2014.

Chapter 6

Forsey, Helen. *A People's Senate for Canada: Not a Pipe Dream!* Toronto: Fernwood, 2015.

Granatstein, J.L., and Norman Hillmer. *Prime Ministers: Ranking Canada's Leaders*. Toronto: HarperCollins, 1999.

Jackson, Robert J. "Westminster Futures: Australia, Canada, New Zealand and the United Kingdom in Comparative Perspective." In Glyn Davis and R.A.W. Rhodes, eds. *The Craft of Governing*. Crows Nest, Australia: Allan and Unwin, 2014.

Robertson, G. *Memoirs of a Very Civil Servant*. Toronto: University of Toronto Press, 2001.

Smith, Jennifer, and D. Michael Jackson, eds. *The Evolving Canadian Crown*. Montréal and Kingston: McGill-Queen's University Press, 2012.

Wells, Paul. *The Longer I Am Prime Minister: Stephen Harper and Canada*. Toronto: Random House, 2013.

Chapter 7

Gunther, J., and C. Winn, eds. *House of Commons Reform*. Ottawa: Parliamentary Internship Programme, 1991.

Jackson, Robert J., and Michael M. Atkinson. *The Canadian Legislative System*, 2nd ed. Toronto: Macmillan, 1980.

Joyal, Serge, ed. *Protecting Canadian Democracy: The Senate You Never Knew*. Montréal and Kingston: McGill-Queen's University Press, 2003.

Smith, David E. *The People's House of Commons: Theories of Democracy in Contention*. Toronto: University of Toronto Press, 2007.

Weaver, R. Kent, and Bert A. Rockman, eds. *Do Institutions Matter? Government Capabilities in the United States and Abroad*. Washington, DC: The Brookings Institution, 1993.

Chapter 8

Baxter-Moore, Nicolas. "Policy Implementation and the Role of the State." In Robert J. Jackson, ed. *Contemporary Canadian Politics*. Scarborough, ON: Prentice Hall, 1987.

Dwivedi, O.P., and James Iain Gow. *From Bureaucracy to Public Management: The Administrative Culture of the Government of Canada*. Peterborough, ON: Broadview Press, 1999.

Johnson, David. *Thinking Government: Public Sector Management in Canada*, 2nd ed. Peterborough, ON: Broadview Press, 2006.

Martin, Lawrence. *Harperland: The Politcs of Control*. Toronto: Viking, 2010.

Osbaldeston, Gordon F. *Organizing to Govern*, vols. I and II. Whitby, ON: McGraw-Hill Ryerson, 1992.

Pal, Leslie A. *Beyond Policy Analysis*, 4th ed. Toronto: Nelson, 2010.

Peters, B. Guy, and Donald J. Savoie, eds. *Taking Stock: Assessing Public Sector Reforms*. Montréal and Kingston: McGill-Queen's University Press, 1998.

Chapter 9

Gall, Gerald L. *The Canadian Legal System*, 4th ed. Toronto: Carswell, 1995.

Greenawalt, Kent. *Fighting Words: Individuals, Communities and Liberties of Speech*. Princeton, NJ: Princeton University Press, 1995.

Hogg, Peter. *Constitutional Law of Canada*, 2nd ed. Toronto: Carswell, 1999.

Kelly, James B. *Governing with the Charter: Legislation and Judicial Activism*. Vancouver: UBC Press, 2005.

Knopff, Rainer, and F.L. Morton. *Charter Politics*. Scarborough, ON: Nelson, 1992.

Manfredi, Christopher P. *Judicial Power and the Charter: Canada and the Paradox of Liberal Constitutionalism*. Toronto: McClelland & Stewart, 1993.

McCormick, P. *Supreme at Last*. Toronto: Lorimer, 2000.

Morton, F.L. *Law, Politics and the Judicial Process in Canada*, 3rd ed. Calgary: University of Calgary Press, 2002.

Sharpe, Robert J., Katherine Swinton, and Ken Roach. *The Charter of Rights and Freedoms*, 2nd ed. Toronto: Irwin Law, 2003.

Slayton, Philip. *Mighty Judgment: How the Supreme Court of Canada Runs Your Life*. Toronto: Penguin, 2012.

Chapter 10

Chenier, J.A., and Scott Duncan, eds. *The Federal Lobbyists, 1999*. Ottawa: ARC Publications, 1999.

Cross, William. *Political Parties*. Vancouver: UBC Press, 2004.

Flanagan, Tom. *Harper's Team: Behind the Scenes in the Conservative Rise to Power*. Montréal and Kingston: McGill-Queen's University Press, 2007.

Ignatieff, Michael. *Fire and Ashes: Success and Failure in Politics*. Toronto: Vintage Canada, 2015.

Lavigne, Brad. *Building the Orange Wave: The Story Behind the Historic Rise of Jack Layton and the NDP*. Toronto: Douglas & McIntyre, 2013.

MacIvor, Heather. "The Charter of Rights and Party Politics: The Impact of the Supreme Court Ruling in *Figueroa v. Canada (Attorney General)*." IRPP Choices, vol. 10, no. 4 (May 2004).

Newman, Peter C. *When the Gods Changed: The Death of Liberal Canada*. Toronto: Dragonmaster Productions, 2012.

OECD. *Lobbyists, Governments, and Public Trust*. Paris: OECD Publishing, 2009.

Plamondon, Bob. *Full Circle: Death and Resurrection in Canadian Conservative Politics*. Toronto: Key Porter, 2006.

Shwartz, Mildred A. *Party Movements in the United States and Canada: Strategies of Persistence*. Lanham, MD: Rowman and Littlefield, 2007.

Smith, Miriam, ed. *Group Politics and Social Movements in Canada*. Peterborough, ON: Broadview Press, 2005.

Chapter 11

Blais, André, et al. *Anatomy of a Liberal Victory: Making Sense of the Vote in the 2000 Canadian Election*. Peterborough, ON: Broadview Press, 2002.

Butler, Peter M. *Polling and Public Opinion: A Canadian Perspective*. Toronto: University of Toronto Press, 2007.

Everitt, Joanna, and Brenda O'Neill, eds. *Citizen Politics: Research and Theory in Canadian Political Behaviour*. Don Mills, ON: Oxford University Press, 2002.

Flanagan, Tom. *Winning Power: Canadian Campaining in the 21st Century*. Montreal and Kingston: McGill-Queens University Press, 2014.

Pammett, Jon H., and Christopher Dornan, eds. *The Canadian General Election of 2011*. Toronto: Dundurn, 2012.

Pilon, D. *The Politics of Voting: Reforming Canada's Electoral System*. Toronto: Edmond Montgomery, 2007.

Studlar, Donley T. *Tobacco Control: Comparative Politics in the United States and Canada*. Peterborough, ON: Broadview Press, 2002.

Tremblay, Manon, and Linda Trimble, eds. *Women and Electoral Politics in Canada*. Don Mills, ON: Oxford University Press, 2003.

Chapter 12

Axworthy, Lloyd. *Navigating a New World: Canada's Global Future*. Toronto: Knopf Canada, 2003.

Holloway, Steven. *Canadian Foreign Policy: Defining the National Interest*. Peterborough, ON: Broadview Press, 2006.

Jackson, Robert J. *Global Politics in the 21st Century*. New York: Cambridge University Press, 2013.

Jackson, Robert J., and Philip Towle. *Temptations of Power: The United States in Global Politics After 9/11*. London, UK: Palgrave Macmillan, 2006.

James, Patrick, Nelson Michaud, Marc O'Reilly, and Marc J. O'Reilly, eds. *Handbook of Canadian Foreign Policy*. Oxford, UK: Lexington Books, 2006.

McDonough, David S., ed. *Canada's National Security in the Post-9/11 World: Strategy, Interests and Threats*. Toronto: University of Toronto Press, 2012.

McRae, Donald. "Arctic Sovereignty? What Is at Stake?" *Behind the Headlines*, vol. 64, no. 1 (2007).

Smith, Graeme. *The Dogs Are Eating Them Now: Our War in Afghanistan*. Toronto: Vintage Canada, 2013.

Chapter 13

Greene, Ian, and David Shugarman. *Honest Politics*. Toronto: Lorimer, 1997.

Langford, John W., and Allan Tupper, eds. *Corruption, Character and Conduct: Essays on Canadian Government Ethics*. Don Mills, ON: Oxford University Press, 1994.

Mancuso, Maureen, Michael M. Atkinson, André Blais, Ian Greene, and Neil Nevitte. *A Question of Ethics: Canadians Speak Out*, rev. ed. Don Mills, ON: Oxford University Press, 2006.

Glossary

Aboriginal rights Historic rights (mostly in the form of land claims) of various groups of Aboriginals, based on Aboriginal occupancy and use of North American land before Europeans arrived. 106

Aboriginal title An Aboriginal claim to land on the basis of traditional occupancy even when no treaty has been signed. 108

adjournment (recess) A break period taken by the House of Commons within a session. 141

advisory bodies Federal organizations whose activities are closely related to the formulation of public policies. They include Royal Commissions, government and departmental task forces, and advisory councils. 171

agencies Include a wide variety of types of non-departmental organizations, including Crown corporations, regulatory agencies, administrative tribunals, and advisory bodies. 170

amendment formula The procedure required to change a constitution. 60

anarchy A lack of government within a society. 6

assistant deputy minister (ADM) One of two or more individuals who heads a branch or bureau and reports directly to the deputy minister (DM). 168

Attitudes Orientations toward political objects that are more differentiated and fleeting than basic values, but that may be more immediate determinants of political behaviour. 22

auditor general An official charged with making a public appraisal of the effectiveness of both public spending and accounting practices to Parliament and, in particular, to the Public Accounts Committee. 178

authoritarian political system A system of government that imposes one dominant interest, that of a political elite, on all others. 7

authority The government's power to make binding decisions and issue obligatory commands. 5

backbenchers MPs on the government side who are not ministers or on the opposition side who are not designated party critics. 142

bicameral Refers to a legislature composed of two Houses. 139

bills Legislation presented to the House of Commons that may be passed into law. There are two categories of bills: public and private. 149

block grant A grant of one large sum of money from the federal government to the provinces to be spent in certain policy fields. 84

British model of parliamentary government A model of government with two Houses—an elected lower House, the House of Commons, and an unelected upper House, the Senate—and a monarch. 10

brokerage theory Maintains that the two oldest parties in Canada have few coherent ideological interests, but rather act as brokers of ideas, selecting those that have the widest appeal and the best likelihood of attracting electoral support. 207

budget A document that primarily sets out the revenue and expenditures required to carry out the government's program. 141, 174

budget debate The four-day (not necessarily consecutive) debate that follows the presentation of the budget. 141

bureaucracy Refers to a form of government organization based on the premise that it should be structured to provide as much efficiency as possible and that this is best achieved through a hierarchically structured decision-making process that minimizes arbitrary decision making. 166

by-election An election held in a constituency to fill a legislative seat that has fallen vacant between general elections. 246

Cabinet The body of the most powerful ministers appointed by the prime minister, which acts in the name of the Privy Council. 123

Canada Assistance Plan (CAP) A program by which the federal government helps to finance welfare and other provincial social services. 85

Canadian Bill of Rights Legislation passed in 1960 that listed fundamental freedoms but was never entrenched in the Constitution. 64

Canadian Security Intelligence Service (CSIS) An intelligence gathering institution. Its operations, headed by a director, are governed by the 1984 *Canadian Security Intelligence Service Act*. 197

Charlottetown Accord An August 1992 agreement in principle on what changes needed to be made to the Constitution; rejected in a countrywide referendum. 69

chief electoral officer (CEO) A permanent public employee appointed by the Cabinet under the authority of the *Canada Elections Act* to head Elections Canada. 236

civil law Regulates relations between or among private individuals and corporations. It is concerned mainly with disputes over property and commercial contracts. 183

Clarity Act Legislation in 1999 that set out the rules by which the government and Parliament of Canada would react to any future separatist referendum.

It concludes that the government will not enter into any negotiations over separation with a province unless the House of Commons determines that (1) the referendum question is "clear" and (2) a "clear" expression of will has been obtained by a "clear" majority of the population. 101

class Refers to a rank or order in society determined by such characteristics as education, occupation, and income. 30

clerk of the House An official responsible for ensuring that relevant documents are printed and circulated and for advising the speaker of the House on the parliamentary business of the day. 146

clerk of the Privy Council The head of the Privy Council Office (PCO) and the whole civil service. 131

closure A measure to terminate debate in the House. 155

coalition government A government formed from more than one party. 124

code A body of legislative laws that are brought together in a single body to provide a relatively complete set of rules in one or more fields of law. 53

collective ministerial responsibility A standard for the federal Cabinet; as a group, ministers are supposed to be held accountable to Parliament for their government's actions. 124

collective rights Entitlements or duties owed to certain groups by the state. 53

commissioner of conflict of interest and ethics An officer of Parliament who administers the Conflict of Interest Code for Members of the House of Commons and the *Conflict of Interest Act* and advises Canadian MPs and public officeholders on how to prevent conflicts of interest between their public duties and private interests. 291

Commissioner of Elections Canada An independent officer responsible for ensuring that political entities fulfill their obligations under the *Canada Elections Act*. 236

commissioner of lobbying An independent agent of Parliament with investigative powers and a mandate to enforce compliance with the *Lobbying Act* and the Lobbyists' Code of Conduct. 227

committee of the whole A committee of the House in which all MPs sit in the chamber as one large committee chaired by the deputy speaker or the deputy chair of committees. 148

common law The precise form of customary law that developed in twelfth-century Britain as a body of established rules based on the principle of *stare decisis*. 53

Commonwealth of Nations An association of 53 states united by a common historical tie. Some owe allegiance to Queen Elizabeth II, some have their own monarchy, and some are republics. 269

Communications Security Establishment (CSE) Established in 1949 as part of the National Research Council to intercept the communications of clandestine organizations. 202

compact theory of Confederation The notion of "two founding nations," which provides French Canadians with a collective claim to equality rather than simple minority status within Canada. 43

competitive party system A system that allows parties to compete for, and have access to, legislative power. 205

comprehensive claim A land claim dealing with cases of Aboriginal title not covered by treaty or other legal means. 108

concurrent powers Power shared between the Parliament of Canada and the provincial legislatures. 78

conditional grants Funds given by the federal government to provincial governments on the condition that they are spent in a certain way. 82

confederation A form of political organization that very loosely unites strong provincial or state units under a weak central government. 75

conflict of interest A situation in which a prime minister, Cabinet minister, member of Parliament, or public servant has a private, personal economic interest sufficient to influence how he or she exercises public duties and responsibilities. 285

constituency A geographical area that elects one MP and is the locus of the local organization of political parties; also known as a *riding*. 216, 233

constitution A body of fundamental rules, written and unwritten, under which governments operate. 51

constitutional law A body of fundamental rules in a constitution, written and unwritten, that influence the making of other laws. 52

constitutional monarchy A form of government in which the head of state is a monarch, but a constitution shapes the arrangements of political power. 10

convention A custom or practice that, while not necessarily a legal necessity, is nevertheless based on accepted reasons and practices. 52

Corrections Canada Government officials responsible for inmates in federal prisons and for parolees. 198

criminal law Pits individuals charged with criminal offences against the state. Unlike civil law, criminal law comes under federal authority in Canada. 183

Crown Refers to the composite symbol of the institutions of the state. The Crown assumes a variety of duties and responsibilities; for example, it may be involved in court proceedings. 115

Crown corporation A semi-autonomous agency of government organized in a corporate form to perform a task or group of related tasks in the national interest. 170

customary law Results from the evolution of norms and customs, which affect the way individuals and groups are expected to act toward one another. 53

debt The accumulation of deficits over the years. 12

declaratory power Allows the federal government to assume jurisdiction over any "work" considered to be for the benefit of Canada as a whole (e.g., uranium exploration). 78

deficit The amount by which government spending exceeds revenues in one year. 12

democratic political system A system of government that reconciles competing interests through competitive elections. 7

Department of Finance One of four central coordinating agencies of the executive, it analyzes policies and the impact of government activity on the economy. 132

Department of Public Safety An organization set up by the federal government in 2003 to monitor national security, crisis management, emergency preparedness, border functions, corrections, policing, and crime prevention. 200

deputy minister (DM) The administrative and managerial head of each department or ministry—its senior public servant. 168

direct taxes Taxes that are collected directly by the government, such as individual income tax, corporate income tax, and succession duties. 81

disallowance The power to disallow provincial legislation, even though the subject matter of the legislation was assigned to the provinces by the BNA Act. 76

dissolution The end of a particular Parliament, which occurs at the request of a prime minister who seeks a new mandate, or whose government has been defeated in the House of Commons. 141, 233

distinct society A term that the Charlottetown Accord called to be added to the Constitution to describe Québec: "Québec constitutes within Canada a distinct society, which includes a French-speaking majority, a unique culture and a civil law tradition." 69

doctrine of parliamentary supremacy A basic premise of British parliamentary democracy. In Canada, it means that, subject to the Constitution, all 11 legislatures have the authority, in theory, to repeal or modify any principle set out in common law. 54

Elections Canada A government agency that administers elections and is responsible solely to the House of Commons. 233

electoral system Refers to the means by which votes cast for candidates are translated into legislative seats. 233

entrenchment Means to embody provisions in a constitution so that they are protected and can be changed only by a formal amendment procedure. 63

equalization payments Unconditional transfer payments to the provinces from the federal government, calculated according to the ability of each province to raise revenue. 83

Established Programs Financing (EPF) A federal block grant program that is essentially conditional in nature. 84

estimates The government's spending proposals for the next fiscal year. 141

ethnic origin Refers to the ethnic or cultural group(s) to which an individual's ancestors belonged; it pertains to the ancestral roots or origins of the population and not to place of birth, citizenship, or nationality. 29

ethnicity Primarily a subjective term used to describe groups of people who share customs, language, dialect, and/or cultural heritage, and sometimes distinct physical or racial characteristics. 4, 29

executive A broad term that refers to the institutions, personnel, and behaviour of governmental power. In modern times, executives are the organizational centre of political systems. 114

expenditure process Brings together the estimated spending requirements of all government departments and agencies for the next fiscal year. 174

Federal Court of Canada Established by Parliament in 1971 to settle claims by or against the federal government on matters relating to maritime law, copyright, patent and trademark law, and federal taxation statutes, and to undertake a supervisory role related to the decisions of tribunals and inferior bodies established by federal law. 185

federal system A system in which legal powers are divided between a central government and regional governments in such a way that each level of government has some kind of activities on which it makes final decisions. 74

federation A form of political organization in which the activities of government are divided between regional governments and a central government in such a way that each level of government has activities on which it makes final decisions. 11, 75

"flexible" constitution A constitution that can be amended easily and adapted to changing circumstances. 57

foreign policy State or government behaviour that has external ramifications. 264

franchise The right to vote. 232

G7 A multilateral organization of the world's seven largest industrialized democracies. It deals with issues concerning the global economy and issues of the day. 267

General Agreement on Tariffs and Trade (GATT) A 1947 agreement that established a trading order based on reciprocity, non-discrimination, and multilateralism among most major industrialized countries. 267

gerrymandering When a party seeks to take advantage of its position in government to redraw electoral boundaries in such a way as to enable it to win more seats in the future. 235

global system The sets of relationships among states and other significant actors in the world. 264

globalization The integration of states through trade, communications, and contact. 268

Gomery Commission A commission headed by retired Justice John Gomery, created to follow up on the auditor general's report on allegations of corruption related to the Québec sponsorship program (a.k.a. AdScam). 291

government The organization of people for the resolution of dispute and conflict. 6

government bill A bill introduced by the Cabinet as government policy. 150

government department An administrative unit of government that is headed by a Cabinet minister and largely responsible for the administration of a range of programs serving the public. 168

governor general The representative of the monarch in Canada, appointed by Her Majesty on the recommendation of the Canadian prime minister and Cabinet. 116

Governor-in-Council The formal executive authority of the governor general applied on the decision of the Cabinet. 127

House leader An MP designated by the leader of each party in the House of Commons to manage party conduct in the House. 146

identity group People who share a characteristic or characteristics that define them and set them apart from others. 29

ideology An explicit doctrinal structure that provides a particular diagnosis of the ills of society plus an accompanying "action program" for implementing prescribed solutions for them. 24

indirect taxes Taxes that are not collected by the government, but by other persons or institutions and passed along to the government (e.g., sales tax). 81

individual ministerial responsibility Refers to the personal responsibility of each minister. As heads of departments, ministers receive confidential advice from public servants, make important decisions, and then are held accountable for those decisions in Parliament and by the populace. 125

individual rights Refers to individual claims against the state. 52

institutions Mechanisms of social order and cooperation; social structures that are organized to achieve goals for society. 2

interest group An organization that engages in activity related to governmental decisions. 223

international relations The broad network of relations among states, including the activities of citizens and non-state institutions. 264

joint standing committee A committee composed of members of both the House of Commons and the Senate. 149

Judicial Committee of the Privy Council (JCPC) The superior court of the United Kingdom, which until 1949, when the Supreme Court of Canada was established, was the court of final appeal in Canada. 56

Keewatin decision A 2014 Supreme Court decision that rejected a claim from the Grassy Narrows First Nation band arguing that Ontario required approval from the federal government before issuing a logging permit on their land. 110

law Consists of a special body of rules issued by government and backed up by the threat of state force. 7

leader of Her Majesty's Loyal Opposition The leader of the party with the second-largest number of seats in the House of Commons. 218

leadership review A party vote that acts as an appraisal of the incumbent party leader; if he or she does not score sufficiently high on a vote, a leadership convention may be held. 220

legislative (statute) law Law created by legislative bodies to supplement customary or common law. 53

legislative committees Committees that are set up to receive bills for examination after they have passed second reading. 149

legislature The branch of government that makes or amends laws. 139

legitimacy When citizens accept that a government should, or has the right to, make decisions for them. 5

letters patent The prerogative instruments defining the office of the governor general that the sovereign makes applicable to each governor general through his or her commission of appointment. 116

lieutenant-governor Appointed by the Governor-in-Council on the advice of the prime minister to represent the monarch in each province. 118

lobbying Activity aimed at securing favourable policy decisions or the appointment of specific government personnel. 225

lobbyists Individuals or organizations who are paid by interest groups to influence government legislation. 225

low income cut-off (LICO) An income inequality measure published by Statistics Canada that is often used to define a poverty line. 32

majority government A government based on the support of only one party in the House of Commons. 124

majority principle System of government in which policy decisions are made by a majority of the people or elected body. 8

Meech Lake Accord An April 1987 agreement, made between the federal Progressive Conservative government and the 10 provinces, for a constitutional amendment. 68

Memorandum to Cabinet (MC) A document, signed by a minister, that begins the process of Cabinet decision making. 127

minister of public safety Cabinet minister responsible for the Correctional Service of Canada and the National Parole Board (as well as CSIS, the RCMP, and other areas). 198

minister of state Like a full Cabinet minister, a minister of state is sworn to the Privy Council and bound by the rules of collective responsibility, but is only allowed to attend meetings of Cabinet on request, and his or her salary and staff allotments are lower than that of full Cabinet ministers. None were appointed by Trudeau. 123

ministerial mandate letter Letter that explains what the prime minister expects the minister to accomplish in his or her department. 122

ministerial responsibility Refers to the personal responsibility of each minister. As heads of departments, ministers receive confidential advice from public servants, make important decisions, and are held accountable for those decisions in Parliament and the country. 172

ministry Larger than Cabinet, the group is composed of all ministers who are appointed by the prime minister. It consists of both full Ministers of the Crown and ministers of state. 123

minority government A government in which the governing party has less than a majority of the members of the House of Commons. 124

monarch The monarch, currently Queen Elizabeth II, is the personal embodiment of the Crown. 115

money bill Government bill for raising or spending money. 150

movement An informal network of groups and individuals that works for social change. It is usually founded on an altruistic idea and tends to have only loose organizational form. 223

multiculturalism A policy that assumes that ethnic customs and cultures should be valued, preserved, and shared within the context of citizenship and economic and political integration. 44

nation Politically conscious and mobilized group of people, often with a sense of territory, who may aspire to greater autonomy or even statehood. 4

nationalism The collective action of a politically conscious ethnic group (or nation) in pursuit of increased territorial autonomy or sovereignty. 93

notwithstanding clause A clause in the Constitution that allows Parliament or a provincial legislature to override most Charter provisions by a simple declaration to that effect when passing legislation. 59

official bilingualism As outlined in the *Official Languages Act*, it ensures the legal equality of English and French languages in the Parliament and courts of Canada and protects the rights of French-speaking minorities in different provinces. It ensures a level of government services in both languages across the country and gives both language groups the right to communicate with the federal government in the official language of their choice. 96

ombudsman A (proposed) independent officer responsible to Parliament for the investigation of citizens' complaints against the bureaucracy. 179

one-party dominant thesis A general theory about Canadian parties, which holds that the Canadian government is normally dominated by one party for long periods of time. 208

Ontario Provincial Police (OPP) Ontario's province-wide police force. 196

Opposition Days (Supply Days) Days on which opposition motions can be debated (20 per session). 147

Oral Question Period A 45-minute period held in Parliament five days a week that provides a forum for the opposition parties to try to embarrass the government, criticize its policies, and force discussion on selected issues. 147

Order Paper The schedule of pending parliamentary business. 151

Orders of the Day The procedures under which the House of Commons deals with the public business placed before it. Orders guide the speaker and direct the officers of the House to pursue particular courses of action. 147

orders-in-council Decisions rendered by Cabinet under the auspices of the Privy Council that carry legal force. 126

parliamentary budget officer An officer of Parliament whose mandate is to provide objective economic and financial analysis to Parliament. 291

parliamentary democracy Parliament exercises power on behalf of the public and is therefore the "repository of popular sovereignty." 139

parliamentary privilege A House of Commons rule that enables MPs to express themselves freely and without intimidation. 144

parliamentary secretary An MP who aids a minister in his or her duties but has no statutory authority. 123

party caucus A group formed by each party in Parliament. Every Wednesday morning when Parliament is in session, all members of the House of Commons, and in some parties all senators, meet in their respective party groups. 153

party discipline The ability of the leaders of a parliamentary party to ensure that its members function as a cohesive group. 153

party leader The individual chosen by party members to fill the pre-eminent role of decision maker, figurehead, and spokesperson in both the parliamentary and the extra-parliamentary branches of the party. 217

party system The relationships among parties in a political system. 205

patriation Bringing a constitutional document to its home country. 58

patronage In the broad sense, concerns the awarding of contracts, employment, and other material benefits to individuals or groups on the basis of partisan support rather than merit. 286

pluralist theory A theory of interest group activity that holds that there are many centres of power in society, and a state's public policy reflects the conflict, cooperation, and compromise of independent interest groups with the government. 223

policy A broadly based framework within which decisions are taken and a pattern of government action or inaction. 7

policy The broad framework within which decisions are taken and action (or inaction) is pursued by governments. 167

political culture The broad patterns of values, beliefs, and attitudes in a society toward political objects. 20

political customs The conventional and accepted practices that are part of the political system. 22

political institutions Institutions that structure democratic expression within states and relate more closely to citizen behaviour; they include parties, interest groups, elections, and the media. 10

political party An organization designed to obtain the power of the state and perhaps form a government. 205

politics The activity that entails making binding decisions about who gets what, when, and how. 6

pork-barrelling An abuse of power whereby politicians extend political favours to whole regions or communities as an inducement for support. 286

power The ability to influence (convince) and/or to coerce (force) others to accept certain objectives or to behave in a particular manner. 6

preferential system An electoral system in which voters rank their candidates in order of preference. 246

prerogative authority Powers of a monarch (or his or her representatives) that have not been bypassed by constitutional or statute law. 115

Prime Minister's Office (PMO) One of four central agencies assisting Cabinet. This is the political office of the prime minister and members are appointed directly by him or her. 130

private bill A bill that confers special power or rights on specific individuals, groups, or corporations rather than on society as a whole. 150

private members' bills A bill sponsored by an individual MP. 150

Privy Council Office (PCO) The main public service organization supporting the Cabinet and prime minister. 130

procedural rights Rights of citizens to access certain processes such as a fair trial. They are intended to protect individuals from arbitrary action by governments. 65

proclamation Involves proclaiming, publishing, or declaring under the Great Seal a statute that thereby becomes law. 151

proportional representation (PR) An electoral system that attempts to ensure that parties receive representation in the House of Commons in proportion to their respective shares of the popular vote. 244

prorogation Closing a session of Parliament. Formally, this is done by the governor general on the advice of the prime minister. 141

public bills Bills that seek to change the law concerning the public as a whole. There are two kinds of public bills: government bills and private members' bills. The vast majority are government bills. 150

public sector integrity commissioner An officer of Parliament appointed to promote and protect whistleblowers. 291

public servants (bureaucrats) Tenured state officials involved in advising government ministers and implementing policies. 166

public service The collective term in Canada for the personnel employed in the administrative arm of government. 173

Queen's Privy Council for Canada A body established at Confederation in the Constitution to assist and advise the governor general. Today, the body is largely ceremonial and members are nominated by the prime minister and appointed for life. 122

racial discrimination The imposition of handicaps, barriers, and different treatment on individuals because of their race. 46

recall A device to promote public participation and force a new election whereby constituents can recall an MP who does not vote or act as they want. 154

referendum A means by which a policy question is submitted directly to the electorate for a decision rather than being decided exclusively by elected representatives. 247

regionalism Refers to territorial tensions brought about by certain groups that demand a change in the political, economic, and cultural relations between regions and central powers *within* the existing state. 35

regulation The imposition of constraints, backed by government authority, that are intended to modify the economic behaviour of individuals in the private sector. 170

religion An organized, institutionalized system of beliefs based on the superior authority of a supernatural being, or beings, the purpose of which is to instruct the faithful in morally responsible behaviour. 41

representative democracy A democracy in which elected officials make decisions with the force of law because they have achieved legitimacy through some form of election. 9

reservation The constitutional ability of lieutenant-governors to reserve provincial legislation for federal approval. 77

residual clause A clause in the Constitution that allows the federal government to legislate in any matter not specifically assigned to the provinces. 77

responsible government The prime minister and Cabinet are accountable to Parliament and may govern only so long as they retain the "confidence" of the majority of the House of Commons. 11

revenue process Concerns the means by which funds are to be raised—by taxation and other measures. 174

rights Legal entitlements owed to individuals or groups as duties by others, or by the government. 52

"rigid" constitution A constitution that is difficult to amend. 57

royal assent When the governor general, sitting in the Senate chambers before the assembled members of both Houses, puts the final seal of approval on legislation. 151

Royal Canadian Mounted Police (RCMP) The police force responsible for enforcing federal statutes; it is also under contract to many provinces and municipalities, and polices the territories to enforce criminal and provincial law. 196

Royal Commissions Widely employed as sources of public policy advice to the executive. They are generally set up by the government to investigate an area of critical public concern and to recommend suitable courses of action. 171

Royal Newfoundland Constabulary The Newfoundland and Labrador police force that shares policing responsibilities with the RCMP. 196

rule of law A guarantee that the state's actions will be governed by law, with fairness, and without malice. No individual should be above the law, and no one ought to be exempt from it. 8, 53

Section 35 Section 35 of the *Constitution Act, 1982* recognizes and affirms the existing rights and treaty rights of Aboriginal peoples, including land claims agreements now and in the future. 107

Section 91 A section of the Constitution that specifies the areas belonging exclusively to the federal government. It also contains a residual clause. 77

Section 92 A section of the Constitution that delineates 16 specific areas of provincial jurisdiction, including direct taxation, hospitals, prisons, property, and civil rights. 77

security certificate process A regulation that was used to jail non-Canadians (foreign nationals or permanent residents) thought to be a threat to national security and then, if necessary, to deport them to a foreign country. 199

Security Intelligence Review Committee An external review committee that monitors the activities of the Canadian Security Intelligence Service (CSIS). 197

session Working period when Parliament is open for business. 140

shared-cost program So-called "50-cent dollar" program in which the federal government pays 50 percent of costs. 82

single-member plurality electoral system Commonly referred to as first-past-the-post, a system by which the candidate who receives the most votes, a plurality in each constituency, wins that constituency. 233

sovereign A sovereign state wields authority and power in that it is capable of maintaining order within its territory, is able to tax its citizens, and is also recognized by the international community as having the right to run its own affairs free from external interference. 5

speaker of the House of Commons A member of Parliament elected to act as an impartial arbiter of the whole House. 145

specific claim An Aboriginal land claim dealing with challenges to existing treaties. 108

Speech from the Throne Delivered by the governor general, it outlines the government's proposed legislative program for the forthcoming session. 141

spending power Refers to the federal government's blanket authority to spend money for any purpose in any field, even if it has no legal jurisdiction over the area. 82

standing committee A committee that is relatively permanent for the life of a Parliament. 148

Standing Orders Contain the rules of the House of Commons that are of a general nature and more or less permanent. 143

state The political unit of an entire territory; it comprises a territory, a population, and a government. It is also an abstraction that incorporates many institutions and rules. 5

state institutions Institutions that are related closely to the Constitution and federalism; they include the executive, legislature, bureaucracy, courts, police, and prisons. 10

substantive rights Fundamental rights as defined in a constitution. 65

supply (appropriation) bills Bills that authorize the spending of money by the government. 150

Supreme Court of Canada Canada's highest court for civil, criminal, and constitutional cases. 183

surplus Money that is left over after a government's bills for a year are paid. 12

stare decisis The principle of following precedents set down in earlier court cases, a principle that also binds lower courts to follow decisions of higher-level courts. 53

Sûreté du Québec (SQ) Québec's province-wide police force. 196

terrorism The systematic use of violence or threat of violence against citizens and/or states to obtain political concessions for a designated enemy. 198

time allocation A device to limit debate in the House. 155

Treasury Board A central coordinating agency that is constitutionally a committee of the Privy Council. 125

Treasury Board secretariat (TBS) An administrative unit of government with a highly qualified staff to assist the six Cabinet members of the Treasury Board. 132

Triple-E Senate A proposal that the Senate be elected, effective, and equal in its representation of all provinces. 160

Tsilhqot'in decision A 2014 landmark Supreme Court decision that awarded the Tsilhqot'in of British Columbia the right to bar mining and commercial logging from their territory. 109

ultra vires A legislative act that is beyond a legislature's jurisdiction on the basis of Canada's federal division of powers. 54

unconditional grants Money from the federal government that the provinces can spend in any way they wish since it is not designated for any specific policy field. 83

unilateral declaration of independence (UDI) A declaration of independence by a province outside constitutional law. 103

unitary system A form of government in which the power and authority to govern is centralized in one government. 11, 74 unwritten constitution A constitution that consists mainly of customs, conventions, or statutes and is not written down in one comprehensive document. 52

Values Shared beliefs that provide standards of judgment about what is right, important, and desirable in society. They are deeply held convictions. 20

veto The power to block legislation or to block a constitutional amendment. 77

visible minorities Defined in the *Employment Equity Act* as "persons other than aboriginal peoples, who are non-Caucasian in race or non-white in colour." 46

ways and means committee A committee of the whole; it considers the resolutions that contain the proposals of the minister of finance. 148

ways and means motions Motions that introduce bills to authorize the raising of money by taxation. 150

whip An MP assigned by each party leader to help maintain party cohesion. 153

writ A document commanding that an election be held, giving the date of the election, the date by which nominations must be received, and the date by which results must be finalized. 236

written constitution The fundamental state law set down in one or more documents. 52

Index

Note: Key Terms and their page numbers appear in boldface.

Gagliano, Alfonso, 290
games analogy, 2–3
GATT. *See* General Agreement on
    Tariffs and Trade (GATT)
Gauthier, Michel, 215, 222
gay rights legislation, 191, 192–193
GDP. *See* gross domestic product
    (GDP)
gender issues, 37–41
General Agreement on Tariffs and
    Trade (GATT), 133, 267
gerrymandering, 235
global economics, 266–276
global system, 264
globalization, 268
Globe and Mail, The, 178, 261, 262
Gomery Commission, 156, 284, 287,
    290–291
Goodale, Ralph, 124
goods and services tax (GST), 157
government
        see also bureaucracy; executive
        authoritarianism, 7
        authority of, 6
        Charter and, 187
        definition of, 6
        democracy, 7–11
        federal powers, 76–77
        responsible, 11, 55
government agencies. *See* agencies
government bill, 150
government departments, 168–169, 170
Government Organization Act, 76
governor general, 11, 39, 115–118
Governor-in-Council, 76, 117, 127
"grandfather clause," 234
Grant, Ulysses S., 270
grants
        block, 84–85
        conditional, 82
        unconditional, 83
Great Depression (1930s), 79, 211
Greece, 2
Green Party, 206, 207, 208, 215–216,
    223, 245, 253
gross domestic product (GDP), 174,
    266
GST. *See* goods and services tax (GST)
Guaranteed Income Supplement (GIS),
    30, 129

H

Halpern v. Canada, 192–193
Hamas, 200
Hans Island, 273
Hansard, 146
Harb, Mac, 292
Harper, Elijah, 68
Harper, Stephen, 36, 39, 42, 49, 89,
    102, 105, 109, 116, 117, 120, 121,
    122, 123, 124, 125, 129, 130, 135,
    136, 137, 141, 155, 156, 160, 161,
    163, 164, 173, 177, 183, 202, 212,
    213, 218, 221, 226, 238, 240, 253–
    261, 259–261, 273, 274, 278, 280,
    282, 284, 291–292
Harris, Mike, 86–87
health care costs, 87–89
Hezbollah (Lebanon), 200
Hillier, General R.J., 280
House leader, 146
House of Commons, 10, 11, 21, 27,
    58, 62, 117–118, 139, 142–153
        committees, 148–149
        functions of, 142
        legislation, passing, 149–153
        members of Parliament (MPs),
            142–143
        organization of, 144–146
        representation in, 37, 234–235
        routine in, 146–148
        rules, 143–144
        Standing Orders, 143–144, 289,
            290
Howe, C. D., 285
Hussein, Saddam, 280
Hyer, Bruce, 215

I

identity group, 29
ideology, 24–25
        schools of, 28–29
Ignatieff, Michael, 102, 130, 211, 221
immigrants, 19, 43–45, 255
Immigration Act (1978), 45
Immigration and Refugee Protection Act,
    199
Income Tax Act, 148, 150
Indian Act (1876), 48, 107, 111
Indian Specific Claims Commission
    (ISCC), 108

indirect taxes, 56, 81–82
individual ministerial responsibility,
    125
individual rights, 52
Individual Rights Protection Act (IRPA)
    (Alberta), 192
Industrial Revolution, 28
institutions, 2–3
        government, 6–7
        political, 10
        state, 10
interest groups, 204–205, 222–230
        definition of, 223
        and lobbying, 225–227
        nature of, 224–225
        pluralist theory, 223
        problems with, 224
        targets of, 227–230
International Labour Organization, 269
international relations, 264
International Security Assistance Force
    (ISAF), 280
Interpretation Act, 76
Inuit, 47, 48, 99, 108, 112
Iran, 282
Iraq, 263, 280, 281
Islamic State (ISIS), 200, 281–282

J

Japanese Canadians, internment of,
    46, 65
Jean, Michaëlle, 39, 116, 117
*John Miron et al. v. Richard Trudel et
    al.*, 191
Johnston, David, 116, 117
Joint Action Plan (JAP), 275
Joint House and Senate Committee on
    a Renewed Canada, 68
joint standing committee, 149
Judicial Committee of the Privy
    Council (JCPC), 56–57, 79, 93,
    183, 186

K

Keewatin decision, 110
Kelowna Accord, 49
Kennedy, John Fitzgerald, 270
Kenney, Jason, 282
Keynes, John Maynard, 26
Keystone Pipeline XL, 273